D1058067

TO J., D., AND P.

Contents

List of Tables	ix
Preface	xiii
Abbreviations	xv

1. Basic Factors — 1
1. Periodization — 1
2. The Tokugawa Heritage — 2
3. Trends in the Infrastructure — 7

2. Out of the Middle Ages, 1868–1885 — 16
1. The Nature of the Meiji Restoration — 16
2. The Expansion of the Infrastructure — 17
3. The Great Economic Reforms — 19
4. Creating a Financial System — 24
5. The Matsukata Deflation — 27
6. Financing the Economy — 29
7. The National Balance Sheet — 32
8. The Financial Achievements of the Transition Period — 33

3. The Takeoff into Sustained Economic Growth, 1886–1913 — 35
1. Changes in Political and Social Structure — 35
2. Changes in the Infrastructure — 37
3. Capital Formation and Saving — 41
4. Money, Prices, Interest Rates, and Asset Prices — 44
5. The Development of the Institutional Structure — 46
6. Financing the Main Sectors of the Economy — 56
7. The Financial Superstructure as a Whole — 64
8. The National Balance Sheet — 67
9. The Financial Achievements of the Takeoff Period — 68

4. The Uncertain Trumpet, 1914–1931 — 71
1. Basic Characteristics of Period — 71
2. Capital Formation and Saving — 77
3. The Development of Financial Institutions — 82
4. Financing the Main Nonfinancial Sectors — 94
5. The Financial Superstructure as a Whole — 101
6. The National Balance Sheet — 103

5. Riding for a Fall, 1932–1945 — 107
1. General Characteristics of Period — 107

2. Capital Formation and Saving   114
3. The Development of Financial Institutions   117
4. Financing the Main Nonfinancial Sectors   124
5. The Financial Superstructure as a Whole   129
6. The National Balance Sheet   129

6. Paradise Regained, 1946–1953   131
1. The Infrastructure   131
2. Causes and Course of the Great Inflation   133
3. Financial Institutions   138
4. The Nonfinancial Sectors   141

7. The Japanese Miracle? 1954–1975   146
1. Basic Changes in the Infrastructure   146
2. Money, Prices, and Interest Rates   151
3. Capital Formation, Saving, and Sectoral Financial Surpluses and Deficits 156
4. Financial Institutions   160
5. The Markets for the Main Financial Instruments   176
6. Financing and Portfolio Structure of the Main Nonfinancial Sectors   188
7. An Overview of Financial Assets and Liabilities   210
8. The National Balance Sheet   213

List of Publications Cited   221
Index   227

Tables

1–1   Long-term Trends in Basic Physical Characteristics of the Japanese Economy, 1885–1978   9

1–2   Rates of Growth of Basic Physical Characteristics of the Japanese Economy, 1886–1975   10

1–3   Trend in Capital Formation and Saving Ratios, 1869–1975   12

2–1   Some Basic Economic Indicators, Annually, 1868–1885   21

2–2   Principal Accounts of National Banks, 1875–1895   26

2–3   Assets of Financial Institutions, 1868–1885   28

2–4   Financial Instruments Outstanding in 1885   32

2–5   National Balance Sheet, 1885   33

3–1   National Product, Consumption, and Capital Formation, 1885–1913   38

3–2   Prices and Interest Rates, Annually, 1885–1913   40

3–3   Capital Formation, 1886–1913   41

3–4   Fixed Capital Formation and Saving, 1905–1913   42

3–5   Net Fixed Capital Stock, 1875–1913   42

3–6   Saving, 1886–1913   43

3–7   Money in Circulation, 1885–1913   45

3–8   Sources and Uses of Funds of Commercial Banks, 1885–1913   48

3–9   Concentration in Commercial Banking, 1900–1945   50

3–10   Savings (Time) Deposits, 1885–1913   53

3–11   Assets of Financial Institutions, 1885–1945   54

3–12   Assets of Main Types of Financial Institutions: Growth Rate, Distribution, Relation to Gross National Product, and New Issue Ratio, 1885–1913   55

3–13   Structure of Assets of Financial Institutions, 1913   56

3–14   Government Saving and Investment, 1883–1912   58

3–15   Distribution of Nonfinancial Corporate Capital, 1885–1913   61

3–16   New Issue Ratios, 1886–1913   65

3–17   National Balance Sheet, 1885, 1900, and 1913   67

3–18   Distribution of National Assets and Relation to Gross National Product, 1885, 1900, and 1913   68

4–1   National Product, Consumption, and Capital Formation, 1913–1931   72

4–2   Price Movements, 1913–1931   73

4–3   Money in Circulation, 1913–1931   76

4–4   Capital Formation, 1914–1931   78

4–5   Net Fixed Capital Stock, 1914–1940   79

4–6   Saving, 1914–1931   80

4–7   Residual and Synthetic Estimates of Household Saving, 1914–1931   81

4–8   Principal Accounts of Commercial Banks, 1913–1931   85
4–9   Deposits and Depositors in Postal Saving System, 1885–1944   86
4–10   Growth and Distribution of Assets of Financial Institutions, 1913–1931   89
4–11   Structure of Assets of All Financial Institutions, 1913–1944   90
4–12   Structure of Assets of Main Groups of Financial Institutions, 1930   91
4–13   Share of Holdings of Securities by Financial Institutions, 1913–1944   92
4–14   New Issue Ratios of Financial Institutions, 1914–1931   93
4–15   Components of the New Issue Ratio of Financial Institutions, 1914–1941   94
4–16   Sources and Uses of Funds of (48 to 75) Large Industrial Corporations,
          1914–1930   96
4–17   Government Debt and Its Financing, 1914–1931   98
4–18   Net New Issue Ratios, 1914–1931   102
4–19   National Balance Sheet, 1913, 1920, 1930, and 1940   104
4–20   National Balance Sheet, 1913, 1920, 1930, and 1940: Distribution and Relation to
          National Product   105
5–1   National Product, Consumption, and Capital Formation, 1931–1944   108
5–2   Basic Economic Characteristics of the 1932–1944 Period   109
5–3   Price Movements, 1931–1945   110
5–4   Money in Circulation, 1931–1945   112
5–5   National Product and War Expenditures, 1941–1945   113
5–6   Capital Formation, 1932–1944   115
5–7   Saving, 1932–1944   116
5–8   Residual and Synthetic Estimates of Household Saving, 1932–1944   117
5–9   Growth and Distribution of Assets of Financial Institutions, 1931–1944   122
5–10   Rate of Increase and Distribution of Main Types of Assets of Financial Institutions,
          1931–1944   123
5–11   New Issue Ratios of Main Types of Financial Institutions, 1932–1944   125
5–12   Sources and Uses of Funds of (287 to 331) Large Industrial Corporations,
          1932–1941   126
5–13   Sources of Funds of Nonfinancial Enterprises, 1932–1944   127
5–14   Government Debt and Its Financing, 1932–1944   127
5–15   New Issue Ratios, 1932–1944   130
6–1   Development of Infrastructure, 1945–1953   131
6–2   National Product, Consumption, and Capital Formation, 1934–1936 and
          1945–1953   132
6–3   Capital Formation and Saving, 1946–1953   132
6–4   Central Government Domestic Borrowing, 1945–1953   134
6–5   Annual Price Movements, 1945–1953   135
6–6   Changes in Money Supply, 1945–1953   136
6–7   Quarterly Price and Currency Movements, 1945–1954   137
6–8   Quantity Equation (Marshallian Form), 1944–1953   138
6–9   Purchasing Power of Money in Circulation, 1945–1953   139
6–10   Financial Institutions, 1945, 1948, and 1953   140
6–11   Bank of Japan during the Inflation, 1944–1953   141
6–12   Structure of Assets of Commercial Banks, 1945–1953   142
6–13   Distribution of Holdings of Government Securities, 1945, 1948, and 1953   143
6–14   Supply of Industrial Funds, 1934–1936 and 1946–1953   144
6–15   Issue Ratios of Nonfinancial Sectors, 1946–1953   144
7–1   Basic Characteristics of Development of Real Infrastructure on Annual Basis,
          1953–1978   149
7–2   Comparison of Growth Rates between 1954–1973 and 1974–1977 Periods   150

7–3   Price Movements, 1953–1978   152
7–4   Money Supply (M_1), 1953–1978   154
7–5   Interest Rates, 1954–1978   155
7–6   Sectoral Financial Surpluses and Deficits, 1954–1977   158
7–7   Structure of Financial Assets and Liabilities of Financial Institutions, 1977   161
7–8   Balance Sheet Structure of Credit Institutions, 1955–1977   164
7–9   Distribution of Financial Assets and Liabilities among Financial Institutions,
         1977   165
7–10   Assets of Main Types of Financial Institutions, 1950–1977   166
7–11   Growth of Assets of Main Types of Financial Institutions, 1951–1977   167
7–12   Distribution of Assets among Financial Institutions, 1950–1977   168
7–13   Assets of Main Types of Banks, 1955–1977   169
7–14   Regional Distribution of Bank Loans and Deposits, 1968, 1973, and 1977   170
7–15   New Issue Ratios of Financial Institutions, 1954–1977   171
7–16   Components of New Issue Ratio of Financial Institutions, 1954–1977   173
7–17   New Issue Ratios of Financial Instruments, 1954–1977   175
7–18   Relation of Assets of Main Types of Financial Institutions to Gross National
         Product, 1950–1977   177
7–19   Distribution of New Issues of Financial Instruments, 1954–1977   178
7–20   Determinants of New Issue Ratios of Nonfinancial Sectors, 1954–1977   179
7–21   Stock Market Developments, 1954–1977   181
7–22   Issuance and Acquisition of Corporate Stock, 1956–1977   182
7–23   Distribution of Holdings of Corporate Stock, 1955–1977   184
7–24   Distribution of Ownership of Listed Corporate Stock, 1945–1975   185
7–25   Distribution of Outstandings and Issuance of Debt Securities, 1953–1977   186
7–26   Distribution of Holdings of Debt Securities, 1955–1977   187
7–27   Uses and Sources of Funds of Public Sector, 1956–1977   189
7–28   Uses and Sources of Funds of Nonfinancial Corporate Business, 1956–1977   191
7–29   Supply of Funds to Industry, 1946–1977   193
7–30   Structure of Assets and Liabilities of Principal Enterprises, 1974   195
7–31   Distribution of Assets of Large Corporations by Group Affiliation, 1955–1970 196
7–32   Intergroup Shareholdings in Three Large Groups, 1954–1966   198
7–33   Uses and Sources of Funds of Personal Sector, 1956–1977   200
7–34   Structure of Uses and Sources of Funds of Personal Sector, 1956–1977   201
7–35   Housing Credit of Financial Institutions to Individuals, 1965, 1970, and 1977 204
7–36   Financial Assets and Liabilities of Households by Income Quintiles, 1974   205
7–37   Penetration of Selected Financial Instruments, 1960–1974   209
7–38   Matrix of Financial Instruments, 1977   211
7–39   Distribution of Financial Assets and Liabilities within and among Main Sectors,
         March 31, 1978   212
7–40   National Balance Sheet, 1955–1977   213
7–41   Structure of National Balance Sheet, 1955–1977   214
7–42   National Balance Sheet, 1955–1977   216
7–43   Structure of Four-Sector National Balance Sheet, 1977   217
7–44   National Balance Sheet Ratios, 1955–1977   218

Preface

Habent sua fata libelli, if one may apply the diminutive to a project comprising three volumes totaling about six hundred pages consisting of parallel volumes on India and Japan and a short volume comparing them with the United States*—and they do so not only after their publication but also during their gestation.

This study of the financial structure and development of Japan since 1869 was started about a decade ago as the first of a planned set of a good half-dozen comparative case studies intended to supplement and illustrate the approach developed in my *Financial Structure and Development* (1969). I soon realized that this plan was beyond the powers of an author then in his mid-sixties and that studies of the two largest Asian countries, which have modern financial systems, would have to stand on their own feet. The book presented here is essentially the result of work done during the years 1970 to 1973, updated and not insubstantially shortened and revised in 1976 and again in 1979. This will explain why statistics, description, and analysis generally end with 1977; why developments before the early 1970s are covered more fully than those of the last few years, and why with a few exceptions nothing published after early 1979 has been taken into account.

I have tried in these volumes to come as close as possible, without becoming tedious and exceeding the publisher's indulgence, to the principle of reproducibility of the statistics used, that is, to permit the reader to derive the figures in the tables from the sources specified in the notes to them. This has not always been possible in the case of figures in the text not taken from the tables, though an attempt has been made to identify the sources of these in the notes where it seemed important.

The source notes to the tables, the footnotes, and the bibliography will indicate the multifarious nature of the materials from which text and tables had to be pieced together. It is only fair to add that the book could not have been written except for the existence of the Bank of Japan's *Hundred-Year Statistics of the Japanese Economy* (1966), its *Economic Statistics Annual*, and its flow-of-funds statistics starting with 1953, and the series of *Estimates of Long-term Economic Statistics of Japan since 1868* of Kazushi Ohkawa and associates.

The tables present the information mostly for benchmark years or as averages for groups of years and, in the interest of comparability, in the form of percentage distributions or other relatives, particularly as relations to national product. However, in almost all cases enough absolute figures have been preserved to enable the reader to recover, or approximate, the underlying absolute values. This procedure has been followed in order to emphasize longer-term developments and structural changes and has in any case been unavoidable in order to keep the book to manageable proportions. Absolute annual figures are shown for only a limited number of

*In addition to this volume, *The Financial Development of India, 1860–1977* and *The Financial Development of India, Japan, and the United States: A Trilateral Institutional, Statistical, and Analytic Comparison* (New Haven and London: Yale University Press, 1983).

xiii

basic series; many others, as well as numerous supplementary tables, were eliminated in shortening the manuscript. It hardly needs to be added that, because of rounding, some totals, products, and ratios do not agree exactly with the sums, products, and ratios of components or factors.

It will be evident to anyone familiar with the literature of a subject as broad as the economic and financial development of Japan over the last century that I can have used only part of the relevant publications, even in the narrower field of financial institutions and instruments. I have also been limited to sources in European languages. My ignorance of Japanese, however, has had one advantage: had I had access to the literature in Japanese and hence felt duty-bound to consult it, the book would never have been finished. All I can hope is that not too many major statistical sources, institutional descriptions, or analytical explanations have escaped me. The list of publications cited is just what it says it is—not a systematic or even selective bibliography of the subject, nor even an enumeration of sources consulted or used.

There are about 25,000 figures in the tables and text of this book. It is obvious that I cannot have avoided mistakes. Again, I can only hope that the percentage is small and that they do not affect any of the main findings or conclusions. While most of the figures come from accepted statistical sources, which does not mean that all of them are accurate, I have not hesitated to make even rough estimates where I felt they were preferable to silence or circumlocution and were likely to shed light on the subject. I shall be only too glad if critics produce better ones; that challenge is indeed a main reason for making estimates.

There is, in summary, not much that I can say *pro illi opere suo* except that I am convinced that the subject is important for understanding financial and hence economic development; that it should have been shorter; that it could have been done better; and that to the best of my knowledge nothing similar to it exists.

The writing of this book has essentially been a solitary job; it has been made possible through the assistance, mainly in the form of travel grants, of the National Science Foundation, which of course is in no way responsible for its contents. I am also grateful for the hospitality and assistance I received on the occasion of my two visits to Tokyo in 1971 and 1976 from the staff of the research and statistics divisions of the Bank of Japan, in particular Professor S. Ishida, then the head of the Bank of Japan's flow-of-funds division. I have not felt justified in asking friends and colleagues to go over hundreds of pages of complex tables and text, so the book may suffer from my (I still feel commendable) considerateness. I am also indebted to Marian Ash of Yale University Press and James Blackman of the National Science Foundation for their patience and understanding during the book's long gestation process. Finally, the manuscript would never have reached the publisher without the efficient help, over many years, of my former secretary, Anne Tassi.

New Haven, Conn.
1982

R.W.G.

Abbreviations

ARNA   Government of Japan, Economic Planning Agency, *Annual Report on National Accounts,* vol. 54, 1979

ARNIS   Government of Japan, Economic Planning Agency, *Annual Report on National Income Statistics*

BJFFA   Bank of Japan, Economic Research Department, *Flow-of-Funds Accounts in Japan, 1954–63* (1964); *1964–71* (1972); *1970–77* (1978)

ELTESJ   Kazushi Ohkawa et al., eds., *Estimates of Long-term Economic Statistics of Japan since 1868,* 12 vols. Tokyo: Toyo Keizai Shimposha, 1965ff.

ESA   Bank of Japan, Statistics Department, *Economic Statistics Annual*

ESJ   Bank of Japan, Statistics Department, *Economic Statistics of Japan,* 1961

ESM   Bank of Japan, Statistics Department, *Economic Statistics Monthly*

HYS   Bank of Japan, Statistics Department, *Hundred-Year Statistics of the Japanese Economy,* 1966

HYSE   Bank of Japan, Statistics Department, *Hundred-Year Statistics of the Japanese Economy.* Supplement, *English Translation of Explanatory Notes,* n.d.

HYSF   Bank of Japan, Statistics Department, *Hundred-Year Statistics of the Japanese Economy.* Supplement, *English Translation of Footnotes,* n.d.

JEG   Kazushi Ohkawa and Henry Rosovsky, *Japanese Economic Growth: Trend Acceleration in the Twentieth Century.* Stanford, Calif.: Stanford University Press, 1973

1   Basic Factors

1. PERIODIZATION

Any attempt to divide the continuous flow of history into sections demarcated by benchmark dates is always dangerous and to a great extent remains arbitrary. Occasionally, however, sharp breaks do occur in the historical continuum which are sufficiently marked over wide areas—in this case on the order of increasing generality in financial development, economic growth and political structure—so that dating the beginning or the end of a period is almost uncontroversial. This, of course, does not mean that no, or even no intensive, connections exist between the flow of events before and after the benchmark.

Financial development in Japan, as well as economic growth and political structure, is characterized by two obvious watersheds. The first, the end of the Tokugawa period, which had started with the battle of Sekigehara in 1600, is marked by the Meiji restoration in early 1868. The second break occurs with the surrender of Japan at the end of World War II in 1945 and the American occupation of the next few years. The years 1974 and 1975, which experienced the first serious postwar recession, may be regarded as the third watershed, terminating the upward phase of a long swing that started in the mid-1950s and is presumably to be followed by a downswing characterized by, on the average, substantially lower rates of growth.

Establishing periods within the stretch of nearly eighty years between the Meiji Restoration and World War II and within the last three decades is much more difficult, particularly if the benchmarks are to separate periods differing not only in financial structure and development but also, if possible, in clearly distinct economic, social, and political character. The four additional benchmarks—1885, 1913, 1930, and 1953—are neither as clear nor as uncontroversial as those of 1868 and 1945 and could be shifted by a few years in either direction. They seem, however, fairly well justified to mark off periods in which the financial and economic characteristics as well as Japan's position in the world differ.

The dates of the first period, 1868 to 1885, are generally accepted as major turning points in Japan's economic development. It was a period of transition, from the still largely feudal and, in international comparison, medieval late Tokugawa period to modern, that is, quasi-Western Japan. The following period, from 1886 to 1913, may be regarded as the period of takeoff into sustained economic growth and financial development and in politics marks the rise of Japan from an obscure Asian country to one of the major powers. By the end of this period Japan had essentially become a modern country, by the standards of the time, of course, in its financial and economic structure, although its standard of living still remained well below that in the West. The period from 1914 to 1931 has perhaps the least unity, financially, economically, and politically, and shows less purposefulness in both the economic and political sphere than any of the others. It is marked by an inconclusive struggle between the economic and political forces who were trying to make Japan more and more resemble a Western country economically and a

1

parliamentary democracy politically and those convinced of the country's divine mission to become the dominating power in Southeast Asia on a specifically Japanese rather than a quasi-Western pattern. By the early 1930s the latter forces, led by the military, had definitely gained the upper hand, aided by the Great Depression, which in Japan started with the financial crisis of 1927. The period 1932 to 1945 is characterized in the financial as in the economic and political sphere by the preparation for war and by actual war.

The first half of the postwar reconstruction period is characterized by a rapid inflation which lifted the price level about one hundred times above that reached at the end of the war. The second half of the period witnessed the long upward swing that seems to have ended in the mid-1970s. The turning point has been located at 1953, somewhat arbitrarily, because by that time the main indicators of economic growth, the gross national product in particular, had reached or slightly exceeded the prewar level. The choice of 1954 as the beginning of the two decades that witnessed a rise of real national product by more than 500 percent and that radically changed Japan's position in the world economy is also motivated by an accidental consideration. The flow-of-funds statistics, which provide the basic quantitative framework for much of the analysis of financial development, start with 1954. Whether 1974–75 is to be regarded historically, as it is here, as another major turning point, separating two decades of extremely rapid expansion from a period of more modest growth, remains to be seen.

These are the main considerations that have led to dividing the century into six periods. Supporting details will be found in the individual chapters:

2. Out of the Middle Ages: 1868–1885
3. The Takeoff into Sustained Economic Growth: 1886–1913
4. The Uncertain Trumpet: 1914–1931
5. Riding for a Fall: 1932–1945
6. Paradise Regained: 1946–1953
7. The Japanese Miracle? 1954–1975

Although this periodization is not primarily based on short- or medium-time cycles, it is fairly compatible with the long swings in Japan's economic development as they have been dated by recent research.[1] The main difference here is that the end of the first period after the takeoff is put at the beginning of World War I, partly for reasons of international comparability, whereas some students are inclined to put it at 1905, the year of the Russo-Japanese War. However, the second and third periods distinguished here cover practically the same time-space as Ohkawa and Rosovsky's first two long swings, 1886 to 1930 compared with 1885 to 1931. Another difference is that period four is limited to the years 1932–45, whereas Ohkawa and Rosovsky's third long swing runs from 1931 through 1954, which is the span covered here by periods four and five.

2. THE TOKUGAWA HERITAGE[2]

Two aspects of the Tokugawa heritage are important, and perhaps crucial, in the financial development of Japan in the century following the Meiji restoration. The first, more obvious and

1. *JEG*, chap. 1. Ohkawa and Rosovsky date the troughs in the long swings at 1901, 1931, and 1956 and the peaks at 1897, 1917, and provisionally at 1962 (p. 25). The periodization adopted here is virtually the same as that used by Takahashi.

2. Because this summary is based on easily accessible standard sources, specific references will be used sparingly. It may be well, however, to list in alphabetical order the main sources consulted, even if only to indicate what the author has missed: R. N. Bellah, *Tokugawa Religion,* 1957; R. N. Benedict, *The Chrysanthemum and the Sword,* 1946; E. S. Crawcour, "The Development of a Credit System in Seventeenth-Century Japan," *Journal of Economic History* 21, no. 3 (September 1961), and "Changes in Japanese Commerce in the Tokugawa Period," *Journal of Asiatic Studies* 22 (1963);

more specific, is the pattern of the country's financial superstructure at the end of the Tokugawa period, the financial instruments and institutions in existence, and the attitudes of the government and the population toward financial matters. The second aspect, possibly even more important in determining the character of the long-term financial development of Japan in the last one hundred years, is represented by some of the basic features of the economic, social, and political structure of Japan during the Tokugawa period, particularly its second half.

Neither of these aspects can be adequately treated here. This section only attempts to summarize those features of Tokugawa Japan, financial and otherwise, that appear to have had a substantial influence on the development of the country's financial superstructure and its relationship with the infrastructure of income and wealth since the restoration.

a. Basic Factors

(i) Although economically "underdeveloped" by present-day standards of living and production techniques, Tokugawa Japan was, in the words of a recent analysis of the country's modern economic development, "a vigorous, advanced and effective traditional society," which "must not be confused with those countries where economic and other types of backwardness were closely combined."[3] This is probably the most important single fact to keep in mind in assessing the importance of the Tokugawa heritage in Japan's financial development.

(ii) Tokugawa Japan was a highly centralized, bureaucratically administered feudal country[4] in which national discipline and loyalty to one's feudal lord, and ultimately to the shogun and the emperor, were emphasized and in which relationships similar to the Roman patron-client nexus (the oyabun-kobun relationship) played an important role.[5] These features outlived the Tokugawa regime, even if in modified and attenuated form, and determined some of the basic economic characteristics of modern Japan.

(iii) With a population of slightly more than 30 million at the end of the Tokugawa period, Japan was in seventeenth- and eighteenth-century terms a "big" country. It was more populous than any European country except Russia and was definitely outranked only by China and Mughal India.[6]

(iv) The Tokugawa population was remarkably stable, at least during the second half of the period, for which a series of censuses, started early in the eighteenth century by the eighth shogun, Yoshimune, provides fairly reliable information. For the seventeen census dates between 1721 and 1852 the reported population fluctuated only within the narrow range of 24.9

E. S. Crawcour and K. Yamamura, "The Tokugawa Monetary System: 1787–1868," *Economic Development and Cultural Change* 18, no. 4 (July 1970); J. W. Hall, *Das Japanische Kaiserreich*, 1968; J. W. Hall and M. B. Jansen, eds., *Studies in the Institutional History of Early Modern Japan*, 1968; E. Honjo, *The Social and Economic History of Japan*, 1935, and *Economic Theory and History of Japan in the Tokugawa Period*, 1965; R. Ishii, *Population Pressure and Economic Life in Japan*, 1937; W. W. Lockwood, *The Economic Development of Japan: The Japanese Experience Since the Meiji Era*, 1954; W. W. Lockwood, ed., *The State and Economic Enterprise in Japan*, 1965; C. Nakane, *Japanese Society*, 1972; E. H. Norman, *Japan's Emergence as a Modern State*, 1940; K. Rathgen, *Japan's Volkswirtschaft und Staatshaushalt*, 1891; E. Reischauer, *Japan—Past and Present*, 1964; C. D. Sheldon, *The Rise of the Merchant Class in Tokugawa Japan*, 1958; K. Singer, *Mirror, Sword and Jewel*, 1973; T. C. Smith, *The Agrarian Origins of Modern Japan*, 1959; M. Takizawa, *The Penetration of the Money Economy in Japan*, 1927; K. Takahashi, *The Rise and Development of Japan's Modern Economy*, 1969.

3. *JEG*, pp. 4 and 7.

4. The specialists disagree about whether or not to call the Tokugawa period "feudal," even within the covers of one book. Thus J. R. Strayer summarizes the situation by asserting that "most students of the European Middle Ages would now admit that feudalism existed in Japan" (Hall and Jansen, p. 3), but Hall feels that this "question is by no means settled, at least for the Tokugawa period" (p. 15).

5. The survival of this characteristic of Japanese society until the present is stressed in Nakane's analysis.

6. France, the most populous European state west of the Russian frontier, had 27 million inhabitants at the first census in 1801 (Institut National de la Statistique, *Annuaire Statistique de la France, 1966 Resumé Retrospectif*, p. 22). The United States did not reach a population of 20 million until 1845, and even in 1868 its population of 38 million was only slightly larger than that of Japan (U.S. Bureau of the Census, *Historical Statistics of the United States*, 1975, p. 8).

million and 27.2 million.[7] In 1852 it was only 5 percent larger than it had been 130 years earlier and 50 percent above the level of the late sixteenth century,[8] indicating an average annual rate of increase of 0.15 percent. Whether the substantial increase in the last decades of the Tokugawa period, 28 percent between 1852 and 1872, or 1.2 percent per year, marks a break with the past or is due, at least in part, to differences between late Tokugawa and early Meiji census coverage is uncertain.

(v) Throughout the Tokugawa period Japan was a predominately agrarian country, like all countries in the world well into the nineteenth century, with the exception of Great Britain and the Low Countries. Agriculture employed about three-fourths of the labor force and accounted for somewhat more than one-half of national product.[9] Japan thus possessed somewhat larger secondary and tertiary sectors than those of some underdeveloped countries even in the mid-twentieth century. The country was also distinguished by a substantial degree of urbanization. Edo (Tokyo), with possibly as many as 1 million or even 1 1/2 million inhabitants (or 3 to 5 percent of the country total), was in the seventeenth and eighteenth centuries one of the most populous cities in the world. Kyoto and Osaka were not too far behind, with about 400,000 inhabitants each, and all cities with more than 10,000 inhabitants, mostly the castle towns in which the feudal lords (*daimyo*) and their retainers (*samurai* or *bushi*) resided, apparently accounted for about one-tenth of the country's inhabitants.[10]

(vi) In the 1860s the national product of Japan appears to have been on the order of ¥ 300 mill.[11] or not much more than ¥ 10 per head, equal at the rate of exchange of the early 1870s to about $10. Although the internal purchasing power of the yen was at that time well ahead of its foreign exchange value, a comparison with the American level ($165 for 1869–73) or even that of Italy (300 lire or $60 in 1870)[12] indicates how far Japan still was from the Western level of output and living.

(vii) No quantitative measures have been developed as yet of the change in national product or its major components during the Tokugawa era. If one can accept the fairly well documented hypothesis that the cultivated area increased markedly, at least in the first half of the Tokugawa period, as a result, in part, of land reclamation,[13] and the more questionable estimate that grain production doubled from 1600 to 1730,[14] national product must have increased considerably, both in the aggregate and per head. One certainly cannot speak of economic stagnation, at least not until the end of the Tokugawa *belle époque* (the *genroku*) in the late eighteenth century. Stagnation and even decline, social and political more than economic, are clearly evident only during the first half of the nineteenth century.

(viii) Inequality in wealth and income was pronounced, although no comprehensive statistical data exist to confirm scattered evidence,[15] but it was not entirely correlated with status. Most of the politically privileged feudal retainer class, the only ones to be permitted to bear arms though forced to live in the local feudal lord's castle town or close to his residence in Edo, had a

7. *HYSE*, p. 1.

8. Based on an estimate of 18 million in 1572–91 (Ishii, p. 3).

9. Crawcour, in Lockwood (1965), p. 21; *JEG*, p. 5.

10. Hall. Another estimate, by Furushima (Smith, 1959, p. 68), puts the proportion of urban population in the middle of the eighteenth century as high as 22 percent.

11. Based on Crawcour's estimate of national income for "the 1860s" of ¥ 400 mill. in 1878–80 prices (1961, p. 21) and a rough allowance for price changes (*HYS*, p. 76).

12. For the United States, Kuznets's estimate (*Historical Statistics of the United States*, 1975, pp. 8 and 231); the estimate for Italy is derived from Istituto Centrale di Statistica, *Sommario di Statistiche Storiche Italiane 1861–1955*, 1958, pp. 40 and 210.

13. For a discussion of the evidence of improvements in agricultural technology and the increase in yields, see Smith, 1959, chap. 7.

14. Hall, p. 198.

15. Ownership of the most important form of wealth—agricultural land—seems to have become more concentrated (Smith, 1959, p. 161 ff.) but evidence is spotty.

standard of living not much above that of the more prosperous farmers and artisans, and below that of many merchants, not astonishing in view of the fact that they were numerous enough to make up, together with their families, about 5 percent of the entire population.[16]

(ix) The linchpin of the economy was the rice crop, produced by millions of peasant households on extremely small farms, held mostly under different forms of tenancy and involving delivery of about two-thirds of the crop to the landlords or to the state.[17] In the eighteenth century about one-fourth of the agricultural land belonged to the shogun in the sense that the operator had to pay a land tax to the owner; about one-tenth of the tax was paid to two dozen branches of the Tokugawa family; another fourth to about 150 feudal lords closely associated with the shogun (so-called *fudai daimyo*); fully one-third to about one hundred less closely affiliated feudal lords (*tozama daimyo*), mostly on the islands of Kyushu and Shikoku; with fully 2 and less than 1 percent held by religious institutions and the imperial court and the nobility (*kuge*), respectively.[18] The shogun and the secondary owners—in theory all land was the shogun's property—of course, distributed most of the rice rents they received, mostly in kind, to government officials and feudal retainers. However, at the end of the Tokugawa period, nearly one-third of the land was held by tenants in the Western sense, having no traditional permanent rights of occupancy.[19]

(x) The characteristic that possibly most clearly differentiated the Tokugawa regime from most of the contemporary world, or for that matter from earlier periods of Japanese history, particularly the sixteenth century, was the rigorously enforced, almost complete absence of any relations with the rest of the world, specifically the absence of a significant amount of foreign trade, travel, or migration. Pursued for more than two centuries, this policy created a wide gap between Japanese and Western technology, both industrial and financial.

b. The Financial Superstructure

The dearth of quantitative data on the financial superstructure of Japan during the Tokugawa period, and the fact that most of the specialized literature is available only in Japanese, limit this section to a brief summary of what appear to be the most important ascertainable facts on financial instruments and financial institutions and their relations to the country's infrastructure of production and distribution.

(i) During the Tokugawa era monetization of the economy made considerable progress, partly as a result of the enforced residence (during alternate years) of the feudal lords, their families, and many of their retainers in Edo.[20] By the first half of the nineteenth century most transactions were monetary with the exception, and an important one it is, of the land tax payable in rice by the farmers. It has been estimated[21] that in the 1860s about 60 to 70 percent of agricultural production, excluding tax rice, which may have constituted about one-third of all farm output, was marketed. Because this proportion is likely to have been higher in the nonfarm sectors, the monetization ratio for the whole economy should have been on the order of three-fourths excluding tax rice but only about three-fifths including it.[22]

(ii) Centered on the rice tax levied in kind by the central government and by the feudal lords on the basis of crop-sharing arrangements, government finance, still quite clearly medieval in character, was probably the weakest link in the financial structure. Because the tax yield

16. Rathgen, p. 42, assuming an average of about four persons per samurai family.

17. Estimates of M. Kimura, cited by Ranis, p. 448.

18. Hall, pp. 166–67.

19. Norman, p. 148.

20. This factor is stressed by Asakura (1967, pp. 274–75).

21. Crawcour, 1961, p. 40.

22. This is based on the very rough estimates of gross national product of about ¥ 300 mill., a rice tax yield of 10 million koku, and a rice price of about ¥ 6 per koku in 1868 (*HYS*, p. 90). The average price for 1868–73 is also close to ¥ 6.

fluctuated with the vagaries of the weather and because of sharp fluctuations in rice prices the government found it quite difficult to plan for expenditures payable in money. From about the middle of the eighteenth century the government was almost continuously in financial difficulties, which it tried to remedy, in the long run without success, through forced loans, currency debasement, and other means.

(iii) Currency was another backward feature of Tokugawa Japan. Even specialists seem far from agreed about what the situation really was, how it changed over two and a half centuries, and how it differed in various parts of the country.[23] There was—as in most of Europe well into the eighteenth century—no uniform currency in circulation, except possibly for a few decades following the 1630s. During the early part of the period, gold, silver, and copper coins of different weight and fineness were issued by various authorities and circulated, silver being used as *numéraire*.[24] Exchanged at fluctuating rates, the coins provided opportunities for profits and influence to exchange brokers and dealers, particularly to a group of large dealers in Osaka known as the Big Ten, who are sometimes regarded as having acted as a sort of monetary authority.[25] Most metallic coins were periodically debased. During the later Tokugawa period, silver coins disappeared from circulation, and near its end several hundred issues of paper money by feudal lords (*hansatsu*) added to the confusion.

(iv) Tokugawa Japan possessed a variety of financial institutions with a substantial amount of division of functions. Such institutions included, apart from the ubiquitous, mostly nonprofessional rural moneylenders, pawnbrokers, exchange brokers, bankers of several types, and *mujin*, a sort of credit cooperative.[26] Modern financial institutions, such as banks of issue, deposit banks, savings banks, long-term credit banks, and life insurance companies, were, of course, missing. The operations of some moneylenders, organized in guilds, were of substantial size, in particular in their dealings with the central government and the great feudal lords.[27]

(v) Notwithstanding an obviously large amount of credit in existence—a well-developed system of short-term trade credit among merchants, often evidenced by bills of exchange— fungible long-term securities of the modern type were virtually absent. The large debts of the feudal lords and their retainers, as well as those of the peasants, apparently short term, were extended for protracted periods but not evidenced by transferable instruments. There were no central or local government bonds. Because corporations were unknown, corporate bonds and stocks were obviously absent.

(vi) Although hard, comprehensive evidence is lacking, as it is in practically every country well into the nineteenth and even the twentieth century, a substantial and apparently increasing amount of indebtedness occurred throughout the Tokugawa period. The main net debtors were, as always, the middle and poorer peasants and the government, in Tokugawa Japan principally the daimyo, but indebtedness seems to have been substantial also among the feudal retainers.[28]

23. For an overview, based as much as possible on quantitative evidence, cf. Crawcour and Yamamura, pp. 489–518.

24. The official rates, fixed in 1609, were 4,000 copper coins for 50 me silver and 1 ryo gold, both gold and silver being legal tender. The gold standard prevailed in eastern Japan, centering in Edo, the silver standard in the West, centered in Osaka.

25. Crawcour, 1961, p. 354.

26. Cf. Asakura, 1967, pp. 274–76. Asakura goes so far as to assert that "the business carried on by exchange brokers was practically the same as that of a modern bank" (p. 275), probably meaning a bank handling deposits subject to check.

27. In 1830 more than 50 exchange brokers, who were also important moneylenders, are reported to have had a capital of more than 200,000 ryo (Asakura, 1967, p. 276). Although the ryo at the Meiji restoration became equal to the yen, which then in turn was equal to the dollar, the purchasing power of the ryo in 1830 was considerably higher, according to Asakura's estimate more than $30 of 1867.

28. A summary of the situation regarding peasants' debt by Smith (1959, p. 158 ff.) may be apposite. Borrowing by peasants "usually originated in poverty rather than enterprise," loans "were usually for trifling amounts," and "interest rates were exceedingly high," 20 percent being the most usual rate, all exactly like the situation in India. As borrowing

The principal lenders were, insofar as larger amounts were involved, city merchants; for smaller amounts, rural moneylenders, often wealthier peasants, performed the service. During the later part of the Tokugawa period, particularly the first half of the nineteenth century, the increasing indebtedness of most of the feudal lords and many of their retainers became a serious economic and political problem, and various remedies, like interest reductions, prolongations, and even outright repudiations, were resorted to without decisive effect.

(vii) Although not strictly financial in nature, the active operation of commodity exchanges, primarily dealing in rice and involving certificates of deposit and loans on them, is another indication of the advanced stage reached in Tokugawa Japan in commercial techniques.

(viii) Not much is known quantitatively about price trends during the first two-thirds of the Tokugawa period, but marked long-term price trends appear to have been absent. Similarly, price movements appear to have been moderate from the late eighteenth century to about 1830. This relative stability in the face of an expanding money supply has been explained by a rising demand for transactions cash in the agricultural sector accompanying its increasing monetization. In the 1830s and again the 1850s inflationary forces clearly gained the upper hand, raising the price level by about one-half. In the last decade before the Meiji restoration the currency, like many other institutions of the Tokugawa regime, collapsed, and consumer prices approximately trebled between 1860 and 1866.[29]

(ix) Regardless of the danger in historical analogy, one cannot help feel that an understanding of Japanese finance during the Tokugawa period is aided by comparing it with that of Western Europe, particularly Italy in the fifteenth and Germany in the sixteenth centuries, with the Osaka merchants and bankers providing parallels to the Bardi, Peruzzi, Medici, and Fugger and the daimyo and the shogun playing the role of the Italian and German princes and the king of Spain. As in Italy and Germany, some Japanese financiers became rich and influential for a while, but most of them were ultimately ruined by their aristocratic debtors' defaults. Unlike the situation in Europe, however, a few of the large Tokugawa firms, such as the house of Mitsui, survived into the modern era, partly, of course, because in Japan the modern era immediately followed the feudal regime, whereas in Europe the two are separated by two or three centuries.

(x) Given the developed credit system and the obviously substantial surplus above subsistence that existed in Tokugawa Japan, what prevented the occurrence of a structural change in the economy similar to that observed in Western Europe in the nineteenth century? The answer seems to be threefold. First, the feudal and traditional elements in the Japanese economy, while slowly attenuated, remained relatively strong. Second, and probably more important, Japan did not experience anything like the European scientific revolution of the seventeenth century and, consequently, failed to produce autonomously the technological advances, particularly in the textile, iron, and mechanical industries, that spearheaded the industrial revolution in the West. Third, the policy of strict isolation effectively prevented the adaptation of Western technology until the 1850s. The objects of financing thus remained the deficits of aristocratic and rural overspenders, not exactly the right basis for a financial system linked to sustained economic growth.

3. TRENDS IN THE INFRASTRUCTURE

The astonishing process of growth, astonishing both in speed and character, that the Japanese economy underwent during the last century cannot be adequately described, let alone explained, in this short section through summary quantitative indicators. All that is intended here is to recall

---

became more common during the second half of the Tokugawa period, peasants increasingly lost their land, although alienation of land was in principle forbidden and led to increasing concentration in landownership.

29. Crawcour and Yamamura, p. 512 ff.

the main phases of this development as it is reflected in the growth and sectoral distribution of real national product; and to review the aggregative measurable factors that may be regarded as being largely responsible for this growth, namely, the supply of labor, reproducible capital, and land. Other important factors, less easily quantifiable or not quantifiable at all, such as changes in human capital, technology, organization, and government policy, are ignored, an unfortunate omission necessitated by the format of this study. Occasional attempts at explanation will be provided, however, in the introductory sections of the following chapters dealing with individual periods.

a. National Product[30]

The centennial growth rate of Japan's gross real national product appears to have been slightly below 4 percent per year, waiving the well-known methodological and statistical doubts regarding the possibility of a consistent measurement of national product, or for that matter of national wealth, over a period of this length that involves, as it does in Japan, drastic changes in economic structure. Because the growth of population has averaged 1.1 percent per year, a statistically less controversial measure, we conclude that product per head has increased over the last century, more correctly the 107 years from the Meiji restoration to 1975, at an annual rate of about 2 3/4 percent.[31] Even substantial revisions of the national product estimates for the first two decades of the period, for which the figures are still uncertain, would not change this figure in a way to affect seriously conclusions about Japan's secular growth rate, although they might well influence our judgment about the contribution of the first phase of 1868 to 1885. Although these rates may seem moderate, it should be realized that maintained for slightly more than a century they imply an approximately 65-fold increase in aggregate gross real national product and a nearly 20-fold increase in real income per head. It must be kept in mind that these calculations are only to a limited extent measures of welfare, or even of economic welfare, because their failure to make full allowance for quality improvements in many types of commodities understates increases in welfare, and, probably more seriously, their failure to allow for many costs and disutilities associated with economic growth overstates the advance.[32]

The growth rate of national product, of course, has varied widely over the past century but has in general shown an increasing trend, as is evident in tables 1-1 and 1-2. It may have been on the order of 2 percent for aggregate and of nearly 1 1/2 percent for per head national product for the years 1869 to 1885. For the takeoff period 1886–1913, for which the estimates are considerably better, the rate is slightly more than 2 1/2 percent for total product and about 1 1/2 percent per year for product per head. The growth rate of aggregate product and of product per head was considerably higher at more than 3 1/2 percent and nearly 2 1/2 percent, respectively, for the following period of equal length extending from 1914 to 1940. This was due primarily to the rapid growth in the World War I period (about 4 1/4 percent per year from 1914 through 1920 for real product per head) and during the 1930s (about 4 percent), whereas the growth rate of real national product per head during the 1920s was minimal. Thus for the entire period from the restoration to 1940 the average annual rate of growth in real product per head was slightly above 2 percent and aggregate national product expanded at an average of about 3 1/4 percent, putting Japan in international comparison near the top for that period. There was, of course, a sharp

---

30. Unless otherwise indicated, the national accounts data (such as national product, capital formation, and saving) are taken for the period 1885 to 1940 from *ELTESJ*, vol. 1 (the more recent estimates of *JEG*, starting with 1905, show only minor differences); and for the postwar period, from various issues of *ARNIS*, particularly the 1976 and 1979 editions.

31. This rate is based on an average growth rate of 4 percent a year for the period 1886 to 1975, for which more reliable estimates exist, and an assumed growth rate of 2 percent for 1869–85. Although the latter figure is conjectural, even two extreme assumptions—no growth at all or a growth rate of 2 1/2 percent, equal to that of 1886–1913—would not make a great deal of difference as they would yield growth rates of 3.5 and 3.9 percent, respectively, for the 107 years between 1868 and 1975. The difference becomes relatively more important, however, if the rate of growth per head is involved.

32. After the discussion of the last few years, this point hardly needs belaboring.

TABLE 1-1. Long-term Trends in Basic Physical Characteristics of the Japanese Economy, 1885–1978

Year	Population (mill.) (1)	Cultivated area (mill. ha.) (2)	Total employment (mill.) (3)	Nonagri-cultural employment (mill.) (4)	Gross national product (¥ bill.)[a] (5)	Consumption per head (yen)[a] (6)	Net capital stock (¥ bill.)[a] (7)
1885	38.43	4.49	21.16	4.84	3.85	86	11.2
1900	44.10	5.02	24.77	7.93	6.23	119	15.8
1913	51.67	5.75	26.42	10.89	8.00	128	22.4
1920	55.39	6.03	26.97	13.24	11.42	153	30.2
1930	63.87	5.87	29.34	15.60	13.88	171	37.9
1940	71.93	5.97	32.23	18.87	22.85	186	60.2
1945	72.75	5.24	·	·	20.11[b]	95[b]	·
1950	83.20	5.05	35.63	19.53	16.24	121	25.0
1955	89.28	5.14	39.26	24.37	25.25	174	42.2
1960	93.42	5.28	43.69	30.57	38.00	243	70.5
1965	98.28	5.09	47.30	36.84	61.10	357	129.0
1970	103.72	5.80	50.94	42.52	105.50	522	242.7
1975	111.94	5.57[c]	52.23	46.05	136.90	612	430.0
1978[c]	115.00	5.50	54.08	48.19	158.50	700	485.0

[a]1934–36 prices.   [b]1944.   [c]Preliminary estimates.

SOURCES: **Col. 1:** 1885–1930, *HYS*, p. 12; 1885–1913, average of January 1 figures; from 1920 on, October 1; 1940–75, *ESA*, 1977, p. 284.   **Col. 2:** 1885–1972, Institute for Developing Economies, *One Hundred Years of Agricultural Statistics in Japan*, p. 120; covers only paddy and dry fields, which in 1960 accounted for 83 percent of total agricultural area; *Japan Economic Yearbook*, 1979, p. 108.   **Cols. 3 and 4:** 1880–1913, Ohkawa, 1957, pp. 145 and 245; 1920–60, *HYS*, p. 53; 1965–75, *ESA*, 1974, p. 257; *ESA*, 1978, p. 279.   **Col. 5:** 1885–1950, *ELTESJ*, 1: 178; 1955, linked to 1951 figure (*ELTESJ*, loc. cit.) by means of *HYS*, p. 51; 1960–75, linked to 1955 value on basis of *ARNIS*, 1976, pp. 102 ff., and *ESM*, February 1976, p. 167.   **Col. 6:** 1885–1950, *ELTESJ*, 1:237–38; 1955–75, linked to 1950 figure on basis of *ARNIS*, 1976, pp. 102 ff., and *ESM*, February 1976, p. 167, assuming an increase in real income per head in 1952 of 9 percent (*HYS*, pp. 13 and 51).   **Col. 7:** 1885–1940, *ELTESJ*, 3:148 ff., net capital stock including livestock plus (1) inventories as estimated by Fujino (1975, p. 190 ff.), converting his estimates in current prices into 1934–36 prices by means of GNP deflator (loc. cit.), and for 1885, (2) the difference between *ELTESJ* estimates of stock of structures other than buildings between 1887 and 1888 and of stock of dwellings between 1885 and 1886 to avoid break in series (*ELTESJ*, 3:149); 1950, rough estimate based on trend from 1952 to 1955; 1955–70, Fujino (1975, p. 192) for net fixed capital stock; for inventories, Fujino's estimates in current prices have been translated into 1934–36 prices by means of GNP deflator (loc. cit.). Fujino's estimates coincide with the national wealth survey figures of the Economic Planning Agency for 1960 but differ for 1955 (particularly for inventories) and 1970. 1975, 1978, extrapolated on basis of net fixed capital stock (*ARNA*, pp. 586–87).

decline in the immediate postwar period, and aggregate real national product and product per head did not reach 1939 levels, the highest of the prewar period,[33] until 1953 and 1957, respectively. From then until 1973 the growth rate has been notoriously spectacular, averaging for the two decades starting in 1956 nearly 9 percent for aggregate and fully 7 1/2 percent for per head gross real national product. Even starting in 1940, the rates are very high, namely, 4.0 percent for per head and 5.2 percent for aggregate gross national product.

During this century radical changes occurred in the sectoral origin of national product, changes that are common in direction though not always in speed as countries develop and as their real income per head grows. In particular, the share of the primary industries, in Japan

33. Based on estimates in *ELTESJ*, 1:214, assuming, in accordance with the estimates of the Economic Planning Agency (*HYS*, p. 51), an increase of 11 percent in 1952 to bridge the gap between a series terminating in 1951 and one starting in 1952.

TABLE 1-2. Rates of Growth of Basic Physical Characteristics of the Japanese Economy, 1886–1975 (Percent Per Year)

Period	Population	Total employment	Nonagricultural employment	Cultivated area	Gross national product[a]	Consumption per head[a]	Net capital stock
1886–1900	.92	1.06	3.35	.75	3.26	2.19	2.32
1901–1913	1.23	.50	2.47	1.05	1.94	0.56	2.75
1914–1920	1.00	.29	2.83	.68	5.22	2.58	4.35
1921–1930	1.43	.85	1.65	−.27	1.97	1.12	2.28
1931–1940	1.12	.94	1.92	.17	5.11	.84	4.75
1941–1945	.22			−2.57	−3.14[b]	−15.46[b]	
1946–1950	2.72	1.01	.34	−.74	3.50	4.11	−8.41
1951–1955	1.42	1.96	4.53	.35	9.23	7.54	11.04
1956–1960	.91	2.16	4.64	.54	8.52	6.91	10.81
1961–1965	1.02	1.60	3.80	−.73	9.96	8.00	12.83
1966–1970	1.08	1.49	2.91	2.65	11.55	7.89	13.48
1971–1975	1.54	.33	1.20	−.80	5.34	3.23	12.11
1886–1913	1.06	.80	2.94	.83	2.65	1.43	2.57
1886–1940	1.13	.77	2.50	.52	3.29	1.41	3.10
1886–1975	1.19	1.00	2.51	.24	4.03	2.20	4.14
1914–1940	1.25	.74	2.06	.14	3.96	1.39	3.72
1914–1975	1.25	1.09	2.32	−.02	4.67	2.55	4.88
1940–1975	1.29	1.35	2.52	−0.20	5.25	3.45	5.78
1956–1975	1.14	1.39	3.13	0.40	8.82	6.49	12.31

[a]1934–36 prices.   [b]1941–44.

SOURCE: Table 1-1.

chiefly the peasant cultivation of food grains, declined from nearly one-half in 1885, and probably more than one-half in the 1860s and 1870s, to less than two-fifths at the beginning of World War I and to less than one-fifth in 1940. After a halt in the 1940s, the decline resumed and even accelerated in the 1950s and 1960s with the result that agriculture contributed not much more than one-twentieth of national product in 1975, a ratio lower than in several developed European countries. Until World War II the shrinkage in the share of agriculture was offset by an increase in the share of secondary sectors, that is, mainly manufacturing. In the postwar period, on the other hand, the share of manufacturing stopped rising in the 1960s and increases were concentrated in the tertiary sectors.

b. Labor Input

The total Japanese labor force has grown between 1885 and 1975 at an average annual rate of 1.0 percent per year. Intraperiod variations can be followed in table 1-2. This rate is slightly below that of the total population, because the labor force participation rate declined from about 55 percent in the late nineteenth century to slightly below one-half beginning in the 1930s. The reasons for these movements—connected with changes in the age and sex structure of the population, in school-leaving age, and in the participation rates and employment shares of women—do not need to be disentangled here. Movements of labor input are, of course, not identical with those in the labor force. Changes in the unemployment rate produce both short-term and sometimes long-term differences. Trends in average hours per day and days per year worked are responsible for differences in long-term movements, apart even from changes in the quality of labor input, which reflect the improved health and education of workers or other factors. The increase in the quality of the labor force that must be added to the increase in numbers has been estimated at about 0.6 percent per year for the 1901–40 period,[34] and at about 1.0 percent per year for the 1952–71 period.[35]

The modernization of the Japanese economy was, of course, accompanied by sharp changes in the sectoral distribution of employment,[36] changes that, in direction, parallel those in the sectoral distribution of output. The share of agriculture in the labor force declined between 1880 and 1975 from nearly four-fifths to about one-eighth compared with a shrinkage in the primary sector's share in national output from nearly one-half to not much more than one-twentieth. In that process the absolute size of the agricultural labor force changed little between 1880 and 1913 and between 1920 and 1940. It declined moderately between 1913 and 1920, and after a temporary increase in the 1940s reflecting wartime dislocation, it was reduced by about two-thirds between 1950 and 1975. There was, thus, absolute rural depopulation from 1913 to 1920 and during the last quarter century and, except during the 1940s, relative rural depopulation for the entire period, when most or all of the natural increase in rural population was absorbed elsewhere.

c. Land

Because Japan is a country of old settlement and only a small proportion of land is usable for agriculture, the expansion of cultivated land during the past century was small. The agricultural area expanded irregularly between 1885 and 1920 at an average annual rate of 0.8 percent per year, the more valuable wet (paddy) fields growing considerably less than dry fields, showed no trend between 1920 and 1940, and fell by 15 percent in the 1940s. In the postwar period the area increased irregularly at an average rate of about 0.4 percent per year. Although the expansion of urban and forest land was more rapid and some expansion probably also occurred in the cultivated area between 1868 and 1885, the increase in the total supply of land during the last century can hardly have been above one-half of 1 percent a year.

d. Capital Inputs

The calculation and evaluation of the long-term growth rate of capital inputs as they contribute to economic growth is conceptually and statistically even more difficult and in the case of Japan quantitatively more important than that of land and labor inputs. Before summarizing the data available on the stock of reproducible capital, it seems appropriate to provide an idea of the growth rate of capital expenditures as the stock at any one date is the result of past capital expenditures and consumption.

(i) THE CAPITAL FORMATION RATIO.[37] If Japan's national product has increased rapidly over the past century, particularly in the postwar period, the rate of growth of capital expenditures and hence of the stock of reproducible capital has been even more spectacular because of the rising secular trend in the capital formation ratio, that is, the quotient of gross or net capital expenditures and gross national product.

The domestic gross capital formation ratio for the first period, late 1868 to 1885, cannot be calculated with a reasonable degree of confidence because of insufficient information. The evidence points, however, to a rather low level, probably on the order of one-tenth of gross national product, which would put the net capital formation ratio at slightly above 5 percent of national product (see table 1-3).

---

34. *JEG,* p. 68.

35. Denison and Chung, "Economic Growth and Its Sources," p. 88.

36. Ohkawa, cited in *HYS,* pp. 56–57.

37. The discussion of capital formation ratios, all in current prices, for the period 1874–1940 is based in the case of fixed reproducible assets on the estimates by Ohkawa and associates (*ELTESJ,* 1:178 ff.) and for inventories on Fujino's figures (1975, p. 190 ff.). For the postwar period the Economic Planning Agency's estimates have been used for reproducible tangible assets as well as for inventory investment (*ARNIS,* 1976, p. 86 ff.).

TABLE 1-3. Trend in Capital Formation and Saving Ratios, 1869–1975
(Percent of Gross National Product)

	Gross fixed capital formation[a] (1)	Net fixed capital formation[a] (2)	Inventory investment[b] (3)	Gross total capital formation (4)	Net total capital formation (5)	Capital imports (6)	Net saving[c] (7)
1869–1885[d]	8	4	2	10	6	2	4
1886–1900	13	5	2	15	7	2	5
1901–1913	15	6	1	16	7	2	5
1914–1921	19	9	3	22	12	−4	16
1922–1931	16	6	1½	17½	7½	1½	6
1932–1941	24	14	4	28	18	−½	18½
1942–1944	22	15	7	29	22	−½	22½
1946–1950	18	13	9	27	22	0	22
1951–1960	25	16	10	35	26	1	25
1961–1970	33	20	4	37	24	½	23
1971–1975	37	24	3	40	27	1	26

[a]Includes military capital formation through 1941; excludes consumer durables, which were equal to 3 percent of national product in 1961–70 and 4 percent in 1971–75. [b]Derived from estimates of inventories and national product in constant prices; hence excludes inventory profits. [c]Col. 5 less col. 6. [d]Rough estimates; cf. discussion in chapter 2.

SOURCES OF BASIC DATA: **Cols. 1, 2, 4, and 5:** tables 3-3, 4-4, 5-6, and *ARNIS*, various issues. **Col. 3:** Fujino, 1975, pp. 190–91, deflated by wholesale price index; *HYS*, p. 51; *JEG*, p. 289; *ARNIS*, various issues. **Col. 6:** *ELTESJ*, 1:178; *ARNIS*, various issues.

From the 1880s, the increase in the ratio was rapid. For the period 1885–1913 gross capital formation averaged nearly one-seventh of national product, at that time not a low ratio in international comparison. The ratio was considerably higher from 1914 through 1921 but fell back to not much more than the prewar level during the 1920s. The ratio moved sharply upward in the forced-draft economy of the 1930s, averaging over one-fourth of national product for the decade, and reached a level of more than one-third at the end of the decade. Because the ratio of capital consumption to gross capital expenditures declined, the net capital formation ratios showed a more rapid rise, namely, from about 7 percent of national product in the late nineteenth century to more than one-fifth at the end of the period, internationally a very high level for that depressed decade.

Although the rate of gross capital formation continued high for 1941 through 1945, net capital formation was probably negative if the extensive war damage to the capital stock is taken into account. This damage has been estimated, probably too liberally, at ¥ 65 bill., or fully one-fourth of the wealth of 1940.[38]

Postwar capital formation ratios, gross or net, have been very high and rising. For the 1950s the gross capital formation ratio averaged more than one-third of national product (including consumer durables), well above the level of the 1930s. For the 1960s and early 1970, it rose, on the average, to over two-fifths of national product if consumer durables are included, a ratio unprecedented in earlier periods in Japan and not duplicated in other free enterprise economies. Even the net ratios averaged more than one-fourth since the 1950s.

(ii) THE STOCK OF CAPITAL. Between 1874, when comprehensive estimates start, and 1940 the net stock of fixed reproducible capital increased at the annual average rate of nearly 3 1/2 percent, or about 2 1/2 percent a year per head, but only at the rates of 2 1/2 and 1 1/2 percent

38. *HYS*, p. 27, assuming wealth in 1936–40 to have grown at the same rate as for the decade of the 1930s (table 4-2, col. 7).

for the gross stock, which is sometimes regarded as a better indicator of productive capacity. However, for the period from 1908 to 1938 the quality improvement in the capital stock is estimated to have increased at a rate of fully 1 percent per year. Fluctuations in the rate of growth within this period of two-thirds of a century were substantial and can be followed in table 1-2.[39] Reflecting the relative neglect of housing in Japanese economic development, the (constant price) value of the stock of residential housing grew only at a rate of 1 percent, slightly less than total population and considerably less than urban population. The stock of nonresidential fixed reproducible capital, including business fixed capital as well as public buildings and structures, however, shows the much more substantial annual growth rate of fully 5 percent, or more than 4 percent per year per head. The public gross fixed capital stock expanded considerably more rapidly than the privately owned part of the stock.[40]

Growth rates of the capital stock were spectacular during the postwar period. A comparison of the results of the national wealth surveys of 1955 and 1970 conducted by the Economic Planning Agency shows a fivefold increase, that is, an average annual growth rate of nearly 12 percent a year, when the figures are adjusted for the rise in prices.[41] Another estimate, which begins with the 1960 national wealth survey, yields practically the same growth rate.[42] A third estimate, using the perpetual inventory method, which covers the two decades ending in 1971 but is limited to private enterprise capital stock, indicates an almost equally striking growth rate of nearly 11 percent.[43,44]

Linking the prewar and postwar growth rates of capital stock is rendered difficult by the sharp discrepancies in the two series that span the gap between 1940 and the early 1950s. The only series that provides estimates for the total net stock of capital puts the 1955 value (in 1934–36 prices) at only 60 percent of the 1940 level (63 percent for fixed assets and 41 percent for inventories) and postpones reaching the prewar level until the end of the 1950s,[45] obviously implying very large war losses that exceed the official estimate of a loss ratio of about one-fourth.[46] An estimate of the Economic Planning Agency[47] that is limited to gross fixed assets, on the other hand, puts the value of the stock in 1955 at 37 percent above the 1940 level and implies that the prewar level had been regained in the late 1940s, that is, a decade earlier than in Fujino's estimate of 1975. For the period between 1955 and 1970 the various estimates are not incompatible. The official national wealth survey, when roughly adjusted for price changes, puts the average annual growth rate for the net stock at nearly 11 percent with only relatively small differences between fixed assets and inventories; Fujino, at nearly 14 percent for fixed assets and 8 percent for inventories; and Denison and Chung at 10 percent for fixed assets and nearly 13 percent for inventories.[48] We may then derive from table 1-1 a centennial growth rate of nearly 4

39. The slow rate of growth during the 1920s is in part attributable to the Kanto earthquake, which caused damage put at ¥ 5.3 bill. (*HYS*, p. 26), 70 percent in Tokyo and 17 percent in Yokohama. This would be equivalent to somewhat more than one-tenth of the reproducible tangible wealth then existing; to about one-third of the national product of 1923; and to approximately two years' total gross capital formation of the period.

40. *ELTESJ*, 1:262, citing estimates of Economic Planning Agency.

41. For national wealth survey results, cf. *HYS*, p. 24, for 1955 and *1970 National Wealth Survey of Japan*, 1:72. The deflators are taken from *ARNIS*, 1976, p. 110 ff.

42. Fujino, 1975, p. 192.

43. Denison and Chung, *Why Has Japanese Economic Growth Been So Rapid?* appendix 1.

44. All available estimates of capital formation and capital stock omit consumer durables. This is not a serious drawback for the prewar period, because the stock of consumer durables appears to have amounted to only about 2 percent of all reproducible assets (Goldsmith, 1975, tables 5-7 and 5-10). By 1970, however, the stock of consumer durables had reached nearly 10 percent of reproducible assets (*1970 National Wealth Survey of Japan*, 1:72, 130) and gross expenditures on consumer durables in the 1960s and early 1970s constituted about one-tenth of total gross capital formation (*ARNIS*, 1976, pp. 86 ff. and 340).

45. Fujino, 1975, p. 190 ff.

46. *HYS*, p. 27.

47. *ELTESJ*, 3:262.

48. Denison and Chung, op. cit.

percent for aggregate net capital stock and of nearly 3 percent for per head stock, making allowance for the relatively slow rate of growth before 1885.

These figures on the level and movements of the capital formation ratio and on the growth rate of capital stock, approximate as they may be, are of great importance in understanding the development of Japan's financial superstructure during the past century, because they indicate the absolute and relative size of the financing task, that is, the size of the funds that had to be provided to the sectors and units making capital expenditures, either internally out of their own saving or externally, and in the latter case either directly by domestic and foreign savers through the sale of financial instruments or indirectly through domestic financial institutions. These relationships will be explored period by period in chapters 2 through 7.

e. The Determinants of Growth[49]

The modern, though not uncontroversial, technique of allocating the rate of change of gross national product, taken as an indicator of the process of economic growth, among contributing factors has not yet been applied in detail to the prewar period. Therefore, all that can be done here is to compare the growth rate of national product with that of the supply of labor, capital, and land, roughly represented by the rates of growth in the labor force, the cultivated land area, and the stock of reproducible capital, and to draw some tentative conclusions from such a comparison. This approach can, in the present state of the basic data, be used only for fairly long periods for which cyclical and other minor fluctuations can possibly be disregarded. Hence, it is attempted here only for three periods, in addition to the century as a whole, namely, 1868 to 1913, 1914 to 1940, and 1953 to 1975.

It is clear from the rates of growth shown in table 1-2 that the growth in input of labor, capital, and land does not suffice to explain the secular rate of increase in gross national product, although it comes close to doing so in the 1914–40 period, which was a period of less dynamic economic growth. For the entire period of 1886 to 1975 an average annual growth rate of real national product of 4 percent compares with increases in the labor force of 1 1/4 percent, in land of possibly as much as one-fourth of 1 percent, and of the stock of reproducible capital of fully 4 percent.

The situation is, however, quite different for the prewar and the postwar periods. Between 1874 and 1953, when war damages had been made good, the labor force increased at a rate of slightly more than 1 percent and by one of nearly 2 percent if adjusted for quality change; land by about one-fifth of 1 percent; and the stock of reproducible capital by about 2 percent, or by 3 percent if adjusted for quality change. This compares with a growth rate of about 2 1/2 percent for real national product. For this period, therefore, the growth in inputs accounts for most of that of output. During the postwar period, 1953–75, in contrast, the growth rate of national product of a bit more than 10 percent was far ahead of the increase in labor input, which has been estimated, in more detail than for the prewar period, at 2 3/4 percent per year, compared to an increase of less than 1 1/2 percent in employment and in increase in the input of land of not much more than one-fourth of 1 percent. It was only the net stock of reproducible capital, with a growth rate of about 10 1/2 percent, that was slightly above that of national product. Output per unit of input rose at a rate of nearly 5 percent a year, the result of increased knowledge and economies of scale, each of which is estimated to have contributed 2 percentage points a year, with improved resource allocation accounting for the remaining 1 percentage point.[50] One is therefore tempted to conclude that the two most important factors in the high secular rate of economic growth of Japan, particularly the spectacular growth rate of the postwar period, were, first, the rapid expansion of the capital stock, reflecting a secular upward trend in the capital

49. There is an immense literature on this problem, growing in statistical and mathematical sophistication, which can neither be listed here nor adequately taken into account in the text.

50. For this, cf. Denison and Chung ("Economic Growth and Its Sources," p. 91) and their more detailed treatment in *Why Has Japanese Growth Been So Rapid?* Some of these figures differ slightly from those in table 1-2.

formation and saving ratios, and, second, the ''residual''—sometimes called our ''measure of ignorance''—which includes such factors as improvements in the education and health of the labor force, technological and organizational advances not directly embodied in capital formation, and economies of scale. These are the bases of the extraordinary expansion of the financial superstructure during the last one hundred years.

2 Out of the Middle Ages, 1868–1885

In January 1868 the Tokugawa regime came to an end, "not with a bang but a whimper," after more than two and a half centuries of existence. Its demise was not occasioned by internal revolution, disregarding numerous local peasant revolts, nor by a foreign war, but as a consequence of the inability to find either a peaceful or a military solution to the gunboat diplomacy of the Western powers, which started with the appearance of Commodore Perry's squadron in Tokyo Bay in 1853. In the following decade the country, under the restored monarchy, underwent far-reaching political, military, economic, and financial changes, again peacefully, with the exception of the brief and locally limited Satsuma rebellion in 1877. After another decade of consolidation the New Japan had by the middle 1880s established the essential features of its real infrastructure and the financial superstructure of its economy that enabled it to "take off" politically and economically and to grow rapidly during the following century. Indeed, many of the characteristics that became evident during this period of transition can still be discerned, naturally often in modified form, among the factors responsible for the country's extraordinary economic growth beginning in the early 1950s.

This chapter starts with a listing, and it cannot be more than that, of a few characteristics of the Meiji restoration that are regarded as important factors in Japan's later financial development. It then turns to a brief review of the main changes in the infrastructure of national product, capital formation, and national wealth. Unfortunately, this review cannot be conducted, as it can in later chapters, on the basis of fairly reliable quantitative measures but will often have to be couched in approximate and qualitative terms, given the lack of, or the disagreement among, existing estimates of the relevant macroeconomic magnitudes. Similar difficulties will be encountered in the remaining sections of this chapter, which deal with the main economic reforms of the early Meiji era, the development of financial institutions and instruments and the financing of the main nonfinancial sectors during the transition period, and the course of inflation and deflation during the second half of this period.

1. THE NATURE OF THE MEIJI RESTORATION[1]

Before turning to the changes in the economic and, in particular, the financial structure of Japan that occurred in the transition period from 1868 to 1885, it is necessary to list the important noneconomic characteristics of the origins and the progress of the Meiji restoration, especially

---

1. This chapter is based primarily, apart from much of the literature listed in footnote 2 to chapter 1 and the standard statistical sources (particularly the Bank of Japan's *HYS, HYSE,* and *HYSF* and the series *ELTESJ* of K. Ohkawa and associates), on the following publications: T. F. M. Adams, *A Financial History of Modern Japan,* 1964; L. Klein and K. Ohkawa, eds., *Economic Growth: The Japanese Experience Since the Meiji Era,* 1968; A. Maddison, *Economic Growth in Japan and the USSR.,* 1969; M. Miyamoto, Y. Sakudo, and Y. Yazuba, "Economic Development in Preindustrial Japan, 1859–1894," *Journal of Economic History* 25 (1965); D. Ott, "The Financial Development of Japan, 1878–1958," Ph.D. dissertation, University of Maryland, 1960, and "The Financial Development of Japan, 1878–1958," *Journal of Political*

those characteristics that, more indirectly than directly, affected financial developments during the transition period.

a. The driving force behind the restoration was political, always keeping in mind the unavoidable oversimplification involved in such statements. It was the desire to safeguard Japan from becoming subject to foreign domination or even merely from losing its freedom of action to a significant extent, a basic psychological attitude for which one might coin the term "xenodoulophobia."

b. Japan's political and economic independence could only be preserved, the authors of the restoration realized, if the country modernized itself militarily and therefore also economically as rapidly as possible at the same time retaining its national identity. Adaptive and selective modernization of the economy was therefore one of the most important objectives of the restoration.

c. The men who had prepared for the restoration since the mid-1850s, and who were largely responsible for its execution through the transition period, came largely from the ranks of the lower samurai of four southwestern *hans* (clans). Although the restoration could not have been carried through successfully without a considerable degree of cooperation from other influential groups, including the leading merchants, it certainly was not a bourgeois revolution.

d. The restoration involved at least four major political reforms, all of which were carried out with remarkable speed within a few years and against relatively little opposition. The first was the substitution of the centralized system of four dozen prefectures for the decentralized feudal domains of several hundred Tokugawa daimyo. After a short period of transition, during which the daimyo acted as imperial delegates in their former domains, they were pensioned off and disappeared from the political scene.

e. Possibly more important was the civilianization of the several hundred thousand samurai, who lost their previous military and political privileges as well as their rice stipends—the commutation will be discussed in section 3c—and became members of the urban labor force, most of them at the modest levels of minor civil servants, for example, policemen, or in comparable occupations. For many of them this signified a formal rather than a substantive change.

f. The demilitarization of the samurai, whose primary loyalty had been to their daimyo, was accompanied by the creation of a conscript army and navy drawn from the entire population, which were officered largely by former members of the upper samurai class and were at the service of the emperor only.

g. The opening of Japan to trade and to other economic and financial contacts with the rest of the world, which may be regarded as another crucial difference between the Meiji and the Tokugawa regimes, had originally been forced upon the country by the Western powers in the 1850s. Two aspects, the restriction of Japan's tariff sovereignty and the limited exterritoriality of foreigners, although resented by the Meiji government, stayed in force throughout the transition period.

h. Meiji Japan remained throughout the transition period a centralized, bureaucratically administered, absolute monarchy without even the facade of a parliamentary democracy.

2. THE EXPANSION OF THE INFRASTRUCTURE

The infrastructure of the Japanese economy, represented by the volume of output and the stock of capital, grew during the transition period from 1868 to 1885 rather slowly, although probably

Economy 69 (1961); H. T. Patrick, "Japan 1868–1914," in R. Cameron, ed., *Banking in the Early Stages of Industrialization*, 1967; H. Rosovsky, "Japan's Transition to Modern Economic Growth, 1868–1885," in H. Rosovsky, ed., *Industrialization in Two Systems*, 1966; K. Yamamura, "Japan 1868–1930: A Revised View," in R. Cameron, ed., *Banking and Economic Development*, 1972.

somewhat more rapidly in its second half, and capital formation and saving were at a low level. This unfortunately is about as much as one can now say with a reasonable degree of confidence if one insists on quantitative evidence. It may, however, be sufficient as a background for what is known about the expansion of the superstructure of financial institutions and instruments and may be acceptable as the denominator of some informative ratios.

Estimates made on the basis of figures now available,[2] which were published before the recent revision in the calculations for the period starting in 1885,[3] yield an average growth rate in constant prices for the years 1865 to 1885 of 2 percent.[4] These estimates must remain in doubt until the record of these two decades is examined more thoroughly. Another recent estimate implies an average annual growth rate of national product of 1.6 percent for the years 1880 to 1885,[5] a period primarily of cyclical downswing, and hence the figure may well be below the average for the entire period from the restoration through 1885. The assumption of a growth rate of about 2 percent per year for aggregate national product, and hence one of about 1 1/4 percent for product per head, would thus seem indicated until specialized research produces better founded estimates.

Changes in the origin of national income seem to have been modest, although presaging in their direction future trends. Thus the share of primary industries, represented to the extent of about nine-tenths by agriculture, is estimated to have declined from a little more than three-fifths in the 1860s and late 1870s to 56 percent in 1885; that of secondary industries to have stayed around one-tenth; and that of the tertiary sector to have risen slightly.[6] Even in 1885 more than three-fourths of the labor force is supposed to have been engaged in agriculture.[7]

Firmer estimates are difficult to obtain because of the uncertainties still surrounding the growth rate of agricultural production, which accounted for considerably more than one-half of national income and for four-fifths of the labor force in the early Meiji era as well as the later part of the transition period and up to the end of the nineteenth century. For the 1870s and early 1880s the rate may have been on the order of 1 1/2 to 2 percent per year.[8]

Two indices are now available, beginning in 1874, for manufacturing. The first index[9] shows an expansion of manufacturing production between 1875 and 1885, based on three-year averages centered on these years, by 45 percent, or 3.8 percent a year. The second index[10] indicates that for the same period the value of manufacturing output, at constant 1934–36 prices, increased by one-third, or at an annual rate of 2.9 percent. Because the manufacturing sector should have been growing rapidly during the decade and because its contribution to national product was small, certainly not more than one-tenth, the growth rate of total national product should have been considerably lower.

Even more frustrating for an analysis of the development of the financial superstructure is the lack of data on capital formation and saving. A rough estimate for the last decade of the

2. In order of age, Yamada (*HYS*, p. 28), for national income; Ohkawa (*HYS*, 32), for national income; and Fujino (1975, pp. 186 and 194), for gross national product in current and constant prices.

3. *ELTESJ*, 1:178 ff.

4. These figures are based on an estimate by Crawcour (in Lockwood, 1965, p. 21) of a level of national income, in 1878–80 prices, of about ¥ 400 mill. for "the 1860s," interpreted as applicable to the middle of the decade; and Ohkawa's estimates of national income in current prices of about ¥ 620 mill. in 1885, which is considerably lower than his later estimate (*ELTESJ*, vol. 1, p. 178), assuming, on the basis of the only index going back to 1868, the wholesale price index of Asahi Shimbun (*HYS*, p. 76), that prices were about the same in 1885 as in 1878–80.

5. This is Fujino's estimate (1975, p. 186).

6. Based on Yamada's estimates (*HYS*, p. 28).

7. Ohkawa's estimate (*HYS*, p. 56).

8. According to Crawcour's estimates (loc. cit.), the volume of primary production in the 1860s was between 60 and 66 percent of that of 1878–80 (nine-tenths accounted for by agriculture), implying annual growth rates of 3.0 and 3.7 percent if his figures represent an average for the decade. One hesitates to accept such high rates without stronger evidence.

9. Shionoya in Klein and Ohkawa, p. 104.

10. Shinohara, *ELTESJ*, vol. 10.

period can be obtained by using figures for the increases in net capital stock.[11] They indicate an increase in net fixed capital between 1874 and 1885 of slightly more than ¥ 1.2 bill. in 1934–36 prices, which should be equivalent to somewhat more than ¥ 500 mill. in current prices using Ohkawa's old national product deflator. A rough estimate of ¥ 8 bill. for gross national product yields a net capital formation ratio of about 6 percent, which might be raised to between 7 and 8 percent if inventories,[12] consumer durables, and military capital formation are included. The ratio for the entire 1869–85 period should then not have been much in excess of 6 percent even if broadly defined. Because net capital imports are estimated at 2 percent of national product, the net domestic saving ratio should not have been in excess of 4 percent of national product.

For the last six years of the period a more recent estimate puts total gross capital formation at nearly 10 percent of national product, all accounted for by fixed capital formation, as net inventory investment was calculated to be slightly negative in a period of depression. The government accounted for one-sixth of the total.[13] Net capital formation should then have been on the order of 5 percent of national product. Because capital imports amounted to nearly 1 percent of national product,[14] the domestic net saving rate would have been in the neighborhood of 4 percent. These should be regarded as upper limits for the entire period from the restoration to 1885.[15]

3. THE GREAT ECONOMIC REFORMS

Although the process of modernizing the economic and financial structure of Japan involves a large number of large and small changes in technology, administration, private decisions and government policies, and economic tastes and attitudes, it nevertheless seems justified to concentrate attention on a small number of measures that are basic to the development of the financial structure of Japan. Each of the measures briefly described in this section had considerable repercussions in the financial sphere, although others also had important effects. The first three of the four "reforms," to which this section is limited, were completed during the first half of the transition period, as were the great political reforms mentioned in chapter 1. The reforms include the introduction of a new monetary system, the reform of the land tax, and the compensation of the expropriated feudal lords and their retainers. The fourth reform, the policy of direct government participation in the process of industrialization, continued through most of the transition period but began to be abandoned near its end.

a. Introducing the Yen[16]

Although the introduction of an efficient monetary system would appear to have been most essential, the monetary system of Japan remained "chaotic"[17] during much of the first decade of the Meiji restoration, not only in fact, but also as far as monetary statistics and the literature

11. *ELTESJ*, 3:139, adjusting for break in one component between 1877 and 1878.

12. Fujino's estimates of inventory investment for the 1880s and 1890s (1975, p. 186) average slightly more than 2 percent of gross national product.

13. 1975, Ibid.

14. *ELTESJ*, 1:192.

15. The available direct estimates of gross capital formation are difficult to accept. These estimates (Emi, 1971), which may refer only to the nonagricultural sector of the economy, put total nonmilitary gross fixed capital formation at ¥ 190 mill. for 1874–85. Because gross national product for this twelve-year period may be roughly estimated at about ¥ 8 1/2 bill., these estimates yield the astonishingly low gross fixed capital formation ratio of not much more than 2 percent. The net domestic fixed capital formation ratio would then have been on the order of 1 percent, given the implied very slow rate of growth of past capital expenditures. The Harrod formula, then, produces the unbelievably low rate of growth of national product of one-fourth of 1 percent. The estimates are equally unbelievable in the face of a gross capital formation ratio of considerably more than 10 percent for the seven years immediately following 1885.

16. See, e.g., Shinjo, chap. 2; *HYS*, pp. 91 ff.; Patrick, 1965.

17. *HYSE*, p. 92.

dealing with the subject are concerned. Originally equal to the Mexican silver dollar, at that time a trading currency in the region, a new currency unit, the "yen," was introduced in 1871, although several types of government paper money and not a few counterfeits, as well as numerous categories of metallic coins, continued to circulate. The situation was complicated by the fact that before the restoration and for some time thereafter, silver was overvalued in Japan in relation to gold, compared to the international prices of the two metals, which led to large outflows of gold and inflows of silver. Exactly how the Japanese economy, and in particular its financial sector, coped with this situation, which seems to have prevailed until the late 1870s, is not evident from the literature available in European languages.

Most of the estimates indicate that the volume of currency expanded greatly from 1868 to 1878, although the available statistics do not provide reasonably accurate quantitative measures of the process. The reported volume of government notes increased from zero at the restoration to a peak of ¥ 139 mill. in 1878,[18] and some contemporary authors assert, in addition, that unreported notes to the extent of ¥ 15 mill. to ¥ 25 mill. were in circulation from 1877 to 1881.[19] During the same period ¥ 23 mill. of new subsidiary silver and copper coins were put into circulation and about ¥ 60 mill. of full-bodied metallic coins, mostly gold, were minted.[20] Because neither the amount of coins leaving the country nor the amount of pre-Meiji feudal paper money or subsidiary coin retired are accurately known, the actual volume of currency in circulation or its increase since the restoration can be only roughly estimated. Three estimates labeled "currency in circulation," which are shown in table 2-1, put it at between ¥ 183 mill. and ¥ 208 mill. in 1880, most of which may be regarded as an addition since the restoration. These figures yield for 1880 a ratio of money in circulation (check deposit money being as yet of very little importance) to national product of about one-fifth, or an income velocity of money of 5, and an average annual money issue ratio (increase in money in circulation divided by aggregate national product) for the period 1868–80 of about 4 percent, a high value in international comparison. Because considerably more than one-half of the increase in currency in circulation consisted of irredeemable government paper money, it is evident that the expansion of the volume of currency in circulation constituted an important form of forced saving and an essential source of funds for the new government. Indeed, from 1868 to 1874 the net issuance of about ¥ 75 mill. of paper money contributed nearly one-fifth of the total revenues of the government and was more than twice as large as its domestic and foreign borrowing.

The statistical material available on money in circulation, prices, wages, interest rates, and national product is unfortunately neither comprehensive nor reliable enough, and at times too contradictory, to permit an analysis of the effects of the changes in the quantity of money on these other magnitudes, particularly insofar as short-term movements are concerned.[21] It is clear, however, from the imperfect data at hand that the sharp expansion of money in circulation from the restoration to 1878, which was particularly rapid in the first four years of the new regime and again in 1877–78 as a result of the expenses involved in putting down the Satsuma rebellion, was followed by a substantial price inflation, but that the lag in the movements of money in circulation and the price level was a long one. The wholesale price level advanced according to one index (Asahi Shimbun) by nearly 40 percent between 1868 and 1872, which corresponds in direction to the sharp increase in currency in circulation. Another index (Tsuru), however, shows an increase of only 13 percent between 1868 and 1871. Money wages, accord-

18. *HYS*, p. 166.

19. Rathgen, p. 463; de la Mazelière, p. 437.

20. The more comprehensive, but possibly more conjectural, calculations of Patrick shown in table 2-1 give a similar figure for 1880 but show only a very small increase since the Restoration, because Patrick puts currency in circulation in 1869 at ¥ 195 mill., mostly in coins (1965, p. 192). Patrick's calculation yields an astonishingly low value of less than 0.5 percent for the money issue ratio for the 1867–80 period.

21. The mammoth 1,000-page *Monetary Analysis and History of the Japanese Economy* (1974) by K. Asakura and C. Nishiyama invalidates this statement only to a limited extent.

TABLE 2-1. Some Basic Economic Indicators, Annually, 1868–1885

| | Currency in circulation (¥ mill.) | | | Gross national product deflator | Wholesale prices | Money wages | Interest rate | Foreign exchange rate | Current account balance |
| | A | B | C | D | deflator | (1885 = 100) | (1885 = 100) | (percent) | (¥ per $) | (¥ mill.) |
	(1)	(2)	(3)	(4)	(5)	(6)	(7)	(8)	(9)	(10)
1868	24	195		24		76	66	14.0		4
1869	50	221		50		92	66	14.0		−13
1870	56	230		56		96	61	13.5		−29
1871	62	230		73		95	65	13.8		−10
1872	72	199		108		105	66	14.6		−17
1873	97	195		140		105	73	12.8		−16
1874	114	185		153		108	76	13.1	0.98	−20
1875	113	173		154		111	78	11.8	1.01	−25
1876	124	177		164		115	79	12.1	1.05	− 8
1877	140	184		175		104	81	10.0	1.04	−16
1878	189	223		222	105	107	87	10.4	1.08	−22
1879	189	221		216	122	110	92	12.0	1.12	−20
1880	183	208	197	204	145	115	100	13.1	1.11	−24
1881	178	195	193	195	160	118	102	14.0	1.11	−13
1882	170	180	190	190	146	111	105	10.1	1.10	− 1
1883	159	166	166	183	114	103	103	7.9	1.11	− 2
1884	153	156	165	178	95	96	99	10.9	1.13	− 8
1885	153	151	155	178	100	100	100	11.0	1.17	− 3

Sources: **Col. 1:** *HYS*, p. 166; for explanation, cf. *HYSE*, pp. 91–95.   **Col. 2:** Patrick, 1965, pp. 192–93.   **Col. 3:** Fujino, 1975, p. 190.   **Col. 4:** Asakura and Nishiyama, p. 882. Inclusion of demand deposits of banks would increase these figures to ¥ 155 mill. in 1875, ¥ 216 mill. in 1880, and ¥ 214 mill. in 1885.   **Col. 5:** Ohkawa (*HYS*, p. 32).   **Col. 6:** *HYS*, p. 76; index of Asahi Shimbun.   **Col. 7:** Tsuru, p. 148.   **Col. 8:** 1874–85, *HSJE*, p. 81; Tokyo bank loans on bills, annual average.   **Col. 9:** *HYS*, p. 318; for 1874–80, annual average; for 1880–85, average of annual high and low.   **Col. 10:** *ELTESJ*, 1:192.

ing to the only available index, advanced by fully one-tenth between 1869 and 1873. Between 1873 and 1878 the increase in wholesale prices was small, regardless of the index used, although money in circulation increased substantially according to the three estimates shown in table 2-1. Most of the indices continued to increase between 1878 and 1881, although money in circulation seems to have declined slightly.

If only the levels at the restoration and in 1881 are compared, the divergence among measures, although somewhat reduced, remains disturbingly large. The two wholesale price indices that cover the entire period agree on a rise by about 30 percent, and money wages advanced by 50 percent. Seemingly not affected by the inflation, interest rates averaged 12 percent for the period, a level that, even if roughly adjusted for the increase in wholesale prices, leaves a real interest rate of over 10 percent.

b. The New Land Tax[22]

It was evident from the early days of the restoration that the government needed substantial and fairly stable monetary revenues to carry through its program of political independence and economic modernization. As Japan in 1868 was still a predominately agricultural country, the transformation of the former feudal rice levies, which seem to have averaged from one-third to two-fifths of the crop, into a comprehensive land tax payable in money was the obvious solution. The transformation was essentially accomplished by the basic land tax reform of 1873.

22. For a detailed discussion of the land tax before the reform and the reform itself, cf. Rathgen, pp. 512–85.

The main result of the complex of reform measures was the establishment of an assessed valuation of all types of land, occasionally changed as time went on, which formed the basis for the tax. Originally levied at a rate of 3 percent, the tax was reduced in 1876 to 2 1/2 percent.

The new land tax yielded in 1873–75, the first years of its application, ¥ 62 mill. on the average, or nearly four-fifths of the total ordinary revenues of the government, a ratio showing its crucial importance. Even after the reduction of 1876, which lowered the yield to an average of ¥ 41 mill. in 1876–78, the tax furnished fully two-thirds of ordinary revenue. Because the yield remained almost unchanged until the end of the century, the tax lost in importance, but by the end of the transition period it still produced about one-half of ordinary revenue.[23] Its relation to national product during the transition period declined more rapidly, from about 15 percent in 1873–75 to 5 percent in 1885.

Although evaluations of the effects of the reform on the various groups subject to the tax differ, it would seem that the reform substantially reduced the burden, compared to the situation before the restoration, particularly for the landowners, though less for tenants. It thus should have increased farmers' capacity to save.[24]

A corollary of the tax reform, the establishment of transferable land titles, is of particular importance for Japan's financial development. Land was made freely salable and mortgageable in contrast to the formal, although often circumvented, inalienability of land during the Tokugawa period.

c. The Commutation of Feudal Pensions[25]

The rice rents received under the Tokugawa regime by the feudal lords and their retainers, a crucial feature of that system, were commuted into monetary pensions evidenced by government bonds. This reform most directly affected the country's financial structure because it created over a period of a few years a new financial instrument exceeding in size all other non-monetary financial instruments then outstanding.

Although the Meiji government had succeeded soon after the restoration in substantially reducing the rice rents received by the samurai, and particularly the daimyo, without arousing strong opposition, two problems remained. First, the pensions constituted a heavy burden on the government's still precarious budget. In 1873, when the land tax revenue was already being collected in full, the pensions absorbed nearly one-third of total ordinary revenues.[26] Second, and more important, the pensions, typically amounting to only ¥ 30 to ¥ 40 a year per family and exceeding ¥ 1,000 in fewer than 600 cases,[27] did not enable even the wealthier ex-samurai and daimyo to enter business as the government desired. The government therefore decided to commute the pensions into government bonds, which the recipients, or at least the larger recipients, could use as capital.

The first attempt, which was made in 1873–74 on a voluntary basis, was not very successful. Only 136,000 pensioners, or a little less than one in three, entitled to a little more than one-fifth of total pensions, accepted the offer. They received more than ¥ 16 mill. in government bonds plus ¥ 19 mill. in cash. Shortly thereafter the government had to agree to repurchase the bonds from the recipients at 80 percent of face value, thus further increasing the

---

23. *HYS,* pp. 130 and 136.

24. It has been estimated that the share of the landowners in the rice crop advanced from 28 percent in the late Tokugawa period to 34 percent at the time of the land-tax reform and sharply increased to 56 percent for the decade following it. The share of the tenants kept close to one-third throughout the period, whereas that of the government fell sharply from more than one-third to one-eighth (Ikeda, in Uchida and Ikeda, p. 58).

25. The operation is treated in varying detail and with varying degrees of clarity in virtually all books dealing with the economic development of the Meiji period. I have found Rathgen's treatment (pp. 447–56) the most satisfactory and have essentially followed it in the descriptive part of this section.

26. *HYS,* pp. 130–31.

27. Rathgen, p. 453.

cash outlay required. In order to pay this amount the government had to borrow £2.4 mill. (nearly ¥ 11 mill.) in London on fairly onerous terms—7 percent bonds maturing in twenty-five years secured by receipts from the rice tax issued at 92 1/2 with a commission of 2 1/2 percent and thus costing the government more than 8 percent.[28] The government recouped part of the costs by levying a progressive tax, at rates of up to 30 percent, on pensions received.

A few years later, in mid-1876, the government felt strong enough to commute the remaining pensions without leaving the recipients a choice. Several types of bonds, totaling ¥ 174 mill., were issued, repayable by drawing over a period of twenty-five years starting in 1882 but salable by recipients after September 1878. The majority of the bonds bore 7 percent interest, and smaller amounts had coupons of 5, 6, or 10 percent. Commutation was regressive among pensioners. The largest holders (pensions of more than ¥ 1,000 per year) received 5 percent bonds equal to seven and a half to five times their annual pension for a total of ¥ 31 mill., and the majority of ex-samurai, with annual stipends of less than ¥ 100, were offered 7 percent bonds equal to eleven and a half to fourteen times their pension if they were entitled to inheritable pensions, with the compensation for life pensions fixed at one-half these amounts.

The first result of this complicated operation, involving the issuance of hundreds of thousands of bond certificates with face values of as little as ¥ 10, was a reduction of the annual charge on the budget from about ¥ 15 1/2 to 11 1/2 mill. Much more important, however, for the development of the financial superstructure of Japan was the distribution within three years of ¥ 190 mill. of government bonds to more than 400,000 holders, or about 5 percent of all households. The size of this operation, at a very early stage of the country's modern history, will be better realized by a few comparisons. The ¥ 190 mill. of bonds represented more than three years' revenue of the central government; they were of the same order of magnitude as total money in circulation; they were probably equal to about one-third of all other financial instruments and were several times as large as all other securities then outstanding; and they were on the order of about one-third of a year's national product and of about one-twentieth of national wealth. Finally, although this must remain conjecture, they probably constituted a large proportion of the recipient's total wealth and certainly represented most of their salable financial assets.

An evaluation of the short- and long-term effects of the commutation operation would require more information than seems to be available on the disposition of the bonds by the recipients. Substantial amounts were used, particularly by the larger recipients, to participate in the capital of the national banks, which was one of the definite objectives of the government when it undertook the operation. This is evident from the fact that nobles and retainers in 1880 owned more than ¥ 30 mill. of stock of national banks, which had been acquired by tendering commutation bonds. Additional bonds were acquired by national banks as investments and thus in effect monetized. Many bonds must have been sold, at prices down to 30 percent below par, to sustain recipients' consumption. A substantial proportion, finally, was retired by the government out of budget surpluses, particularly in the early 1880s.

Some idea of these shifts can be obtained by looking at the distribution of government bonds in 1885 because very few bonds were issued in the decade following 1876. At that date the national banks were reported to hold ¥ 48 mill. of the bonds (more than half to cover their own note issues) and the Yokohama Specie Bank held another ¥ 3 mill., or together more than one-fifth of all domestic government bonds outstanding.[29] Although the holdings of other financial institutions are not known, they must have been small, except for those of the Deposit Bureau of the Finance Ministry, which may have been on the order of ¥ 10 mill.[30] Thus nearly three-

---

28. Adams, 1964, p. 21.

29. *HYS*, p. 272.

30. This assumes that most of the assets of the Deposit Bureau of ¥ 11.6 mill. (Rathgen, p. 511) were invested in government bonds.

fourths of the bonds must have been held by the private sector, which at that time essentially meant households. How many of these bonds were still in the hands of the original recipients or their heirs and how many were in the hands of people who had acquired them in the open market does not seem to be known.

d. The Government as a Pioneer of Modernization and Industrialization

Although not embodied in basic legal enactments, specific measures were undertaken by the Meiji government during the transition period to modernize the economy. These measures included the establishment of Western-type industrial organizations and the introduction of Western technology. Following occasional smaller similar activities in the closing decade of the Tokugawa regime, foreign experts were employed and Japanese were sent abroad to study. This phase was virtually completed at the end of the transition period in 1885.

The government's active financial participation in the early industrialization of Japan[31] began with the restoration. The government invested, it has been calculated, ¥ 35 mill. in government enterprises. About equally divided between the 1868–74 and 1875–80 periods,[32] these investments represented about two-fifths of the government's total nonmilitary capital expenditures from 1868 through 1880 and were equal to about 5 percent of its total expenditures. Most of the investments were financed out of ordinary revenue or, it might be argued, during the first period out of the receipts from paper currency issues.

Beginning in 1880, the government disposed of these enterprises, which it had promoted, owned, and managed, to private business, often to leading groups like Mitsui, and usually realized considerably less than its original investment. For thirteen enterprises, for example, about one-eighth of the government's total investment, sales receipts were slightly below one-half of the original investment.[33] Although the reasons for the disposal seem to have been primarily financial—the need to raise cash[34] and the avoidance of continuous deficits—by that time the government also felt that it had fulfilled its role as an industrial pioneer, and that private business was in a position, both administratively and financially, to operate and expand the enterprises.

Equally important in the modernization process was the advancement of technological knowledge, in fields far exceeding that of the manufacturing industry. By employing foreign experts, usually for relatively short periods, and by sending students abroad for academic study and practical experience, the government advanced the technological base in various industries. The program was of considerable size, particularly in comparison with what other then underdeveloped countries were doing. Total expenditures have been calculated at about ¥ 20 mill. for the period: about ¥ 15 mill. for foreign experts and ¥ 5 mill. for students going abroad.[35] Although these sums are small in comparison to national product—on the order of 0.1 percent for the period 1868–85—they constituted a substantial drain on the budget and on limited foreign exchange resources.

4. CREATING A FINANCIAL SYSTEM

The first two attempts of the Meiji government to create a commercial banking system in its first decade failed; but near the end of the transition period it succeeded in establishing a central bank. All, except the first emergency measure, were copies of foreign institutions, as were so many of the institutional changes of that period. The commercial banks followed an American model and the central bank a European model.

31. The main source of information is Smith, 1955.
32. Emi, 1971, p. 227.
33. Smith, 1955, pp. 90–95.
34. Smith, 1955, pp. 100–103.
35. Emi, 1963, pp.114–24. Cf. also Hara.

The first attempt, immediately after the restoration, to organize banklike companies (*kawase kaisha*), which would issue notes to provide funds to lend to business and government, never really got off the ground. Only a half dozen of these companies were formed by groups of merchants, apparently under substantial pressure by the new government. Within a few years, all but one had closed their doors, partly because the public, remembering the han notes, was suspicious of paper money and partly because of poor management.[36]

The second attempt, although better prepared, was not more successful.[37] After studying the situation in leading foreign countries, the government concluded that the recently created national banking system of the United States provided the best model for Japan, having as it did the advantages of introducing a sound currency and at the same time assisting in financing government and business. The law of November 1872, however, had two flaws. First, it made the notes issued by the national banks against the collateral of government bonds redeemable in metal, which, given the public's attitude toward paper money and the deficits in the current balance of payments, made it very difficult to keep the notes in circulation. Second, the terms of the law did not provide the banks with a sufficient margin of profit. As a result, only five national banks were organized from 1873 to 1876, the first and largest of them only as a result of substantial pressure by the Ministry of Finance on Mitsui, Ono, and other leading merchant houses.[38] The total assets of the first national banks never seem to have exceeded ¥ 10 mill., a risible amount even in the early Meiji period. Their note issues did not even reach ¥ 2 mill., compared to more than ¥ 100 mill. of government paper money.

Learning from this experience, the government in April 1876 drastically revised the National Bank Act: the notes were made inconvertible, capital could be contributed in commutation bonds, and the banks' profit margin was enlarged. Having thus been provided with both a source of capital and a profit incentive, a veritable boom in the organization of national banks occurred in the three years following the amendments. When the number of banks reached 151 in 1879, with a paid-in capital of ¥ 41 mill. and notes amounting to ¥ 34 mill., still only one-fourth of government paper money outstanding, the government called a halt and refused to license additional banks. The government probably regarded the banks as contributing to the inflation, and by then, in any event, it had decided to concentrate note issuance in a central bank of the European type. Organized in 1882, the Bank of Japan was beginning to operate on a more than token scale in 1886. Although the number of national banks had begun to decline, falling to 139 in 1885 and to 133 ten years later, the operation of the banks expanded for another decade and a half, with the number of offices increasing from 82 in 1879 to 119 in 1885 and to 180 in 1895. The total assets of national banks expanded rapidly from 1877 to 1895, increasing from about ¥ 40 mill. (main assets or liabilities and capital; aggregate balance sheets were apparently not published) to more than ¥ 100 mill. in 1885 and to a peak of more than ¥ 300 mill. a decade later (table 2-2). In 1885 their assets were equal to nearly 15 percent of national product, whereas the ratio of their issues to aggregate national product for the period 1877–85 was on the order of 1 1/2 percent.

During this period the share of funds provided by capital and reserves, primarily contributed in the form of commutation bonds, was in excess of two-fifths. Former daimyo and samurai contributed a large proportion of the original capital, but the contributions by merchants and landowners were also substantial and increased at the expense of the contributions of the samurai. The share of notes was close to one-third, whereas that of deposits doubled from one-eighth in 1877 to one-fourth in 1885. Even so, however, the increase in deposits between 1876 and 1885 of ¥ 25 mill. was equal to only about one-third of 1 percent of the period's gross national product. Current deposits, which might be regarded as part of the money supply, in

36. On this episode, see the eyewitness account of E. Shibuzawa in Okuma, pp. 488–90.

37. On the creation of the national banking system, see, e.g., *HYSE*, pp. 103–04; Shinjo, passim; Adams, 1964, pp. 9 ff.

38. See again Shibuzawa, loc. cit.

TABLE 2-2. Principal Accounts of National Banks, 1875–1895

	1875	1880	1885	1890	1895
I. Amounts (mill. yen)					
Assets	5	102	113	198	307
Government securities	3	44	48	40	20
Lendings	2	58	65	158	287
Deposits	1	15	27	34	75
Notes	1	34	30	26	21
Borrowings	—	1	2	11	23
Paid-in capital and reserves	3	45	50	61	68
II. Distribution (assets = 100)					
Government securities	60	43	42	20	7
Lendings	40	57	58	80	93
Deposits	20	15	24	17	24
Notes	20	33	27	13	7
Borrowings	—	1	2	10	8
Paid-in capital and reserves	60	43	44	54	22
III. Relation to GNP (percent)[a]					
Assets	1.0	10.4	14.0	18.8	19.8
Government securities	0.6	4.5	6.0	3.8	1.3
Lendings	0.4	5.9	8.0	15.0	18.5
Deposits	0.2	1.5	3.3	3.2	4.8
Notes	0.0	3.5	3.7	2.5	1.4
Borrowings	—	—	0.2	1.0	1.5
Paid-in capital and reserves	0.6	4.6	6.2	5.8	4.4
IV. Number of banks					
	4	151	139	134	133

[a]Roughly estimated at ¥ 500 mill. for 1875.

SOURCES: *HYS*, pp. 196–97 and 272, except borrowings (Goto, p. 45).

1885 amounted to only about ¥ 10 mill., or 1.2 percent of national product and 6 percent of currency in circulation.

Of the national banks' main assets, more than two-fifths consisted until 1885 of government securities, mostly commutation bonds representing contributed capital but also partly resulting from open market purchases. These securities in 1885 were equal to about one-fifth of the domestic government bonds then outstanding. Loans and overdrafts, presumably mainly to business, accounted for the remaining three-fifths; bills discounted were relatively small. Most of the loans went to traders, as agriculture accounted for only about one-tenth of the total, but about one-sixth of the loans went to nobles and retainers, probably in part to assist in setting up business and in part for consumptive purposes.

Although the government by the end of the transition period had managed to set up an effective note-issuing commercial banking system and a foreign trade bank—the Yokohama Specie Bank organized in 1880, which rapidly grew to assets of about ¥ 20 mill. in 1885—practically unregulated banks without issue privileges and various types of quasi banks, which combined commercial with financial activities, developed without official statistics taking much note of them. As a consequence, only fragmentary information is available. The private ordinary banks, including the first, the bank of the House of Mitsui, which was organized in 1876, were the most important among these institutions. In 1885 more than 200 of them were reported, practically all organized from 1879 on, with a paid-in capital of ¥ 19 mill., or more than two-fifths of the capital of the 139 national banks then operating.[39] If it is assumed that the lendings

39. *HYS*, pp. 198–99.

and deposits of the ordinary private banks bore the same ratio to their capital as was the case for national banks, they would have amounted to about ¥ 30 mill. and ¥ 12 mill., respectively. They thus would have added in 1885 about 4 and 1 1/2 percent, respectively, to the ratio of bank assets and deposits to national product and about 0.5 percent to the banks' issue ratio during the 1881–85 period.

Still less is known about the numerous quasi banks, which numbered in 1885, as far as reported, about 750 with a capital of ¥ 15 mill. compared to only 120 with ¥ 1.2 mill. capital five years earlier. Thus their average capital was only about ¥ 20,000 compared to an average of ¥ 85,000 for private ordinary banks and ¥ 320,000 for national banks. Because deposits were small, the lendings of quasi banks probably did not exceed capital substantially, adding less than one-fifth to the funds of national banks.[40]

Although the numerous pawnshops and credit cooperatives (mujin) may have played a substantial role in the financial structure during the first part of the transition period, by 1885 their assets were too small to be significant. They nevertheless were an important source of funds for large sectors of the population, mainly small farmers, merchants, and artisans, who did not have access to other financial institutions.[41]

Table 2-3 attempts to bring together the scattered and often not too reliable information on the assets and issues (regarded as equal to the change in assets) of financial institutions during the transition period, occasionally filling gaps with rough estimates. Notwithstanding these defects, two conclusions emerge. First, the absolute and relative size of financial institutions increased considerably during the transition period, particularly during its second half. Second, they were still small, both in international comparison and in relation to later levels in Japan. Thus the assets of financial institutions were equal at the end of the period to about one-third of a year's national product, although this ratio rises to nearly one-half if government paper currency is included. The increase was substantial compared to 1875 when the ratio seems to have been on the order of one-fifth of a year's national product, even including government paper currency, which was then the largest liquid financial instrument. At the time of the restoration this ratio may have been as low as one-tenth (excluding metallic currency), although a meaningful comparison is hardly possible in view of the very different institutional structures and the absence of reliable data. The issue ratio of financial institutions during the transition period, including government paper money, cannot have been much in excess of 2 percent and may have been substantially less if paper money in circulation in 1868 has been underestimated. It almost certainly was higher during the second half of the period, particularly if government paper money is excluded.

5. THE MATSUKATA DEFLATION[42]

The deflation that Count Matsukata, who became minister of finance late in 1881, carried through during the next few years marks the end of the transition period and the inflation that had prevailed during most of the 1870s. It also marks the establishment of a substantial degree of stability in public and private finance, a basis from which the system could rapidly expand during the following decades. Its triple goal was to balance the budget, halt price inflation, and eliminate the disagio of the yen in terms of silver. Matsukata reached these goals by 1885 at the expense, it is true, of sharp declines in commodity prices, wages, and land values, along with a

40. Asakura, 1965, p. 30.

41. In the mid-1870s about 25,000 pawnshops were reported with loans of ¥ 25 mill., then quite a substantial amount, although only ¥ 1,000 per shop (Asakura, 1967, p. 34).

42. Strangely enough, no detailed, or by modern standards acceptable, study of this interesting episode, interesting particularly for monetarists, appears to exist in Western languages; for a brief treatment, cf. Rosovsky, "Japan's Transition to Modern Economic Growth," pp. 132–39.

TABLE 2-3. Assets of Financial Institutions, 1868–1885

	Assets[a]			Change in assets[a]		
	1868	1875	1885	1869–75	1876–85	1869–85
	I. Amounts (¥ mill.)					
1. Bank of Japan	—	—	52	—	52	52
2. Yokohama Specie Bank	—	—	20	—	20	20
3. National banks	—	5	113	5	108	113
4. Ordinary private banks	—	—	30	—	30	30
5. Postal saving system	—	0	9	—	9	9
6. Deposit Bureau	—	—	11	—	11	11
7. Quasi banks	b	b	20	b	20	20
8. Pawnbrokers	·	25	17	25	−8	17
9. Credit cooperatives	·	·				
10. Insurance companies	—	—	1	—	—	1
11. Total	·	31	273	31	242	273
12. Government paper currency	24	99	88	75	−11	64
	II. Relation to gross national product (percent)[c]					
1. Bank of Japan	—	—	6.5	—	0.7	0.5
2. Yokohama Specie Bank	—	—	2.5	—	0.3	0.2
3. National banks	—	1.2	14.1	0.2	1.5	1.0
4. Ordinary private banks	—	—	3.7	—	0.4	0.3
5. Postal saving system	—	0.0	1.1	—	0.1	0.1
6. Deposit Bureau	—	—	1.4	—	0.1	0.1
7. Quasi banks	b	b	2.5	·	0.3	0.2
8. Pawnbrokers	·	5.0	2.1	0.7	−0.1	0.2
9. Credit cooperatives	·	·				
10. Insurance companies	—	—	0.1	—	—	0.0
11. Total	·	6.2	34.0	0.9	3.5	2.5
12. Government paper currency	6.8	19.8	11.0	2.1	−0.2	0.6

[a]Generally only main assets or liabilities and capital.   [b]Very small.   [c]Gross national product roughly estimated at ¥ 0.35 bill. for 1868 and ¥ 0.50 bill. for 1875 and set at ¥ 0.81 bill. (Ohkawa) for 1885, ¥ 3.5 bill. for 1868–75, and ¥ 7.0 bill. for 1876–85.

SOURCES: Lines 1–5: Taken from or based on *HYS*, pp. 192–99, 206, and 244. Line 6: Rathgen, p. 511. Line 7: Based on Asakura, 1965, p. 30. Line 8: 1875, Asakura, 1965, p. 34; 1885, *HYSE*, p. 127. Line 10: *HYS*, pp. 236–39. Line 12: *HYS*, p. 166.

high level of farm foreclosures, urban bankruptcies, and suicides. In addition, the rate of growth of real national product was also probably reduced.[43]

The centerpiece of Matsukata's policy was, following quantity theory orthodoxy, though possibly not consciously, reduction of the money supply, primarily by retiring government paper currency out of budget surpluses. Debt retirements had started in earnest as far back as 1877 and government notes in circulation had reached their high in 1878. Matsukata thus only accelerated and intensified policies begun earlier. According to the official statistics, the volume of government notes declined in the three years 1879–81 by ¥ 20 mill., or 15 percent. In the following four years Matsukata reduced it by ¥ 30 mill. more, or another 25 percent. Total money in circulation may even have decreased by a larger amount if it is true that during the period the "unreported" notes of about ¥ 20 mill. were also withdrawn from circulation. Thus, the total money in circulation (including subsidiary coins but not specie, the amount in circulation not being known) may have declined from 1879 to 1885 by as much as ¥ 60 mill. or about 30 percent.

43. Fujino's estimate (1975, p. 194) of real national product declined by more than 10 percent between 1880 and 1883.

Regardless of the actual degree of shrinkage in the money supply, the effects are clearly visible in a decline in wholesale prices between 1881 and 1884, the low point, by about one-fourth.[44] The consumer price index fell even more, namely, by 30 percent, the price of rice being halved. The only available index of money wages indicates a decline of only 6 percent, although some reported specific wage rates show sharp declines.[45] The effects of Matsukata's policies are also evident in Japan's international transactions, with the deficit in the current account, which had exceeded ¥ 20 mill. a year, then about 2 percent of national product, in 1878–80 being reduced to an average of ¥ 2 mill. in 1882–85.[46] Finally, the disagio of the yen against silver, then still the base of the system, which had reached 45 percent in 1881, disappeared in 1885.

The effects of the Matsukata deflation are also evident in the financial sphere. A sharp break occurred in the rapid expansion of national banks; their lendings declined from ¥ 78 mill. in 1881 to ¥ 63 mill. two years later, and the upward trend resumed only in 1886. Reported interest rates decreased sharply from 14 percent in 1881 to a low of 8 percent in 1883 and in 1884–85 at 11 percent were still below the 13 percent level of 1879/80. Bankruptcies increased from an average of ¥ 1.3 mill. of liabilities in 1880–82 to ¥ 3.8 mill. in 1883–85 and fell back to ¥ 1.8 mill. in 1886–88. Suicides rose to over 7,000 in 1885–86, compared to about 5,000 in the early and late 1880s.[47]

6. FINANCING THE ECONOMY

For this period of the financial development of Japan a comprehensive treatment of the process of financing the main sectors of the economy, starting from estimates of investment and saving and sectoral financial surpluses and deficits and leading to the calculation of measures like the issue ratios of financial institutions and nonfinancial sectors and of the various types of financial instruments, a treatment that will be attempted in chapters 3 to 7 for the later periods, is unfortunately as yet beyond reach. The estimates now available on national product and its distribution and on capital formation and saving and even the figures on less complex magnitudes like prices, wages, and money in circulation are, as has become painfully evident in the preceding sections, so scarce, so contested, and sometimes so contradictory that nothing short of an intensive restudy of all available primary data, mainly available only in Japanese, could provide a sufficiently firm foundation for such a venture. All that is offered in this section are a few conjectures intended to define orders of magnitude and to provide the basis for very rough comparisons with later periods and with other countries.

a. The Overall Picture

If the estimates of capital formation now available are accepted, investment during the transition period must have been low—about 6 percent on a net basis—but not abnormally so for a country in as early a stage of development as Japan was, a country in which capital-intensive sectors like manufacturing, railroads, and power were practically absent and in which housing required relatively little investment per unit. Saving must have been even lower—around 4 percent of national product—because net capital imports amounted to nearly 2 percent of the period's national product.

On the other hand, a not negligible amount of domestic saving is indicated by financial statistics. Even if one makes some allowance for the unrecorded reduction in some pre-restora-

---

44. The index of the Committee on Monetary System Research declined by 10 percent, but between 1879 and 1882; that of the Asahi Shimbun by 19 percent from 1881 to 1884; Tsuru's by 24 percent; Yoshino's by 22 percent; Takahashi's by 20 percent, and the Hitotsubashi index by 27 percent.

45. *ELTESJ*, 8:243 ff.

46. *ELTESJ*, 1:192.

47. Rathgen, p. 488.

tion financial instruments (cancellations and write-downs, such as occurred in the debts of hans and the shogunate at the time of the restoration, of course, should not enter into the calculation any more than the noncash issue of commutation bonds), for the financial instruments outstanding in 1868, and for the fact that some of the lending was for consumption purposes and thus represents dissaving for the borrowers, it is difficult to put the issue of financial instruments that represented saving at much less than ¥ 1 bill. for the entire transition period, starting from the outstandings in 1885 shown in Table 2-3. Moreover, by every historical analogy, there should have been a considerable amount of saving not evidenced by the issuance of financial instruments, that is, saving by farmers, artisans, and urban merchants in the form of agricultural improvements, utensils, and structures that was financed out of these units' current saving. One is thus led to put total net financial saving for 1869–85 at close to ¥ 1 bill. and total saving at well in excess of that amount. These guesses—and they cannot be more than that—yield a domestic net saving ratio of about 7 percent for the entire transition period. Although these guesses are considerably higher than the available saving estimates for that period, they at least avoid the sudden quantum jump between the years just before and just after 1885 shown in the figures now in use.

b. Financing the Main Sectors

The difficulties in arriving at reasonable estimates of total national investment and saving are small when compared with the situation in the separate sectors of the economy, except possibly the government. Hence this section provides only a few clues to the situation.

(i) THE GOVERNMENT. The estimate of government capital formation for most of the transition period is ¥ 185 mill. for the years 1874 to 1885[48] and about ¥ 230 mill. for the entire period. Consequently, the ratio of gross government capital expenditures to national product was about 1 1/2 percent, so that the ratio for net capital expenditures should have been close to 1 percent.

Because the government borrowed only small amounts to partly finance capital expenditures, mostly for railroads, government saving may be regarded as having been nearly equal to capital expenditures if the entire transition period is considered and if the issuance of government paper money is not regarded as borrowing. In the latter case, most capital expenditures made until the end of the 1880s could be regarded as financed by currency issues, because these were well in excess of capital expenditures from 1868–75 and half as large in 1876–80. From 1881 to 1885, however, when government debt was considerably reduced, all capital expenditures must be regarded as internally financed. Thus, from the late 1870s the government contributed to capital formation as well as to saving but did not absorb significant amounts of saving of other sectors.

Total net cash issues of the government other than currency during the transition period totaled only about ¥ 30 mill., or less than 0.3 percent of gross national product. They included ¥ 16 mill. from foreign bonds issued in 1870 and 1873 and ¥ 15 mill. of borrowings, mostly from the Fifteenth National Bank, in 1877–78. However, net issues of paper money, which are a form of government debt but are better included among the issues of financial institutions, amounted to more than ¥ 60 mill. excluding notes issued in exchange for pre-restoration paper money. Total net government issues would then equal less than 0.1 percent of national product of the transition period.

(ii) NONAGRICULTURAL BUSINESS. Not enough is known quantitatively, indeed practically nothing, about sources and uses of funds of the nonagricultural business sector to determine either total volume of investment and saving or their financing. It is likely that a substantial part of the lending of financial institutions, a net of a little more than ¥ 100 mill., went to this sector, as did most of the ¥ 40 mill. in capital stock of corporations existing in 1885. Most of the

48. Rosovsky and Emi estimate (HYS, p. 34).

increase in trade credit, and it may have been substantial, reaching ¥ 200 mill. was, of course, provided within the sector. Thus total issues of the nonfinancial business sector may well have reached ¥ 400 mill., equal to 3 1/2 percent of the period's national product. Most of the issues were raised in the second part of the decade.

(iii) AGRICULTURE. Estimates of rural indebtedness in 1885, reported to have totaled ¥ 330 mill., of which about two-thirds was mortgage debt,[49] are just about the only comprehensive figures available. This would have been equal to about one-fifth of total farmland value,[50] a quite substantial, but not disturbingly high, ratio. Assuming that most of this debt was incurred after the restoration, when land became freely transferable, the issue ratio of agriculture would have been on the order of 2 percent of the period's national product.

The greater part of this debt appears to have been provided at very high rates, often on the order of 20 percent a year, by quasi banks, pawnbrokers, and rural moneylenders. The banking system, mostly private banks,[51,52] is reported to have provided only about one-sixth of the total.

(iv) HOUSEHOLDS. Still less is known in quantitative, comprehensive terms about the financing of nonfarm households, (excluding unincorporated businesses). Their debt burden would seem, however, to have been relatively light. They must have been responsible for most of the residential mortgage debt of ¥ 35 mill., about 3 percent of the value of residences,[53] and for part of the ¥ 17 mill. borrowings from pawnbrokers. Thus their total debt would seem to have been only about ¥ 50 mill. in 1885, which, even if all accumulated since 1868, would yield an issue ratio of less than one-half of 1 percent of national product.

(v) FOREIGN FINANCING. Undertaken mostly by the government, long-term borrowing abroad was very small, occurred in the first years of the Meiji regime, and had been repaid by 1885. The balance of payments estimates show substantial short-term net capital imports totaling nearly 2 percent of the gross national product of the 1869–85 period, almost one-half being attributed to the first six years of the period. However, as these figures include errors and omissions in other positions of the balance of payments, their significance is in doubt.

c. National Issue Ratios

It is only with great hesitation that the following table, which brings together the issue ratios (net issues as percent of gross national product) for the different sectors, is presented. These guesses, based on table 2-4, are expressed as a range and given only for the entire transition period, although there is little doubt that most of the ratios were considerably higher during the second part of the period.

Financial institutions	3.0–3.5
Nonfinancial sectors	5.4–6.4
Government	0.3
Nonagricultural business	3.0–3.5
Agriculture	1.7–2.2
Nonagricultural households	0.4
Nation	8.4–9.9

Notwithstanding their crudity, these ratios seem to permit two conclusions. First, the ratios are high for a country in such an early stage of modern economic development in which

49. For total farm debt, see Asakura (1965, p. 36); for farm mortgage debt, Mayet (*Agricultural Insurance*, cited by Ott, 1961, p. 123). For evidence of increasing farm indebtedness during this period, cf. also Ott, loc. cit., and Rathgen.

50. Asakura, loc. cit.

51. Ott, loc. cit., estimated that total farm debt doubled between 1878 and 1885, only about one-fifth of the total being held by financial institutions.

52. *ELTESJ*, 1:192.

53. Goldsmith, 1969, p. 332.

TABLE 2-4. Financial Instruments Outstanding in 1885

Item	Amount (¥ mill.)	Source
Issued by nonfinancial sectors		
Central government: securities	231	*HYS*, p. 158
Central government: borrowings	15	*HYS*, p. 158
Farm mortgages	330	Asakura, 1965, p. 36
Residential mortgages	35	Rathgen, p. 292.
Corporate stock	30	*HYS*, p. 324; par value
Borrowings from financial institutions		
Commercial banks	90	Lendings of national banks (*HYS*, p. 196) and ordinary banks (estimated)
Bank of Japan and Yokohama Specie Bank	10	*HYS*, pp. 192 and 206
Quasi banks	30	Rough estimate (twice capital of quasi banks as given by Asakura, 1965, p. 30)
Borrowings from pawnbrokers	17	*HYS*, p. 127
Trade credit	350	Assumed equal to inventories (Goldsmith, 1975, p. 148)
Total (approximately)	1150	
Issued by financial institutions		
Government paper money and subsidiary coin	119	*HYS*, p. 166
National bank notes	30	*HYS*, p. 166
Deposits in all banks	60	Estimated on basis of 1888 (*HYS*, p. 194)
Paid-in capital of all banks	66	*HYS*, p. 194
Deposits and notes of Bank of Japan	36	*HYS*, p. 192
Other liabilities and capital of Bank of Japan	16	*HYS*, p. 192
Postal saving deposits	9	*HYS*, p. 244
Deposits with quasi banks and pawnbrokers	15	Rough estimate
Liabilities of Trust Fund Bureau	11	Rathgen, p. 511
Others	40	Rough estimate
Total (approximately)	400	

real income per head was quite low. Second, the net issue ratio of the nonfinancial sectors was about twice as high as that of financial institutions, a relatively low value considering again Japan's position. Both findings are evidence of the fact that Japan, even in this first phase of its modern economic development, was quite different in its financial structure from the "under-developed" Asian and African countries of the twentieth century, a difference that may be attributed, as are so many features of its economic development, at least in part to its Tokugawa heritage.

7. THE NATIONAL BALANCE SHEET

These fragments of quantitative information can be combined with an estimate of the current value of the national wealth to yield the rough national balance sheet for Japan in 1885 that is shown in table 2-5. A balance sheet cannot be more reliable than its components, of course, but it may suffice for comparisons with similar, and gradually improving, balance sheets for later benchmark dates.

The financial interrelations ratio (financial assets divided by tangible assets), the relation-

TABLE 2-5. National Balance Sheet, 1885

	Amounts (¥ bill.)	Distribution (percent)	Relation to national product (percent)[d]	Relation to national wealth (percent)
I. Tangible assets	5.05	78	627	105
1. Land[a]	2.32	36	288	48
a. Agricultural[a]	1.70	26	211	35
b. Other	0.62	10	77	13
2. Reproducible tangible wealth	2.73[b]	42	339	57
a. Residential buildings	0.93	14	115	19
b. Other buildings and structures	0.82	13	102	17
c. Producer durables	0.17	3	21	4
d. Inventories	0.35	5	43	7
e. Livestock	0.41	6	51	9
f. Consumer durables	0.05	1	6	1
II. Financial instruments	1.52	22	190	32
1. Issued by financial institutions[c]	0.39	6	49	8
2. Issued by nonfinancial sectors	1.13	16	141	23
a. Government domestic debt	0.24	4	30	5
b. Business debt (excluding c)	0.14	2	18	3
c. Trade credit	0.35	5	44	7
d. Agricultural debt	0.33	4	41	7
e. Residential mortgages	0.04	1	5	1
f. Corporate stock	0.03	1	4	1
III. Net foreign assets	−0.24	−4	−30	−5
IV. National assets (I + II)	6.57	100	817	137
V. National wealth (I + III)	4.81	73	597	100

[a]Including forests (0.40).   [b]Estimated by Fujino (1975, p. 190) at ¥ 3.03 bill.   [c]Including government paper money (0.09).   [d]Ratios to national product are based throughout the volume on its year-end value, assumed equal to the average of the value of year and the year following.

ship most important for financial analysis, stood at three-fourths. This value, as will soon be seen, is well below later values for Japan but is not lower than it is in many underdeveloped countries in the mid-twentieth century.

The financial intermediation ratio (issues by financial institutions divided by issues by nonfinancial sectors), a second important relationship, is slightly more than one-third including, but only fully one-fourth excluding, government currency. This indicates that financial institutions held less than about one-fourth of the issues of the nonfinancial sectors and that indirect external financing (borrowing from financial institutions) was equal to less than one-fourth of direct external financing. These ratios are characteristic of a rather early stage in a country's financial development.

8. THE FINANCIAL ACHIEVEMENTS OF THE TRANSITION PERIOD

By the end of 1885 Japan had the rudiments, and not much more, of a modern financial system, modern, of course, in comparison only to the financial institutions and instruments that then existed in Western countries. Specifically, by that date Japan possessed:

a. A uniform currency system, using both metallic and paper money but based on silver, which was then rapidly losing its position in the international monetary system.

b. A modern central bank that was just beginning to get into actual operation.

c. A fairly extensive system of note-issuing commercial banks.

d. A substantial number of other banks and quasi banks, many of which were still premodern, that, engaged primarily, as did the note-issuing banks, in short-term lending.

e. A special government-owned bank for the financing of foreign trade.

f. A postal saving system.

g. A few very small private savings banks.[54]

h. A brand-new Deposit Bureau in the Ministry of Finance that was destined to become one of the largest financial institutions.

i. One life insurance company and one marine insurance company.

On the institutional side, Japan thus lacked, compared with Western countries of the later nineteenth century, long-term credit banks, specialized savings institutions (until 1880), credit cooperatives (except the premodern mujin), investment companies, and investment bankers.

Turning to financial instruments, Japan was familiar with the usual short-term instruments and such long-term instruments as central government bonds and farm and urban mortgages. Although a few corporations existed, their shares as yet were hardly marketable. Thus, among the securities then common in the West, mortgage bonds, local government bonds, and corporate bonds were as yet absent.

The rudimentary character of the Japanese financial system, however, is evident not in the types of modern financial institutions and instruments that were introduced since the restoration, which were usually copies or successful adaptations of European and American models, but in the small size of most of these institutions and instruments in relation to national product and wealth in comparison to similar ratios in developed Western countries. Thus the total assets of financial institutions (including government paper money) at the end of the transition period were equal to only about half a year's national product and to 6 percent of national wealth. All financial assets, both those issued by financial institutions and by other sectors, however, already amounted to nearly twice national product and to nearly one-third of national wealth. Although similar ratios cannot be calculated for the beginning of the period, they undoubtedly were much lower.

The financial achievements of the transition period are thus quite remarkable—the creation of a framework of financial institutions and instruments that, expanded but not radically changed during the following decades, proved capable of providing the funds for the accelerated growth of the Japanese economy until World War II and, one might even assert, for the entire period of Japan's modern growth.

This achievement appears to be, like so much in Japan's economic development, the combined result of successful adaptive copying from abroad, unsuccessful experimentation—the early development of the commercial banking system during the transition period is an example—government planning and support, individual initiative, and luck. Like many other aspects of Japan's economic development, although possibly less so than in later periods, factors common to many countries in the process of industrialization and modernization seem to have been combined successfully with traits specific to Japan's historical inheritance, as reflected in the nature of its social structure and the character of its population.

---

54. Asakura, p. 36.

3   The Takeoff into Sustained Economic Growth, 1886–1913

During the last three decades of the Meiji era[1] Japan took off both economically and politically. By the time World War I ended the old order that had prevailed since Waterloo, notwithstanding many changes, Japan was acknowledged as a major power, indeed the most important power in Southeast Asia. By that time it was equally obvious that Japan had joined Europe and North America in the process of sustained economic growth that the West had witnessed since the early or mid-nineteenth century. Japan's growth rates were at least equal to those experienced by the then developed countries, even though its real income per head in 1913 was still much lower than that of Western Europe or North America. In the financial sphere, too, it was evident that Japan had caught up, or was close to doing so, in terms of financial institutions and instruments as well as in terms of the relative size of its financial superstructure.

1. CHANGES IN POLITICAL AND SOCIAL STRUCTURE

Although the first two decades after the Meiji restoration have been called the Japanese "Sturm und Drang" era,[2] the following generation passed without major, or at least without visible major, changes in the country's political and social structure. The facts relevant to economic and financial development may therefore be summarized very briefly.

    a. Although Japan copied another Western feature in 1891, a written constitution and a bicameral legislature, the differences to genuine parliamentary democracy were greater than the similarities. The constitution was "granted" by the emperor, not voted by the legislature; the parliamentary vote was restricted to a small proportion of the adult male population; and political parties, such as they were, had no mass basis and were dominated by the other elites.

    b. In the middle decade of the period Japan fought and won two wars conducted exclusively on foreign soil, two of the most effective political and economical military operations in modern history, considering the costs and benefits.[3,4] The military expenditures directly

---

    1. This period is often regarded as having ended in 1905, e.g., by Ohkawa and Rosovsky (*JEG*), mainly because this year marks the end of the first long swing in Japan's economy. Extending the period through 1913 is motivated primarily by the fact that World War I produced a marked change in Japan's international economic and political position and, possibly more important, by the feeling that the years 1906–13, quite apart from the fact that the Meiji era ended only in 1912, seem to be nearer in their economic and social characteristics to the two decades starting in 1885 than to Japan between the two world wars.

    2. Emi, 1963, p. 109.

    3. A detailed description of the costs of these two wars and their financing will be found in Ono and Ogawa, two studies sponsored by the Carnegie Endowment. For the Marxist point of view, cf. Takao, pp. 440–49.

    4. A thorough economic cost-benefit analysis of these two wars, taking account of the long as well as the short run, would be most interesting. It is not performed in Boulding and Gleason's "War as an Investment: The Strange Case of Japan," notwithstanding its title.

attributable to the Sino-Japanese War of 1895–96 seem to have been on the order of ¥ 200 mill., or about 7 percent of that period's gross national product. They were more than offset by the indemnity of ¥ 365 mill. that Japan received in the following year from the unfortunate Chinese government, a sum that provided Japan with the international reserves needed to ensure the transition to the gold standard. The government's debt increased in 1894 and 1895 by about ¥ 140 mill., about 10 percent of a year's national product, not all for extra military expenditures. The Russo-Japanese War was much more expensive. The extra military expenditures amounted to about ¥ 1,700 mill. during the years 1904–06, equal to about one-sixth of that period's national product; the government's debt increased by about ¥ 1,500 mill., about a half year's national product; and most of the loans, namely, about ¥ 1,050 mill., had to be contracted abroad, thus creating for the first time in Japan's history a substantial foreign debt. The benefits of the war, however, were larger, even if not immediately transferable into cash-in territory, in the possibility of exploiting China and in international standing. The internal borrowing of nearly ¥ 500 mill., largely from the banking system although not from the Bank of Japan, was a substantial factor in the expansion of the financial superstructure during the period.

c. The three decades from the 1880s to World War I may with some justification be regarded as the period that was decisive for the development of a basic characteristic of modern Japan's political, social, economic, and financial structure, the symbiosis of the elites, although its origins antedate this period and even the Meiji restoration and although it reached its apogee only before and during World War II. A substantial degree of cooperation among political, social, and economic elites and among and within the industrial, commercial, and financial elites has existed in virtually all large modern nation states. When the influence of business leaders and parliamentary politicians increased, beginning in the middle of the nineteenth century, such cooperation was probably strengthened. But it would seem that the symbiosis was so much closer and enduring in Japan, and sufficiently different in character, that it may be regarded as a basic characteristic of modern Japan.

A pentagon of elites is involved, although their number and character are necessarily to some extent arbitrary.[5] They are, the order of listing not implying relative importance, the imperial court nobility (in Japanese often called *genro*); the military establishment (*gumbatsu*) and the clans (*hanbatsu*) who preceded them; the civilian higher bureaucracy (*kambatsu*); the politicians (whom one could in Japanese, where *batsu* means "clique," call *seitobatsu*); and the business elite, especially the large combines (*zaibatsu*), which might be further subdivided into the industrialists (*sangyobatsu*) and the financiers (*ginkobatsu*), although these two groups are often difficult to separate. The relative importance and the makeup of these five elites have, of course, varied over the century following the Meiji restoration. They have been reduced to three since World War II by the practical disappearance of the court nobility and the military establishment as elites. Oversimplyfying but, it is hoped, not seriously distorting the situation, one might say that during the transition period the imperial court and the upper bureaucracy, then much more closely connected with the genro than in the twentieth century, were the leading elites; that during the takeoff period the business leaders and the higher civil servants gained greatly in importance; that it was only during the period from World War I to the mid-1920s that the politicians gained a substantial share of power; and that from the early 1930s through World War II the military elite and the higher civil bureaucracy became preeminent, although they obtained the close, even if not always deepseated, cooperation of the two business elites. In the postwar period, the situation, of course, has changed greatly. The politicians recovered some of their influence and the civil service retained most of theirs, with the two business elites apparently exercising effective leadership.

Some may wonder at the omission of the landowners and the labor unions. The interests of

5. On these, cf. Morley, mostly on 1920–25 period; Ino; and Ward and Rüstow.

the landowners—at least the large landowners, who were very heterogeneous in character—were attended to by the court nobility; those of the small farmers, mainly in the postwar period, were looked to by the politicians and at times, chiefly in the interwar years, by the military. Labor leaders never constituted a powerful group except during the early years of the American occupation.

This digression, if such it is, is essential to an understanding of the economic and financial development of modern Japan. Although Japanese entrepreneurs, as well as farmers and workers, are strongly influenced by the profit motive, as in all countries not subject to a centrally planned dictatorship, and even in them to some extent, there seems little doubt that considerations not strictly pecuniary in nature have had more influence on Japanese entrepreneurs than on their counterparts in the West and even more than on their colleagues in the noncommunist Third World. One does not need to overstress the community-centered character of Japanese business to acknowledge this difference and to find evidences of its effects. Popular slogans are not scientific explanations, but neither should they be summarily brushed aside. There remains substance, and for the economic and financial development of Japan considerable substance, in the devices coined early in the Meiji period such as "A rich country and a strong army" (*fukoku kyohai*), "Japanese spirit and Western technology" (*wakon yosai*), or even more specifically "Encouraging industrialization and fostering the entrepreneurial spirit" (*shokusan kōgyō*).

2. CHANGES IN THE INFRASTRUCTURE

As in the preceding chapter, only the briefest of summaries can be presented of the changes in output and its components, in prices, and in international economic relations, stressing those that seem to have had substantial influence on the country's financial development. For this period, fortunately, there is sufficient quantitative evidence to substantiate a reasonable confidence about the main trends, even though specialists still disagree on some important features. A few of the most important annual series are shown in table 3-1.

a. Reasonable agreement appears now to have been established that the average growth rate of real product in the period 1885–1913 was about 2 3/4 percent,[6] considerably lower than estimates current one or two decades ago. Because population grew at the rate of slightly more than 1 percent, the more significant annual increase of real national product per head was slightly more than 1 1/2 percent. Such a rate is of the same order as that then prevailing in some developed countries and is not higher than the rates at which these countries seem to have grown in the mid-nineteenth century when they were closer to the phase of economic development in which Japan found itself in the takeoff period.[7]

b. Facts about level and changes in the standard of living of the Japanese people in this period are scarce. Consumption per head in constant prices increased at a rate of 1.4 percent per year between 1885 and 1913 (2.2 percent from 1885 to 1900; 0.5 percent from 1900 to 1913).[8] At the end of the period, consumption per head was on the order of ¥ 75 per head, or nearly $40 at the current exchange rate. Although the internal purchasing power of the yen was considerably above this rate, the low level of the Japanese standard of living is illustrated by the fact that

6. Okhawa's revised (*ELTESJ*, 1:178) estimates yield a rate of 2.8 percent, which agrees with Taira's conclusion, p. 6, and with Maddison's estimate of 2.7 percent for 1878–1913, pp. 30–33. A more recent estimate by Ohkawa starting in 1905 (*JEG*) yielded a growth rate of 2.4 percent for 1906–13 instead of the older estimate of 2.1 percent (*ELTESJ*).

7. The average growth rate of output per head between 1870 and 1913 for twelve Western countries was 1.6 percent, ranging from 0.7 percent for Italy to 2.2 percent for the United States and 2.3 percent for Sweden (Maddison, pp. 197, 30). Japan with a rate of probably not much more than 1 1/2 percent for that period was thus just hitting the average, although it was still in an early stage of its modern economic growth and thus might have been expected to be nearer the upper end of the range for the developed countries.

8. *ELTESJ*, 1:238.

TABLE 3-1. National Product, Consumption, and Capital Formation, 1885–1913

	Gross national product			Personal consumption per head 1934–36 prices (yen) (4)	National product deflator (1934–36 = 100) (5)	Gross fixed capital formation ratio (percent) (6)	Current foreign balance (¥ mill.) (7)
	Current prices (¥ bill.) (1)	Constant (1934/36) prices					
		Amount (¥ bill.) (2)	Change (percent) (3)				
1885	0.81	3.85	·	86	20.9	12.1	− 3
1886	0.80	4.08	+6.0	91	19.6	12.6	7
1887	0.82	4.34	+6.4	97	18.8	12.2	− 7
1888	0.87	4.45	+2.5	98	19.5	15.4	4
1889	0.96	4.72	+6.1	104	20.2	14.8	1
1890	1.06	4.58	−3.0	100	23.0	14.5	−30
1891	1.14	5.03	+9.8	108	22.6	14.0	17
1892	1.13	4.95	−1.6	106	22.7	13.6	18
1893	1.20	5.23	+5.7	113	22.9	13.8	0
1894	1.34	5.46	+4.4	110	24.5	16.4	−11
1895	1.55	5.80	+6.2	115	26.8	16.2	118
1896	1.67	5.77	−0.5	118	28.9	18.5	23
1897	1.96	5.70	−1.2	117	34.3	20.5	−57
1898	2.19	5.91	+3.7	123	37.1	19.4	−40
1899	2.31	6.32	+6.9	124	36.6	16.2	28
1900	2.41	6.23	−1.4	119	38.7	16.2	−51
1901	2.48	6.47	+3.9	120	38.4	15.3	16
1902	2.54	6.36	−1.7	118	39.9	13.2	26
1903	2.70	6.39	+0.5	117	42.2	13.6	− 6
1904	3.03	7.08	+10.8	119	42.7	12.0	−131
1905	3.08	6.77	−4.4	111	45.6	16.8	−326
1906	3.30	6.73	−0.6	110	49.0	16.3	−24
1907	3.74	6.99	+3.9	123	53.5	16.9	4
1908	3.77	7.19	+2.9	123	52.4	17.6	−63
1909	3.78	7.36	+2.4	124	51.3	15.8	4
1910	3.93	7.83	+6.4	127	50.1	17.6	−74
1911	4.46	7.92	+1.1	124	56.3	19.3	−100
1912	4.77	7.93	+0.1	126	60.2	18.0	−108
1913	5.01	8.00	+0.9	128	62.7	17.2	−14

SOURCES: **Cols. 1, 2, and 5:** Ohkawa, *ELTESJ*, vol. 1.   **Col. 4:** Shinohara, *ELTESJ*, 6: 140–41.   **Col. 6:** Ohkawa's revised estimate divided by col. 1.   **Col. 7:** Yamamoto, *ELTESJ*, vol. 1.

average consumption per head in 1913 (at current exchange rates) amounted to about $300 in the United States, $270 in England, and about $100 even in Italy.[9]

c. During this period Japan for the first time developed short and long cyclical movements of the type observed in the West since the second quarter of the nineteenth century, movements that were due primarily to fluctuations in investment activity. The upward phase of the first long swing from 1885 to 1897 was followed by a downward phase extending from 1898 to 1905. The second long swing's upward phase, lasting from 1905 to 1919, extends somewhat beyond the end of the takeoff period as defined here.[10] Within these long swings there were shorter cycles

9. For the United States, *Historical Statistics*, pp. 7 and 139; for England, B. R. Mitchell, *Abstract of British Historical Statistics*, 1962, pp. 10 and 370; for Italy, Istituto Centrale di Statistica, *Sommario di statistiche storiche italiane*, 1958, pp. 39 and 210.

10. *JEG*, p. 25.

with troughs in 1868, 1876, 1883, 1890, 1901, and 1909.[11,12] The period used here begins and ends at practically the same short-term cyclical position, namely, a recession, thus avoiding a bias in growth rates calculated from 1885 to 1913.

d. During the takeoff period agriculture continued to account for not much less than one-half of national income, although its share declined from about one-half in 1885 to below two-fifths in 1913, and its share in the labor force fell from more than three-fourths to about three-fifths. There is still considerable debate about the trend of agricultural output in this period, the latest estimate putting it at 1.8 percent per year for the period from 1878–82 to 1918–22,[13] which should not differ much from a figure for the 1885–1913 period. Agricultural output thus increased only slightly more rapidly than population, much of the increase being attributable to improvements in productivity rather than to larger inputs.[14]

e. The takeoff period is, of course, characterized by considerable expansion and, in many important cases, the establishment of modern manufacturing, power, and transportation industries, almost doubling the share of secondary industries in national product, but even then lifting this share to only one-fifth in 1913. The output of manufacturing industries increased at an average rate of nearly 5 percent from 1884–86 to 1912–14.[15] However, even in 1913 the level of Japan's industrialization, particularly in the heavy industries, was still moderate in comparison to the leading Western countries.

f. From the financial point of view the growth of the capital-intensive railroads was of particular importance. With growth being especially rapid during the 1890s, the total length of lines increased from only 580 km in 1885 to about 10,600 km in 1913, a level reached in Great Britain in 1850. Up to 1905 most of the railways were privately financed and owned, at that date to the extent of two-thirds, but between 1905 and 1907 the government acquired most of the private lines, and in 1913 it owned nearly seven-eighths of the railway network.

g. During the period Japan's international economic relations intensified to a significant extent. Indeed, one might say that Japan's integration into the world economy dates only from this period. Thus foreign trade (imports plus exports) increased sharply from about ¥ 65 mill., or 8 percent of national product, in 1885 to ¥ 1,500 mill., or 28 percent, in 1913. At least two important domestic industries, cotton and silk, became decisively dependent on foreign markets. This development naturally required a substantial expansion of the mechanism of foreign trade financing.

h. An important step in Japan's integration into the world market was the adoption of the gold standard in 1897.[16] Japan's clinging to silver had led to a depreciation of the yen in terms of the leading currencies. The disagio, which had stood at about 15 percent in 1885 when Matsukata had succeeded in reestablishing the parity between yen notes and silver bullion, increased to about 50 percent a decade later. Although this depreciation of its currency may have given Japan some advantage in its foreign terms of trade, which improved by about one-fifth between 1882 and 1896,[17] by the end of the nineteenth century Japan would have been the only major country, other than China, not linked to the gold standard mechanism of currency and finance.

i. Japan also for the first time called to a substantial extent on foreign capital markets;

11. Based on Fujino's equipment cycles with an average duration of nearly eight years. Fujino (1966) also distinguishes inventory cycles with an average length of two and a half years.

12. For an older and different dating, cf. Thorp, pp. 343 ff.

13. Yamada and Hayami, p. 19. Four other estimates range from 1.0 percent (Nakamura) to 2.4 percent (*ELTESJ*, vol. 9).

14. Yamada and Hayami, p. 13. The agricultural labor force actually decreased by 5 percent between 1885 and 1913, whereas the area under cultivation expanded by 12 percent between 1890 and 1910 (*HYS*, p. 19).

15. Shinohara, *ELTESJ*, 10:145. Shionoya's index (in Klein and Ohkawa, pp. 104–05) shows an increase of 5.2 percent per year for the same period.

16. Cf. Matsukata.

17. Noda, 1972, p. 18.

TABLE 3-2. Prices and Interest Rates, Annually, 1885–1913

	GNP deflator (1)	Wholesale prices 1934–36 = 100 (2)	Consumer prices[a] (3)	Wages (¥ per day) (4)	Interest rates (percent) (5)	Dividend yield of stocks (6)	Foreign exchange (¥ per $) (7)
1885	20.9	26.9	·	0.19	·	·	1.19
1886	19.6	27.3	28.5	0.18	9.1	6.0	1.30
1887	18.8	28.9	30.3	0.18	9.1	6.3	1.31
1888	19.5	29.5	29.8	0.18	9.8	9.6	1.34
1889	20.2	30.4	31.6	0.18	10.2	13.4	1.31
1890	23.0	31.8	33.7	0.18	10.1	13.7	1.19
1891	22.6	30.6	32.3	0.19	9.3	10.9	1.11
1892	22.7	32.4	30.1	0.22	8.4	8.8	1.42
1893	22.9	34.2	30.4	0.22	7.2	7.3	1.63
1894	24.5	35.7	31.4	0.22	9.3	7.9	1.78
1895	26.8	35.8	34.4	0.23	9.6	6.1	1.98
1896	28.9	39.5	37.8	0.24	9.3	16.8	1.97
1897	35.2	44.0	42.2	0.30	10.2	4.9	2.01
1898	37.1	46.3	45.7	0.34	11.3	6.8	2.04
1899	36.6	47.5	43.1	0.37	8.9	6.4	2.02
1900	38.7	48.3	48.5	0.40	10.9	6.6	2.03
1901	38.4	46.9	47.4	0.39	11.8	11.0	2.02
1902	39.9	47.4	49.3	0.39	10.3	9.2	2.01
1903	42.2	50.4	51.7	0.40	8.6	9.4	2.02
1904	42.7	53.0	52.9	0.42	8.5	11.5	2.04
1905	45.6	56.9	55.0	0.43	9.2	13.8	2.02
1906	49.0	58.6	56.0	0.43	8.7	21.0	2.02
1907	53.5	63.2	61.9	0.49	8.6	11.2	2.02
1908	52.4	60.9	59.8	0.52	9.6	15.3	2.02
1909	51.3	58.1	57.4	0.51	8.6	10.1	2.02
1910	50.1	58.8	57.6	0.51	7.3	6.0	2.02
1911	56.3	61.0	61.9	0.59	7.1	12.0	2.02
1912	60.2	64.6	65.3	0.56	7.9	5.1	2.02
1913	62.7	64.7	67.3	0.58	9.0	7.8	2.02

SOURCES: **Col. 1:** *ELTESJ*, 1:232.   **Col. 2:** 1901–13, *HYS*, p. 76, extrapolated for 1880 to 1886 on basis of index of Asahi Shimbun (loc. cit.).   **Col. 3:** *ELTESJ*, 8:135.   **Col. 4:** For 1899 to 1913, *ELTESJ*, 8:247, col. 5, average daily male wage in manufacturing; linked for 1885–98 to wage rate shown in Fujino, 1975, p. 190.   **Col. 5:** *HYS*, p. 81; average rate for loans on bill by Tokyo banks. Interest rates on bank loans were between 1.9 percent (1888) and 0.6 percent (1913) higher (Teranishi and Patrick, p. 41).   **Col. 6:** Fujino, 1975, pp. 194–95.   **Col. 7:** *HYS*, pp. 318–20; average of highest and lowest rate of year.

foreign holdings of Japanese securities, which had been negligible in 1885, were close to ¥ 2 bill. in 1913, equal to nearly two-fifths of a year's national product. Three-fourths of this total, however, represented government bonds sold abroad in 1904–05 to help finance the Russo-Japanese War.[18] Foreign sales of corporate securities remained small and foreign direct investments remained negligible, reflecting the extreme suspicion of both government and business of potential foreign influence on the Japanese economy.

    j. Although Matsukata had succeeded in the early 1880s in sharply reducing the level of prices and wages, the upward movement resumed soon after and continued practically without interruption to the end of the period. The rate of inflation, however, slowed down considerably after the shift to the gold standard and the stabilization of foreign exchange rates. Wholesale

18. *HYS*, p. 317.

TABLE 3-3. Capital Formation, 1886–1913

	Total[a]	Private	Government total	Government nonmilitary	Capital consumption allowances	Net capital formation[a]
			Gross capital formation			
			I. Amounts (¥ bill.)			
1886–1900	4.01	3.13	0.87	0.51	1.97	2.04
1901–1913	8.16	5.55	2.62	1.79	3.99	4.17
1886–1913	12.17	8.68	3.49	2.30	5.95	6.21
			II. Distribution (percent)			
1886–1900	100.0	78.2	21.8	12.8	49.1	50.9
1901–1913	100.0	67.9	32.1	22.0	48.9	51.1
1886–1913	100.0	71.3	28.7	18.9	48.9	51.1
			III. Relation to gross national product (percent)			
1886–1900	18.7	14.6	4.1	2.4	9.2	9.5
1901–1913	17.5	11.9	5.6	3.8	8.6	9.0
1886–1913	17.9	12.8	5.1	3.4	8.8	9.1

[a]Includes inventories (and inventory profits) of ¥ 0.92 bill. in 1886–1900 and ¥ 1.03 bill. in 1905–13, or 23 and 13 percent of gross capital formation and 4.1 and 2.1 percent of gross national product.

SOURCE OF I: *ELTESJ*, 1:183 ff., for fixed assets; Fujino, 1975, p. 186, for inventories.

prices increased by more than 140 percent, or at an annual rate of 3.2 percent, between 1885 and 1913,[19] the rate of increase declining from 4.1 percent for 1885–97 to 2.6 percent for 1897–1913. This is the more remarkable as international prices were falling in the first subperiod but substantially rising during the second. The cost of living increased at an annual rate of 2.9 percent between 1885 and 1913. The national product deflator more than tripled from 1885 to 1913 by rising at an average annual rate of 4.1 percent a year, the increase again being more rapid in the first subperiod (4.4 percent a year from 1885 to 1900; 3.8 percent from 1900 to 1913).

3. CAPITAL FORMATION AND SAVING

a. Capital Formation[20]

The most recent set of estimates covering the entire period (table 3-3) puts gross domestic capital formation at 18 percent of gross national product with hardly any difference between the two halves of the period, although substantial cyclical annual variations occurred. The net fixed capital formation ratio is put at slightly above 9 percent. These figures provide an idea of the financing task facing the Japanese economy in this period.

The estimates show three main characteristics of capital formation in Japan during this time span. The first is the large share of public capital formation of nearly three-tenths, which was still nearly one-fifth if military expenditures are excluded. The fact that public capital expenditures were divided about evenly between construction and durables[21] indicates that the Japanese government financed not only the usual infrastructure of public buildings and roads but

19. *HYS*, p. 76. For this period, fortunately, differences among various indexes are small.

20. Annual estimates of gross fixed capital expenditures in current and constant (1934–36) prices are given in great detail, both for the government and all private sectors together, in part 3 of Emi, 1971, pp. 224–330. These figures, however, are considerably lower for private capital expenditures for 1886–1900 than those of table 6-3, at ¥ 4.1 bill. (ibid., pp. 224–25) against about ¥ 8 bill.

21. Rosovsky, 1964, pp. 207–08.

TABLE 3-4. Fixed Capital Formation and Saving, 1905–1913

	Amounts (¥ bill.) (1)	Distribution (percent) (2)	Relation to GNP (percent) (3)
Fixed capital formation			
Private	3.53	62.6	9.85
Dwellings	0.88	15.6	2.45
Other	2.65	47.0	7.39
Government	2.11	37.4	5.89
Nonmilitary	1.45	25.7	4.05
Military	0.66	11.7	1.84
Total gross fixed capital formation	5.64	100.0	15.74
Capital consumption allowances	3.09	54.8	8.62
Total net fixed capital formation	2.55	45.2	7.11
Domestic net saving	2.43	43.1	6.78
Private sector	1.35	23.9	3.76
Government			
Including military	1.08	79.1	3.01
Excluding military	0.42	7.4	1.17
Capital imports	0.71	12.6	1.98

SOURCE OF COL. 1: *JEG*, pp. 290 and 296.

TABLE 3-5. Net Fixed Capital Stock, 1875–1913 (1934–36 Prices)

	Total[a] (1)	Residential buildings (2)	Other buildings (3)	Other structures (4)	Producer durables (5)	Livestock and plants (6)
I. Rate of growth (percent per year)						
1875–1885	−.35	−.15	4.90	3.78	4.58	.77
1886–1900	2.55	1.06	1.12	6.09	6.38	.63
1901–1913	3.17	1.12	1.87	5.18	7.83	1.71
1875–1913	1.99	.76	2.37	5.16	6.40	1.04
II. Distribution (percent)						
1874	100.0	60.4	18.7	4.7	3.1	13.1
1885	100.0	52.7	24.7	6.5	4.2	12.4
1900	100.0	46.4	23.0	12.1	8.1	10.4
1913	100.0	38.0	21.4	16.4	15.1	9.1
III. Relation to gross national product (percent)						
1874	583	353	109	30	18	76
1885	251	135	62	16	11	31
1900	207	95	48	25	17	21
1913	231	88	49	38	35	21

[a]Absolute figures about ¥ 7.2 bill. in 1874, about 10.0 ¥ bill. in 1885 (the two figures adjusted for change in coverage), ¥ 13.1 bill. in 1900, and ¥ 18.6 bill. in 1913.

SOURCE OF BASIC DATA: *ELTESJ*, 3:149, tentatively corrected for break in estimates of col. 2 between 1885 and 1886 and in col. 4 between 1877 and 1878; *ELTS*, vol. 1, for gross national product, except for 1874, which is roughly estimated at ¥ 1,500 mill. in 1934–36 prices.

TABLE 3-6. Saving, 1886–1913[a]

	Total net saving	Private	Government Total	Government Civilian	Government Military
		I. Amounts (¥ bill.)			
1886–1900	1.17	1.14	0.03	−0.33	0.36
1901–1913	1.86	1.25	0.61	−0.21	0.82
1886–1913	3.03	2.39	0.64	−0.53	1.18
		II. Distribution (percent)			
1886–1900	100	97	3	−28	31
1901–1913	100	67	33	−11	44
1886–1913	100	79	21	−17	38
		III. Relation to gross national product (percent)			
1886–1900	5.5	5.3	.2	−1.5	1.7
1901–1913	4.0	2.7	1.3	− .5	1.8
1886–1913	4.4	3.5	.9	− .8	1.7

[a]May exclude inventory accumulation.

SOURCE: *ELTESJ*, 1:190.

also a substantial part of the expenditures for equipment in transportation and some other sectors. The second characteristic is the sharp increase in the proportion of producer durables in total private capital expenditures, rising from less than one-fifth in 1887–96 to almost two-fifths in 1907–16 and reflecting, among other things, the increasing importance of the manufacturing industries. The third characteristic, the low and shrinking share of residential construction expenditures, is of considerable importance for the development of the financial superstructure. They declined from nearly one-half of private capital expenditures in 1887–96 to less than one-fourth in 1907–16, and from one-fifth to less than one-tenth of total gross capital expenditures.[22] Although the low level, in international comparison, of the latter ratios may be explained by the flimsy character of most Japanese housing, their sharp decline in a period of fairly rapid urbanization remains puzzling.

A more recent and more detailed estimate, limited to the years 1905–13 (table 3-4), shows about the same picture if it is remembered that it does not cover inventory investment.

The results of net capital formation are visible in the growth of the capital stock (table 3-5). The figures show an average annual rate of increase of only 2 percent on a net basis for the 1875–1913 period, leaving per head growth rates of only 1 percent. Such rates indicate that Japan's economic growth in this takeoff period cannot have been capital-intensive, a conclusion confirmed by statistical and other factual evidence that indicates the continued prevalence of traditional labor-intensive methods of production in light of manufacturing industries. Another indication, for example, is the fact that the average fixed capital-output ratio was the same in 1913 as in 1885, namely, 2.3, and the marginal net capital-output ratio was at the same level. It is remarkable, however, that as the period progressed the growth rate of the presumably modern components of the capital stock, particularly producer durables and nonresidential structures, accelerated substantially and were far above the rates for residential and other buildings.

Estimates from another source[23] show a share of the public sector in the total capital stock of 31 percent in 1913, substantially up from 27 percent in 1905, when this series starts, an increase that implies growth rates for the eight-year period of 6.1 percent a year for the public, compared with 3.4 percent for the private, capital stock.

22. Ibid.
23. Economic Planning Agency, cited in Ohkawa, 1965, p. 262.

b. Saving

For this period an overall view of the volume of savings and its relation to national product is best obtained on the basis of the conceptual equality of gross or net national saving with the difference between gross (net) national capital formation and net capital imports.

For the period as a whole net capital imports seem to have aggregated about ¥ 1 1/2 bill.[24] This would be equivalent to 2 percent of national product and to about one-fourth of total net domestic capital formation. Hence the national net saving ratio is 2 percent lower than the national capital formation ratios, that is, it would be equal to about 6 1/2 percent of national product with little difference between the two halves of the period.

The figures in table 3-6, which are derived by a different method, show lower figures of only 4 1/2 percent of national product, possibly because they omit saving in the form of inventories, and of less than 3 percent if military saving of the government is excluded. The saving rate of the private sectors, mostly attributable to households and unincorporated business, is put at 3 1/2 percent, declining rather astonishingly from 5 percent in the first half of the period to only 2 1/2 percent in the second.[25]

4. MONEY, PRICES, INTEREST RATES, AND ASSET PRICES

Matsukata's deflation proved to be but a brief interruption in the secular inflation that has accompanied Japan's financial development. Depending on which wholesale price index one prefers, the previous high of 1881 was passed early or late in the 1890s. Using the Bank of Japan's index, wholesale prices advanced by nearly 80 percent between 1885 and 1900, or by nearly 4 percent a year. Almost all of the increase occurred after 1891, partly a reflection of the fall of the price of silver and Japan's shift to the gold standard at an exchange rate, starting in 1896, that was about 40 percent lower than it had been in 1885. The increase from 1900 to 1913 was much slower, about 35 percent, but the annual average rate of 2.3 percent was still faster than in most of the rest of the world. (The U.S. index, e.g., advanced at a rate of 1.7 percent per year over the same period.) The movements in the general price level (national product deflator) were similar but a little more pronounced—up by about 85 percent from 1885 to 1900 and by another 60 percent from 1900 to 1913, for a total of 200 percent, or nearly 4 percent a year. Equally important, there was no period during which the price level declined substantially or for more than two years in a row (table 3-2).

Asset prices naturally could not escape this inflationary tendency, but documentation of their movements is much inferior. Agricultural land prices seem to have increased sharply, possibly by nearly 500 percent, from their very depressed level of 1885 until the turn of the century and to have risen by another 50 percent from then to World War I.[26] The advance in stock prices appears to have been more moderate for the period as a whole but was accompanied by very sharp short-time fluctuations,[27] reflecting the as yet highly speculative, restricted, and far from mature character of the market for corporate stock.

Interest rates showed a definite downward trend but remained high in comparison to those prevailing in developed countries. Thus the rate charged on bank loans declined from about 14 percent in the early 1880s[28] to about 12 percent by the turn of the century and to about 9 percent for the average of the years 1909–13.[29] Government bond yields declined from more than 9 percent in the early 1880s (commutation bonds) to about 5 percent in 1913. This trend, which

24. *ELTESJ*, 1:178.

25. An attempt to measure saving from the financial side was made by Emi (1965), but, if only in view of the unsatisfactory data available, it cannot be regarded as successful.

26. Goldsmith, 1975, p. 142.

27. Cf. charts 1 and 2 in *History of Yamaichi Securities Co., Ltd.*, 1958 (in Japanese).

28. Adams and Hoshii, p. 14.

29. Ott, 1960, p. 302.

TABLE 3-7. Money in Circulation, 1885–1913 (¥ Mill.)

	1885	1890	1895	1900	1905	1910	1913
			I. Amounts (¥ mill.)				
1. Government notes	88	34	11	—	—	—	—
2. Bank notes[a]	34	129	201	228	313	406	434
3. Subsidiary coin	31	38	48	85	102	144	149
4. Total currency[b]	153	201	260	313	415	550	583
5. Current bank deposits	20	24	104	248	456	518	512
6. Total	173	225	364	561	871	1068	1095
			II. Ratio to gross national product				
1. Government notes	0.11	0.03	0.01	—	—	—	—
2. Bank notes	0.04	0.12	0.14	0.09	0.10	0.10	0.09
3. Subsidiary coin	0.04	0.04	0.03	0.03	0.03	0.03	0.03
4. Total currency	0.19	0.18	0.16	0.13	0.13	0.13	0.12
5. Current bank deposits	0.03	0.02	0.07	0.10	0.14	0.12	0.10
6. Total	0.21	0.20	0.23	0.23	0.27	0.26	0.22
			III. Alternative estimates (¥ mill.)[c]				
1. Asakura and Nishiyama[d]	198	248	410	707	1059	1509	1634
2. Fujino	155	173	298	535	717	966	1000

[a]Excluding the notes of the Bank of Taiwan and the Bank of Chosen.   [b]Includes currency held by banks, the proportion rising from one-sixth to one-third of total.   [c]Excluding holdings by banking system.   [d]Currency and demand deposits in ordinary banks.

SOURCES: Line I: *HYS*, pp. 166 and 197–99; total private deposits have been allocated to current and other deposits on the basis of the reported totals for these two categories. Line III, 1: Asakura and Nishiyama, pp. 822–23. Line III, 2: Fujino, 1975, pp. 190–91.

does not seem to have been investigated in detail and on the basis of a broader spectrum of interest and yield rates, together with a reduction in the differentials between localities and types of loans,[30] may be regarded as a reflection of the transformation of the Japanese capital market from its premodern to its semimodern phase.

It is difficult to find a satisfactory explanation for the movements of prices and interest rates for the takeoff period of Japan when statistical data are still limited, the scope of what may be regarded as money changed, and the whole financial structure expanded rapidly. In the face of a full doubling of real national product between 1885 and 1913 (more than 60 percent from 1885 to 1900; nearly 30 percent from 1900 to 1913), currency in circulation, which constituted the bulk of money until close to the turn of the century, doubled between 1885 and 1900 (table 3-7). If allowance is made for the increase in the current deposits of banks, the volume of money seems to have more than tripled between 1885 and 1900, an increase that is in line with the product of increases in real output and in the price level reflected in the tripling of national product in current prices. From 1900 to 1913 money in circulation appears to have approximately doubled, that is, again to have expanded in line with national product in current prices.[31] Thus the velocity of circulation does not seem to have changed appreciably. In 1913 it was slightly above one-fifth of national product, insignificantly below the ratios of 1900 and 1885.[32]

30. Cf. now, however, Teranishi and Patrick, pp. 10 ff.

31. If Fujino's estimates of "deposit currency" are used (*HYS*, p. 98), which are substantially in excess of the official figures for "current deposits" used in table 3-6, the increase in money in circulation is in excess of that of national product in both periods and its ratio to national product rises from 0.20 in 1885 to 0.23 in 1900 and 0.24 in 1913. Even then, however, the parallelism in the rates of increase of money in circulation (7.6 percent per year) and national product (7.0 percent) is fairly close.

32. Hoekendorf's calculations show a slight but irregular upward drift in the ratio from 4.4 in 1886–90 to 4.6 in 1909–13.

The degree of modernization of the Japanese money supply in this period, however, was startling. Between 1885 and 1913 the share of subsidiary coin declined from 18 to 14 percent and that of bank notes from 70 to 40 percent, government notes being replaced by those of the central bank, whereas the share of bank deposits rose from 12 to 47 percent.[33]

5. THE DEVELOPMENT OF THE INSTITUTIONAL STRUCTURE

Compared to the complete overhaul of Japan's financial system, and indeed the creation de novo of most of it, that took place during the transition period, basic changes in the institutional structure between the mid-1880s and World War I were limited. In this sphere the period that marked the takeoff of Japan as an economic and political power was characterized rather by a rapid expansion in the size of the institutions and instruments that had been created during the closing decade of the transition period. The development of the main institutions and instruments during this period will be briefly reviewed in the subsections that follow. At this point a summary of the main features of this process will suffice.

(i) The Bank of Japan, organized in 1882, developed into an effective central bank and the sole issuer of bank notes.

(ii) The commercial banking system was unified by the liquidation of the note-issuing national banks and the rapidly fading importance of the credit institutions carried over from the pre-Meiji era.

(iii) An effective system of thrift institutions for small savers was created.

(iv) Around the turn of the century the by then fairly developed short-term credit system was supplemented by the creation of a system of long-term credit banks, initiated by the government and with government participation, which were financed largely by the issuance of their own debentures.

(v) Mainly as a result of the Sino-Japanese and Russo-Japanese wars, the government issued large amounts of long-term bonds, which became an important constituent of institutional and private investors' portfolios.

(vi) The corporation became accepted as the standard form of organization of sizable enterprises, and corporate debentures and shares began to be acquired to a substantial extent by both financial institutions and individual outside investors.

(vii) The large combines (zaibatsu), which were later to acquire a predominant position in Japanese business, made considerable progress and developed the forms of organization and operation they were to maintain until the end of World War II.

a. The Bank of Japan

Following the process of selective copying so common in Japan during the transition period, the Bank of Japan was modeled after the Banque Nationale de Belgique, regarded after considerable study as representing the type best fitted to Japanese conditions. Following that example, the bank was nominally independent from the government; one-half of its shares were held by private financial institutions; the discounting of commercial bills was to be its main lending activity; and the issuance of bank notes its main source of funds. The government, however, acquired the other half of the shares and retained substantial supervisory powers. As a matter of fact, the bank, from its beginnings, has been regarded, and regarded itself, much more as an integral part of the internal and international financial activities of the government than was the case in most of the central banks of that era. The first governor and vice governor, for example, were before their appointment—by the emperor—high officials in the Ministry of Finance, a situation often repeated during the bank's later history.

During the first years operations expanded rapidly, partly as a result of the exchange of the

33. Using Fujino's estimate of deposit money, their share even rises to nearly 55 percent in 1913.

bank's notes for those of the government. By 1885 its assets were not much more than ¥ 50 mill. They were slightly more than ¥ 300 mill. in 1900 and by 1913 approached ¥ 700 mill. Assets thus were equal to about one-fourth of those of commercial banks (excluding the Yokohama Specie Bank) in 1885 and to nearly one-third in 1900 but only to about one-fifth in 1913. From 1900 on, after the retirement of both government and national bank notes, the bank was the sole supplier of paper currency, and its notes constituted between one-half and three-fourths of its total liabilities and net worth. The notes, in turn, declined from 9 percent of gross national product in 1900 to 8 percent in 1913, whereas in 1885 government and national bank notes together had amounted to 15 percent of national product. The close connection with the government is indicated by the substantial importance of government deposits, particularly in the first few years of the bank's operations when government deposits supplied one-fifth to one-third of the bank's total funds and again in 1896–97 and in 1905–07 in connection with the two wars. Both tendencies—the decline in the central banks' assets in comparison with the assets of commercial banks and the decline in the ratio of paper currency to national product—are commonly found in financial development.

Of the three main assets, the metallic reserve showed the largest fluctuations, being bolstered in 1896 by the receipt of part of the Chinese war indemnity. The bank's assets also showed its close connection to the Ministry of Finance. Loans to the government and holdings of government securities were rarely below one-fifth of total assets and sometimes exceeded one-third. Lending to business rose from less than ¥ 40 mill. in 1890 to about ¥ 150 mill. in 1900 and 1913. They thus were equal to about one-fifth of the lendings of commercial banks in 1890 and 1900 but to less than one-tenth in 1913.

The influence of the Bank of Japan on the commercial banks and on the entire range of financial institutions, or even on the financial activities of nonfinancial business enterprises, is not adequately reflected in these figures. It was one of the peculiarities of the Japanese financial system during this period, as it still is today, that the bank's powers of moral suasion were very great, reflecting the close interconnection of the business and governmental elites.

b. The Commercial Banks

The commercial banking system underwent extraordinary expansion from 1885 to 1913. The number of commercial banks, excluding private and quasi banks, which rapidly lost in importance, rose from about 350 to over 1,600; and although there was still only one office (including the main one) for each 14,000 inhabitants, the number of offices also increased, from a little more than 300 in 1893 to more than 2,000 in 1913. The total assets of commercial banks (excluding the Yokohama Specie Bank), which in 1885 seem to have been on the order of ¥ 200 mill., shot up to ¥ 835 mill. in 1900 and to nearly ¥ 2,700 mill. in 1913, implying a rate of increase for the period as a whole of over 10 percent per year. As a result, the relation of commercial banks' assets to gross national product increased from about one-fourth in 1885 to more than one-third in 1900 and more than one-half in 1913. The expansion of the commercial banking system thus reflected more than the increase in national product, which proceeded at the rapid rate of nearly 7 percent a year, by combining an annual increase in real product of nearly 3 percent with a secular inflation rate of 4 percent a year.

The national banks, which had been the most important component of the commercial banking system until the mid-1890s, lost their note-issuing privileges and converted to ordinary commercial banks, which had been provided with a revised legal basis in 1893. From then on, all commercial banks were subject to the same regulations. Under the provisions of the act, many of the still operating private and quasi banks became ordinary banks, a shift that accounts for the increase in the number of ordinary banks from 270 in 1892 to 1,005 in 1896.

A variety of changes occurred during this period in the uses and sources of funds of commercial banks, shown in table 3-8, changes that again are similar to those observed in other countries in the early development of the banking system. Thus the share of own funds (paid-in

TABLE 3-8. Sources and Uses of Funds of Commercial Banks, 1885–1913 (¥ mill.)

| | Holdings | | | | Changes | |
| | 1885 | | | | | |
	National and ordinary banks (1)	Private and quasi banks (2)	1900 (3)	1913 (4)	1886 to 1901 (5)	1901 to 1913 (6)
Number of banks	357	962	1802	1614	483	−188
1. Total assets	148	50	835[c]	2664[c]	637	1829
2. Lendings	85	50	663	1671	528	1008
3. Government securities	48[a]	—	51	163	3	112
4. Other securities	—	—	51[d]	114[d]	51	63
5. Other assets	15	5	70	719	50	649
6. Deposits, total	40	16	437	1444	381	1007
7. Deposits, current	17	·	168	379	151	211
8. Deposits, other private	16	·	262	1047	·	785
9. Deposits, public	7[a]	·	7	18	·	11
10. Notes	30	—	—	—	−30	—
11. Borrowing	} 8	—	71	147	} 118	76
12. Other liabilities		—	55	559		504
13. Paid-in capital	65[b]	34	239	392	140	153
14. Reserves	5[a]	—	33	122	28	89

[a]National banks only.   [b]Of which 44 for national banks.   [c]Total assets, as well as some other items, are considerably below estimates of Teranishi and Patrick.   [d]Includes ¥ 43 mill. of shares in 1900 and ¥ 60 mill. in 1913 (Ott, 1960, p. 199).

SOURCES: **Col. 1:** Mostly rough estimates based on figures for national banks (*HYS*, pp. 166, 116 ff., 266 ff.).   **Col. 2:** Number of banks and line 12, from Asakura, 1965, p. 30. Other figures are rough estimates.   **Cols. 3 and 4:** Lines 1, 2, 13, 14, Bank of Japan, Research Department. Lines 3, 6, 7, 9, *HYS*, pp. 198–99, pp. 266 ff. Lines 4, 5, 8, 12, derived as residuals. Line 12, Goto, p. 87.

capital and reserves) decreased from about one-half in 1885 to one-third in 1900 and to one-eighth in 1913.[34] Deposits became increasingly important as sources of funds, furnishing nearly two-thirds of all funds between 1885 and 1900 and fully one-half between 1900 and 1913. Within deposits, "current deposits" supplied a declining share, about two-fifths between 1885 and 1900 and one-fifth between 1900 and 1913. Commercial banks thus developed into true financial intermediaries, whereas they had been primarily lenders of own funds in the 1870s.[35]

"Lendings" constituted throughout the period the main use of funds, namely, about 80 percent from 1885 to 1900 and 55 percent from 1900 to 1913, the decline being mainly a result of a very sharp increase in the unspecified residual of other assets. Increases in holdings of securities absorbed less than one-tenth of total uses of funds.

There apparently is no comprehensive set of statistics covering the whole period, or benchmark dates near its beginning and end, to determine the amounts or proportions of loans made available to the various sectors of the economy or the terms on which these funds were supplied. This is unfortunate because information of this type is essential to the debate among students of Japanese banking who are concerned with how closely the lending and investment policies of Japanese commercial banks approached the German or the British type of operations, that is, to what extent they represented the short-term financing of inventories and of accounts

34. The decline is considerably smaller, namely, from 44 percent in 1888 to 26 percent in 1913, in a more recent estimate (Teranishi and Patrick).

35. This is a point emphasized by Teranishi and Patrick.

receivable in internal and external trade as against actually medium-term loans to finance fixed capital expenditures, particularly in industry, or the acquisition of corporate securities.[36] The truth seems to lie, as usual, somewhere between the two extreme points of view, although it is probably nearer to the view that before World War II the differences between the Japanese system and the contemporary German commercial banking system, whose investment financing proclivities have been exaggerated, were greater than the similarities.

Fairly comprehensive and detailed statistical evidence is available only for an early date (1894) and covers ¥ 124 mill. of bank loans out of total bank "lendings" of ¥ 325 mill. as reported in the official statistics.[37] These figures suggest that most of the loans (41 percent of the total, but 69 percent excluding loans to unidentified borrowers) were made to commercial unincorporated enterprises. The share of borrowers in agriculture was modest (13 percent including, and 21 percent excluding, unidentified borrowers), and corporations and local bodies accounted for about 12 and 15 percent, respectively, of identified borrowers. Loans to "industrial" borrowers came to not much more than 2 percent of the identified total.[38] The smallness of the average loan is remarkable: ¥ 560 for the 22,000 loans covered, ranging from ¥ 140 for loans to agriculturalists to ¥ 3,700 for the nearly 2,300 loans to companies, and from ¥ 240 for loans on real estate to ¥ 2,300 for nearly 19,000 loans collateraled by shares.

It is difficult to argue from these figures for a substantial involvement of commercial banks in medium-term industrial financing, at least at this early date. The data contain, however, two ratios that seem to indicate that a substantial proportion of lending was not of short-term, self-liquidating character. They are, first, the fact that two-fifths of the loans were made for terms exceeding one year, although less than one-fifth of the loans were renewed at all and only one-tenth more than once, and second, the high proportion of slightly more than one-third of the loans reported as collateraled by corporate shares, which was more than twice as much as loans on real estate collateral.[39] The question must, therefore, remain undecided until the specialists come forth with more convincing quantitative evidence, in which the degree of representativeness is known, particularly with evidence for a date nearer the end of the takeoff period.

A closer look at developments, which cannot go far on this occasion, shows a substantial difference between the two subperiods 1886–1900 and 1901–13. During the first subperiod the expansion of the commercial banking system was very rapid and almost nonselective. During the second, consolidation of the system led to a substantial decline in the number of banks, from a maximum of 1,867 with an average number of branches of 0.78 per bank and average assets of ¥ 0.47 mill. in 1901 to slightly more than 1,600 from 1909 to 1913 with an average of 1.30 branch offices and average assets of ¥ 1.65 mill. in 1913.

The system, then, even on the eve of World War I, was one of many small local banks, which accounted for most of the resources, coexisting with a few city banks that had already reached considerable size—not too different from the situation in the United States. In 1910 the five largest banks, four of them affiliated with one of the big combines, held fully one-fifth the deposits of all commercial banks (table 3-9). This growth is rather remarkable because two of the five banks (Mitsubishi and Sumitomo) were less than twenty years old in 1913 and even the three oldest banks went back only to 1880 (Yasuda), 1876 (Mitsui), and 1872 (Dai Ichi, Shibuzawa's First National Bank), although some of them had Tokugawa antecedents in the form of finance

36. For two recent summaries taking essentially one or the other side of this controversy, see Patrick, 1967, and Yamamura, 1972.

37. The source of these much used figures is Juishi Soyeda, an official of the Ministry of Finance, (pp. 479–81), who does not explain how the figures were obtained. The coverage of bank loans would be higher if the table refers only to loans and overdrafts (total of ¥ 155 mill. in official statistics), not including bills discounted (¥ 137 mill. for national banks alone).

38. These were, obviously, mainly loans to artisans to judge by the average amount of ¥ 235.

39. If Soyeda's statistics exclude bills discounted, which were considerably larger than loans and overdrafts combined, the significance of the high ratios for loans over one year and of loans collateraled by corporate shares would diminish sharply.

TABLE 3-9. Concentration in Commercial Banking, 1900–1945
(Percent of Deposits of All Commercial Banks)

	Mitsui	Mitsubishi[b]	Sumitomo	Yasuda[a]	Dai Ichi	Total	
						1 + 2	1 to 5
1900	6.1	2.7[b]	·	·	·	8.8	·
1910	7.6	2.9	3.7	2.9	4.5	10.5	21.6
1919	6.1	4.1	6.1	2.3	6.5	10.2	25.1
1930	7.5	6.8	7.7	7.3	7.3	14.3	36.6
1941	6.6	7.0	10.2	9.8	8.7	13.6	42.3
1945	12.9[c]	11.8	10.3	13.5	c	24.7	48.5

[a]After 1945 Fuji.   [b]Banking Department of Mitsubishi Limited partnership.   [c]Teikoku = Mitsui + Dai Ichi.

SOURCES: 1900, Shibagaki, p. 563; 1910–45, Ehrlich, p. 268.

departments in the big combines. To judge by the movements of the share of two of the four banks (Mitsui and Mitsubishi), the degree of concentration in 1910 was only slightly larger than at the turn of the century.

c. The Yokohama Specie Bank

Set up by the government in 1880, the Yokohama Specie Bank was the only important financial institution that did not closely follow a Western model. Rather, it was created to meet the specific needs of a country attempting to enter the network of international trade and struggling with the additional difficulty of remaining on the silver standard in a world that was increasingly using the gold standard. It is typical of Japanese conditions that the bank throughout its history was used as an arm of the government's international commercial and financial policy. The establishment of a Japanese national institution was also prompted by the typical desire not to permit foreign institutions to preempt or dominate an important economic activity, in this case the functions performed by foreign banks, a precedent observed, undoubtedly with misgivings, in India, China, and other countries in Southeast Asia.[40]

The bank, with an initial capital of ¥ 3 mill., equal to 7 percent of the capital of all 151 national banks then in operation, grew rapidly. Its assets increased from ¥ 23 mill. in 1885 (12 percent of the assets of all commercial banks) to ¥ 153 mill in 1900 (18 percent) and ¥ 424 mill. in 1913 (16 percent),[41] thus maintaining its status as the largest single short-term credit institution in Japan. By 1913 its assets were nearly two-thirds as large as those of the Bank of Japan. Foreign trade financing always constituted the main use of the bank's assets, with the loans and discounts of the bank's foreign branches acquiring increasing importance as time went on and by 1913 absorbing more than one-fourth of the bank's total assets. Assuming that all the bank's loans and discounts served to finance Japan's foreign trade, they would have been equal to about one-fourth of the country's exports and imports in 1885, 1900, and 1913. But even if all loans and discounts were not so used, the share of the bank in financing Japan's foreign trade was substantial and probably well in excess of that of any single other financial domestic or foreign institution.

Although the bank's capital was increased during this period from ¥ 3 to ¥ 30 mill., its share in sources of funds declined from 13 percent in 1885 to 7 percent in 1913. Deposits of Japanese government agencies played an important role in the early period, and in the last decade

40. An indication of the standing of the bank is the ownership of one-fourth of its stock by the imperial household (London Stock Exchange Official Intelligence, 1914, p. 419).

41. For annual balance sheets of Yokohama Specie Bank, cf. HYS, pp. 206–07.

before World War I deposits collected in overseas branches constituted a substantial source of funds. Among private domestic deposits, current deposits dominated until close to the end of the century, but by 1913 time deposits were nearly three times as large as current deposits.

d. Long-term Credit Banks[42]

In the mid-1890s the Japanese government decided to introduce into Japan the last major type of Western financial institution that they had not already copied or adapted, namely, long-term credit, or mortgage, banks. Operating on the Continent, although not in Great Britain or the United States, for more than half a century, the mortgage banks had there become an important pillar of the capital market. But here, too, the Western institution was adapted to the peculiarities of the financial structure of Japan, in this case by the much greater emphasis on long-term credit to industry and the much smaller role of urban residential mortgage credit, a difference that reflects the backward position of housing in Japan's infrastructure.

The first mortgage bank, the Hypothec (Kangyo) Bank, was organized in 1897. It was followed in 1898–1900 by 46 Agricultural and Industrial Banks, one for each prefecture; in 1900 by the Hokkaido Colonial (Takushoku) Bank, to answer the needs of this backward and financially neglected northernmost main island; and in 1902 by the Industrial Bank of Japan. These institutions grew rather slowly until about 1905. By that time their aggregate assets of ¥ 122 mill. were equal to less than one-tenth of the assets of commercial banks. Growth then accelerated, however, and by 1913 the fully ¥ 600 mill. of assets of these institutions had reached nearly one-fourth of those of the commerical banking system.

The main source of financing were long-term debentures backed by mortgages, which were implicitly if not legally guaranteed by the Japanese government. Issues were initially small, averaging for the first decade only ¥ 6 mill. per year, but accelerated considerably from about 1905 on. By 1913 the amount outstanding totaled slightly more than ¥ 300 mill., still a modest amount when compared to the long-term domestic bonds of the national government of nearly ¥ 2,600 mill., although they were about equal in size to local government bonds and about one-fourth in excess of corporate bonds outstanding. A substantial part of the issues was absorbed by various government institutions and funds, mainly the Deposit Bureau, and small amounts were acquired by commercial banks and by insurance companies.[43] The majority, therefore, should have been absorbed by individual investors, although no specific statistics about the distribution of bank debentures outstanding seem to be available.

Nor are there, apparently, statistics of the recipients of the banks' long-term loans. It is likely, however, that the bulk of their loans was divided between agriculture and industry. Whatever the distribution, the total net amount of loans made between 1897 and 1913 of just under ¥ 400 mill. was equal to about 7 percent of the period's total private fixed capital formation, although it is likely to have constituted a substantial fraction of the total in some sectors and for some types of capital expenditures. In the last five years of the period, when lendings were at the considerably higher annual rate of about ¥ 55 mill. per year, the ratio to all private fixed nonhousing capital expenditures was on the order of one-sixth, attesting to their importance.

e. Thrift Institutions

Modern specialized thrift institutions were first introduced in 1893 in the form of privately owned stock saving banks, although the government had copied Gladstone's British postal saving system as early as 1875. By 1885 the system had accumulated ¥ 9 mill. of deposits, a small absolute figure—about 1 percent of a year's gross national product—but three times the

---

42. For a description of origin and early operation of these banks, cf. *HYSE*, pp. 134 ff.

43. According to Ott (1960, pp. 199 and 212), commercial banks in 1913 held ¥ 35 mill. of bank debentures and corporate bonds and insurance companies another ¥ 16 mill. Even if most of these holdings consisted of bank debentures, they would have accounted for not more than about one-eighth of all bank debentures outstanding.

reported time deposits of national banks. In 1893 when private savings banks began operating, the deposits of the postal saving system had risen to ¥ 25 mill., about 2 percent of national product and three-fifths of the reported time deposits of all commercial banks. Then, for a decade, deposits hardly increased, possibly reflecting the competition of the new private savings banks. After the turn of the century, however, deposits rose from ¥ 29 mill. in 1902 to ¥ 204 mill. in 1913, an annual growth rate of nearly 22 percent, the rise nearly equaling 4 percent of national product. The postal saving system followed no investment policy of its own, lodging its net receipts with the Deposit Bureau of the Ministry of Finance.

Private savings banks expanded rapidly in number in the first few years, from 419 in 1900 to 489 in 1913, with nearly 1,000 branches, mainly because a number of existing premodern institutions adopted this form of organization, which was introduced by law in 1893. Assets grew more regularly, exceeding ¥ 100 mill. in 1900 and approaching ¥ 500 mill. in 1913.[44] At that time savings banks' assets were equal to nearly one-fifth of those of all commercial banks and nearly one-tenth of national product, and there was one main or branch office for almost every 35,000 inhabitants. Much of the banks' funds were supplied by savings and time deposits, fully one-half in both 1900 and 1913. Current deposits were not negligible, accounting for about one-tenth of total funds. Capital and reserves furnished more than one-sixth at both dates. The banks generally kept a very liquid position, cash and deposits equaling one-fourth of total assets in 1900 and 1913. In addition, the banks held substantial amounts of government and other securities, which constituted about one-fifth of assets. As a consequence, the banks had only about one-half of their assets available for loans, and it appears that a substantial proportion of the loans were similar to those made by commercial banks.

During this period a substantial number of premodern thrift and lending organizations continued to operate, but their average and aggregate size were undoubtedly small and they rapidly declined in importance compared with the modern types. Because their significance is negligible and because no comprehensive or continuous figures on their activities are available,[45] no attempt is made to include them in the statistics.

An idea of the relative importance of the different types of modern thrift institutions, including commercial banks, is given in table 3-10. The figures, however, refer to both time and saving deposits and there is no way to ascertain which part of the total represented thrift deposits of households and which temporary investments of business. Taking the totals as representing one important type of private saving, the increase of ¥ 260 mill. between 1885 and 1900 is equal to about 1.2 percent of the period's national product, rising to 2.5 percent for the period 1901 to 1913 for an increase of slightly more than ¥ 1,200 mill. as the result of an annual rate of growth of 14 percent. Even in 1913 commercial banks still accounted for more than three-fifths of all reported time and savings deposits, although probably for a lower proportion of household thrift deposits, as they had in 1900.

f. The Deposit Bureau[46]

The Deposit Bureau, organized in 1896 as a division of the Ministry of Finance, began to acquire some importance during this period, although in 1913 it was still far from the position in the financial structure of Japan that it was to reach later after several reorganizations. Its name was changed after World War II to the Trust Fund Bureau.

The bureau's funds increased from less than ¥ 20 mill. in 1885 to about ¥ 65 mill. in 1900 and to nearly ¥ 300 mill. in 1913, most of its funds during this period apparently coming from the postal saving system. Until 1901 most of the bureau's assets were invested in government securities, the bureau at that time holding about one-fifth of the amount outstanding. In the following decade the bureau absorbed only ¥ 40 mill. of domestic government securities, or 7

---

44. For annual balance sheets of savings banks, see *HYS*, pp. 202–03, and Ott, 1960, pp. 201 ff.

45. *HYSE*, pp. 107 ff.

46. See *HYS*, p. 242, for total funds. For early history, see *HYS*, pp. 149 ff.

TABLE 3-10. Savings (Time) Deposits, 1885–1913[a]

	Amounts (¥ mill.)			Percent of gross national product		
	1885 (1)	1900 (2)	1913 (3)	1885 (4)	1900 (5)	1913 (6)
1. National banks	6	—	—	0.8	—	—
2. Ordinary private banks	3	182	913	0.4	7.4	18.7
3. Long-term credit banks	—	2	38	—	0.1	0.8
4. Yokohama Specie Bank	0	6	79	0.0	0.2	1.6
5. Savings banks	—	58	259	—	2.4	5.1
6. Post office saving system	9	24	204	1.1	1.0	4.2
7. Total	18	272	1493	2.2	11.1	30.6

[a]All lines refer to "time deposits" except lines 5 and 6, which refer to "savings deposits" except ¥ 8 and ¥ 93 mill. time deposits in savings banks in 1900 and 1913, respectively.

SOURCE: Cols. 1–3: *HYS*, pp. 197, 199, 202, 206, 208 ff., 244.

percent of the increase in such securities outstanding. During the same period the bureau acquired about ¥ 80 mill. of bank debentures, which represented about two-fifths of the total increase in its assets and more than one-fourth of the total issues of such debentures, which probably made it the most important holder of this type of security.

g. Insurance Companies[47]

In the insurance field Japan again copied Western models fairly closely, although many small informal insurance-like mutual-aid societies had operated in the Tokugawa period.

The first modern Japanese marine insurance firm (Tokyo Marine Insurance Company) was organized with the assistance of the government in 1879 and had no domestic competition until 1897 and only two competitors until 1905. In the following two years, however, six additional companies were organized. By 1913 there were 18 reporting marine and other transportation insurance companies with a capital of more than ¥ 110 mill., in part probably not paid-up. Developments were similar in fire insurance. The first company (Tokyo Fire), organized in 1887, was rapidly followed by three other companies. After a spate of new company creations in the 1890s, their number stayed between 19 and 25 with nearly ¥ 60 mill. capital in 1913.[48]

Modern life insurance started with the organization of the Meiji Life Insurance Company, with a capital of only ¥ 100,000, in 1881, a company that was to remain among the leaders throughout the following century. But here again, a sudden burst of new company formation occurred in the closing years of the century, with the number rising to 43 in 1900; the number declined to 32 in 1906, however, as a law passed in 1900 forced liquidations and amalgamations. But by 1913 the number had recovered, rising to 42 with a capital of ¥ 20 mill.

Insurance companies were of little importance in the capital market throughout this period. In 1900 their total assets amounted to only ¥ 25 mill. (1.0 percent of national product), although by 1913 they had risen sharply to ¥ 175 mill., nearly three-fourths thereof being accounted for by life companies, still only a little more than 3 percent of national product and less than one-eighth of saving and time deposits in credit institutions. The increase in their assets between

47. On the early development of Japanese insurance companies, cf. Mizushima, pp. 29–47. (Mizushima's *Formation and Development of Modern Insurance* was not accessible to me and may exist only in Japanese.) For statistics, cf. *HYS*, pp. 236 ff. and Ott, 1960, p. 207.

48. Many of the small and short-lived companies apparently do not appear in the official statistics (*HYS*, p. 236) because reports became compulsory only with the Insurance Regulation Law of 1900, which for the first time provided for the supervision of all types of insurance companies.

TABLE 3-11. Assets of Financial Institutions, 1885–1945
(¥ Mill. to 1913; ¥ Bill. from 1920)

	1885 (1)	1900 (2)	1913 (3)	1920 (4)	1930 (5)	1940 (6)	1945 (7)
1. Bank of Japan	52	312	673	2.80	2.18	6.14	79.15
2. Yokohama Specie Bank	23	153	424	1.14	1.25	3.41	333.43[b]
3. Commercial banks	198	835	2664	10.31	15.77	38.00	138.12
4. Bank trust accounts	—	—	—	—	1.58	3.52	6.68
5. Savings banks	—	97	438	2.26	1.61	4.56	7.52
6. Post Office Saving System	9	24	204	0.88	2.40	8.14	48.55
7. Long-term credit banks	—	48	623	1.59	2.94	5.72	40.48
8. Mutual loan and savings banks	—	—	—	0.03	0.15	0.91	2.58
9. Credit cooperatives	—	—	46	0.36	1.89	6.97	66.03
10. Deposit Bureau	17	64	285	1.10	3.12	11.55	65.76
11. Life insurance companies	0	35	128	0.40	1.56	4.92	12.17
12. Other insurance companies	1	15	47	0.27	0.41	0.81	2.55
13. Post Office life insurance	—	—	—	0.03	0.48	2.07	6.13
14. Total	388[a]	1583	5532	21.17	35.34	96.72	809.15[c]

[a]Including ¥ 88 mill. government paper money.   [b]September 30.   [c]¥ 475.72 bill. excluding Yokohama Specie Bank.

SOURCES: Line 1: *HYS*, p. 192. Line 2: Ott, 1960, p. 169, for cols. 1–5. For cols. 6 and 7, communication from Yokohama Specie Bank obtained through R. Mikitani. Figure in col. 7 is exaggerated by transactions in Japanese-occupied territories. Line 3: 1885, 1900 from table 3-8. From 1913 on, Ott, 1960, p. 192. The figure for 1885 is compatible with Teranishi and Patrick's recent estimate of bank funds for 1888 (¥ 232 mill.), but their estimates of ¥ 1,038 mill. for 1900 and ¥ 2,950 mill. for 1913 (p. 40) are considerably below those used here. Line 4: *HYS*, p. 217. Line 5: Estimates based on paid-in capital, deposits, and lendings (*HYS*, pp. 202–03). Line 6: *HYS*, pp. 244–45. Line 7: To 1930, Ott, 1960, p. 175 ff. Including Hypothec Bank (excluding unpaid capital), Industrial Bank of Japan, Industrial and Agricultural Banks, and Hokkaido Colonial Bank. Line 8: Ott, 1960, p. 230. Line 9: *HYS*, p. 223 ff., and Ott, 1960, pp. 221 ff. Line 10: *HYS*, p. 242. Figures refer to outstanding balance plus reserves on March 31 of the following year. Lines 11 and 12: 1885–1900, rough estimates based on contracts outstanding (*HYS*, pp. 236 ff.); 1913–46, *HYS*, pp. 236 ff. Line 13: *HYS*, p. 246; 1920 estimated on basis of insurance in force.

1900 and 1913 equaled 0.3 percent of the period's national product and one-eighth of the increase in time and savings deposits.

In 1913 about one-fifth of the companies' funds were held in the form of bank deposits, one-tenth in government securities, and nearly one-fourth in other securities, about equally divided between bonds and stocks. This left one-fourth for investment in loans, part of which were call loans rather than long-term credit. Thus the direct contribution of insurance companies to long-term financing was apparently very modest.

h. All Financial Institutions

An overview of all financial institutions will be presented in the form of seven tables, some of which show the data for the seven benchmark dates between 1885 and 1945, or the six periods between them, first, to provide a longer perspective and, second, to avoid the repetition of similar tables in chapters 4 and 5. These tables should be studied, rather than commented upon in detail. Whatever comments are offered will be limited to the period from 1885 to 1913, as those for the two following periods, 1914–30 and 1931–45, will be deferred to chapters 4 and 5.

Table 3-11 provides the background in the form of data on the assets of thirteen types of financial institutions for the seven benchmark dates. These figures are used in table 3-12 to show the growth rates between benchmark dates, to indicate the distribution of total assets among the thirteen types, to compare assets with national product, and to show the new issue ratio, that is, the ratio of the changes in assets between benchmark dates to the periods' national product.

TABLE 3-12. Assets of Main Types of Financial Institutions: Growth Rate, Distribution, Relation to Gross National Product, and New Issue Ratio, 1885–1913 (Percent)

	Growth rate		Distribution			Relation to gross national product			New issue ratio	
	1886 to 1900 (1)	1901 to 1913 (2)	1885 (3)	1900 (4)	1913 (5)	1885 (6)	1900 (7)	1913 (8)	1886 to 1900 (9)	1901 to 1913 (10)
Bank of Japan[a]	12.7	6.1	36.6	19.8	12.2	6.5	12.8	13.8	0.77	0.74
Yokohama Specie Bank	13.5	8.2	6.0	9.7	7.7	2.9	6.3	8.7	0.58	0.55
Commercial banks	10.3	9.3	50.0	52.7	48.2	24.6	34.2	54.6	2.88	3.74
Savings banks	—	12.3	—	6.1	7.9	—	4.0	9.0	0.44	0.70
Post Office Saving System	6.8	17.9	2.3	1.5	3.7	1.1	1.0	4.2	0.07	0.37
Long-term credit banks	—	21.8	—	3.0	11.3	—	2.0	12.8	0.22	1.17
Cooperative banks	—	·	—	—	0.7	—	—	0.9	—	0.09
Deposit Bureau	9.2	12.2	4.4	4.0	5.2	2.1	2.6	5.8	0.21	0.45
Life insurance companies	·	10.5	0.0	2.2	2.3	0.0	1.5	2.6	0.16	0.19
Other insurance companies	19.8	9.2	0.3	0.9	0.9	0.1	0.6	0.9	0.06	0.07
All financial institutions	9.9	10.1	100.0	100.0	100.0	48.2	64.7	113.5	5.39	8.08

[a]Including government paper money: 22.7 percent in col. 3; 10.9 percent in col. 6; −0.40 percent in col. 9.

SOURCE OF BASIC DATA: Table 3-11.

Table 3-13, finally, exhibits the distribution of assets of the seven largest financial institutions among six main assets in 1913. It should be noted that the totals for all institutions do not eliminate claims of one type of financial institution against another type and hence are above consolidated totals. On the other hand, the tables do not cover premodern lenders, whose importance, though declining, remained substantial throughout the period, particularly in the financing of agriculture and small business. It has been estimated, for example, that loans by pawnbrokers early in the period (around 1884) amounted to 70 percent of the total lendings to the private sector by national banks.[49] The overall picture, however, would not be substantially changed if premodern lenders could be included in the statistics.

During the period as a whole as well as during the two subperiods, the short-term banking system (Bank of Japan, Yokohama Specie Bank, and ordinary commercial banks) dominated the picture, but this predominance declined over the period. From 1886 to 1900 financial institutions outside the short-term banking system, with a new issue ratio of only slightly more than 1 percent of national product, accounted for less than one-fifth of the aggregate ratio for all financial institutions. Between the turn of the century and World War I, in sharp contrast, the new issue ratio of financial institutions outside the short-term banking system rose to 3 percent of national product and accounted for nearly two-fifths of the aggregate ratio of all financial institutions, thus doubling its relative importance.

Between 1885 and 1913 total assets of all financial institutions increased at a rate of 10 percent per year, the rates for individual types ranging from 6 percent for the Bank of Japan to 16 percent for property insurance companies.

These differences are reflected in the changes in the shares of individual groups in the assets of all financial institutions. These were modest for the largest group, commerical banks, but substantial for the institutions newly organized during the period, such as the long-term credit banks and life insurance companies, which in 1913 together accounted for 5 percent of the

49. Teranishi and Patrick, p. 17, citing Asakura.

TABLE 3-13. Structure of Assets of Financial Institutions, 1913
(Total Assets of Each Institution = 100)

Institution	Cash	Deposits with others	Loans and discounts	Central government securities	Other securities	Other (residual)[a]
Bank of Japan	34.4	4.9	21.8	8.4	—	30.5
Yokohama Specie Bank	5.2	4.5	80.6	0.5	5.2	4.0
Commercial banks	5.1	1.8	62.7	6.1	4.2	20.1
Long-term credit banks	0.2	8.7	26.0	2.4	2.4	60.3
Savings banks	3.3	13.5	45.6	8.4	8.5	20.7
Deposit Bureau	5.4	—	15.5	34.5	44.6	—
Insurance companies	—	23.9	38.1	11.6	26.4	—
All institutions	7.7	4.9	50.2	7.4	6.8	23.0

[a]Mostly unpaid capital and interoffice accounts.

SOURCE OF BASIC DATA: Ott, 1960, pp. 160 ff.

total, and for the monetary authorities, whose share fell precipitously from more than one-third in 1885 to one-eighth in 1913.

Because the resources of financial institutions expanded much more rapidly than national product, they increased from less than a half year's product in 1885 to considerably more than one year's in 1913, that of the commerical banks alone rising from three to more than six months' product.

The new issue ratio of all financial institutions almost doubled between the first and second half of the period, from nearly 5 1/2 to more than 8 percent, that of the three bank groups rising from 4 1/4 to 5 percent, and that of the two types of thrift institutions operating throughout the period (saving banks and Post Office Saving System) doubling, from 0.5 to 1.1 percent. The new issue ratio, however, showed very sharp annual fluctuations, ranging from minus 1 percent in 1893, one of the three years in which current national product declined, to between 18 and 19 percent in 1905–06, the inflationary years of the Russo-Japanese War. There is no close relationship between the level of the ratio and changes in real national product.

In 1913 the main types of financial institutions together held one-eighth of their assets in cash or deposits with other institutions; one-seventh in securities, divided about equally between central government and other securities; one-half in loans and discounts (two-thirds if miscellaneous assets, mainly unpaid capital and interoffice accounts were excluded), which always contributed the backbone of their resources. The structure of assets, however, varied greatly among institutions, the differences being evident in table 3-13.

6. FINANCING THE MAIN SECTORS OF THE ECONOMY

a. The Public Sector

The importance of the public sector for the process of investment and saving in Japan is evident from the facts that total government capital expenditures from 1885 to 1913 represented more than one-fourth of total national capital expenditures and still accounted for nearly one-fifth of the total if military expenditures are excluded.

After Count Matsukata had restored a balanced budget and generally put the country's public finances on a sound footing, institutional changes were relatively minor and the only serious problems were created by the financing of the two wars. By Western and modern standards the proportion of national product appropriated by the government during this period was moderate—slightly less than one-seventh—although it increased moderately from about 12 percent in the first decade of the period to 16 percent in the third, the period of the Russo-Japanese War.

Three features of the government's activities that are of particular interest, its capital formation, its borrowing, and its saving, are summarized in table 3-14 for the three decades 1883 to 1912, a time span that practically coincides with the period considered here.[50]

Capital formation was heavy, equaling fully one-third of current revenue, and rose from about one-fifth in the first decade to one-third in the third, after having exceeded two-fifths in the second decade. Civilian capital expenditures predominated to the extent of two-thirds, representing by themselves nearly one-fourth of current revenue. The increase was even more pronounced in relation to national product, namely, from 2.5 to 5.4 percent including, and from 1.7 to 3.9 percent excluding, military capital expenditures.

Capital expenditures were almost entirely financed from current revenue during the first decade. During the second decade the increase in debt equaled not much more than one-fourth of total gross capital expenditures. If allowance is made for net borrowing in 1895 of about ¥ 80 mill. to cover the expenditures of the Sino-Japanese War, four-fifths of total gross capital expenditures and the entirety of civilian investment may be regarded as covered by current revenue. The situation in the third decade, which included the Russo-Japanese War, is complex. According to table 3-14 the increase in debt was less than one-half of total capital expenditures. If it is first allocated to military capital expenditures, the remaining increase in debt equaled less than one-fifth of civilian capital expenditures of the government. For the period as a whole, net borrowing equaled less than two-fifths of total gross capital expenditures and only 6 percent of gross civilian capital expenditures if military capital expenditures are statistically regarded as financed by borrowing. If the calculation is based on net expenditures, as is more reasonable from the point of view of national accounting, the share of government capital expenditures financed out of current revenue would, of course, be considerably lower.

From the point of view of the saving process and the capital market, it is primarily the amount of net cash issues of government debt instruments and the character of the buyers that matter, particularly the distinction between foreign and domestic buyers and among the latter, the distinction among the banking system, other financial institutions, and the nonfinancial sectors.

By 1896 the government had managed to retire the entire small, old foreign debt, which by 1885 had already been reduced to ¥ 8 mill.—1 percent of national product and about one-fifth of a year's exports—from the high point of ¥ 16 mill. in 1873. In 1899 the government appealed to the international capital markets for the first time since the early years of the Meiji era, now confident that such borrowing could not endanger or even affect its political or economic freedom of action. The terms of the loan of £10 mill. (¥ 80 mill.)—4 percent interest rate, issue price of 90 percent, maturity of 55 years,[51] no specific security pledge—reflected the low level of international interest rates of the period as well as the excellent credit standing of Japan. The bonds' yield to maturity at an issue price of less than 4 1/2 percent was less than 2 percent above that of the era's prime security, British consols. The proceeds were to be used primarily for expanding the government's railroad system and for industrial development.

This loan was soon dwarfed by the series of borrowings, primarily in London, but also in New York and Berlin, that were necessitated by the expenditures, foreign as well as domestic, connected with the Russo-Japanese War. Between May 1904 and November 1905 the government borrowed through an international group of underwriters, including the Yokohama Specie Bank, £107 mill. (¥ 1,045 mill) through two medium-term (seven years) and three long-term

50. Emi's estimates (1965) are used, although it is difficult to reconcile his figures with some of the official figures in *HYS*, possibly because no detailed description of the sources and derivation of his estimates is available. It is, e.g., not clear how the acquisition of most of the then operating private railroads during the third decade was treated.

51. Adams and Hoshii, p. 46.

TABLE 3-14. Government Saving and Investment, 1883–1912
(Percent of Gross National Product)

	1883 to 1892	1893 to 1902	1903 to 1912	1883 to 1912 (percent)	1883 to 1912 (¥ bill.)
1. Revenue	11.8	11.2	16.6	14.3	9.31
2. Capital expenditures	2.5	4.9	5.7	5.0	3.26
a. Civilian	1.7	2.9	3.9	3.2	2.13
b. Military	0.8	2.0	1.9	1.8	1.13
3. Increase in financial assets	0	0.1	1.7	0.9	0.63
4. Increase in debt	0.2	1.4	2.6	2.0	1.26
5. Gross savings					
a. Including military capital expenditures	2.3	3.6	4.7	4.1	2.63
b. Excluding military capital expenditures	1.5	1.6	2.8	2.3	1.50

SOURCES: Lines 1, 3, and 4: Emi, 1965, p. 10, except line 2b, which is taken from Emi, 1971, pp. 224–25.

(twenty to twenty-five years) issues. This time terms were not as easy, partly reflecting the rise in international interest rates, 6 percent nominal and about 8 1/2 percent effective for the short-term loans and 4 1/2 and 5 percent for the long-term bonds issued at 90, and the revenues of customs and the tobacco monopoly had to be pledged as security. These loans entailed an annual interest charge of more than ¥ 50 mill., equal after the war to about 3 percent of government annual revenue, to about 1 1/2 percent of national product, and to about one-eighth of a year's exports.

Net foreign borrowing between 1906 and World War I was relatively small, the foreign debt increasing only from ¥ 1.15 to ¥ 1.53 bill. in 1913, then fully one-fourth of a year's national product. This was the result of gross borrowing of nearly ¥ 650 mill. in seven issues[52] and repayments of about 250 mill. of the debt contracted for the Russo-Japanese War, mainly the ¥ 215 mill. of seven-year bonds retired as early as 1907. The proceeds of the new loans were used mainly for retirement of domestic debt, partly in connection with the acquisition of most of the private railroad network.

Most of the increase in domestic debt was connected with the two wars. Of the total increase in domestic government debt between 1885 and 1913 of ¥ 1.23 bill. (including ¥ 0.32 bill. for local governments that began to issue bonds only in 1889), ¥ 0.15 bill. occurred in 1894–95 and about ¥ 0.6 bill. in 1904–06. Thus the net increase during the remaining twenty-three years was on the order of only ¥ 0.5 bill. Net issues totaled only ¥ 0.24 bill. from 1886 to 1900 and ¥ 1.47 bill. between the turn of the century and World War I. These amounts were equal to 1.1 percent and 3.0 percent, respectively, of national product and to 7 percent and one-fifth of a year's gross capital formation. Although small amounts of Treasury bills were out-standing between 1901 and 1912, including some issued abroad in 1905–06, and borrowings from financial institutions ranged between ¥ 10 mill. (1889) and ¥ 144 mill. (1905), the net increase in borrowings over the period amounted to less than ¥ 90 mill. The bulk of the government's domestic debt thus consisted of long-term bonds, increasing from ¥ 0.22 bill. in 1885 to ¥ 1.18 bill. in 1913, of which ¥ 0.13 bill. were domestic bonds of local governments.

This increase, of course, was the result of considerably larger new issues of, and the retirement of, most of the bonds that had been outstanding in 1885. Thus from 1886 to 1900 ¥ 0.39 bill. of domestic bonds of the central government were issued and ¥ 0.22 bill. retired, mainly through refunding operations at reduced interest rates between 1887 and 1893. From

52. *HYS*, p. 250.

1900 through 1913 new issues of ¥ 1.83 bill., ¥ 0.82 bill. in 1904–06 and ¥ 0.72 bill. in 1909–10, compared with ¥ 1.14 bill. of retirements,[53] nearly half of which took place in 1910 on the occasion of refunding part of the bonds issued in connection with the Russo-Japanese War. Among the bonds retired during this period was the bulk of the commutation bonds issued in the mid-1870s. Soon after their issuance most of these bonds apparently had been sold or exchanged for stock of the national banks by the original recipients.[54]

A substantial, although not dominating, part of the government's domestic securities was held by the banking system, about one-fourth in 1885, nearly one-third in 1900, and nearly one-fourth in 1913. In addition, the Deposit Bureau, unimportant in 1885, held about one-eighth of government debt outstanding in 1900 and nearly one-tenth in 1913. Because the holdings of other financial institutions were small, the majority of the government's domestic bonds—about three-fifths for the period as a whole but only about two-fifths in the first half compared to about three-fourths in the second half—must have been absorbed by the nonfinancial sectors, presumably mostly by households. The amounts involved were well below ¥ 0.1 bill. in the first half of the period but in the second seem to have exceeded ¥ 0.5 bill., equal to possibly 1/2 percent and 1 1/2 percent, respectively, of personal disposable income.

Except for the Bank of Japan, the Deposit Bureau, and the national banks, government securities did not absorb a dominating or even a large part of the funds of any of the major financial institutions. Thus government securities from 1898 to 1913 constituted on the average only 7 percent of the assets of commercial banks and never exceeded 11 percent.

Government securities and loans accounted for a substantial proportion of the Bank of Japan's total assets during most of the period, for example, nearly one-third in 1885 and fully one-fourth in 1900, but by 1913 had declined to not much more than one-tenth. Over the period as a whole the bank absorbed only ¥ 60 mill. of government debt, one-seventh of the increase in its total assets and less than 7 percent of the increase in the total domestic debt of the government.

b. Agriculture

Although agriculture during this period employed about two-thirds of the country's labor force and produced nearly half of its income, the share of agriculture in capital formation was below 5 percent according to the available estimates.[55] Even if these figures should underestimate capital formation in agriculture, particularly that part generated by farmers themselves, it is evident that the share of agriculture in national capital formation was low—probably under one-tenth.[56]

No reliable estimate of agricultural saving for this period exists. It seems likely, however, that farmers' share in national saving was considerably below their share in national income. Unless farmers accumulated a large proportion of financial assets absorbed during this period by the private sector, and there is no evidence that they did, their share in national saving would have been low even if they had not increased their indebtedness. Although the estimates of farm debt are of the roughest,[57] there is little doubt that it increased considerably during this period. The available estimates indicate an increase by about ¥ 200 mill. between 1885 and 1900 and another considerably larger rise by nearly ¥ 500 mill. between 1900 and 1913. These figures are considerably in excess not only of the probable net but also of gross fixed capital formation in agriculture. Even if these figures understate the "true" level of capital formation in agriculture, it is difficult to believe that the level of capital formation could even have been equal to the

53. It is not clear from the statistics whether the issues of the central government were all for cash or whether a small fraction was issued in exchange for securities of private railroad companies being taken over.

54. Adams, 1964, p. 28.

55. Inferred from data on capital stock (*ELTESJ*, 3:148 ff.).

56. The amount of capital formation in forestry and fishing was so low (*ELTESJ*, 3:156) that it can be neglected.

57. Cf. Ott, 1960, p. 123.

increase in agricultural debt. Hence, any net saving of agriculture must essentially have taken the form of an increase in financial assets.

There certainly were increases of this type. Farmers must have accounted for a not negligible proportion of the increase in money in circulation and in time deposits, which amounted between 1885 and 1913 to more than ¥ 0.8 bill. and nearly ¥ 1.5 bill, respectively. But the farmers' share would have had to be substantial to make up the difference between estimated net capital expenditures and the increase in agricultural debt and would have had to be very high to leave a substantial surplus. Much of the net saving, that is, the excess of net capital formation plus the increase in currency and time deposits over the increase in indebtedness, would have had to be in such forms as government bonds, bank debentures, and corporate bonds and shares. Some sectors of agriculture, particularly the larger landowners, undoubtedly acquired such assets, but there is no evidence that ownership was widespread among the small and middle-sized farmers, particularly among the mass of the tenantry. It is hard to see how agricultural saving between 1885 and 1913 could have amounted to even 5 percent of total income of ¥ 23 bill.[58,59]

Compared to the total value of agricultural capital, including land, the burden of indebtedness remained light, as a result of the substantial increase in land prices beginning in the 1890s. Thus total farm indebtedness seems to have stayed on the order of slightly less than one-tenth of the value of the tangible wealth of agriculture.[60]

There is no comprehensive information about the sources of agricultural indebtedness, but by the end of the period a substantial part, particularly mortgage loans, must have been supplied by the mortgage banks and the prefectural agricultural and industrial banks.[61] The share has been estimated at four-fifths in 1885 and three-fifths in 1901 and 1914.[62]

c. Nonfinancial Business

For this period no comprehensive statistics, let alone sources and uses of funds statements, exist for the nonfinancial business sector, and the scattered information is often contradictory. Practically nothing at all is known in quantitative terms about unincorporated nonfinancial business. There is no question, however, that this was the period in which the corporate form became at first important and finally dominant in the nonfinancial business sector.

At the beginning of the period, the number of nonfinancial corporations was not much in excess of 1,000. Most corporations were small as is indicated by the average paid-in capital of about ¥ 20,000, from which one can infer a total of assets of not more than ¥ 50,000 to ¥ 100,000 for the average corporation.[63]

Of the total paid-in capital of nonfinancial corporations of only ¥ 25 mill. in 1885, or 3 percent of gross national product, nearly one-half was accounted for by the railroads (table 3-15). The corporate form was still rare in manufacturing, with fewer than 500 corporations with a capital of only ¥ 4 mill., or an average of less than ¥ 10,000. Most of the larger manufacturing enterprises during this period were apparently still conducted in the form of partnerships or

---

58. *ELTESJ*, 1:204.

59. In view of the difficulties of using the difference between receipts and expenditures disclosed in small samples of households as a measure of their saving, even in much more recent periods when sampling methods and survey techniques have improved decisively, one must hesitate to use the few figures of the type available in Japan for this early period (*HYS*, pp. 358–59), which, when blown up, lead to unreasonably high estimates of agricultural saving.

60. This is the 1913 ratio of an agricultural debt of ¥ 0.9 bill. (Ott, 1960, p. 123) and a value of agricultural land (Goldsmith, 1975, p. 141) of ¥ 6.0 bill. and of reproducible assets of ¥ 4.0 bill., derived from *ELTESJ*, 3:154–55 and 164, and 8:158–59 and 165–66.

61. About one-half of the loans of the Hypothec Bank and fully two-thirds of those of the prefectural Agricultural and Industrial Banks had been made to agriculture (Kato, 1970), i.e., a total of nearly ¥ 200 mill. This would be equivalent to less than one-fourth of total estimated farm debt.

62. Ott, 1960, p. 123. Another estimate (Teranishi and Patrick, p. 17) puts it above nine-tenths.

63. For number and capital of corporations, cf. *HYS*, pp. 324 ff.

TABLE 3-15. Distribution of Nonfinancial Corporate Capital, 1885–1913

	Total[a]	Manufacturing	Trading	Transportation
		I. Distribution (percent)		
1885[b]	100	15	35	50
1900	100	20	50	29
1913	100	41	47	11
		II. Percent of gross national product		
1885[b]	3.1	0.5	0.1	1.5
1900	31.9	6.5	16.1	9.3
1913	40.7	16.9	19.3	4.5
		III. Change as percent of gross national product		
1886–1900	3.51	0.73	1.78	1.01
1901–1913	2.58	1.41	1.16	−0.04

[a]Absolute amounts: ¥ 25 mill. for 1885; ¥ 780 mill. for 1900; ¥ 1,983 mill. for 1913; includes small amounts for agriculture.   [b]Authorized capital reduced to paid-in capital in proportion of 1890 for each sector.

SOURCE OF I: HYS, pp. 324–25.

sole proprietorships, including the manufacturing enterprises of the zaibatsu, which were not too numerous at that date and were mostly concentrated in mining.

From the middle 1880s on, however, the corporate sector (joint stock and other companies called *kaisha*) grew rapidly. The number of corporations rose by about 550 percent between 1885 and 1900 and increased by another 80 percent to World War I. At that time the number of nonfinancial corporations had risen to more than 15,000, or, according to another statistic, which apparently includes a number of still smaller companies, to nearly 20,000.[64] Corporate paid-in capital increased even more, by more than 30 times, between 1885 and the turn of the century and by another 150 percent between 1900 and 1913. It is likely that a considerable part of this increase resulted from the conversion of partnerships into corporations, which is known to have happened on a substantial scale within the zaibatsu.[65] On the other hand, some reductions in capital occurred in the case of railroads following the takeover of most of them by the government shortly after the turn of the century. Unfortunately, Japanese specialists do not seem to have analyzed the figures from this point of view, which is crucial for their use in interpreting the position of corporate security issues in the capital market. Nor are there adequate estimates of corporate saving, which would permit assessment of its importance within national saving. It is fairly clear, however, from the relatively small size of the paid-in capital of nonfinancial corporations and their dividend payments, which averaged ¥ 1,650 mill. and ¥ 110 mill., respectively, in the five years before World War I, that the contribution of corporate saving to national saving must have been fairly small. For 1906 to 1913 corporate saving has been estimated at less than ¥ 150 mill.,[66] or one-fourth of private saving, 8 percent of total net saving, one-half of 1 percent of national product, and not much more than 1 percent per year of paid-in capital.[67]

The growth of corporations since the 1880s was thus much more rapid than that of the economy in general. The relation of the paid-in capital of nonfinancial corporations to gross

64. HYS, p. 330.
65. Shibagaki.
66. ELTESJ, 1:190.
67. This estimate is higher than two others. Emi (1965) puts corporate saving for the decade 1903–12 at only ¥ 115 mill., or ¥ 12 mill. per year. Sakurai (p. 59) cites an estimate by Matsunari and associates, according to which saving of the main industrial corporations for 1897 through 1913 amounted to ¥ 150 mill., or less than ¥ 10 mill. a year. Emi's estimate is only 0.3 percent of national product, only about 1 percent of the paid-in capital of nonfinancial corporations, about one-eighth of dividends paid by all corporations (HYS, p. 330), and less than 4 percent of total national saving—all figures so low as to raise serious doubt about their comprehensiveness.

national product rose from about 3 percent in 1885 to more than 30 percent in 1900 and to nearly 40 percent in 1913. At the beginning of World War I the total assets of nonfinancial corporations may therefore have been close to a year's national product. The average size of nonfinancial corporations also increased substantially, reaching almost ¥ 130,000 in 1913 or considerably more than 1,000 times per head national product.

During these three decades considerable shifts occurred in the main sectors of nonfinancial corporations as measured by their paid-in capital, the only comprehensive measure we have. The outstanding feature was the decline of the share of transportation, mainly railways, from about one-half of the total of all nonfinancial corporations in 1885 to about one-third in 1900 and to not much more than one-tenth in 1913, reflecting the nationalization of a large part of the private railroads.

Over the period as a whole there was also a substantial change in the relationship between the two other main groups, manufacturing and trading. Although the paid-in capital of commercial corporations had been twice as large as that of manufacturing corporations in 1885, by 1913 the first group was only slightly larger than the second, most of the relative increase in the share of manufacturing corporations occurring after 1905. This, of course, is in line with the general tendency of the Japanese economy to become more industrialized.

There is no comprehensive information on the sources and uses of funds of all nonfinancial corporations. For the main industrial corporations there exists a set of estimates of the sources of their funds, although not of the uses. The absolute figures of this set of statistics, however, are difficult to accept, as they would mean that this group of corporations accounted for practically all the issues of stocks and bonds of the entire corporate sector[68] and showed bank borrowing in excess of the total reported increase in all bank loans.

d. The Growth of the Zaibatsu

One of the crucial developments in nonfinancial business, particularly the corporate sector, during this period is the rise of the combines (zaibatsu).[69] Although the two main zaibatsu (Mitsui and Sumitomo) have their origins in the Tokugawa period, and the Mitsui group played an important economic role in the establishment of the Meiji regime, the three other zaibatsu (Mitsubishi, Yasuda, and Dai Ichi) were the creation of pioneering modern entrepreneurs— Iwasaki, Yasuda, and Shibusawa—during the first two decades of the Meiji regime. All of them may be said to have had a hand in establishing the main features that characterize the development of the zaibatsu during the generation before World War I. Unfortunately, Japanese economists apparently have not yet managed to develop statistical information that would enable one to relate the importance of the zaibatsu within nonfinancial business in a quantitative way, for instance through such characteristics as the share in business and corporate investment, both in the aggregate and for important individual industries; in business and corporate saving; in corporate security issues; and in business and corporate borrowing. Although comparative quantitative evidence is lacking, it is likely that the zaibatsu even during this period controlled a larger share of the country's nonfinancial business than was the case in any other country for similar groups.

However, three important features of the development of the zaibatsu during this period seem sufficiently clear. The first is the participation of the original commercial enterprises in a number of industries, mainly mining and textiles, that is, the transformation of the zaibatsu, in the Marxist terminology favored by many Japanese economists, from commercial to industrial capitalists. However, most of the zaibatsu remained dominant in both domestic and international trade. How important these interests were is indicated by the fact that the largest zaibatsu alone (Mitsui) accounted at the turn of the century for about one-tenth of the imports and one-fifth of

68. Matsunari, cited in footnote 67.

69. For some information on the development of the zaibatsu during this period, see Shibagaki, p. 335 ff.

the total exports of the country.[70] Rather than concentrating on establishing monopolistic positions in one or a very few industries, the zaibatsu became similar to modern conglomerates. With the creation of five major and a number of minor zaibatsu, the Japanese economy acquired during this period the oligopolistic structure that has characterized it ever since.

Second, practically all the components of the zaibatsu adopted the corporate form, whereas most of them had earlier been conducted in the form of partnerships. More important, these corporations were set up as or became subsidiaries of a top holding company or a layer of holding companies, which laid down general policies for the entire group but left current management to the component companies, the degree of centralization or decentralization of decision making and financing differing among zaibatsu and changing over time.[71] Financially, however, with few exceptions, each zaibatsu, including its nonfinancial, banking, and other financial components, could be regarded as a closed group in the sense that the top holding company arranged for, or at least had a hand in, external financing in its different forms and that the nonfinancial components of each group were treated as preferred customers of the financial members.

Third, the shares in the top holding company of each zaibatsu were entirely or predominantly held by members of one family or their very close associates, control often being even more centrally vested in a single individual under house rules. Although such close control over large economic empires has not been uncommon in other countries in the early phases of industrialization, and to a much more attenuated extent even to World War I, it persisted in Japan in its rigid form until abolished after World War II at the behest of the American occupation authorities.

e. Nonfarm Households

Nonfarm households were the largest single sector in the Japanese economy during the takeoff period. Unfortunately, there is no direct information available on the sources and uses of their funds.

One statement, however, can be made with a considerable degree of confidence: the gross or net capital formation of the nonfarm private household sector was small, in absolute terms or in relation to household disposable income, provided that unincorporated nonfarm enterprises are excluded or that only the change in nonfarm households' equity in these enterprises is taken into account.

Residential construction expenditures dominated private household capital formation, of course. Such expenditures were astonishingly small if the estimates now available are accepted. Gross capital expenditures on residential structures were on the order of ¥ 1 1/2 bill. for the period 1886 to 1913,[72] about equally divided between farm and nonfarm dwellings.[73] Total gross investment in nonfarm housing thus was equal to about 2 percent of national product. Net capital formation through residential housing might then be estimated at well below ¥ 1 bill., representing not more than 1 percent of national product and not much more than one-tenth of total net capital formation, although about one-sixth of its private component. Only about one-half of these figures are attributable to nonagricultural households, so that net housing investment could hardly have equaled more than 1 percent of their income.

The little quantitative evidence available, along with qualitative supplementary information, points to a low ratio of debt to land and structure value in residential housing and hence to a large ratio of net saving of nonfarm households in the form of housing to net housing capital expenditures. In the middle 1880s the ratio of residential mortgage debt, presumably excluding

70. For exports and imports of Mitsui Bussan, cf. Shibagaki, p. 550.

71. For such difference between the two largest zaibatsu, see H. Morikawa, "The Organizational Structure of Mitsubishi and Mitsui Zaibatsu, 1868–1922," *Business History Review* 44 (1970).

72. Rosovsky, 1961, pp. 207–08.

73. *ELTESJ*, 1:184.

that on farm homes, which was included in the total farm mortgage debt, was not much above one-tenth of the structure value of nonfarm residences,[74] although it was considerably lower in relation to the total value of dwellings including land. The ratio does not seem to have increased substantially during the following decades.[75] One reason for these low ratios is, apart from the flimsy character of urban houses, which are mostly one-story wooden structures, the apparently prevailing opinion that a citizen in good standing would acquire a house only when he could do so without having to borrow.

The net investment in consumer durables may practically be disregarded in calculations of this rough sort. Total expenditures on furniture and household utensils were quite small; these items were not very durable; and those durables that now constitute the bulk of this category did not yet exist. This statement is in contrast to the figures shown in some of the old, official Japanese national wealth estimates in which furniture and other household equipment, probably also including clothing, is put at relatively high proportions of the value of the houses themselves.[76]

7. THE FINANCIAL SUPERSTRUCTURE AS A WHOLE

Four ratios, and their components, will be used to characterize quantitatively Japan's financial structure and its development during the takeoff period.[77] First, the new issue ratios of financial institutions and the nonfinancial sectors, which express the issues of the different types of financial instruments in terms of national product or, in the stock dimension, express the amounts outstanding of such instruments in terms of national wealth; second, the financial intermediation ratio, that is, the relation between the issues of financial institutions and those of the nonfinancial sectors or between the amounts outstanding of the two classes of financial instruments, a ratio that provides an indication, although not an exact measure, of the relative importance of direct and indirect (intermediary) finance;[78] third, the financial interrelations ratio, which relates the size of the financial superstructure measured by the total amount of financial assets to that of the real infrastructure measured by tangible assets; and fourth, the ratio between the issues of financial instruments and the period's gross or net capital formation. The statistical material available for Japan's takeoff period permits only approximate measurement of these ratios, but the figures should be accurate enough to avoid distortion of the main trends if proper attention is paid to possible margins of error.

Although the ratios for financial institutions are fairly firm if their conceptual limitations are accepted, the parallel ratios for the main types of financial instruments issued by nonfinancial sectors, shown in table 3-16 for the periods 1886–1900 and 1901–13, are in several cases extremely precarious. This is true in particular for three large items, trade credit, other business debt, and corporate stock, but for different reasons.

74. Based on urban home mortgage debt of ¥ 0.4 bill. and a value of residential buildings of ¥ 0.93 bill. (Goldsmith, 1975, p. 146), of which about one-half might belong to nonagricultural households.

75. The estimates for 1900 and 1913 (table 3-17) of ¥ 0.2 bill. and 0.4 bill. are equal to 6 and 9 percent of the structure value of all residential buildings (Goldsmith, 1975), although to almost twice as much in relation to nonagricultural dwellings only, but again the ratios are substantially reduced if account is taken of the value of the underlying land.

76. Cf. estimates of ¥ 1.6 bill. for "furniture" in the Bank of Japan's estimate of national wealth in 1913 (HYS, p. 20), which would be equal to nearly one-half of the value of all privately owned buildings.

77. For a more detailed discussion of these ratios, cf. Goldsmith, 1969, particularly chap. 2, and 1970.

78. The increase in the assets of financial institutions is slightly in excess of the new issues acquired by nonfinancial sectors because part of the issues was absorbed by other financial institutions, either within the same group (e.g., interbank deposits) or among other groups (e.g., bank shares acquired by insurance companies). A second, generally minor cause of overstatement is the inclusion among assets of items that do not represent issues of financial instruments but bookkeeping entries, such as valuation changes and reserves. It has not been possible to adjust for these differences; indeed, such adjustments are often omitted even for more recent periods in other countries where statistical data are much richer.

TABLE 3-16. New Issue Ratios, 1886–1913 (Percent of Gross National Product)

	1886 to 1900	1901 to 1913	1886 to 1913
		I. Financial institutions	
Total	5.8	8.5	7.7
		II. Nonfinancial sectors	
Government domestic securities and loans[a]	1.1	2.2	1.8
Corporate bonds	0.1	0.2	0.1
Other business debt (excluding 4)	2.6	4.5	3.9
Trade credit	3.2	4.5	4.1
Farm debt	0.4	1.0	1.9
Nonfarm residential debt	0.8	0.4	0.5
Corporate stock	3.7	2.6	2.9
Total	11.9	15.3	14.3
		III. All sectors	
Total	17.7	21.1	22.0

[a]Of which, local governments 0.2 percent in all three periods.

SOURCE: Table 3-17, using differences in outstandings between 1885 and 1900, 1900 and 1913, and 1885 and 1913.

a. New Issue Ratios

Accepting provisionally the figures of table 3-16, it appears that the main types of issues by nonfinancial sectors were equal during both subperiods to 12 and 15 percent of national product. (Households' equity in unincorporated business enterprises is not regarded as a financial instrument, given the close interrelation between the household and business activities of farmers and owner-operators of unincorporated nonfarm businesses, which makes a distinction conceptually almost meaningless, apart from its being statistically unfeasible.) This figure is overstated because it assumes that the difference in corporate stock outstanding represented cash issues, whereas it is known that a substantial part, particularly of issues of nonfinancial corporations, is nothing but the equity of partnerships that adopted the corporate form. On the other hand, the use of the figure for lendings of commercial banks to represent all business debt other than corporate bonds and trade credit probably[79] understates the new issues of the nonfinancial sectors. It is not likely that the difference between these two partly offsetting items overstates the ratio for the period as a whole by more than 1 percentage point. The main substantial margin of doubt that remains concerns trade credit. It has been assumed that trade credit was approximately equal in size to inventories, an assumption that must be based hazardously on the fact that this was the ratio existing in Japan in the late 1950s, the first period for which there are statistical data for these magnitudes.[80] Although it is impossible to attach a well-founded estimate of the margin of error to the figures shown in table 3-16, it is felt that the margin is not in excess of 2 percent. Although the range of the new issue ratio of financial instruments issued by nonfinancial sectors would then be from 12 and 14 and 14 and 16 percent for both subperiods, it is regarded as more likely that it would be between 11 and 13 and 14 and 16 percent.

79. One must say "probably" because not all lendings of commercial banks represent business borrowing, and the part that does not may exceed the otherwise unrecorded borrowing of business.

80. Figures for trade credit are from the Bank of Japan's flow-of-funds statistics; inventories are from the Economic Planning Agency's estimates for 1955 and 1960 (*ESA*, 1970, pp. 277–79). The ratio increased sharply in the 1960s and to more than 2 in 1970, but it is felt that such high ratios are inapplicable to Meiji Japan.

b. The Financial Intermediation Ratio

The financial intermediation ratio, the quotient of the issues of financial institutions, which represent indirect financing of the nonfinancial sectors, and of the issues of the nonfinancial sectors that may be absorbed either by financial sectors (indirect financing again) or by nonfinancial sectors (direct financing), rose slightly from nearly one-half in the first subperiod, 1886–1900, to 55 percent from 1901–13. In the stock dimension the ratio between the value of the outstanding financial assets of financial and nonfinancial sectors increased slowly from 35 percent in 1885 to 45 percent in 1900 and to 52 percent in 1913.[81] The level of both ratios is higher than it should be, first, because intersectoral holdings among financial institutions are not eliminated and, second, because the denominator probably understates the relative importance of premodern lenders. Adjustment for the difference between the paid-in and the market values of corporate shares would lower the level of the stock ratio and moderate its upward movement, but only slightly. In any case, a distinct, though not radical, increase in the institutionalization process, that is, the ratio of indirect to direct financing, appears to have taken place during the takeoff period, particularly during its first half.

c. The Financial Interrelations Ratio

The most concise single measure of the relative importance of the financial superstructure, the financial interrelations ratio, that is, financial assets divided by tangible assets, advanced slowly from 30 to 34 percent from 1885 to 1900. From then to World War I, however, the rise accelerated sharply, bringing the ratio to more than three-fifths in 1913, both components, the ratios of issues of financial and nonfinancial sectors to tangible assets, approximately doubling in an interval of only thirteen years. Factoring the ratio differently, its sharp rise between 1900 and 1913 is due to a combination of a substantial decline in the capital-output ratio from 6 to 5 and a sharp increase in the ratio of financial assets to national product from 0.21 to 0.32. One may then regard the first decade of the twentieth century as the takeoff in Japanese finance, the period during which the country moved from ratios characteristic of financially underdeveloped countries to close to the levels characterizing developed countries.[82]

Using the formula for factoring the financial interrelations ratio that has been used in the preceding chapters, we obtain

$$FIR = \tau \times \alpha \times \beta^{-1} (\varphi + \delta) (1 + \nu) + F_{1885}/ T_{1913} \text{ or}$$
$$0.60 = 0.85 \times 15.9 \times 0.19 \times (0.13 + 0.07) (1.05) + 0.06,$$

which is quite close to the observed ratio of 0.62.

d. New Issues and Capital Formation

The ratio of domestic new issues of the nonfinancial sector to capital formation increased on the basis of gross capital formation from more than two-thirds in the first subperiod to almost four-fifths in the second and on the basis of net capital formation from one and one-third to one and one-half. For the private sector alone the ratios were even higher, namely, four-fifths for the first subperiod, nearly unity for the second, and nine-tenths for the period as a whole on the basis of gross capital formation; no estimates of net capital formation of the private sector alone are available. This does not mean that almost all capital expenditures of the takeoff period were externally financed, including the sale of corporate stock, because a part of all issues was raised for other purposes. It indicates, however, that the ratio of external financing to capital formation

81. The more straightforward method of directly measuring the share of each instrument held by financial institutions cannot be applied generally because of lack of appropriate data.

82. The value of the 1913 financial interrelations ratio has been roughly estimated at between 0.70 and 0.90 for the United States, France, and Germany (Goldsmith, 1969, p. 338). The distance between these values and the Japanese ratio of about three-fifths is, however, larger than appears because the former make no or only inadequate allowance for trade credit.

was high, a fact known to be true for business, and that it increased from the first to the second subperiod.

8. THE NATIONAL BALANCE SHEET

The national balance sheet, some components of which have already been used in the preceding section, provides a convenient overview of Japan's financial structure and the changes in it during the takeoff period. Table 3-17 shows the rough estimates in absolute figures, and table 3-18 puts them in perspective by expressing them in relation to national assets and to gross national product.

The main ratios that can be derived from the national balance sheet have already been discussed in the preceding section. Here, therefore, a few changes in the structure of tangible and financial assets will be examined. The three most important changes in the distribution of tangible assets are the declines in the shares of agricultural land and in residential and other buildings and the increasing share of producer durables. Among financial assets, the changes include the increasing shares of instruments issued by financial institutions, of business debt to banks (relatively overstated because of the probable underestimates of business debt to premodern lenders), and of corporate stock, which would be even more pronounced if allowance

TABLE 3-17. National Balance Sheet, 1885, 1900, and 1913 (¥ Bill.)

	1885	1900	1913
I. Tangible assets	5.05	15.25	26.14
1. Land[a]	2.32	7.10	11.03
a. Agricultural[a]	1.70	5.00	7.76
b. Other	0.62	2.10	3.27
2. Reproducible tangible wealth	2.73	8.15	15.11
a. Residential buildings	0.93	3.20	4.30
b. Other buildings and structures	0.82	2.25	3.91
c. Producer durables	0.17	0.72	2.17
d. Inventories	0.35	1.00	3.08
e. Livestock	0.41	0.88	1.43
f. Consumer durables	0.05	0.10	0.22
II. Financial assets	1.52	5.13	16.20
1. Issued by financial institutions[b]	0.39	1.58	5.53
2. Issued by nonfinancial sectors	1.13	3.55	10.67
a. Government domestic securities	0.24	0.46	1.46
b. Corporate bonds	—	0.01	0.10
c. Other business debts (except d)	0.14	0.68	2.75
d. Trade credit	0.35	1.00	3.08
e. Farm debt	0.33	0.42	0.90
f. Residential mortgages	0.04	0.20	0.40
g. Corporate stock[c]	0.03	0.78	1.98
III. Net foreign assets	−0.24	−0.24	−1.04
IV. National wealth (I + III)	4.81	15.01	25.10
V. National assets (I + II)	6.57	20.38	42.34

[a]Including forests.   [b]Including government paper money and subsidiary coin: 1885, ¥ 0.12 bill.; 1900, ¥ 0.09 bill.; 1913, ¥ 0.15 bill.   [c]Excluding stock of financial institutions included in line II = 1; par value.

SOURCES: Lines I-1 and I-2: Goldsmith, 1975, pp. 140 and 145–46. Somewhat different estimates are given in Fujino, 1975, pp. 190–91, namely, for I-2: ¥ 3.03 bill., ¥ 8.60 bill., and ¥ 14.14 bill.; and for I-2d and 2e: ¥ 0.38 bill., ¥ 1.30 bill., and ¥ 2.33 bill. Line II-1: table 3-10. Line II-2a: HYS, pp. 158 and 162. Line II-2b: Ott, 1960, p. 102. Line II-2c: 1885, table 3-8; 1900 and 1913 commercial bank lending (Teranishi and Patrick, p. 40) plus lendings of long-term credit banks (Ott, 1960, pp. 175 ff.). Line II-2d: Assumed equal to inventories excluding livestock. Line II-2e and 2f: Ott, 1960, p. 123. Line II-2g: HYS, pp. 324–25.

TABLE 3-18. Distribution of National Assets and Relation to Gross National Product, 1885, 1900, and 1913

	Distribution			Relation to gross national product		
	1885	1900	1913	1885	1900	1913
I. Tangible assets	0.78	0.75	0.62	6.27	6.24	5.36
1. Land	0.36	0.35	0.26	2.88	2.90	2.26
a. Agricultural[a]	0.26	0.25	0.18	2.11	2.04	1.59
b. Other	0.10	0.10	0.08	0.77	0.86	0.67
2. Reproducible tangible assets	0.42	0.40	0.36	3.39	3.33	3.10
a. Residential buildings	0.14	0.16	0.10	1.16	1.31	0.88
b. Other buildings and structures	0.13	0.11	0.09	1.02	0.92	0.80
c. Producer durables	0.03	0.03	0.05	0.21	0.29	0.44
d. Inventories (including livestock)	0.12	0.09	0.11	0.94	0.77	0.93
e. Consumer durables	0.01	0.01	0.01	0.06	0.04	0.05
II. Financial assets	0.22	0.25	0.38	1.89	2.10	3.32
1. Issued by financial institutions[b]	0.06	0.08	0.13	0.48	0.65	1.13
2. Issued by nonfinancial sectors	0.16	0.17	0.25	1.40	1.45	2.19
a. Government domestic securities	0.04	0.02	0.03	0.30	0.19	0.30
b. Corporate bonds	—	0.00	0.02	—	0.00	0.02
c. Other business debts (excluding d)	0.02	0.03	0.06	0.17	0.28	0.56
d. Trade credit	0.05	0.05	0.07	0.43	0.41	0.63
e. Agricultural debt	0.04	0.02	0.02	0.41	0.17	0.18
f. Residential mortgages	0.01	0.01	0.01	0.05	0.08	0.08
g. Corporate stock[c]	0.01	0.04	0.05	0.04	0.32	0.41
III. Net foreign assets	−0.04	−0.01	−0.02	−0.30	−0.10	−0.21
IV. National wealth	0.73	0.74	0.60	5.98	6.14	5.15
V. National assets	1.00	1.00	1.00	8.16	8.34	8.69

[a]Including forests.   [b]Including government paper money and subsidiary coin.   [c]Excluding stock of financial institutions included in II-1; par value.

SOURCE: Table 3-17.

were made for the excess of market over par value[83] and the decline of the shares of agricultural debt and government securities. Most of these changes are observed in the early phases of financial development in other countries.

9. THE FINANCIAL ACHIEVEMENTS OF THE TAKEOFF PERIOD

1. On the eve of World War I, and even a few years earlier, Japan had acquired, essentially as the result of developments during less than half a century, a financial structure that was

83. Although stocks were issued at, or on the average very close to, par, it is known that stock prices deviated from par, and it appears that they were above par and had a slight upward trend during the period (see chart 1 in *History of Yamaichi Securities Co., Ltd.*). For prices of about a dozen of the most actively traded stocks during the years 1893–98, cf. Matsukata, table 42. The ratio of the market value of issues of the nonfinancial sector to national wealth could not have been markedly affected in 1885, when the total paid-in capital of corporations was on the order of ¥ 0.1 bill., or 2 percent of national wealth. The understatement might, however, have amounted to as much as 5 percent of national wealth in 1913. It thus might raise the ratio of financial instruments to tangible assets to about two-thirds. There is one indication that in 1913 the difference between par and market value is not likely to have been drastic for all corporate stock outstanding. The amount of dividends paid by business corporations in 1913 is given at about ¥ 135 mill. (*HYS*, p. 330), which at the relatively high interest and yield rates then prevailing in Japan does not indicate a market value substantially in excess of the paid-in capital of ¥ 2.0 bill. The average price of shares traded on the Tokyo Stock Exchange, a figure that can be used only with great reservations as an indicator of price trends, rose from about ¥ 58 in 1900 to ¥ 71 in 1913, compared to a standard par value of ¥ 50 and a somewhat smaller average paid-in value. These figures again point to only a moderate excess of market over paid-in values, although one increasing between 1900 and 1913.

qualitatively and quantitatively not too dissimilar from, even if still slightly behind, those built up in contemporary Western countries in about twice to three times that time span.

2. The broadest quantitative characteristics of this catching-up process are an issue ratio of financial institutions of nearly one-tenth in 1909–13; an issue ratio of nonfinancial sectors of about one-eighth; a financial intermediation ratio of more than three-fifths; and a financial interrelations ratio of more than three-fifths in 1913.

3. Japan had created, indeed essentially copied, practically the full panoply of Western financial institutions, most of which covered the entire country rather than being limited to a few large urban centers: a modern central bank; a commercial banking system combining a small number of fairly large institutions with a branch system of limited size and a large number of small local banks; long-term credit banks for agriculture and industry; three nationwide systems of thrift institutions—private savings banks, the postal saving organization, and agricultural credit cooperatives; and life and property insurance companies, the first still quite small. Premodern lenders, however, still played an important role in financing agriculture and small business.

4. The degree of concentration within the commercial banking system, by far the largest financial institution, remained modest.

5. The main gaps in the institutional system were the absence or negligible size of investment bankers, investment companies, and urban credit cooperatives, but such banks were also missing in many Western developed countries, not only early in the twentieth century, but until after World War II.

6. The government played a much more important role in the financial structure than did the government in any developed Western country. The government had a decisive role in shaping the policies of the central bank, which in turn had very considerable influence on the activities of the commercial banks, both through moral suasion and because the large commercial banks often borrowed from the Bank of Japan. In addition, the government operated one of the three systems of thrift organizations, and the system of long-term credit banks was partly owned and strongly influenced by the government.

7. Japan also had developed the main types of financial instruments to provide both long-term funds to nonfinancial sectors and outlets for household saving—central and local government bonds, mortgage bank debentures, and corporate bonds and stocks. It apparently had managed to distribute them fairly widely, although the proportion of these securities held by financial institutions was probably larger and the proportion of households owning the remaining majority share smaller than in most Western countries. The market for mortgages, particularly those on residential properties, however, was very narrow.

8. Short-term credit was available freely, Japanese banks always having been apparently more liberal in this field than those in most Western countries.

9. As everywhere and at all times, small enterprises had considerably more difficulty in securing funds than large ones, particularly for the intermediate and long term.

10. The large family conglomerates (*zaibatsu*) became firmly established and essentially developed the form of organization they retained until after World War I, although their share in both the financial and nonfinancial sectors of the economy was smaller on the eve of World War I than it was to become in the next three decades. In distinction to later developments, the shares of the top holding companies, as well as of the operating members of the conglomerates, remained closely held and no part of them was offered to the general public.

11. Secular inflation at an average rate of nearly 4 1/2 percent (national product deflator) or 3 1/4 percent (wholesale and consumer price indices), more than tripling (or more than doubling) the price level between 1885 and 1913, apparently did not interfere with the development of financial institutions and instruments based on fixed monetary values, and money illusion seems to have been complete.

12. The level of nominal and even of real interest and yield rates remained rather high

except for government bonds and instruments directly or implicitly guaranteed by the government, but local and other interest differentials diminished.

13. In comparison to the growth of financial institutions and financial instruments, the development of a capital market lagged far behind. Public issues of bonds and stocks were relatively small, and most of the large amounts of funds required by corporate and unincorporated business were provided either internally, apparently sufficient for only a minority of requirements, or externally by the banking system, namely, by the commercial banks and premodern lenders for short-term needs and by the mortgage banks or the government for long-term needs.

14. The financial development of Japan during the takeoff period owed relatively little to foreign funds and, after the turn of the century, to foreign technical assistance. Net capital inflows were absent for the 1886–1900 period. Although they amounted to about ¥ 0.8 bill. for the period 1901–13, equal to nearly 2 percent of gross national product and about one-fifth of net domestic capital expenditures, they were, statistically, more than accounted for by the government's borrowing for the Russo-Japanese War. Even at a disaggregated level, focusing attention on the use of individual loans, foreign funds were of importance only in financing the capital expenditures of railroads and local governments.[84] They were negligible in the rest of the economy, whether in the form of purchases of Japanese securities or of direct foreign investment in Japanese business enterprises.

84. Local governments between 1906 and 1913 increased their net foreign indebtedness by ¥ 173 mill. (Ott, 1960, p. 97), which was equal to about one-fifth of their total gross fixed capital expenditures during this period (Emi, 1971, pp. 246 ff.). Foreign capital was probably of considerably smaller relative importance in financing railroad capital expenditures.

4   The Uncertain Trumpet, 1914–1931[1]

1. BASIC CHARACTERISTICS OF PERIOD[2]

a. The nearly two decades from 1914 to 1931 is divided into two subperiods of very different character: World War I and its immediate aftermath, and what may loosely be called the 1920s, that is, the years 1922 through 1931. The dividing line between the two subperiods has been put at the end of the short business (inventory) cycle immediately following and causally connected with World War I.[3] The first subperiod comprises, therefore, the eight years 1914 through 1921, and the second subperiod embraces the decade starting in 1922. For financial purposes, the second subperiod may be further divided into two segments of five years each separated by the financial crisis of 1927. A half dozen of the basic economic indicators are shown on an annual basis in table 4-1.

b. Although formally a belligerent in World War I, Japan was, in fact, essentially neutral and reaped all the benefits of this status. Total military expenditures attributable to the war were small, less than ¥ 0.9 bill.,[4] or not much more than 2 percent of the 1914 to 1918 national product and about one-tenth of total government expenditures. They were, from almost any point of view, largely overcompensated by the economic and political gains of the period.

c. The two primary economic features of the war years were a sharp expansion in exports, crucially assisted by the preoccupation of most of Japan's competitors with the war,[5] and an acceleration of the process of industrialization, which proved permanent. The real value of exports more than doubled between 1913 and 1918, and their share in gross national product rose from less than 10 percent to nearly 15 percent. During the same period manufacturing production expanded by two-thirds.[6]

---

1. Considerable use has been made in this chapter of the following: H. M. Bratter, *Japanese Banking* (U.S. Dept. of Commerce, Trade Promotion Series, 116), 1931; E. E. Ehrlich, "The Role of Banking in Japan's Economic Development," Ph.D. dissertation, New School for Social Research, 1960; H. G. Moulton, *Japan: An Economic and Financial Appraisal*, 1931; H. T. Patrick, "The Economic Muddle of the 1920's," in J. W. Morley, ed., *Dilemmas of Growth in Prewar Japan*, 1971; L. S. Presnell, ed., *Money and Banking in Japan*, 1973, a translation of a Japanese publication of the Economic Research Department of the Bank of Japan, 1969.

2. One may, as always, argue about the exact delimitation of any period in the continuous process of economic development. In this instance in particular, one might prefer 1929 as the terminal year in order to bring the periodization in line with that applicable to other industrial countries. In the case of Japan, however, it can be argued that the depression started, particularly if attention is centered on financial developments, as early as 1927. On the other hand, the abandonment of the gold standard in the fall of 1931, the initiation shortly afterward of reflationary and increasingly nationalistic economic and financial policies, and the disappearance of party government seem to mark 1932 more clearly as a decisive turning point.

3. Cf. Fujino, 1966, p. 66.

4. Moulton, p. 576.

5. For a description of Japan's foreign trade, cf. Yamasaki and Ogawa.

6. Based on an increase in production of the manufacturing sector (*ELTESJ*, 1:229).

TABLE 4-1. National Product, Consumption, and Capital Formation, 1913–1931

	Gross national product			Personal consumption per head 1934–36 prices (yen) (4)	Current foreign balance (¥ bill.) (5)	Gross fixed capital formation ratio (percent) (6)
	Current prices (¥ bill.) (1)	Constant (1934–36) prices				
		Amount (¥ bill.) (2)	Change (percent) (3)			
1913	5.01	8.00	+1.0	128	−0.10	17.2
1914	4.74	8.06	+0.8	123	−0.01	17.0
1915	4.99	8.53	+5.8	128	0.22	15.9
1916	6.15	9.23	+8.2	134	0.62	16.8
1917	8.59	10.06	+9.0	138	0.96	21.1
1918	11.84	10.93	+8.6	145	0.83	22.8
1919	15.45	11.48	+5.0	158	0.38	19.0
1920	15.90	11.42	−0.5	153	−0.07	22.6
1921	14.89	12.15	+6.4	163	−0.25	19.3
1922	15.57	11.83	−2.6	171	−0.18	19.1
1923	14.92	11.29	−4.6	172	−0.52	16.8
1924	15.58	12.70	+12.5	174	−0.64	18.8
1925	16.27	12.33	−2.9	174	−0.24	16.6
1926	15.98	12.42	+0.7	174	−0.38	17.9
1927	16.29	12.84	+3.4	176	−0.13	17.7
1928	16.51	13.67	+6.5	176	−0.12	16.6
1929	16.29	13.74	+0.5	175	0.09	17.3
1930	14.67	13.88	+0.1	171	0.04	15.8
1931	13.31	13.94	+0.4	172	−0.08	14.6

SOURCE: *ELTESJ*, 1:178, 193, 225, 237, and 239.

d. Real gross national product increased between 1913 and 1921 by one-half in the aggregate. The average annual rate of growth per head of fully 4 percent was considerably above the rates experienced in the Meiji era. The sharpest increases, averaging more than 8 percent per year per head, occurred in the middle part of the period (1916–18), surpassing the best previous periods of similar length (1886–89 and 1893–95) by about 5 percent each. In no year did real aggregate product decline.

e. The accelerated industrialization of the country is evident in the increasing share of the manufacturing industry in net domestic product: more than one-fourth in 1920 compared with one-fifth in 1913 and one-sixth around the turn of the century.

f. The end of the war was followed, as in most of the world, after a sharp but brief recession, by a short cycle that terminated in a trough in the spring of 1921, which may be regarded as signaling the end of the immediate postwar readjustment and the longer cycle that had started with the war.[7]

g. Financially, the war period and its immediate aftermath through 1921 was characterized by an open inflation of substantial dimensions, which originated in the private rather than the government sector. The price level (national product deflator), as well as the consumer price index, more than doubled between 1913 and 1920, mostly between 1915 and 1919, and declined by only about one-tenth in the adjustment of 1921. Table 4-2 shows the annual movements in the relevant price indices.

h. Japan's balance of payments showed large surpluses on current account from 1915

7. For a discussion, cf. particularly Patrick, 1971, and in the financial field, Adams, 1964, chap. 3.

TABLE 4-2. Price Movements, 1913–1931

	National product deflator	Wholesale prices	Consumer prices	Wages	Stock prices	Interest rates (percent)	Rural land prices 1934–36 = 100)	Foreign exchange (yen per $)
			1934–36 = 100					
	(1)	(2)	(3)	(4)	(5)	(6)	(7)	(8)
1913	62.7	64.7	67.3	31	·	9.6	70	2.02
1914	58.8	61.8	62.0	31	58	9.9	64	2.03
1915	58.5	62.5	58.0	31	86	9.6	59	2.04
1916	66.6	75.6	62.7	32	112	8.9	63	2.00
1917	85.4	95.1	76.9	43	111	8.5	75	1.98
1918	108.3	124.6	103.5	56	113	8.3	103	1.95
1919	134.7	152.6	137.7	94	144	8.7	170	1.98
1920	139.2	167.8	144.0	95	74	10.6	139	2.02
1921	122.5	129.6	132.0	110	82	10.9	142	2.08
1922	131.6	126.7	130.0	107	104	11.0	148	2.08
1923	132.2	128.9	128.8	107	85	11.1	110	2.04
1924	122.6	133.6	130.0	111	87	11.1	136	2.38
1925	131.9	130.5	131.6	111	92	10.2	135	2.45
1926	128.6	115.7	125.6	114	106	10.7	139	2.13
1927	126.9	109.9	123.7	115	117	10.4	133	2.11
1928	120.7	110.6	119.0	116	98	9.9	131	2.15
1929	118.6	107.8	116.2	115	86	9.6	127	2.17
1930	105.9	888.5	104.4	108	59	9.7	119	2.02
1931	95.5	74.8	92.4	102	44	9.4	100	2.04

SOURCES: **Col. 1:** *ELTESJ*, 1:232.   **Col. 2:** *HYS*, p. 76.   **Col. 3:** *ELTESJ*, 8:135–36.   **Col. 4:** *ELTESJ*, 8:247, col. 5; average daily male wage in manufacturing.   **Col. 5:** *HYS*, p. 252, for 1921–31; for 1914–20, *ESJ*, 1961. **Col. 6:** Average rate on bank loans (Ministry of Finance as cited in Ott, 1960, p. 302).   **Col. 7:** Average of March prices for ordinary and paddy fields. *HYS*, pp. 88–89.   **Col. 8:** *HYS*, p. 320.

through 1919, totaling ¥ 3.0 bill., or 6 percent of gross national product, which were only offset to a small extent by the deficits of 1920 and 1921. The total surplus of the 1914–21 period of ¥ 2.6 bill. was used to increase the country's gold stock (¥ 1.2 bill.) and to finance long-term investments abroad (¥ 1.8 bill.), part of which, in China and Russia, had to be written off in the 1920s, leaving a small balance of net short-term borrowing or errors and omissions.

i. Compared to the rapid economic expansion and the optimism of the 1914–21 period, the following decade was one of slow growth, accompanied by serious economic, financial, social, and political difficulties and a lack of direction. The reasons for the unsatisfactory development of Japan during this decade are far from clear, but the evidence of growth retardation is evident. It is ironical, and no causal relation is claimed, that this decade of on the whole unsatisfactory economic and social performance was also the period in its history, at least until 1945, during which Japan became most Westernized in its internal politics and social structure and the least nationalistic in its international posture.

j. Aggregate real national product in 1931, the highest level during the decade, was only 15 percent higher than it had been ten years earlier. If the increase in population is taken into account, there was even a small decline. In no other decade since 1868 had growth been as slow.

k. Economic and financial fluctuations within the decade were fairly pronounced, three short (trough-to-trough) cycles being distinguished, which ended late in 1922, 1926, and 1930.[8] By the test of real gross national product the only annual periods of substantial growth were 1924

8. Fujino, loc. cit.

with 12 1/2 percent and 1928 with 6 1/2 percent. Aggregate national product actually declined in 1922–23 by an average of 3 1/2 percent, partly as a result of the great Kanto earthquake, which is estimated to have caused damage to national wealth of more than ¥ 5 bill.,[9] equal to one-third of one year's national product, nearly two years' gross capital formation, and about one-tenth of the value of reproducible tangible assets in Japan.[10]

l. In view of these trends, it is not astonishing that real consumption per head increased by only 0.5 percent per year between 1921 and 1931 compared with a rate of 3 percent per year for the period 1913–21 and an annual average of 1.3 percent for the three decades before World War I.[11] This failure of the standard of living to improve noticeably or as rapidly as during the preceding decade may be connected to the malaise characterizing the period.

m. One factor contributing to the stagnation of output in the 1920s was the slowing down of the remarkable growth of agricultural production in the preceding generation. From 1920 through 1935 agricultural output increased only at an annual rate of 0.9 percent, that is, by 0.4 percent less than the growth of population, compared with annual growth rates averaging 2.0 and 1.6 percent for the two preceding twenty-year periods.[12] This slowdown occurred in the face of an increase between 1913–17 and 1928–32 of 3 percent in the arable land area, 15 percent in fixed capital, and 80 percent in nonfarm current inputs but was accompanied by a reduction in the agricultural labor force by more than 10 percent.[13]

n. Another factor contributing to the slowdown of the 1920s is a reduction in the gross domestic capital formation ratio from fully 20 percent in 1914–21 to 18 percent in 1922–31,[14] although the latter ratio was still above that for 1901–13 and 1886–1900. As a consequence, the growth rate of the net stock of fixed capital increased at an annual average rate of only 2.4 percent from 1922 to 1931 against a rate of 4.1 percent for 1914–21, and thus remained slightly below the rate of 2.8 percent for 1886–1913.[15]

o. The growth of the nonagricultural labor force also slackened considerably, notwithstanding the continued influx from agriculture. The average rate of growth in the 1920s declined to 1.7 percent, from 2.8 percent in 1913–20 and nearly 3 percent in 1885–1913, although the rate of increase in total population in the 1920s was the highest observed.[16]

p. These figures suggest that the increase in productivity, which had been sharp in the 1914–21 period and substantial in the preceding thirty years, practically came to a standstill in the decade 1922–31.

q. This stagnation is rather astonishing in view of the fact that the shares of the secondary and tertiary sectors of the economy continued to rise; in terms of national income (from 71 percent in 1920 to 85 percent in 1930) and the labor force (from 46 to 50 percent), the secondary and tertiary sectors rose even more rapidly than in the 1914–20 period.[17]

r. From 1922 to 1927 the general price level showed only minor fluctuations around a slightly downward trend. The following years, however, were characterized by a sharp deflation, which started and ended earlier than in most industrialized countries. In 1931 the general price level was one-fourth lower than it had been four years earlier. Retail prices were fairly

9. *HYS*, p. 26.

10. The estimate for 1920 (Goldsmith, 1975, p. 126) is ¥ 48 bill.; investment-goods prices declined by nearly 10 percent between the end of 1920 and 1923 (*ELTESJ*, 8:158), but the net real capital stock increased by 7 percent (*ELTESJ*, 3:149–50). The *ELTESJ* estimates do not make allowance for earthquake losses.

11. *ELTESJ*, 1:237.

12. Yamada and Hayami, p. 9. Quadrennial rates of growth for the six periods from 1913–17 to 1938–42 are: 13, 6, 0, 7, 6, and 0 percent (ibid., p. 24).

13. Ibid., p. 25.

14. Fixed capital formation ratio (table 4-1) plus inventory accumulation ratio (Rosovsky, 1961, p. 208).

15. *ELTESJ*, 3:148 ff.

16. Cf. table 1-2.

17. *JEG*, p. 282.

stable until 1925 but declined substantially in 1930 and 1931. At that time they were about 30 percent below the level of 1925 and 35 percent below that of 1920, although still about 50 percent above that of 1914.[18]

s. The money supply increased sharply during the war and its immediate aftermath, rising between the end of 1913 and 1920 at an annual rate of between 15 and 21 percent, depending on the estimate used.[19] Deposit currency apparently expanded a little more rapidly than cash currency. From 1921 through 1929 fluctuations were minor, but a sharp decline by nearly one-fifth took place in the depression of 1930–31. As the money supply moved roughly in step with, although a little ahead of, national product, income velocity did not show a persistent or marked trend, although it exhibited considerable annual fluctuation (table 4-3).

t. During this period, particularly its first half, the stock market gained considerably in importance and for the first time began to play a substantial role in the economy and in the financing of business. The sharp rise in business profits during the war years led to a considerable increase in the volume of trading and in the level of stock prices. In 1919 the volume of stocks traded on the Tokyo stock exchange was four times as high as in 1910–14, and the average level of stock prices at their peak in January 1920 was two and a half times as high as in July 1917, an advance only slightly in excess of the rise in the general price level, although the index was in excess of 400 percent for several favored industries.[20] After a sharp setback, culminating in the panic of March 1920, stock prices moved irregularly until 1928, reflecting the mediocre performance of corporate profits and the panic and temporary closure of the exchange in the spring of 1927, which resulted from the banking crisis (section 3). The level of stock prices then fell by October 1931 to less than one-half of that of 1921 and probably to not more than three-fourths of the 1913 level, although the price level was more than 50 percent higher than before World War I. The volume of trading followed similar movements.

u. Agricultural land prices, the only type of real estate for which this information is available but for this period probably the most important one,[21] rose by nearly 150 percent between 1913 and 1919, reflecting both the general rise in the price level and the profitability of agriculture; fell by nearly 20 percent in the following year; and trended downward during the rest of the period, slowly to the end of the 1920s and rapidly in the depression of 1930–31, which hit agriculture with particular severity. In the spring of 1932 farmland prices were only 40 percent above the level of 1913, compared with a rise in the general price level of commodities and services by about one-half.

v. In view of the conventional and controlled nature of most Japanese interest rates, reported movements can be used only as indicators of levels and trends. The Bank of Japan's discount rate, which was changed only 15 times during this period of 18 years, ranged between slightly more than 5 percent (in 1917–18 and 1930–31) and 8 percent, a level at which it remained without change from November 1919 in the middle of the first postwar recession to April 1925. The average rate on bank loans, which is probably more representative of changes in the demand/supply situation than bond yields, ended the period at approximately the same level at which it started, namely, slightly below 10 percent. The lower level during World War I of about 8 1/2 percent is rather puzzling, given the rapid increase in output and in the price level, and probably reflected the cartelized nature of the bank credit market and the official cheap money policy that is evidenced in the relatively low discount rates of the Bank of Japan, which

18. The decline is somewhat sharper if the Tokyo retail price index (*HYS*, p. 50) is used.

19. All statements about money supply and related matters for this period must be expressed with great caution as no official or other authoritative series appears to exist. Table 4-3 brings together the figures now available, which in some respects are not compatible with each other, although the main trends are similar.

20. Adams, 1964, pp. 73 and 93; *HYS*, p. 252.

21. Both in 1913 and 1930 farmland accounted for about one-third of the total value of all land and buildings (Goldsmith, 1975, pp. 140 and 146, and *ELTESJ*, 3:154–55).

TABLE 4-3. Money in Circulation, 1913–1931 (¥ Mill.)

	Currency			Bank deposits			
	HYS[a] (1)	Fujino (2)	A and N (3)	HYS[b] (4)	Fujino (5)	A and N (6)	Money in circulation (7)
1913	584	395	638	379	689	996	805
1914	525	374	583	391	694	1009	785
1915	575	351	637	507	754	1246	849
1916	754	417	835	590	1091	1697	1060
1917	1041	553	1120	853	1451	2353	1315
1918	1418	773	1543	1045	1953	3073	1780
1919	1869	988	2087	1276	2186	3896	1974
1920	1647	1202	1936	1165	2887	4369	2371
1921	1772	1150	2112	1217	3345	4780	2323
1922	1725	1179	2096	1328	3562	4696	2334
1923	2045	1251	2164	1458	3421	4559	2427
1924	1997	1249	2131	1418	3257	4476	2347
1925	1963	1207	2098	1444	3264	4573	2270
1926	1902	1164	2028	1455	3192	4580	2250
1927	2021	1285	2148	1411	3349	4704	2327
1928[c]	2098	1233	2200	1347	3548	4662	2280
1929	2011	1269	2122	1258	3398	4925	2235
1930	1785	1133	1889	1112	3147	4132	1951
1931	1683	1055	1799	975	2959	3818	1760

[a]Excluding notes of Banks of Taiwan and Chosen but including subsidiary coin.   [b]Current private deposits of ordinary banks.   [c]In an article that seems to have been generally overlooked, Kurt Singer estimated, after carefully surveying the evidence, the total amount of money effectively in circulation in 1928 at between ¥ 2.35 bill. and ¥ 2.55 bill., consisting of ¥ 1.40 bill. deposit balances, ¥ 0.85 to ¥ 0.95 bill. bank notes, and ¥ 0.10 to ¥ 0.20 bill. subsidiary coins (*Economic Journal*, 1936, p. 274). His figures thus are very close to those of col. 7.

SOURCES: **Cols. 1 and 4:** *HYS*, pp. 166–67, 199–200, current deposits in ordinary banks; the reported figures apparently cover only fully two-thirds of all such deposits.   **Cols. 2 and 5:** *Hitotsubashi Journal of Economics*, 1961; reprinted in *HYSE*, p. 99.   **Cols. 3 and 6:** Asakura and Nishiyama, pp. 822–23; demand deposits in ordinary banks.   **Col. 7:** Hoekendorf, pp. 225–26.

was connected with the bank's accumulation of international assets. The higher level prevailing throughout most of the 1920s, leading to rates around 11 percent from 1921 to 1924, contrasts with the rather lackluster performance of the economy but may reflect, particularly in the years 1923–24, the effects of the Kanto earthquake and the credit demands following it. The more sensitive and volatile call money rate peaked in the crisis of 1921, whereas the tightly controlled yields on government bonds remained at the artificial 5 percent level throughout the period and those of industrial bonds showed a downward trend, declining by about one-fourth between 1916 and 1930. Rates paid on deposits remained high throughout the period; postal savings deposits fluctuated, with only three changes, between 4.2 and 5.0 percent, and commercial banks paid between 5 and 7 percent for time deposits.[22]

w. The unfavorable balance of payments on current account, partly reflecting the fact that the Japanese price level fell less than that of most of its competitors, totaled ¥ 2.2 bill. for the period 1922–31. Although constituting only 1.4 percent of national product, it caused considerable difficulties in the country's international financial affairs, which were aggravated by the continuation of long-term capital exports, mainly to dependent areas, of ¥ 1.1 bill., or on an annual basis only one-half the level of the 1914–21 period. The deficit was met to the extent of

22. Cf. detailed data on interest rates, *HYS*, pp. 257 ff.

¥ 0.7 bill. by net gold exports. To what extent the remaining large deficit shown in the balance of payments represents short-term borrowing abroad or errors and omissions in the estimates, it is difficult to say.

x. In the face of the slow growth of the real infrastructure of income and wealth in the 1920s, it is remarkable that the financial superstructure of financial instruments and financial institutions continued to increase rapidly, although not without serious difficulties and pronounced structural modifications and, of course, not as rapidly as during the hectic World War I period. The bulk of this chapter will describe financial developments and will attempt to explain the apparent disparity between the trends in the financial superstructure and in the real infrastructure.

2. CAPITAL FORMATION AND SAVING

a. Capital Formation

For the entire period 1914–31 gross domestic capital formation averaged nearly one-fifth of national product, slightly above the ratio for the preceding three decades. The net ratio of 9 percent was also hardly above the previous level.[23] Hence the task of financing capital formation was of approximately the same magnitude as during the later part of the Meiji era.

There were, however, considerable differences between the World War I years and the 1920s. Thus the gross capital formation ratio of the 1914–21 period of more than one-fourth of national product was well in excess of that of both halves of the 1920s by about 15 percent. The difference, however, is primarily due to the change from heavy inventory accumulation during World War I and its immediate aftermath to a decumulation equal to 1 percent of national product during the 1920s. The ratio of gross fixed capital formation was only slightly lower in the 1920s than in the 1914–21 period. Fluctuations during the second subperiod were small until 1929, but the effect of the Great Depression is evident in the low level of the ratio in 1930–31 when it fell below 15 percent, the lowest since 1909. Taking the entire period together, total gross fixed capital formation was divided between the government and the private sectors in the ratio of approximately 2 to 3, which was not very different from the situation in the 1901–13 and 1886–1913 periods. One-fourth of the government's gross capital expenditures were of military character. Of private capital expenditures, one-third was for construction (of which nearly two-fifths were residences), one-half for equipment, and one-seventh for inventories. The pattern of distribution of total fixed capital expenditures, however, showed considerable fluctuation over the period, reflecting the phases of the business cycle and such extraneous events as World War I and the Kanto earthquake. These can be followed in panel II of table 4-4, which shows the relevant figures for three subperiods of five to seven years length. Because capital consumption allowances are put at about one-tenth of national product in all subperiods, the net capital formation ratio in the 1920s was only 5 percent, one-third of the 1914–21 period and well below the 8.5 percent of 1886–1913.

The results of net capital formation are visible in the growth of the capital stock and its distribution shown in table 4-5. Between 1913 and 1930 the real net fixed capital stock grew by more than 70 percent, or by 3 1/4 percent a year, which was substantially above the growth rate of 2 percent for the 1875–1913 period but only equal to that of the last dozen years of the Meiji period. The rate was considerably lower with 2 1/2 percent for the 1920s (no allowance is made in the estimates for the loss resulting from the Kanto earthquake) than for the inflationary 1914–20 period with 4 1/4 percent. Because the main components of the stock grew at quite different rates, its distribution changed considerably, the share of residences declining sharply

---

23. In view of the conventional nature of the estimates of capital consumption allowances, particularly in the case of the government, all figures for net saving can be used only with a good deal of caution.

TABLE 4-4. Capital Formation, 1914–1931

		Gross fixed capital formation					Capital consumption allowances (7)	Net capital formation (8)
	Total (1)	Total (2)	Private (3)	Government civilian (4)	Government military (5)	Inventory investment[a] (6)		
				I. Amounts (¥ bill.)				
1914–21	21.50	15.80	11.90	2.89	1.70	5.70	8.23	13.27
1922–26	12.28	13.32	7.71	4.38	1.23	−1.04	8.20	4.08
1927–31	11.66	12.21	6.63	4.62	0.96	−0.55	7.43	4.23
1914–31	45.44	41.33	26.24	11.89	3.89	4.11	23.86	21.58
				II. Distribution (percent)				
1914–21	100.0	73.5	55.3	13.4	7.9	26.5	38.3	61.7
1922–26	100.0	108.5	62.8	35.7	10.0	−8.5	66.8	33.2
1927–31	100.0	104.7	56.9	39.6	8.2	−4.7	63.7	36.3
1914–31	100.0	91.0	56.2	26.2	8.6	9.0	52.5	47.5
			III. Relation to gross national product (percent)					
1914–21	26.0	19.1	14.1	3.5	2.1	6.9	10.0	16.0
1922–26	15.7	17.0	9.8	5.6	1.6	−1.3	10.5	5.2
1927–31	15.1	15.8	8.6	6.0	1.2	−0.7	9.6	5.5
1914–31	19.1	17.4	11.0	5.1	1.7	1.7 ·	10.0	9.0

[a]Includes inventory profit.

SOURCES OF I: **Cols. 2–5 and 7:** *JEG,* pp. 290 and 296.   **Col. 6:** Fujino, 1975; difference between value of inventory at benchmark dates.

from nearly two-fifths to not much more than one-fourth. On the other hand, the share of producer durables rose from 15 to 24 percent, an indication of the country's continuing industrialization.

b. Saving

An analysis of aggregate saving by sector or form is practically precluded for this period as the only data consistently fitting into a system of national accounts are derived indirectly (from the equality of capital formation and saving) and distinguish only two extremely broad sectors, government and nongovernment. The estimate for the private sectors is simply the difference between total national saving, obtained by adjusting domestic capital formation for net capital imports or exports, and the saving of the government, which is derived from the budget.[24]

Although net capital exports were negligible for the period as a whole, they were very large for the first subperiod, amounting to more than 3 percent of national product, and were almost offset by substantial capital imports, averaging more than 1 1/2 percent of national product, for the second subperiod. As a result, the saving ratio, very high with 13 1/2 percent in the 1914–21 period, fell precipitously to 5 1/2 percent in the 1920s, resulting in a ratio for the entire period of 8 percent, compared to one of 4 1/2 percent in 1886–1913. Private saving was even slightly below the ratio of the preceding three decades.

For the period as a whole saving is characterized, apart from its failure to rise significantly above its rate in the late Meiji period, by, first, the dominating position of government saving, which accounted for more than three-fifths of national saving compared with less than one-fourth in 1886–1913, and, second, the relatively small contribution of corporate saving, with only 8

24. The estimates of Ohkawa and Rosovsky for the sum of private and government saving are slightly lower—by about 1 1/2 percent of national product—than the sum of net domestic fixed capital formation, inventory investment, and foreign balance (tables 4-6 and 4-1). The reason for this discrepancy is not evident.

TABLE 4-5. Net Fixed Capital Stock, 1914–1940 (1934–36 Prices)

	Total[a]	Buildings residential	Buildings other	Other structures	Producer durables	Livestock and plants
			I. Rate of growth (percent per year)			
1914–20	4.20	1.54	1.83	4.20	12.31	2.48
1921–30	2.60	1.19	3.71	5.21	1.76	3.22
1931–40	3.71	1.46	2.49	4.10	6.57	2.30
1914–40	3.42	1.39	2.66	4.52	6.20	2.68
			II. Distribution (percent)			
1913	100.0	38.0	21.4	16.4	15.1	9.1
1920	100.0	31.7	18.2	16.4	25.6	8.1
1930	100.0	27.6	19.7	21.1	23.6	8.6
1940	100.0	22.2	17.5	21.9	31.0	7.5
			III. Relation to gross national product (percent)			
1913	232	88	50	38	35	21
1920	210	67	38	34	54	17
1930	231	64	44	49	54	20
1940	222	49	39	49	69	17

[a]Absolute figures (¥ bill.): 18.59 for 1913, 24.79 for 1920, 32.05 for 1930, 46.13 for 1940.

SOURCE OF BASIC DATA: *ELTESJ*, 3:149–51.

percent of private saving, 3 percent of national saving, and 6 percent of dividend payments. The structure of saving differs considerably between the expansionary and inflationary World War I period and the often depressed 1920s. Thus, although private saving was equal to 8 1/2 percent of national product for 1914 through 1921, it almost vanished in the following decade. In the case of the government, on the other hand, its saving bore a not too dissimilar ratio to national product—between 4 and 6 1/2 percent—in the three subperiods. The importance of civilian government saving even increased, from 3 to more than 8 percent of national product, whereas military saving became negative in the 1920s. As a result, civilian government saving was more than five times as large as private saving in the 1920s and still larger, more than 60 percent, for the period as a whole.

Accepting the estimates of corporate saving, there remain household savings (including the saving of unincorporated business) of about ¥ 7 bill. for the entire period, resulting from net savings of nearly ¥ 7 bill. in the first subperiod and of virtually nothing in the second subperiod, equal to about 8 percent and zero percent of national product. These were very low ratios for the second subperiod but high for the first if it is remembered that they would have to be raised by nearly one-half when expressed in terms of disposable personal income rather than in relation to national product.

Total household saving is, of course, the sum of the increase, excluding valuation changes, in (a) the household sector's holdings of tangible assets, that is, mainly residential structures; (b) other structures, equipment, livestock, and plantations in agriculture and in the unincorporated business sectors; and (c) intangible assets, among which changes in claims against financial institutions and net purchases or sales of securities constitute the principal components; less (d) increases in household and unincorporated business debt. It is, therefore, necessary to see whether the estimates of household saving derived indirectly as a quadruple residual (gross domestic capital expenditures less capital imports less depreciation allowances less net government saving less net firm saving) is in accord with a combination of more direct estimates of the main components of net household saving. Such a comparison is necessary not only as a check against the indirect residual method but also in order to be able to study the

TABLE 4-6. Saving, 1914–1931

	Total net saving (1)	Private saving			Government saving		
		Total (2)	Corporate (3)	Other (4)	Total (5)	Civilian (6)	Military (7)
I. Amounts (¥ bill.)							
1914–21	11.06	7.00	0.30[a]	6.70	4.06	2.36	1.70
1922–26	3.73	−1.35	0.00[b]	−1.35	5.08	3.87	1.21
1927–31	4.85	1.83	0.30[c]	1.53	3.02	5.93	−2.91
1914–31	19.64	7.48	0.60	6.88	12.16	12.16	0.00
II. Distribution (percent)							
1914–21	100	63	3	60	37	22	15
1922–26	100	−36	0	−36	136	104	32
1927–31	100	38	6	32	62	122	−60
1914–31	100	38	3	35	62	62	0
III. Relation to gross national product (percent)							
1914–21	13.4	8.5	0.4	8.1	4.9	2.9	2.0
1922–26	4.8	−1.7	0	−1.7	6.5	4.9	1.5
1927–31	6.3	2.4	0.4	2.0	3.9	7.7	−3.8
1914–31	8.2	3.1	0.3	2.8	5.1	5.1	0.0

[a]1914–20.   [b]1921–27.   [c]One-half of 1928–34.

SOURCE OF I: *JEG*, p. 296, except for col. 3, which is Ohkawa's estimate (*Keizai Kenkyu*, 1972, p. 132).

structure of household saving, which is essential for financial analysis. The main components that can be roughly estimated are brought together in table 4-7.[25]

Although the two estimates happen to be similar for the first subperiod, the synthetic estimate is far above the residual estimate in the 1920s, even though in estimating the particularly doubtful components of the synthetic estimate, such as the net purchases of securities by households, the tendency has been to underestimate rather than overestimate. Indeed, the synthetic estimate would be well above the residual estimate even if the unrealistic assumption were made that households did not account for any part of the substantial net purchases of government and corporate securities attributable to the nonfinancial sectors of the economy. The difference would be even greater if allowance had been made for net saving through tangible assets by unincorporated enterprises within and outside of agriculture, which, however, might have been offset by an increase in bank borrowing and net trade borrowing by nonfarm unincorporated business enterprises.

For the 1920s the estimates thus are incompatible. The residual estimate is practically zero compared to a personal saving ratio of about 10 percent of personal disposable income for 1914–21. The synthetic estimates also show a decline in the saving ratio, from about 11 to less than 9 percent of personal disposable income, but it is very much smaller than the sharp drop shown by the residual estimate. Both calculations are extremely rough; a reasonably confident conclusion about the level of the household saving ratio of the 1920s awaits both considerably better basic data and much more intensive analysis.

25. Several years ago Emi made an attempt to measure national and personal saving from the financial side (pp. 1–19) and hence for the personal sector in a way similar in principle to the synthetic method used here, but a final footnote suggests that he had considerable doubts about the results. His estimate of personal saving is nearly ¥ 13 bill. for each of the decades 1913–22 and 1923–32, (no annual figures being given). For the two periods together, Emi's estimate of about ¥ 26 bill. is about one-fifth higher than the synthetic estimate of table 4-7, allowing for the fact that his period includes two years (1913 and 1932) not covered by the synthetic estimate.

TABLE 4-7. Residual and Synthetic Estimates of Household Saving, 1914–1931

	1914–21	1922–26	1927–31	1922–31	1914–31
I. Residual estimates, ¥ bill.	6.7	−1.4	1.5	0.2	6.9
II. Synthetic estimate, ¥ bill.[a]	7.7	6.8	5.4	12.2	19.9
1. Net residential construction[b]	12	13	13	13	13
2. Net agricultural investment	8	9	9	9	9
3. Claims against financial institutions	77	59	65	61	67
4. Securities					
a. Government bonds[c]	4	6	0	3	4
b. Corporate bonds[c]	4	4	9	7	6
c. Corporate stock	47	18	17	17	29
5. Home mortgage debt	6	7	9	8	8
6. Other consumer debt[d]	0	1	4	2	2
7. Farm debt	44	0	0	0	17
8. Total	100	100	100	100	100

[a]Sum of lines 1–4 less sum of lines 5–7.   [b]Other tangible assets might well add another ¥ 2 to ¥ 4 bill. for the period as a whole.   [c]Domestic securities only.   [d]Only policy loans.

SOURCES: Line I: Table 4-6.   Line II-1: One-half of gross residential construction expenditures (JEG, p. 290). Line II-2: Change in net stock of fixed reproducible capital (including livestock) in agriculture, forestry, and fisheries (ELTESJ, 3:154 ff.) adjusted for changes in price level of investment goods (ELTESJ, 8:134).   Line II-3: HYS, pp. 199H, 217, 244; Fujino's estimate for currency (HYSE, p. 99).   Line II-4: One-half (lines 4a and 4c) or one-fourth (line 4b) of absorption by nonfinancial sectors obtained by subtracting holdings of financial institutions from total domestic outstandings (Ott, 1960, passim).   Lines II-5–7: Rough estimates; cf. text.

The analysis of the structure of personal saving must use the synthetic estimate. It then appears that throughout the period the acquisition of financial assets, here again the accumulation of claims against financial institutions, was the decisive component, continuing a basic characteristic of the Japanese financial process. If the increase in home mortgage and in farm debt is deducted from the net investment in tangible assets, the accumulation of financial assets accounts for almost the entire personal net saving for the period as a whole, although the share would be somewhat reduced—probably not below three-fourths—if allowance had been made for net saving in the form of tangible assets other than dwellings. In the first subperiod financial saving was even in excess of total saving by ¥ 2 bill., as farm debt increased considerably more than net farm investment. Even in the 1920s net tangible investment represented not much more than one-eighth of total personal net saving if limited to dwellings, although possibly as much as one-fourth if other tangible assets are included.

Within the accumulation of financial assets, claims against financial institutions, more than ¥ 13 bill. for the period as a whole, far exceeded net purchases of securities, about ¥ 7 bill., which can be estimated only with a much larger margin of error. The securities consisted mainly of corporate stock, but the estimation of their value is particularly precarious and is overstated because they partly reflect exchanges of stock for equity in nonfarm unincorporated enterprises. There were substantial differences between the two subperiods in the composition of financial saving. From 1914–21 the increase in claims against financial institutions was only about 50 percent larger than net purchases of securities, whereas they were more than twice as large in the 1920s, indicating a shift from direct to indirect forms of placement of funds.

For the period as a whole, monetary claims accounted for not much more than one-tenth of all personal saving through claims against financial institutions. They were outranked by deposits in thrift institutions (including time deposits with commercial banks), which constituted nearly two-thirds of all saving in the form of claims against financial institutions and about two-fifths of all personal saving. Equity in insurance contracts, finally, accounted for one-seventh of saving through financial institutions and nearly one-tenth of total personal saving.

This distribution, however, is the result of the different patterns prevailing in the three subperiods. The share of monetary claims showed a sharply declining trend, becoming negative in the 1927–31 period, which includes the banking crisis and the Great Depression. The share of equity in insurance contracts, on the other hand, moved up continuously, from about 6 percent of total personal saving and more than 7 percent of claims against financial institutions in 1914–21 to about 30 percent and 45 percent, respectively, in 1927–31.

3. THE DEVELOPMENT OF FINANCIAL INSTITUTIONS[26]

a. The Main Types of Institutions

(i) THE BANK OF JAPAN. The activities and economic role of the Bank of Japan differed sharply in the two halves of the 1914–31 period. During World War I and in the years immediately following, the assets of the bank expanded sharply, mainly reflecting the accumulation of international assets that resulted from large surpluses in foreign trade. And the bank did nothing to prevent this expansion from exercising its effect on the volume of money and the rise in incomes and prices. In the following decade, in sharp contrast, the bank had to contend almost continuously with difficulties in the balance of payments and in the domestic banking and credit structure; it shrank in size, although it did not lose in importance in the domestic financial structure.

The expansion in the bank's assets during and immediately after the war was dramatic. Total assets increased from less than ¥ 0.7 bill. in 1913 to ¥ 2.8 bill. seven years later, a rise compared to national product, from about 13 percent to 18 percent. The share of the bank in the assets of all financial institutions, however, advanced only marginally.

The basis of this expansion was the increase in foreign assets from less than ¥ 0.4 bill. in 1913 to about ¥ 1.8 bill. in 1919–21. The increase in other assets was by comparison small, not much more than ¥ 200 mill. in loans and discounts and less than ¥ 150 mill. in government securities.

The counterpart of this rise in assets was an increase in bank notes issued, which at that time still constituted a large proportion of total money in circulation, from not much more than ¥ 0.4 bill. in 1913 to more than ¥ 1.4 bill. in 1920, and a sharp rise in government deposits, from very small amounts to more than ¥ 1 bill. in 1918–21.

These developments were accompanied during the war years by a rather passive easy money policy. The bank's discount rate on commercial bills was reduced from the 7.3 percent level introduced in fall of 1914 and continued to the spring of 1916, to 5.1 percent from March 1917 to September 1918. It was only in the credit stringency following the war that the rate was increased in four steps to 8.0 percent, a rate that prevailed from November 1919 to April 1925, that is, throughout the postwar depression, the following recovery, and the Kanto earthquake.

The almost continuous deficits in the current balance of payments, which started in 1920, were reflected in a slow reduction in the bank's foreign assets from a peak of about ¥ 1.8 bill. to about ¥ 0.9 bill. in 1928 and in a further cut to about ¥ 0.5 bill. in 1931. Because loans and discounts to the banking system expanded only moderately and erratically, reflecting the generally depressed state of business activity, and because there was hardly a net increase in the holdings of government securities, a reflationary policy being ruled out by the attempt to adhere to, and later to return to, the gold standard at the old parity, the bank's total assets declined from nearly ¥ 3 bill. in 1919–21 to less than ¥ 2 bill. in 1931, or from nearly one-fifth of about one-seventh of national product. The decline, however, was much more dramatic in relation to the assets of all financial institutions, which continued to expand quite rapidly during the 1920s, namely, from more than 12 percent of the total in 1921 to less than 6 percent ten years later.

---

26. Most of the statistics used in this section are taken from either the tables or *HYS, HYSE,* or Ott, 1960. The descriptive parts rely in part on the publications listed in footnotes to chaps. 3 and 4.

Most of the decline was reflected in a sharp reduction of government deposits from ¥ 1.1 bill. to less than ¥ 0.3 bill., the volume of notes issued showing no definite trend in absolute terms or in comparison to total money in circulation or to national product.

The main preoccupation of the bank during the 1920s was to prevent, or to mitigate, a crisis in the credit and banking system. The difficulties originated in an overexpansion of credit during the immediate postwar boom and were compounded by the losses suffered by business in the Kanto earthquake. For a number of years the bank discounted, in part backed by a guarantee of the government, a substantial volume of bills representing these doubtful engagements, but in 1927 most of them finally had to be written off, causing considerable losses to, and forcing the liquidation of, some banks.

The Yokohama Specie Bank continued throughout this period to operate as an adjunct of the Bank of Japan abroad and in financing Japan's foreign trade. Its assets increased sharply from less than ¥ 0.4 bill. in 1913 to nearly ¥ 1.5 bill. in 1919 and stayed between ¥ 1.0 bill. and ¥ 1.5 bill. throughout the 1920s. Most of the assets consisted of bills, in yen or foreign currencies, connected with Japanese exports and imports.

(ii) COMMERCIAL (ORDINARY) BANKS. As did many other aspects of Japanese finance between 1914 and 1931, the development of the commercial banking system also differed greatly in the two subperiods, 1914–21 and 1922–31. In the first subperiod the system expanded rapidly in nearly every direction and indeed overexpanded in some of them. During the following decade, consolidation and concentration were the order of the day.

From 1913 to 1921 the assets of commercial banks increased without interruption from ¥ 2.4 bill. to ¥ 10 bill., or at an average rate of nearly 20 percent a year, expansion being relatively most rapid in 1917 and 1918 with about 40 percent each. The share of commercial banks in the assets of all financial institutions, however, remained in the neighborhood of one-half, whereas their ratio to national product rose from 50 percent in 1913 to nearly 65 percent in 1920, with most of the increase occurring during the later part of the period when bank assets continued to expand at a still substantial rate and national product ceased to grow. The rapid expansion of the banking system from 1914 to 1920 reflected the export-led growth of the economy and the inflation induced, or at least not interfered with, by the policy of the government and the Bank of Japan.

Changes in the structure of assets of the banking system, shown in table 4-8, were moderate, at least among the broad types of assets distinguished in the statistics. Loans and discounts dominated to the extent of about two-thirds of total assets (excluding interoffice accounts), although their share declined from 69 percent in 1913 to 63 percent in 1921. Data on the breakdown of loans by type of borrower, size, and duration, which would be more important for economic analysis, do not seem to be available. The share of holdings of government and corporate securities increased slightly, and the proportion of all domestic securities held by commercial banks rose from about 6 to 10 percent. The structure of the portfolio did not change much. The share of government securities declined slightly and that of corporate securities remained close to one-third. Corporate bonds increased their share from 13 to 21 percent, whereas that of shares declined from 23 to 12 percent. In 1921 the book value of corporate shares held was equal to only 2 percent of the par value of all corporate stock outstanding, whereas the banks' holdings of corporate bonds represented nearly one-fifth of total outstandings. The ratio of cash (including deposits with correspondents) to total assets remained in the neighborhood of one-tenth. As is to be expected in a period of rapid asset expansion, the share of own funds (paid-in capital and reserves) to deposits declined from fully one-fifth in 1913 to one-seventh in 1921.

The expansion of the banking system was not, however, limited to the partly inflationary rapid growth of assets and liabilities. Although the number of banks continued to decrease slowly, more than 1,600 in 1913 to not much more than 1,300 in 1921, the number of branch offices grew fairly rapidly, from 2,100 in 1913 to more than 3,100 in 1921, one-half of the increase occurring in 1920 and 1921.

The situation facing the banking system in the 1920s was entirely different from that in the preceding period. In 1931 gross national product was one-sixth lower than it had been in 1920. The fact that total assets of commercial banks increased between 1920 and 1931 by 15 percent if interoffice accounts are eliminated and account is taken of the approximately ¥ 1.7 bill. of assets of the 500 savings banks, which converted to ordinary banks in 1922, points to a slow continuation of the expansion of the banking system. In terms of assets the system grew in every year until 1926, when its assets were more than 60 percent larger than in 1920 (only by half as much if interoffice accounts and former savings bank assets are excluded), although national product was the same. From 1926 to 1931 assets declined in every year but 1928, and for the five-year period shrank by more than one-tenth, which was still less than the decline in national product by one-sixth. As a result, the relation of bank assets to national product rose sharply from 65 percent in 1920 to 105 percent in 1926 and increased further to more than 110 percent in the following five years.

Changes in the structure of assets, so far as reflected in the broad categories reported, were relatively small and tended in the same direction as those observed in the 1914–20 period. The share of loans and discounts continued to decline from 66 percent of assets (excluding interoffice accounts) in 1920 to 55 percent in 1931. Government securities advanced from less than 7 to nearly 10 percent, and the share of corporate securities increased even more, from less than 6 percent in 1920 to 15 percent a decade later. In 1931 the holdings of commercial banks equaled about one-fifth of all domestic government securities outstanding, those of corporate bonds remained in the neighborhood of one-fourth, and those of corporate stock around 2 percent. The cash ratio (including interbank deposits) fell from 10 to less than 8 percent. The ratio of own funds to deposits stayed slightly above one-fifth.

What characterizes this period and determines its role in the overall development of the Japanese banking system are not these relatively minor changes in the size of the system and the composition of its assets and liabilities but the structural changes that basically resulted from the existence of too many small and poorly managed banks and from the accumulation of loans that became endangered first as a result of the postwar recession and then as a consequence of the heavy losses of business structures, equipment, and inventories caused by the Kanto earthquake in September 1923.[27]

For several years both types of distress loans were nursed along by the commercial banks and by the Bank of Japan, which provided special rediscount facilities for "earthquake bills" on the basis of a government guarantee against losses. In the spring of 1927 the collapse of a large combine (Suzuki), which had been heavily in debt to one of the large banks (the home office of the Bank of Taiwan), led to widespread runs on a number of banks, some of which had to close, although others survived with the assistance of the Bank of Japan. As a result, a new, somewhat stricter banking law was enacted, and the government pressured smaller and weaker banks to amalgamate with larger and stronger institutions. At the same time the hitherto unacknowledged losses on loans and securities that had accumulated since the early 1920s were written off.

The effects of this policy, as well as the continuation of the tendency toward mergers, is evident in the decline of the number of commercial banks from nearly 1,800 in 1922 (when its total had been increased by the accession of nearly 500 savings banks with more than 1,500 offices) to not much more than 1,400 in 1926, prior to the banking crisis. The process then accelerated and by 1931 the number of commercial banks had fallen to 680, less than two-fifths of those operating a decade earlier. This time, however, in contrast to developments in the preceding two decades, the number of branches also declined, beginning in 1925, from a peak of more than 6,300 to 4,500 in 1931, about one-tenth less than in 1922. Consequently, average assets per bank increased from less than ¥ 8 mill. in 1922 to ¥ 22 mill. in 1931, whereas assets per office expanded much more slowly, from ¥ 2.0 mill. to ¥ 2.9 mill., the average number of

---

27. For a description of the banking difficulties, cf. Bratter, pp. 24 ff.

TABLE 4-8. Principal Accounts of Commercial Banks,
1913–1931 (Percent of Total Assets)[a]

	1913	1921	1926	1931
1. Cash[b]	9.1	9.8	8.2	7.5
2. Lendings	69.2	62.8	64.3	55.1
3. Government securities	6.6	8.5	6.8	9.6
4. Other securities	4.6	6.6	8.3	14.9
5. Paid-in capital	16.2	10.6	10.5	10.5
6. Reserves	5.0	3.4	4.6	4.5
7. Deposits	59.8	64.9	64.1	69.2
8. Assets, ¥ bill.	2.41	9.94	14.33	11.95

[a]Excludes interoffice accounts.   [b]Includes deposits with, and due from, other correspondents and agencies.

SOURCES OF BASIC DATA: Lines 1 and 8: Ott, 1960, pp. 191ff.   Lines 2, 6, and 7; Ministry of Finance, *Ginkokyoku nenpo* (Banking Bureau Annual). Lines 3 and 5: *HYS*, p. 266 ff.

branches per bank rising from 2.8 to 6.7. The number of banks with a capital of more than ¥ 2 mill. increased between 1921 and 1929 from 128 to 191, or from 10 to 22 percent of all banks, whereas the number of banks with a capital of less than ¥ 0.5 mill. fell, from 770 to under 250.[28]

As a result of the merger movement, as well as of the increasing urbanization of Japan, city banks grew much more rapidly than local banks, whose share in the assets of all commercial banks declined from more than 80 percent in 1913 and about 75 percent in 1920 to 65 percent in 1930. Similarly, the share of the Big Five (four of which were affiliated with large zaibatsu) in all commercial bank deposits rose from a little more than one-fifth in 1910 and one-fourth in 1919 to considerably more than one-third in 1930.[29]

(iii) THRIFT INSTITUTIONS. During the first part of the period the savings banks remained the most important specialized thrift institutions, disregarding the savings deposits in commercial banks and some unorganized institutions. They accounted for nearly two-thirds of the total assets of this group, which also included the Post Office Saving System, the rural credit cooperatives, and the still very small mutual loan and savings banks and urban credit cooperatives, which started operations during World War I. In 1913 the two types of thrift institutions then existing held nearly one-eighth of the assets of all financial institutions, and their assets were equal to a similar fraction of national product. By 1920 the now five groups had increased their share in the assets of all financial institutions to one-sixth, growing at an average annual rate of more than 25 percent; and the relation of their assets to national product had advanced to more than one-fifth. This expansion had been aided by the organization of a substantial number of new institutions of this type. Thus the number of savings banks increased from 489 to 636, and the number of individually very small rural cooperatives increased from fewer than 8,000 to more than 11,000. The two new types of thrift institutions were also gaining ground, with more than 200 mutual loan and savings banks and nearly 100 urban credit cooperatives in 1921.

Following a change in the banking law, most of the savings banks, about three-fourths in number and assets, in 1922 converted to ordinary commercial banks. If allowance is made for this shift, thrift institutions continued to grow rapidly during the 1920s, their assets increasing at an average annual rate of 13 percent between 1922 and 1926, which was well in excess of the

28. Moulton, p. 167; *HYS*, pp. 198 ff.
29. Cf. table 3-9.

rate of growth in the assets of all financial institutions of 6 percent and contrasted with the virtual stagnation of national product. These differences were dramatically accentuated during the financial difficulties and the depression of the 1927–31 period. During these five years the assets of thrift institutions rose by a little less than 80 percent, whereas national product declined by one-sixth. As a result, the share of thrift institutions in the assets of all financial institutions (after the departure of most of the former savings banks but including the trust accounts of banks, which started in the early 1920s) increased between 1922 and 1931 from less than one-tenth to nearly one-fourth, and the relation of their assets to national product shot up from one-seventh to more than three-fifths. Of the total increase in the assets of thrift institutions between 1922 and 1931 of ¥ 6.1 bill., savings banks accounted for only ¥ 1.0 bill., and credit cooperatives, the postal saving system, and the trust accounts of commercial banks each contributed approximately ¥ 1.7 bill. The 1920s may be regarded, therefore, as the period in which the thrift institutions came into their own, accounting for about one-half of the increase in resources of all financial institutions and for 4 percent of the decade's national product. The rapid expansion of thrift institutions was probably helped by the difficulties of many commercial banks, which reduced savers' confidence in them.

Data about the number of accounts and average balances are available only for the postal saving system. They are summarized in table 4-9.

Reflecting mainly the rapid growth of the postal saving system, which provided it with about three-fourths of its funds, the Deposit Bureau of the Ministry of Finance became an important element in the country's financial structure. Its total assets increased from less than ¥ 0.3 bill. in 1913 to more than ¥ 1.1 bill. in 1921 and to nearly ¥ 3.5 bill. in 1931, thus rising from about 5 percent of national product in 1913 to 9 percent in 1921 and to more than 25 percent in 1931. Although the bureau's share in the assets of all financial institutions remained in the neighborhood of 5 percent from 1913 to 1926, it increased considerably during the late 1920s, reaching 10 percent in 1931. The share of the bureau's assets invested in direct government securities rose from about one-eighth in 1921, the first year for which the breakdown is available, to nearly 45 percent in 1931. At that time the bureau's holdings represented about 15 percent of all domestic (central and local) government securities outstanding compared with about 4 percent in 1921. The increase in the bureau's holdings over the decade of ¥ 920 mill. was equal to fully one-fifth of total net issues of government securities during the decade. The

TABLE 4-9. Deposits and Depositors in Postal Saving System, 1885–1944

| March 31 of following year | Deposits (¥ mill.) (1) | Accounts (mill.) (2) | Account (3) | Deposits (yen) per Inhabitant | | Accounts |
				Current (4)	1934–36 prices (5)	Inhabitants (percent) (6)
1885	12	0.42	29.0	0.3	1.0	1.1
1900	25	2.40	10.4	0.6	1.2	5.5
1913	200	12.89	15.5	3.9	6.3	25.1
1921	901	25.43	35.4	16.1	12.4	45.3
1926	1254	32.41	38.7	20.8	16.8	53.8
1931	2816	39.07	72.1	43.4	46.3	60.2
1936	3483	49.24	70.7	50.1	45.4	70.8
1941	9975	110.16	90.6	139.3	81.2	153.9
1944	30375	193.79	156.7	411.4	196.2	262.6

Sources: **Cols. 1 and 2:** Ministry of Posts and Telecommunication, *Tokyo Centenary Statistics of Posts and Telecommunication*, 30:36 ff. (in Japanese).   **Col. 5:** Deflated by consumer price index for calendar year (*ELTESJ*, 8:135).

remaining assets of the bureau consisted of corporate bonds and loans, mostly of and to other government financial institutions, particularly the long-term credit banks, and government-connected nonfinancial corporations. In 1931 the bureau's holdings of corporate bonds were equal to about one-sixth of all corporate domestic bonds outstanding, but the share was probably considerably higher for the debentures of long-term credit banks. Thus one of the important aspects of the bureau was that it enabled the government to operate in many sectors of the capital and credit markets, if necessary, rapidly and without publicity.

With the exception of the postal saving system, which kept most of its assets in the form of deposits with the Deposit Bureau, the most important assets of thrift institutions have been loans and discounts and securities. Although statistical information on the character and recipients of the loans is generally lacking, it may be assumed that in the case of credit cooperatives the borrowers were exclusively or predominantly members. In 1930, for example, loans and discounts represented more than one-fourth of the assets (excluding interoffice accounts) of savings banks and about two-thirds of those of credit cooperatives. Holdings of securities were relatively small, except for savings banks, among which central government and other securities, mostly acquired during the 1920s, each absorbed more than one-fourth of total assets. Credit cooperatives kept about one-fourth of their assets in the form of deposits with either their own central organizations or with other financial institutions.

(iv) INSURANCE ORGANIZATIONS. The period between World War I and the beginning of the 1930s was decisive in the development of insurance in Japan, particularly life insurance. In 1913 the assets of all insurance organizations, then dominated to the extent of nearly three-fourths by private life insurance companies, amounted to only ¥ 175 mill., equal to only a little more than 3 percent of either national product or of the assets of all financial institutions. Assets grew between 1913 and 1921 at an annual average rate of 20 percent, which brought them to more than 4 percent of national product. The rate of growth of assets during the 1920s, which slowed down to 13 percent a year, was sufficient to increase the share of insurance organizations in 1931 to nearly 8 percent of the assets of all financial institutions and to one-sixth of national product, five times the 1913 relationship. It is likely, therefore, that the share of life insurance in personal saving increased substantially. In 1931 private life insurance companies still accounted for nearly two-thirds of the assets of all insurance organizations, and the Post Office life insurance organization, which began operations in 1916, accounted for more than one-fifth; insurance companies other than life accounted for the remaining one-seventh.

This sharp increase in the relative position of life insurance organizations in the 1920s may be regarded as evidence that the structure of financial institutions in Japan had begun to approximate that in Western countries. Thus in 1929 life insurance companies in the United States accounted for more than one-eighth of the assets of all financial institutions, compared with only 6 1/2 percent in Japan in 1931 (including Post Office life insurance), but the ratio of the assets of U.S. companies to national product of fully one-sixth was not much higher than the corresponding Japanese ratio.

The private insurance companies, which during this period accounted for between 100 (1913) and nearly 80 percent (1931) of the assets of all insurance organizations, were heavy investors in securities. In 1931 more than one-fifth of their total assets were invested in corporate bonds, nearly 15 percent in corporate stock, and about one-tenth in government bonds. More than one-half of their remaining assets were made up of mortgage and short-term loans and more than 15 percent were kept in the form of bank deposits. The structure of assets over the preceding two decades showed no marked changes. In 1931 insurance companies held about one-sixth of the securities other than central government obligations in the portfolios of all financial institutions, a substantial increase from the share of not much more than one-tenth in 1913.

The Post Office life insurance organization acted essentially as a conduit to other governmental financial organizations, particularly the Deposit Bureau. In 1931 its assets consisted of about two-fifths each of loans to the government and of bonds of the central and local governments. The only substantial outside investments were policy loans, which absorbed fully one-tenth of total assets.

The number of insurance companies increased only slowly in the face of the rapid absolute and relative expansion of their activities. In the life insurance field the number of operating companies actually declined from 42 in 1913 to 40 in 1931, and the degree of concentration of assets remained high. Throughout the period most of the large companies were controlled by one of the zaibatsu. It is quite likely that the large insurance companies allocated a substantial part of their funds to loans to, and securities of, companies belonging to the controlling zaibatsu.

(v) LONG-TERM CREDIT BANKS. Organized around the turn of the century by the government, long-term credit banks continued to concentrate on long-term credits to agriculture and industry, financed to the extent of 50 to 70 percent of their total funds by the issue of debentures, a considerable portion of which was acquired by other financial institutions. They grew fairly rapidly during the 1910s but more slowly during the following decade. As a result, their share in the assets of all financial institutions declined from 11 percent in 1913 to 8 percent in 1920 and remained at that level during the decade. The ratio of their assets to national product increased from 12 to 22 percent and the ratio of their assets to total fixed reproducible wealth nearly doubled from 6 to 10 percent, whereas the relation of the increase in their assets to gross private fixed capital formation declined from 14 percent in 1914–20 to 10 percent in 1928–31.

In the 1920s some of the prefectural agricultural and industrial banks began to merge with the central Nippon Kangyo Bank, reducing their number from 46 to 19 in 1931. This process continued in the following period, and the five banks remaining in operation from 1938 on were merged in 1945 with Nippon Kangyo Bank.

b. Financial Institutions as a Whole

The discussion of the main financial institutions as a whole will be limited to four aspects: the differentials in growth rates of assets with the resulting changes in the distribution of total assets of financial institutions among the main groups; the distribution of total assets among the main categories; the share of financial institutions in the total of the main types of securities outstanding; and the relation of the total assets and the net new issues of financial assets to national product.[30]

(i) CHANGES IN DISTRIBUTION OF ASSETS AMONG INSTITUTIONS. Because the growth rate of the main types of financial institutions showed considerable differences, the share of the various types in the total assets of all financial institutions necessarily also changed. These developments can be followed in table 4-10 for each of the subperiods, 1914–21, 1922–26, and 1927–31, as well as for the entire period.

Differences in growth rates and changes in shares were relatively small in the period 1914–21, which was dominated by inflation. In particular, the shares of the four broad groups of institutions, namely, the banking system (the Bank of Japan, the Yokohama Specie Bank, and the commercial banks), the thrift institutions, the long-term credit banks, and the insurance organizations, did not change substantially, with the banking system accounting for slightly more than two-thirds of the total in 1920 as well as in 1913. The increase in the share of thrift institutions from 12 to 16 percent and the decline of the share of the long-term credit banks from 11 to 8 percent are, however, of some significance.

---

30. The following tables are based, as are many others used throughout this study, on the reported aggregate assets of the different types of financial institutions. The elimination of claims and liabilities within and among financial institutions, such as interoffice accounts, interbank deposits, holdings of bank deposits and bank debentures by non-bank financial institutions, and deposits with the Deposit Bureau, to produce more relevant figures of financial institutions' claims against and liabilities to nonfinancial sectors is an adjustment that cannot be done exhaustively on the basis of available data, at least not without an effort that is impossible within this study. Although such a procedure would produce somewhat different figures, it is not believed that the main movements would be significantly different from those based on reported total assets.

TABLE 4-10. Growth and Distribution of Assets of Financial Institutions, 1913–1931 (Percent)

	Annual growth rate				Distribution				Relation to gross national product		
	1914–21	1922–26	1927–31	1914–31	1913	1921	1926	1931	1913	1920	1930
1. Bank of Japan	19.8	-3.8	-3.3	6.2	12.2	12.6	7.7	5.6	13.8	18.2	15.6
2. Yokohama Specie Bank	11.3	3.1	-1.0	5.4	7.7	4.4	3.8	3.1	8.7	7.4	8.9
3. Commercial banks	19.9	5.2[a]	-2.3	10.0	48.2	50.0	55.4	42.2	54.6	67.0	112.0
4. Bank trust accounts	.	.	21.0	.	—	—	2.1	4.6	—	—	11.3
5. Savings banks	23.5	11.1[a]	8.6	7.9	7.9	10.4	3.7	4.8	9.0	14.7	11.5
6. Post Office Saving System	21.1	4.8	17.4	15.3	3.7	4.2	3.9	7.5	4.2	5.7	17.2
7. Deposit Bureau	20.3	7.3	14.2	14.8	5.2	5.5	5.9	9.7	5.8	7.1	22.3
8. Mutual loan companies	.	42.0	13.9	.	—	0.1	0.3	0.4	—	0.2	1.1
9. Credit cooperatives	33.2	25.9	10.5	24.5	0.7	1.7	4.1	5.9	0.9	2.3	13.5
10. Long-term credit banks	11.4	6.4	4.3	9.1	11.3	7.9	8.0	8.5	12.8	10.3	21.0
11. Life insurance companies	18.1	16.5	10.4	15.4	2.3	2.1	3.4	4.8	2.6	2.6	11.2
12. Other insurance companies	24.5	4.7	3.4	12.7	0.9	1.2	1.1	1.1	1.0	1.8	2.9
13. Post Office life insurance	—	56.1	33.8	.	—	0.1	0.5	1.7	—	0.0	3.4
14. All financial institutions	19.3	6.0	3.2	10.9	100.0	100.0	100.0	100.0	113.5	137.4	252.6

[a]Adjusted for conversion of most savings into commercial banks.

SOURCES OF BASIC DATA: Line 1: *HYS*, 192.   Line 2: Ott, 1960, p. 169–70.   Line 3: Ibid., p. 191–92.   Line 4: *HYS*, p. 202–03; deposits, paid-in capital, and reserves.   Line 5: *HYS*, p. 244.   Line 6: *HYS*, p. 217.   Line 7: *HYS*, p. 242–43; refers to March 31 of the following year until 1923; then to end of calendar year.   Line 8: Ott, op. cit., p. 175 ff.   Line 9: Ibid., p. 230; total assets less unpaid capital.   Line 10: Ibid., p. 221, 236, 249; *HYS*, p. 226.   Line 11 and 12: *HYS*, p. 237 ff.   Line 13: *HYS*, p. 246 for 1926–31; Ott, op. cit., p. 241 for 1919–25; rough estimates for 1916–18.

The diversity of the growth rates of assets and hence changes in the distribution of the assets of all financial institutions were much more pronounced in the 1922–26 and 1927–31 periods, particularly the latter. Thrift and life insurance organizations grew more rapidly than the banking system or the long-term credit banks in both periods. As a consequence, their combined share (excluding savings banks that became commercial banks) rose from nearly 10 percent in 1921 to 13 percent in 1926 and to 20 percent in 1931. This movement reflects the fact that personal saving in the form of savings deposits and life insurance contracts continued at a high level throughout the decade (this problem will be discussed further in the following section), whereas the volume of money, which is an important determinant of the size of assets of the banking system, shrank, particularly in the depression years at the end of the period.

Within the banking system, the ordinary banks gained at the expense of the Bank of Japan and the Yokohama Specie Bank as they continued to expand, in terms of assets, until 1928 and as their assets shrank less than those of the Bank of Japan from 1929–31. As a result, the share of the commercial banks in the assets of the entire banking system increased from 72 percent in 1920 to 81 percent in 1927 and 83 percent in 1931, whereas the assets of the Bank of Japan declined from 20 to 11 percent.

(ii) DISTRIBUTION OF TYPES OF ASSETS. Because the asset structure of the different types of financial institutions is far from identical, the changes in the distribution of the assets of all financial institutions among the main types of assets, as they are shown in table 4-11, are the combined result of shifts in, first, relative importance in terms of total assets of the different types of institutions, which was discussed in the preceding section, and, second, of shifts in the structure of assets of individual types of institutions.

The main trend in the distribution of the assets of all financial institutions by type was an increase in the share of securities at the expense of that of loans and discounts, primarily during the late 1920s. As a result, the share of central government securities increased from 8 to 10 percent and the share of other (i.e., mainly corporate) securities advanced more sharply from 7 to 15 percent. By way of compensation, the share of loans and discounts declined from 49 to 43 percent and that of other, mostly interfinancial, assets fell from 23 to 19 percent. Most of these changes were the result of shifts in the relative size of the main types of financial institutions, particularly an increase in the share of thrift and insurance organizations, which keep a larger proportion of their assets in the form of securities, rather than of changes in the portfolio structure of the various types of financial institutions.

In many countries such a relative shift from loans and discounts to securities would be interpreted as a move in the direction of substituting direct financing through the securities market for indirect loan financing by financial institutions. Such an interpretation is hardly warranted in Japan, for during this period, as well as before and after, most securities were

TABLE 4-11. Structure of Assets of All Financial Institutions, 1913–1944 (Percent)

	1913	1920	1925	1930	1935	1940	1944
Reported total assets	100	100	100	100	100	100	100
Cash and deposits	13	15	13	12	9	10	11
Other assets[a]	23	25	23	19	21	20	4
Loans and discounts	49	45	47	43	34	29	32
Central government	8	6	8	10	17	20	38
Other securities	7	9	10	15	19	22	14
Reported total assets; ¥ bill.	5.4	21.1	28.5	33.9	41.0	91.6	230.1

[a]Including unpaid capital and interoffice accounts.

SOURCE OF BASIC DATA: Ott, 1960, passim.

TABLE 4-12. Structure of Assets of Main Groups of Financial Institutions, 1930
(Total Assets of Each Institution = 100)

Institution	Total	Cash	Deposits with others	Loans and discounts	Central government securities	Other securities	Other assets
Bank of Japan	100.0	40.8	1.5	36.1	8.1	—	13.5
Yokohama Specie Bank	100.0	1.5	11.8	55.8	16.3	12.0	2.6
Long-term credit banks	100.0	1.1	5.9	80.8	1.6	3.9	6.7
Commercial banks	100.0	6.2	2.2	43.2	8.4	11.5	28.5
Savings banks	100.0	1.5	6.5	19.5	20.1	18.6	33.8
Deposit Bureau	100.0	—	8.1	19.1	27.6	40.8	4.4
Prefectural credit associations	100.0	0.4	23.1	34.8	3.5	19.5	18.7
Rural credit cooperatives	100.0	—	25.2	68.0	1.1	5.7	—
Mutual loan companies	100.0	0.7	11.4	24.8	—	0.7	62.4
Urban credit associations	100.0	1.1	17.9	55.0	1.5	11.9	12.6
Central Cooperative Bank	100.0	—	19.0	67.0	0.8	9.9	3.3
Insurance companies	100.0	0.1	16.6	23.1	6.6	43.1	10.5
Post office life insurance	100.0	—	9.5	56.5	14.5	14.7	4.8
Bank trust accounts	100.0	—	2.0	63.4	6.6	23.9	4.1
All institutions	100.0	5.8	6.0	43.5	10.2	15.5	19.0

SOURCE OF BASIC DATA: Ott, 1960, passim.

acquired by financial institutions directly from issuers or through the intermediation of some government agency.

The structure of the assets of the different groups of financial institutions in 1930 can be followed in table 4-12. It shows, of course, pronounced differences among institutions and also in some cases substantial changes from the situation in 1913 (table 3-13). Loans and discounts, generally the core of the assets of financial institutions, for example, range from about one-fifth of total assets among savings banks, the Deposit Bureau, and insurance companies to more than two-fifths for commercial banks, two-thirds for trust accounts of commercial banks and for rural cooperatives, and four-fifths for long-term credit banks.

(iii) THE SHARE OF INSTITUTIONAL HOLDINGS OF SECURITIES. Financial institutions have held a substantial and increasing proportion of all domestic securities outstanding in Japan (table 4-13). The share increased from below one-fifth of the total in 1913 to about one-fourth in 1920 and 1925 and to more than one-third in 1930 if it is assumed that securities are valued at or close to par in institutional balance sheets, which is likely in the case of bonds but doubtful for stocks.

The share of institutional holdings has differed greatly, however, as between types of securities. Financial institutions have always held a substantial, and since the 1920s dominating, proportion of the central government's domestically issued securities, the share having risen to close to two-thirds in 1930, and the net increase in institutional holdings in the 1914–30 period has equaled nearly three-fourths of total net issues during these seventeen years. In the case of other securities (local government and corporate bonds, long-term credit bank debentures, and corporate stock), the share increased from about one-eighth in 1913 to nearly one-fifth during the 1920s. Financial institutions held only relatively small amounts of stock, 4 to 6 percent of the total outstanding if differences between par, book, and market values are disregarded.[31] These

31. Financial institutions seem to have absorbed only about 6 percent of total stock issues during the period as a whole, their share varying from about 4 percent in 1914–21 to 11 percent in 1922–27 and 1 percent in 1927–31 if the comparison is based on the book value of institutional stockholdings and the par value of paid-in capital of corporations. Because book values reflect to some extent stock price changes, the ratios given above probably overstate the correct ratio in the first two subperiods and almost certainly understate it for the 1927–31 period.

TABLE 4-13. Share of Holdings of Securities
by Financial Institutions, 1913–1944 (Percent)[a]

	Central government securities	Other securities		All securities
		Total	Stocks	
	Holdings at end of year			
1913	34	12	4	18
1920	47	19	4	25
1925	57	18	5	26
1930	64	21	6	34
1935	74	32	8	44
1940	79	37	11	55
1944	58	51	11	55
	Increase in holdings during period			
1914–20	56	23	4	29
1921–25	78	15	8	27
1926–30	84	51	8	58
1931–35	89	74	20	82
1936–40	83	46	15	68
1941–44	53	60	12	55
1914–30	72	28	6	37
1931–44	58	62	14	57

[a]Book values for institutional holdings; par value for outstandings.

SOURCE OF BASIC DATA: Ott, 1960, passim.

trends are the combined result of an increase in the share of securities in total assets of some groups of financial institutions and of the more rapid growth of those institutions, mainly insurance companies, which customarily keep a relatively high proportion of their assets in the form of securities.

(iv) THE ISSUE RATIO OF FINANCIAL INSTITUTIONS. For economic analysis, the possibly most interesting characteristic in the development of financial institutions is the new issue ratio, that is, the ratio of the net new issues of these institutions to national product. Starting with the crudest of the various possible measures, namely, the ratio of the change in reported total assets of financial institutions to national product, it is seen in table 4-14 that the ratio averaged one-eighth for the period as a whole, but that the often observed differences among subperiods are visible in this measure too. Thus the ratio averaged 21 and 8 percent, respectively, for the two major subperiods, 1914–21 and 1922–31, whereas the ratios reached a peak with an average of 32 percent and a range of only 27 and 37 percent for the years 1916–19, sharply declining to a relatively narrow range of 8 and 13 percent in the 1920s and falling to zero in the depression and deflation years 1930–31. If the annual level and changes are compared with those in nominal and real national product, a slight positive association is evident. Generally, the higher the rate of increase in national product, the higher the issue ratio. The outstanding exception to this relation is provided by the earthquake year 1923 in which the emergency expansion of credit contrasted with a decline in real national product.

The movements of the issue ratios of individual financial institutions will deviate from those of the overall ratio to the extent of differences in the growth rates of the assets of the different types of financial institutions, differences that were discussed in the preceding section. Similarly, the distribution of the overall ratio among the component ratios will be equal to the distribution of the differences in the absolute changes in assets over one year or a group of years. It is, therefore, to some extent repetitious to state that for the period as a whole, the banking

TABLE 4-14. New Issue Ratios of Financial Institutions, 1914–1931
(Percent of Gross National Product)

	1914–21 (1)	1922–26 (2)	1927–31 (3)	1914–31 (4)
	I. Individual institutions			
1. Bank of Japan	2.64	−0.65	−0.48	0.55
2. Yokohama Specie Bank	0.70	0.20	−0.07	0.28
3. Commercial banks	10.55	6.94[a]	−2.39	5.17[a]
4. Savings banks	2.34	−1.58[a]	0.75	0.54[a]
5. Post Office savings bank	0.90	0.32	1.90	1.04
6. Trust banks	—	0.81	1.31	0.69
7. Mutual loan banks	0.02	0.08	0.09	0.06
8. Credit cooperatives	0.43	2.10	1.06	0.85
9. Deposit Bureau	1.16	0.67	2.17	1.33
10. Long-term credit banks	1.40	0.87	0.74	1.01
11. Life insurance companies	0.43	0.70	0.86	0.66
12. Other insurance companies	0.27	0.09	0.08	0.15
13. Post Office life insurance	0.02	0.16	0.59	0.25
	II. Groups of institutions			
1. Banking system (1–3)	13.89	6.49[a]	−2.94	6.00[a]
2. Thrift institutions (4–8)	3.69	1.73[a]	5.12	3.19[a]
3. Insurance organizations (11–13)	0.73	0.96	1.54	1.07
4. Long-term credit banks (10)	1.40	0.87	0.74	1.06
	III. All financial institutions			
5. Total[b]	20.87	9.67	6.61	12.57

[a]In 1922 most savings banks converted into ordinary banks, hence cols. 2 and 3 need to be combined for comparison.   [b]In addition to II, lines 1–4, the total includes Deposit Bureau, which is essentially duplicative with some institutions included.

SOURCES OF BASIC DATA: Table 3-11 and corresponding annual data.

system accounted for less than 5 percent, savings banks for 1 1/2 percent, long-term credit banks for 1 percent, thrift institutions for 3 percent, and insurance organizations for fully 1 percent out of an overall issue ratio of financial institutions of 12 1/2 percent.

For economic analysis, the task is to explain the ratios just cited. This explanation is possibly better directed to the ratio of consolidated rather than combined changes in the assets of all financial institutions. Although it is not possible to cancel out accurately all loans and security holdings among financial institutions, this objective may be approximated by two methods that may be presumed to indicate the lower and upper boundaries of the conceptually desirable adjustment. The average of these two methods suggests that the unadjusted ratio should be reduced for the first subperiod by about one-fourth and for the second by about one-sixth to approximate the adjusted ratio, which eliminates interfinancial issues. This yields roughly adjusted new issue ratios of financial institutions of approximately 16 percent for 1914–21 and of nearly 7 percent for 1922–31. It is these ratios that have to be explained.

The changes in the assets of financial institutions and hence the level and changes in the adjusted issue ratios may be attributed to three components: the issuance of money, the incurrence of non-monetary deposit liabilities to households, and a catchall remainder that includes non-monetary liabilities to domestic government and business and to foreigners as well as increases in paid-up capital and reserves.[32] In the present state of the data such an allocation

32. For a similar breakdown and some discussion of this approach to an analysis of the net issue ratio, cf. Goldsmith, 1973, chap. 1.

TABLE 4-15. Components of the New Issue Ratio
of Financial Institutions, 1914–1941
(Percent of Gross National Product)

	New issue ratio of financial institutions		Money issue ratio (3)	Household saving ratio[b] (4)	Residual (5)
	Unadjusted (1)	Roughly adjusted[a] (2)			
1914–21	20.9	15.5	4.1	7.9	3.5
1922–26	9.7	8.0	−0.2	4.6	3.6
1927–31	6.6	5.5	−0.4	5.3	0.6
1932–36	13.9	12.0	1.1	7.4	3.5
1937–41	42.2	33.0	6.6	17.2	9.2

[a]Eliminating claims within financial system.   [b]Time deposits in commercial banks, deposits in thrift institutions, and assets of life insurance organizations.

SOURCES: **Col. 1:** Tables 4-14 and 5-11.   **Col. 2:** Based on table 4-11.
Col. 3: Fujino's estimates (tables 4-3 and 5-3) extrapolated for 1941 by Asakura's estimates (tables 4-3 and 5-3).

among the three components and the further breakdown of the second component cannot be done satisfactorily, for there is not even a generally accepted series on money supply. Using the data now available, it appears that money in circulation increased from 1913 to 1921 by 4 percent of the period's national product, whereas it fell from 1922 to 1931 by 0.3 percent of national product.[33] This leaves ratios of about 11 1/2 and 8 percent for the two other components of the adjusted issue ratio.

The first of the two remaining components may be approximated on the basis of time deposits of commercial banks, deposits of thrift institutions, and the assets of life insurance organizations. These increased by about ¥ 6 1/2 bill. from 1914 through 1921 and by another ¥ 7 1/2 bill. in the following decade, equal to about 8 and about 4 1/2 percent of national product. This leads to an estimate of the residual of about 3 1/2 percent for both the first and second subperiods.

Three conclusions may be drawn from this extremely rough disaggregation of the adjusted new issue ratio of financial institutions in the 1914–31 period as it is summarized in table 4-15.[34] First, that the issuance of money was only a secondary influence; second, that household non-monetary saving through financial institutions accounted for the bulk—more than three-fifths—of the ratio; and third, that the contribution of the non-monetary deposits of business and other components of the residual were of considerable importance in both subperiods. These conclusions are entirely compatible with what is known about the financial process in these two decades. This is probably as much as should be claimed for this exercise.

4. FINANCING THE MAIN NONFINANCIAL SECTORS

a. Nonagricultural Nonfinancial Business Enterprises

During World War I business, particularly nonfinancial corporations, expanded rapidly and operated very profitably, although a substantial part of increased profits only reflected the

33. Somewhat different results are obtained if other estimates of money in circulation (e.g., Asakura and Nishiyama) are used.

34. The adjustment shown in table 4-15 is the average of two adjustments, which are regarded as close to the lower

rise in the price level and inventory appreciation. The 1920s, by contrast, were a period of, first, considerable losses and retrenchment and then of slow expansion, with an only moderate level of profits, although the corporate sector and the large conglomerates continued to make inroads on the share of small unincorporated enterprises. The statistical material is insufficient for a satisfactory analysis of the financing of business during this period. No sources-and-uses-of-funds statements meeting the requirements of comprehensiveness, detail, and reliability exist. The observer is therefore reduced to obtaining a picture of financial developments by piecing together partial sets of data, which occasionally contradict each other. The main features of the picture, however, are fairly clear for the corporate sector, even though they often cannot be quantified as much as would be desirable. Practically nothing is known in quantitative terms on the financial development of unincorporated enterprises, although they continued to account for a substantial proportion of employment, output, assets, and debt of the nonagricultural nonfinancial business sector.

The number of nonfinancial corporations, the roughest indicator, rose from nearly 20,000 in 1913 to more than 38,000 in 1921, with the most rapid increases occurring during the boom of 1918–20. Expansion continued at a rapid pace during the 1920s, with only a slight interruption in 1924, and by 1931 nonfinancial corporations numbered 69,000, three and a half times as numerous as they had been in 1913. Paid-in capital and reserves shot up from about ¥ 2 1/2 bill. in 1913 to ¥ 17 bill. in 1921. Expansion slowed down considerably during the 1920s, so that capital remained below ¥ 20 bill. in 1931. Average capital and reserves per corporation, after rising from about ¥ 0.14 mill. in 1913 to ¥ 0.53 mill. in 1921, declined considerably after the mid-1920s and by 1931 had fallen to less than ¥ 0.40 mill.[35]

Corporate profits during the war years and immediately afterward were undoubtedly very high, although no comprehensive aggregates appear to be available. Dividends for the period 1914–21 are reported as ¥ 3.80 bill. (including relatively small amounts for financial corporations in 1917–20), rising from about ¥ 0.15 bill. a year in 1914–15 to a peak of ¥ 0.80 bill. in 1920. For the period, they averaged about 10 percent of paid-in capital. For a small group of large corporations, for which more detailed figures are available, net profits before depreciation averaged about one-third and dividends about one-fourth of paid-in capital, reflecting the extraordinarily high profits during World War I and implying a retention ratio of nearly 30 percent. Profits and dividends effectively stagnated during the 1920s to decline substantially in 1930–31.

A little more information is available for a small group of 48 to 75 enterprises, which accounted for fully one-eighth of the paid-in capital of all nonfinancial corporations in 1914 and for nearly one-fourth in 1929. Some of their sources and uses of funds are summarized in table 4-16. The net worth of these large industrial corporations rose by about 270 percent between 1914 and 1921, that is, somewhat more slowly than the roughly comparable capital of all nonfinancial corporations. During the 1920s, however, the situation was reversed. The net worth of the large enterprises continued to expand at a fairly rapid rate, more than doubling between 1921 and 1931, whereas the increase was on the order of one-third for the capital of all nonfinancial corporations. Total funds of these selected enterprises trebled between 1914 and 1921 in line with national product. In the following decade total funds again trebled, whereas national product declined slightly. Even though it is almost certain that all corporations expanded considerably more slowly than these large enterprises, the weight of nonfinancial corporations in the economy is likely to have increased substantially. For these large enterprises, the external financing ratio amounted to only one-fourth during the 1914–21 period but rose to nearly one-

---

and upper limits of the correct adjustment. The narrower adjustment is based on the estimate of intermediary holdings of assets (Ott, 1960, pp. 284 ff.) plus the deposits of the postal savings system with the Deposit Bureau (*HYS*, pp. 242–43). The second, broader adjustment, using figures of Ott, 1960, eliminates all changes in assets of financial institutions except those in loans and discounts and in securities held.

35. *HYS*, p. 330.

TABLE 4-16. Sources and Uses of Funds
of (48 to 75) Large Industrial Corporations, 1914–1930[a]

	1914–21[b]	1922–26	1927–30[c]
I. Amounts (¥ bill.)			
Paid-in capital	0.74	0.96	0.44
Reserves	0.30	0.25	0.12
Corporate bonds	0.10	0.66	0.69
Other outside liabilities	0.23	0.40	0.30
Sources	1.37	2.27	1.55
Fixed assets	1.41	1.13	1.12
Inventories	0.13	0.11	−0.00
Other current assets	0.55	0.30	0.39
Uses	2.09	1.54	1.51
II. Distribution (percent)			
Paid-in capital	54	42	28
Reserves	21	11	8
Corporate bonds	7	29	45
Other outside liabilites	18	18	19
Sources	100	100	100
Fixed assets	68	73	74
Inventories	6	7	0
Other current assets	26	20	26
Uses	100	100	100
III. Relation to gross national product (percent)			
Paid-in capital	0.90	1.23	0.69
Reserves	0.36	0.32	0.19
Corporate bonds	0.12	0.84	1.08
Other outside liabilities	0.28	0.51	0.47
Sources	1.66	2.90	2.43
Fixed assets	1.71	1.44	1.76
Inventories	0.16	0.14	−0.00
Other current assets	0.67	0.38	0.61
Uses	2.53	1.97	2.37

[a]Incomplete, e.g., financial assets, trade credit, and retained earnings are omitted; hence sources do not equal uses.   [b]From June 30, 1914, to end of
1921.   [c]From December 31, 1926, to June 30, 1930.

SOURCE: *HYS*, pp. 334–35.

half and nearly two-thirds during the early and late 1920s when profits were much lower, the increase in the share of debentures being particularly pronounced. The structure of uses did not change much, fixed assets absorbing between two-thirds and three-fourths of the total. It is doubtful to what extent these relationships apply to the universe of all nonfinancial corporations.

There is hardly any information about the financial affairs of small and medium-scale business. It is generally assumed that these enterprises had to rely to a large extent on financing through trade credit, through credit cooperatives, and in the unorganized credit markets, and that they could raise only very limited amounts of funds in the capital market through the issuance of corporate stocks and bonds. This is confirmed by the results of two sample inquiries undertaken near the end of the period, which showed that the small business enterprises investigated had raised about one-fourth of their borrowed funds from banks and about one-tenth from credit associations or a total of about one-third from financial institutions. The rest was obtained from moneylenders (about one-third of the total), from commission merchants (one-tenth and more than one-fifth, respectively, in the two inquiries), and from various lenders other than financial institutions.[36]

The available data thus do not permit the construction of a sources-and-uses-of-funds statement for all nonfinancial corporations. However, from scattered information some conclusions regarding the process of capital formation and financing in Japan in these nearly two decades can possibly be drawn. Among these are the considerable differences in the characteristics of the three subperiods; the larger volume of external financing, compared to national product, in the first subperiod than in the second and third; the larger role of borrowing from financial institutions in the second subperiod and through corporate bonds in the second and third subperiods compared to stock financing; and finally, if the figures now available are accepted, the astonishingly low share of corporate net saving.

Although there is scattered evidence of the further increase of the large combines in the operations, investments, assets, and profits of the nonfinancial business sector, particularly and possibly exclusively in the 1920s, no comprehensive quantitative data seem to exist to document these surmises. In particular, it is not possible to determine the share of the combines in the total of funds raised by the business sector and possible changes in this share.

b. The Government

The central government borrowed fairly continuously during the period, except in 1914–16, but on a relatively moderate scale. Its net issues were equivalent to approximately 2 percent of national product for the entire period as well as for the three subperiods and were all placed in Japan. The increase in debt of ¥ 4.4 bill. was, however, more than offset by gross capital expenditures of nearly ¥ 16 bill., of which one-fourth was military, and should have been also well below net capital expenditures (table 4-17).

The government's foreign debt was fractionally lower in 1931 than it had been in 1913, and the ratio of foreign to total debt, which had been close to three-fifths in 1913, had been reduced to one-fifth in 1931. New foreign borrowing during this period was limited to four long-term loans. Early in 1924 a loan was floated in New York and another in London, partly to provide foreign exchange to meet the extraordinary import requirements caused by the Kanto earthquake. In May 1930 two more loans, again in New York and London, were sold, shortly after Japan's return to the gold standard. These two pairs of loans yielded approximately ¥ 500 and ¥ 250 mill., respectively, but amortizations and retirements of old loans during the period were sufficient to offset these amounts.[37]

36. Some evidence of the differential rate of growth of large, small, and medium-sized nonfinancial corporations is provided by the differences in the development of some important indicators for all nonfinancial corporations, on the one hand (*HYS*, p. 324 ff.), and of a small group of 50 to 75 enterprises, on the other (table 4-16), given below (percentage change for period):

	All nonfinancial corporations		Large corporations	
	1914–21	*1922–30*	*1914–21*	*1922–30*[a]
Paid-in capital	+345	+ 45	+216	+133
Reserves	+335	+ 60	+360	+ 97
Corporate bonds	+214	+205	+ 56	+866
Profit[b]	.	− 8[c]	+398	+ 39
Dividends	+369	+ 1	+423	+ 32

[a]To June 30, 1930.
[b]Apparently before depreciation.
[c]1923–30.

37. Adams, 1964, pp. 80–81.

TABLE 4-17. Government Debt and Its Financing, 1914–1931

	1914–21	1922–26	1927–31	1914–31
1. Increase in debt (¥ bill.)				
a. Central government	1.64	1.30	1.43	4.37
b. Local government	0.34	0.86	1.02	2.22
c. Total	1.98	2.16	2.45	6.59
2. Rate of increase (percent per year)	6.9	7.6	6.1	6.8
3. Relation to national product (percent)	2.4	2.7	3.3	2.7
4. Distribution of central government debt increase				
a. Banking system	57	17	15	32
b. Other financial institutions	27	30	78	44
c. Other domestic institutions	18	29	−7	13
d. Borrowings	8	17	13	12
e. Foreigners[a]	−10	8	1	−1
5. Gross capital expenditures (¥ bill.)	4.59	5.61	5.58	15.78

[a]Foreign holdings assumed equal to foreign currency bonds outstanding (Ott, 1960, p. 95).

SOURCES: Lines 1a and 1b: *HYS*, pp. 158–59, 162.   Lines 4a–4e: *HYS*, pp. 158–59, 272 ff.   Line 5: Table 4-4.

For the period as a whole, financial institutions absorbed about four-fifths of the net increase in the central government's domestic debt. As a result, the share of financial institutions in the central government's total domestic debt increased from one-third in 1913 to more than two-thirds in 1931. The total amount of central government securities held outside the financial system in 1931, ¥ 1.3 bill., was hardly twice as large as it had been in 1913, and its relation to national product declined from 1.3 to 1.0 percent.

Among financial institutions, commercial banks were the leading holders of domestic central government securities (now omitting the relatively small direct borrowings of the government), absorbing for the period as a whole about one-fourth of total net issues, although their share was considerably larger, with two-fifths, in the first subperiod than from 1922 to 1931 when it averaged only one-seventh. The savings banks bought another one-eighth of net new issues, particularly in the 1927–31 period. In terms of net absorption, however, the Deposit Bureau ranked first, as the expansion of its holdings, with more than one-fourth of the total increase in outstandings, was slightly in excess of net purchases of commercial banks for the period as a whole. Its net purchases in 1927–31 were four times as large as those of the banks and equaled nearly three-fifths of the total increase in net central government debt. They were thus crucial for the support of the market. The Bank of Japan and the Yokohama Specie Bank were also substantial purchasers and each absorbed about 5 percent of total net issues.

The net issues of local governments, mostly for financing public works, were for the period as a whole about half as large as those of the central government, but the proportion rose from only one-fifth in 1914–21 to more than two-thirds in 1922–31. Foreign loans, totaling about ¥ 100 mill., issued by the cities of Tokyo and Yokohama, provided a modest proportion of the total, particularly in the late 1920s, after foreign issues outstanding had been reduced by 30 percent between 1913 and 1925.

Financial institutions were the most important buyers, together absorbing nearly two-thirds of total net issues of local government securities over the period as a whole and in the 1927–31 period absorbed more than the increase in total outstandings. Among financial institutions the Deposit Bureau was the dominating factor, accounting for two-fifths of all net purchases by financial institutions and absorbing over the entire period one-fourth of total net issues of domestic local government securities. From 1927 to 1931 the bureau and the Post Office life insurance system, which was also under control of the Ministry of Finance, accounted for more than two-thirds of net purchases by financial institutions and for more than one-half of all net issues of local government securities.

Domestic nonfinancial buyers, presumably mostly households, thus absorbed nearly two-fifths of the total supply of local government securities, but their share declined from nearly two-thirds in 1914–21 to one-half in 1922–26 and fell precipitously to one-fifth in 1927–31. The absolute volume of net nonfinancial purchases equaled about 0.25 percent of national product in 1914–21 and 0.4 percent from 1922 and 1931.

c. Agriculture

Although agriculture during this period contributed about one-fourth of national product, its role in investment and in the financial structure was small. However, a lack of statistics does not permit an even moderately reliable measurement.

In the absence of information on capital expenditures in agriculture, one is forced to rely on estimates of changes in the gross capital stock.[38] These show for the entire period from 1914 to 1931 the astonishingly low total of only about ¥ 0.7 bill. excluding residences, which might add nearly ¥ 1 bill. Assuming that the national ratio of gross capital formation to the increase in gross capital stock of 1.6[39] could be applied to agriculture, its gross capital formation would be on the order of at most ¥ 3 bill., or approximately 8 percent of the national total. The net figure, which is relevant for comparisons with increases in debt, would of course be substantially reduced, by two-thirds, if the national net gross ratio is used. The figures indicate a share in agricultural income on the order of 6 percent on a gross basis and 2 percent on a net basis, compared to national ratios of 15 and 5 percent.

Agricultural debt increased sharply during the 1914–21 period—according to the far from satisfactory available estimates, from ¥ 0.9 bill. in 1914 to ¥ 4.3 bill. in 1933[40]—compared to a doubling of the value of agricultural land. During the following decade no substantial net change seems to have occurred in accordance with the generally depressed situation of agriculture. If these figures are accepted, the increase in agricultural debt was far in excess of net or even slightly above gross capital expenditures for the period as a whole, particularly for the inflationary first subperiod, whereas capital formation exceeded debt change by a moderate amount during the remainder of the period.

This rapid increase in farm debt was sufficient to raise the ratio of the debt to the value of farmland[41] and reproducible assets, a ratio that can be estimated only with a large margin of uncertainty, from about 5 percent in 1913 to more than one-tenth in 1921. The burden of farm debt thus measured continued to increase during the 1920s as a result of the decline in land prices, although the volume of debt remained unchanged and by 1931 was on the order of one-fifth.

The estimates available put the share of financial intermediaries in total farm debt at about two-fifths throughout the period.[42] In the earlier part of the period the numerous small local commercial banks were probably the main source of organized short- and even long-term credit to agriculture. During the twenties the importance of the agricultural and industrial banking system is likely to have increased for long-term credit, and rural credit cooperatives certainly became a gradually more important source of short-term credit. In 1913 their loans were equal to about 5 percent of estimated total farm debt and to one-tenth of agricultural loans ascribed to

38. *ELTESJ*, 3:154–55.

39. Cf. table 4-4 for capital formation; *ELTESJ*, 3:154, for gross capital stock (after rough adjustment to current prices).

40. Cf. estimates assembled by Ott, 1960, p. 123.

41. Goldsmith, 1975.

42. In 1912 ordinary banks, savings banks, mutual loan associations, and long-term credit banks supplied only 36 percent of the total farm debt of ¥ 743 mill., as estimated by the Ministry of Finance's survey. Individuals were equally important as suppliers; together with moneylenders, they provided nearly three-fifths of the total of farm credit reported. The situation was not much changed in 1929, at which time long-term credit banks accounted for 16 percent of the total, ordinary and savings banks for 13 percent, cooperatives for 14 percent, and individuals and others for 56 percent (Asakura, cited in *HYSE*, pp. 123–24).

financial institutions.[43] By 1923 these ratios had risen to nearly one-tenth of total farm debt and more than one-fifth of the part supplied by financial institutions. Because the volume of loans by agricultural cooperatives more than doubled between 1923 and 1931, their share in total agricultural debt advanced to one-fifth and that in loans from financial institutions to one-half, making the credit cooperatives the most important single source of agricultural credit, which was due, to a good extent, to the funds made available to them by the Deposit Bureau.[44]

In the absence of macroeconomic estimates of saving in agriculture, one may be tempted to extrapolate the information from the data on a very small number of sample households.[45] Blowups from these samples of fewer than 100 households to the approximately 6 million farm households are, however, so much in conflict with the available macroeconomic evidence that the attempt is inadvisable.[46]

d. Households

If households are defined to exclude the business activities of the proprietors of unincorporated enterprises, there is little doubt, notwithstanding the absence of many of the relevant statistics, that their total financing requirements, as well as their use of external funds, were very small throughout the period.

The main evidence is the low level of expenditures on residential construction and the consequently small amounts of home mortgage loans outstanding. Expenditures on the construction of nonagricultural residences may be estimated at ¥ 1.2 bill. for 1914–21 and at ¥ 1.8 bill. for 1922–31,[47] equal to slightly less than one-tenth of total gross capital formation and to 1 1/4 percent of gross national product. Given the general disinclination in that period to borrow to finance one's home, it is unlikely that this volume of residential construction would have generated an increase in the home mortgage debt outstanding of as much as ¥ 1/2 bill. in the first subperiod and ¥ 3/4 bill. in the second. These very rough estimates are not in conflict with similar estimates based on the value of all residential real estate. The net stock of residences has been valued at nearly ¥ 4 1/2 bill. in 1913 and at nearly ¥ 8 1/2 bill. in 1930,[48] figures that should be substantially increased to allow for the value of land. Assuming an overall debt-to-value ratio of one-fifth and allocating about one-third of the value of residences to agriculture, the total mortgage debt would not have been much more than ¥ 1/2 bill. in 1913 and ¥ 1 1/4 bill. in 1931, involving an increase of about ¥ 3/4 bill., an increase lower than that suggested by the figures for construction expenditures. Even more liberal assumptions regarding propensity to borrow in order to finance residential construction would hardly lead to estimates much in excess of ¥ 1 bill. for the period as a whole. A considerable portion of this total represented borrowing from other households or from unorganized moneylenders.

No statistics are available on household borrowing for other purposes, that is, mainly to buy consumer durables; to acquire securities, primarily corporate stock; and to finance temporary or continuous deficits. In view of the extremely low level of expenditures on consumer durables during this period, borrowings to purchase them may well be disregarded. Policy loans

43. *HYS*, p. 225.

44. *HYSE*, p. 121.

45. *HYS*, pp. 358 ff.; Institute for Developing Economies, *One Hundred Years of Agricultural Statistics in Japan*, pp. 218–19.

46. Multiplying the per household sample figures by an estimated 6 million farm households leads, using data for 1925, to an estimate of total farm household income of about ¥ 10 bill., which is equivalent to approximately three-fifths of total national product and hence two and a half times as high as the figure ought to be (*JEG*, p. 282). Similarly, the total value of farm assets works out at about ¥ 90 bill., which is again about three times what macroeconomic estimates indicate (*ELTESJ*, 3:153, for reproducible tangible assets and Goldsmith, 1975, p. 141, for land). The blown-up value of farm debt of nearly ¥ 3 bill., on the other hand, is of the right order of magnitude and is even about one-third lower than the macroeconomic estimate.

47. Emi, 1971, p. 262.

48. *ELTESJ*, 3:148 ff., roughly adjusted for price changes as shown in *ELTESJ*, 8:158.

by the Post Office life insurance system, the only type of consumer credit for which information is available, amounted to 11 percent of assets in 1931.[49] If the same ratio is applied to life insurance companies, the total of policy loans would have come to approximately ¥ 250 mill. in 1931, involving an increase since 1913 of nearly the same amount. Other borrowing for consumption was probably not negligible, but most of it presumably occurred among households or between households and unincorporated business enterprises. It therefore seems unlikely that the household sector could have used external funds to the total extent of as much as, say, ¥ 2 bill. for the entire period 1914–31. This would be equal to less than 1 percent of the period's national product, to about 5 percent of total saving, and to about 10 percent of the increase in the loans and security holdings of financial institutions.

Sample data on household finances for this period are rare and unreliable. Three surveys taken in 1921 and 1926 show a "balance between income and expenditure" equal to 14, 11, and 10 percent, respectively, for urban worker's households.[50,51] It is doubtful that the average level of the saving ratio, about one-eighth of income, indicated by these surveys can be regarded as representative of all urban households. It would point to aggregate urban household saving on the order of ¥ 1 bill. a year, which would be in the neighborhood of one-half of the estimate of aggregate saving derived from the national accounts. The value of these samples for financial analysis is small, because they do not provide information on the structure of saving with the exception of savings deposits. For savings deposits, the samples show an average net increase in deposits of nearly ¥ 9 per household in 1921 and ¥ 6 in 1926, equal to 8 and 5 percent of household income. Blown up to cover all urban households, these figures imply net increases in savings deposits of about ¥ 1.0 bill. in 1921 and ¥ 0.7 bill. in 1926. This is far above the average figures from banking statistics, although much less so in 1926 than in 1921,[52] even if it is assumed that, as is reasonable, substantial parts of urban worker household saving deposits were kept with commercial banks.

5. THE FINANCIAL SUPERSTRUCTURE AS A WHOLE

a. The Issues of Nonfinancial Sectors

Table 4-18 documents, even accepting the substantial margins of error in some of the issue categories, particularly in trade credit,[53] the dominating importance of nonagricultural business, and here again corporate business, as the issuer of financial instruments outside financial institutions. For the period as a whole nonagricultural business accounted for about four-fifths of all such issues, the central and local governments contributing only 13 and 7 percent, respectively, and the household and farm sectors small amounts, equal to probably less than one-tenth, which are omitted from table 4-18. The share of business was substantially smaller only in the depression-dominated period, 1927–31, when the volume of its issues was extraordinarily low in relation to national product, whereas that of the central and local governments reached a peak. Within the issues of the nonagricultural business sector, corporations seem to have accounted for

49. Ott, 1960, p. 241.

50. HYS, pp. 356–57.

51. Another household inquiry, referring to 1926–27, gives similar results, namely, a ratio of "surplus" to household income of about 10 percent for both wage earners and salaried workers (cited Lockwood, 1954, p. 422).

52. HYS, pp. 199 ff., 202, 217, and 244.

53. Of all financial assets, the volume of trade credit is probably the most difficult to estimate and unfortunately also of large absolute size. In the absence of any direct eivdence of the volume of trade credit before the early 1950s, it has seemed best, or least unobjectionable, to tie the level and movements of trade credit to that of inventories, which, of course, is also subject to a wide margin of error of estimation. It has been assumed rather arbitrarily that in 1913 trade credit was about the same size as inventories and that the ratio rose slowly until the early 1940s to the value of about 1.5, with which it appears in the flow-of-funds accounts in the mid-1950s. The movement of the resulting very rough estimates has been compared with the trend in national product and with changes in the wholesale price level to ensure that as far as possible the estimates are not patently unreasonable.

TABLE 4-18. Net New Issue Ratios, 1914–1931 (Percent of Gross National Product)

	1914–21	1922–26	1927–31	1922–31	1914–31
I. Financial institutions[a]	20.87	9.67	6.61	8.20	12.57
II. Nonfinancial sectors[b]	20.50	15.12	5.67	10.47	13.96
1. Central government	2.19	1.53	1.83	1.68	1.86
2. Local governments	0.45	1.00	1.30	1.15	0.91
3. Business	17.86	12.59	2.53	7.64	11.19
a. Corporate bonds	0.68	1.00	1.65	1.32	1.10
b. Corporate stocks	8.41	3.30	2.31	2.80	4.75
c. Borrowings	8.27	4.47	0.78	2.68	4.62
d. Trade credit	0.50	3.83	−2.21	0.84	0.72
III. Foreign issues	3.25	−2.58	−0.26	−1.43	0.17
IV. All sectors	47.62	22.21	12.02	17.24	26.70

[a]Including interfinancial issues.　　[b]Domestic issues only.

SOURCES OF BASIC DATA: Line I: Table 4-16.　　Line II-1 to 3b: *HYS*, pp. 158, 162, 317, 330.　　Line II-3c: Ott, 1960, pp. 110–11 (net loans and discounts of all financial institutions).　　Line II-3d: Assumed to increase from 1.0 to 1.4 times inventories (Goldsmith, 1975, pp. 110–11).　　Line III: Table 4-1, col. 5.

70 to 90 percent of the total, depending on how loans from financial institutions and trade credit are allocated, necessarily in a rather arbitrary fashion, between corporate and unincorporated business.

The distribution of business issues by type shows some significant changes among the three subperiods. Trade credit, the weakest link in the estimates, was considerably reduced in absolute amount in the period from 1927 to 1931, reflecting both the sharp fall in prices and the substantial reduction in turnover. If trade credit is disregarded, there appears a substantial increase in the share of corporate bonds, which is particularly marked in the 1927–31 period and is evidence of an important change in the Japanese capital market. Corporate stocks accounted for about two-fifths for the period as a whole, but their share varied greatly among subperiods. Because these figures are based on changes in the paid-in capital of all corporations, they do not necessarily correctly reflect either the trend in the volume of stock bought by the general public or, consequently, the trend in the development of the market for new share issues; in addition, the figures may be overstated by the inclusion of shares issued in exchange for the equity in unincorporated business enterprises.

b. The Financial Intermediation Ratio

A comparison of the new issue ratios for the financial and nonfinancial sectors provides a rough measure of the extent of the institutionalization of the financial process. For that purpose, the issue ratio of financial institutions must, however, be adjusted to exclude interfinancial issues. If this is done, the following picture emerges (in percent of gross national product).

	Issues of nonfinancial sectors	*Issues of financial institutions*		*Ratio (3):(1)*
		Unadjusted	*Roughly adjusted*	
1914–21	20.5	20.9	15.5	0.76
1922–26	15.1	9.7	8.0	0.53
1927–31	5.7	6.6	5.5	0.96
1922–31	10.5	8.2	6.5	0.62
1914–31	14.0	12.6	10.0	0.71

These figures yield a value for the financial intermediation ratio of about two-thirds for the period as a whole if allowance is made for the relatively small issues of the household sector. They indicate that about two-thirds of all net issues of financial instruments by nonfinancial sectors were absorbed by financial institutions and testify to a rather high degree of institutionalization of the financial process. Because of the unavailability of figures for some minor components and because of the possibility that trade credit is underestimated, it is likely that the issues of the nonfinancial sectors have been understated and that the true value of the ratio may well be somewhat lower than that indicated.

The financial intermediation ratio does not seem to have differed greatly between the first and second subperiods, being slightly lower in the second. Within the 1920s, however, the ratio was considerably higher in the 1927–31 period, when financial institutions appear to have absorbed about nine-tenths of the net new issues of the nonfinancial sectors, than from 1922 to 1926, when the ratio is calculated at about one-half. More intensive recourse to financial institutions during a depression rather than during a more prosperous period would not be unreasonable.

6. THE NATIONAL BALANCE SHEET

The most important fact disclosed by the rough national balance sheet (table 4-19) is the sharp increase in the financial interrelations ratio, the quotient of financial and tangible assets, that occurred during the 1920s.

From 1914 through 1920 the value of the stock of tangible assets increased under the influence of the sharp increase in land prices and construction costs by slightly more than the volume of financial instruments outstanding with the consequence that the financial interrelations ratio declined slightly from 0.62 to 0.59. If net foreign assets are regarded as part of tangible wealth, that is, national wealth is used as the denominator, the decline is more pronounced—from 0.65 to 0.57—because the substantial net foreign debt position of 1913 changed to a substantial foreign balance in 1920. This reduction was the result of the combination of a small increase in the ratio of the assets of financial institutions to tangible assets from 0.21 to 0.24 and a substantial decline, from 0.41 to 0.35, in the ratio of the issues of nonfinancial sectors to tangible wealth.

The dramatic change in the financial interrelations ratio, however, occurred in the 1920s when it doubled from 0.59 to 1.20, although stock prices were cut in half over the period. This movement was due to a combination of a decline in the value of tangible assets by one-fifth, which reflected the sharp price deflation, and a large increase in the volume of financial instruments outstanding (by about 60 percent), both for issues of nonfinancial sectors and for those of financial institutions. This decade, therefore, witnessed one of the most intensive phases in the growth of the financial system compared to national wealth and income, the ratio of financial assets to gross national product rising from a bit more than 3 in 1920 to more than 5 1/2 in 1930.

The national balance sheet also permits the calculation of net new issue ratios of the nonfinancial sectors for the two periods 1914 to 1920 and 1921 to 1930 on a somewhat more comprehensive basis than the annual data basis that is used in table 4-18. Here again the ratio is considerably lower for the 1920s with 13 percent than for the 1914–20 period with 26 percent. This is true particularly for business borrowing from financial institutions, trade credit, agricultural debt, and the issuance of corporate stock. In contrast, the ratios are of about the same order in the two periods for government securities and residential mortgages. There is only one instrument, corporate bonds, for which the ratio is considerably higher in the 1920s than in the 1914–20 period.

The distribution of national assets among components and their relation to national product can be followed in table 4-20. Changes in the distribution of tangible assets were small,

TABLE 4-19. National Balance Sheet, 1913, 1920, 1930, and 1940 (¥ Bill.)

	1913	1920	1930	1940
I. Tangible assets	26.14	87.25	69.48	174.43
1. Land	11.03	39.53	31.91	60.21
a. Agricultural[a]	7.76	27.23	22.91	37.45
b. Other	3.27	12.30	9.00	22.75
2. Reproducible tangible wealth	15.11	47.72	37.57	114.22
a. Residential buildings	4.30	14.28	8.40	26.56
b. Other buildings and structures	3.91	15.65	12.85	37.94
c. Producer durables	2.17	8.88	6.13	22.32
d. Inventories	3.08	4.48	5.89	17.00
e. Livestock	1.43	3.93	3.05	7.90
f. Consumer durables	0.22	0.50	1.25	2.50
II. Financial assets[b]	16.20	51.65	83.37	245.63
1. Issued by financial institutions[c]	5.53	21.17	35.37	96.72
2. Issued by nonfinancial sectors[b]	10.67	30.48	48.00	148.94
a. Government securities[d]	1.46	3.15	7.74	33.89
b. Corporate bonds[d]	0.10	0.46	2.67	4.35
c. Business borrowing (excluding b and d)	2.75	8.48	13.41	25.65
d. Trade credit	3.08	5.50	7.50	24.00
e. Agricultural debt	0.90	3.50	4.30	8.00
f. Residential mortgages	0.40	0.90	1.90	3.00
g. Corporate stock, par value	1.98	6.49	11.68	25.02
h. Corporate stock, market less par value[e]	0.00[f]	2.00	−1.20	25.00
III. Net foreign assets	−1.04	3.72	1.50	1.25
IV. National wealth (I + III)	25.10	90.97	70.98	175.68
V. National assets (I + II)	42.34	138.90	152.85	420.06

[a]Including forests.   [b]Corporate stock at market.   [c]Total liabilities and capital of financial institutions; hence includes interfinancial assets.   [d]Domestic issues only.   [e]Excluding stock of financial institutions.   [f]Assumed approximately equal to par.

SOURCES: Line I: Goldsmith, 1975, pp. 140, 146. Somewhat different estimates for lines I-2 and I-2c (or I-2c and I-2d) are given by Fujino, 1975, p. 191 (¥ bill.):

	Reproducible tangible assets	Inventories
1913	14.14	2.33
1920	51.89	7.99
1930	36.97	6.02
1940	107.64	26.59

Line II-1: Table 3-11.   Line II-2a: *HYS*, pp. 158–59, 162.   Line II-2b: Ott, 1960, p. 99.   Line II-2c: Assumed equal to net loans and discounts by all financial institutions (ibid., pp. 110–11). Very similar values are given for lendings by all banks in *HYS*, pp. 194–95.   Line II-2d: Assumed to increase from 1.0 to 1.4 times inventories (Goldsmith, 1975, p. 145).   Line II-2e and 2f: Rough estimates; cf. discussion in sections 4c and 4d.   Line II-2g: Rough estimates based on stock price index.   Line III: Cumulated balance of payments figures (*ELTESJ*, 1:178, 191).

particularly during the first part of the period. For the period as a whole, the share of residential structures and inventories and of the total of reproducible assets declined, whereas that of land advanced slightly. Within financial assets, the share of issues of financial institutions, which is exaggerated because of the inclusion of interfinancial claims, increased from one-third in 1913 to somewhat more than two-fifths in 1920 and 1930. Among the issues of nonfinancial assets, government securities increased their share slightly from fully one-eighth to one-sixth, all in the 1920s. The share of corporate stock rose from less than one-fifth in 1913 to more than one-fourth in 1920 and 1930, reflecting in the first period mainly advancing stock prices and in the second

TABLE 4-20. National Balance Sheet, 1913, 1920, 1930, and 1940:
Distribution and Relation to National Product (Percent)

	Distribution (percent)				Ratio to gross national product			
	1913	1920	1930	1940	1913	1920	1930	1940
I. Tangible assets	61.7	62.8	45.5	41.5	5.22	5.49	4.74	4.43
1. Land	26.1	28.5	20.9	14.3	2.20	2.49	2.18	1.53
a. Agricultural[a]	18.3	19.6	15.0	8.9	1.55	1.71	1.56	0.95
b. Other	7.7	8.9	5.9	5.4	0.65	0.77	0.61	0.58
2. Reproducible tangible wealth	35.7	34.4	24.6	27.2	3.02	3.00	2.56	2.90
a. Residential buildings	10.2	10.3	5.5	6.3	0.86	0.90	0.57	0.67
b. Other buildings and structures	9.2	11.3	8.4	9.0	0.78	0.98	0.88	0.96
c. Producer durables	5.1	6.4	4.0	5.3	0.43	0.56	0.42	0.57
d. Inventories	7.3	3.2	3.9	4.0	0.61	0.28	0.40	0.43
e. Livestock	3.4	2.8	2.0	1.9	0.29	0.25	0.21	0.20
f. Consumer durables	5.2	3.6	0.8	0.6	0.04	0.03	0.09	0.06
II. Financial assets[b]	38.3	3.7	54.5	58.5	3.23	3.25	5.68	6.23
1. Issued by financial institutions[c]	13.1	15.2	23.1	23.0	1.10	1.33	2.41	2.45
2. Issued by nonfinancial sectors[b]	25.2	22.0	31.4	35.5	2.13	1.92	3.27	3.78
a. Government securities[d]	3.4	2.3	5.1	8.1	0.29	0.20	0.53	0.86
b. Corporate bonds[d]	0.2	0.3	1.7	1.0	0.02	0.03	0.18	0.11
c. Business borrowing (excluding b and d)	6.5	6.1	8.8	6.1	0.55	0.53	0.91	0.65
d. Trade credit	7.3	4.0	4.9	5.7	0.61	0.35	0.51	0.61
e. Agricultural debt	2.1	2.5	2.8	1.9	0.18	0.22	0.29	0.20
f. Residential mortgages	0.9	0.6	1.2	7.1	0.08	0.06	0.13	0.08
g. Corporate stock, par value	4.7	4.7	7.6	6.0	0.40	0.41	0.80	0.64
h. Corporate stock, market less par value[e]	0.0	1.4	−0.8	6.0	0.00	0.13	−0.08	0.63
III. Net foreign assets	−2.5	2.7	1.0	0.3	−0.21	0.23	0.10	0.03
IV. National wealth (I + III)	0.6	65.5	46.4	41.9	5.01	5.72	4.84	4.46
V. National assets (I + II)					8.45	8.74	10.42	10.66

NOTE: [a]Including forests.   [b]Corporate stock at market.   [c]Total liabilities and capital of financial institutions; hence
includes interfinancial assets.   [d]Domestic issues only.   [e]Excluding stock of financial institutions.

SOURCE: Table 4-19.

new stock issues. Corporate bonds jumped from about 1 to more than 5 percent, mainly in the
1920s. The share of business borrowing, on the other hand, stayed at somewhat above one-
fourth. That of trade credit fell from three-tenths to one-sixth, mainly in the first period, as its
estimates are tied to those of inventories. Net foreign assets, finally, changed sides from minus 2
1/2 percent in 1913 to plus 2 1/2 percent in 1920, but by 1930 their share had declined to 1
percent.

The ratio of national assets to national product rose from 8 to more than 10 1/2, most of the
increase occurring in the 1920s. The relative movements of the components necessarily reflect
those of their shares in total national assets. Thus the ratio nearly doubled for financial assets
from 3 to more than 5 1/2 whereas that of tangible assets stayed close to 5.

The national balance sheet, finally, permits calculation of the financial interrelations ratio
according to the formula

$$FIR = \tau\alpha\beta^{-1} (\delta + \varphi) (1 + \nu) + \frac{F_{t-n}}{W_t} (1 + \nu')$$

used in chapter 3 for the 1885–1913 period. For the years 1914–40 this yields:

$$0.88 \times 13.6 \times 0.23 \times (0.26 + 0.21)(1.06) + 0.09\,(1.10),$$

which produces a calculated financial interrelations ratio of 1.47 for 1940 compared with an observed ratio of 1.41 obtained from the national balance sheet. The sharp increase over the value for 1913 is due mainly to the high level of the new issue ratios for both nonfinancial sectors and financial institutions and to the high financial intermediation ratio (φ/δ) of 0.81. The effect of these ratios is partly offset by a reduced value of the multiplier (α), which reflects a more rapid average increase in gross national product in current prices. The difference between the observed and the calculated value of the financial interrelations ratio is due to the roughness of the formula and the irregularities in the movements of several components over the period of observation.

5   Riding for a Fall, 1932–1945

1. GENERAL CHARACTERISTICS OF PERIOD[1]

a. The fourteen-year period from 1932 through 1945 is more explicitly bounded by the (second) abandonment of the gold standard and the Manchurian "incident" in September 1931 and the surrender in Tokyo Bay in August 1945. The period derives a considerable degree of unity from the accelerating trend in armament expenditures, military operations, deficit financing, credit expansion, and inflation, which ultimately led to the near collapse of the country's economic, financial, political, and social system at the end of World War II.

b. The period, nevertheless, is not homogeneous, and three subperiods of approximately equal length may be distinguished. When the data are limited, as here, to annual figures, the most appropriate division appears to be 1932 through 1936, 1937 through 1941, and 1942 through 1945, with the Peking incident of July 1937, which marked the beginning of large-scale military operations in China, and the start of the war with the United States in December 1941 providing the dividing dates between the subperiod.[2,3]

c. The main trends in the basic characteristics of the Japanese economy during the period can be followed in table 5–1 on an annual basis and in table 5–2 in relative terms for the entire period and the three subperiods.

d. The first subperiod of 1932–36, from the first (Shanghai) to the second (Marco Polo Bridge) China "incident," already showed a rapid acceleration of military expenditures, which were nearly two and a half times as large in 1936 as in 1931. In internal politics the period witnessed the crucial transition from party government to an effectively bureaucratic-military government, although the forms of parliamentary democracy were preserved. It might be argued, nevertheless, that the main characteristics of the subperiod were rather those of a general upswing, particularly in investment, set off by a sharp depreciation of the international value of

1. In addition to the publications listed in note 1 to chap. 4, considerable use has been made in this chapter of the following: T. A. Bisson, *Japan's War Economy*, 1945; J. B. Cohen, *Japan's Economy in War and Reconstruction*, 1949, and *Japan's Postwar Economy*, 1958; U.S. Strategic Bombing Survey, *The Effects of Strategic Bombing on Japan's War Economy*, 1946, hereafter cited as USSBS.

2. Because many of the long-term statistical series end in 1940 and figures for 1945 are often unavailable, e.g., national income accounts, it is sometimes necessary to define the last two subperiods as comprising the years 1937 through 1940 and 1941 through 1944.

3. The two first subperiods distinguished here do not coincide with the three (inventory) business cycles identified during the years 1931–41, which cover roughly speaking the years 1931 through 1933 for the first cycle, the years 1934 through 1937 for the second, and the period from the spring of 1938 to the spring of 1941 for the third trough-to-trough cycle (Fujino, 1966, p. 66). Together, however, these ten years are very close in timing to the equipment cycle dated by Fujino to run from late 1930 to mid-1941. Ohkawa and Rosovsky's dating of long swings characterizes the years 1931 to 1937 as the relatively short upward phase of a long cycle, the long downward phase extending from 1938 through 1956 (*JEG*, p. 25).

TABLE 5-1. National Product, Consumption, and Capital Formation, 1931–1944

	Gross national product					
	Current prices (¥ bill.) (1)	Constant (1934–36) prices		Personal consumption per head 1934–36 prices (yen) (4)	Gross fixed capital formation ratio (percent) (5)	Current foreign balance (¥ bill.) (6)
		Amount (¥ bill.) (2)	Change (percent) (3)			
1931	12.52	13.89	+3.1	166	14.6	−0.08
1932	13.04	14.07	+1.3	163	14.8	0.04
1933	14.33	14.66	+4.2	161	16.1	0.04
1934	15.67	16.24	+10.8	162	17.2	0.01
1935	16.73	16.62	+2.3	155	18.3	0.23
1936	17.80	17.15	+3.2	157	18.7	0.23
1937	23.43	21.31	+24.3	163	24.8	−0.56
1938	26.79	21.97	+3.1	160	30.2	−0.56
1939	33.08	22.09	+0.6	152	31.5	0.17
1940	39.40	20.63	−6.6	135	31.7	0.13
1941	44.90	20.91	+1.4	131	·	−1.02
1942	54.38	20.82	−0.4	124	·	−1.07
1943	63.82	21.09	+1.3	116	·	−0.91
1944	74.50	20.11	−4.6	95	·	−0.38

SOURCE: *ELTESJ*, 1:179, 214, 238. Col. 6 for 1941–44 is balance of trade in goods and services, which differs from current account balance shown for 1931–40.

the currency and fueled by increasing government deficits and credit expansion, an upswing in which both the private and civilian sectors of the economy fully participated.

e. In the five years between 1931 and 1936 real gross national product increased by nearly one-fourth, or by more than 4 percent a year. Although manufacturing production, and within it the output of the heavy industries, considerably exceeded the expansion of total national product, real personal consumption continued to increase slowly, although not more slowly than during the 1920s; and agricultural output continued to expand at a rate of 3½ percent, well ahead of population growth. The expansion of military expenditures, rising by more than 140 percent between 1931 and 1936, however, already greatly exceeded the growth of total government expenditure or national product.

f. The slack in the Japanese economy in 1931 was sufficiently large to permit expansion in the volume of real national product by about one-fourth by 1936 with an increase in the general price level (national product deflator) of 12 percent. The wholesale price index, it is true, advanced by nearly 40 percent under the influence of the depreciation of the yen, compared to gold by 65 percent (table 5–3). On the other hand, retail prices rose by only 10 to 20 percent.[4] Thus by Japanese standards, the degree of inflation during this period was moderate.

g. The balance of payments on current account showed a substantial surplus, mainly limited to 1935–36, in contrast to the large deficits of the twenties. This was more than offset by large long-term capital exports, mainly to dependent areas, whereas net gold movements were small. However, the substantial short-term capital imports (slightly above ¥ 1 bill. for 1932–36) may reflect errors and omissions in the other categories.

h. The modest degree of inflation accompanying this first step-up in military operations

4. The increase amounted to 11 percent according to the consumer price index of Ohkawa and associates (*ELTESJ*, 8: 135) and to 17 percent according to the Tokyo retail price index (*HYS*, p. 50).

TABLE 5-2. Basic Economic Characteristics of the 1932–1944 Period

	1936 / 1931	1941 / 1936	1944 / 1941	1945 / 1941	1944 / 1931
	I. Ratios				
1. National product, current prices	1.42	2.52	1.66	·	5.95
2. National product, constant prices	1.23	1.22	0.96	·	1.45
3. National product deflator	1.16	2.07	1.72	·	4.11
4. Agricultural production	1.19	0.88	0.85	0.65	0.89
5. Manufacturing production	1.65	1.45	1.01	0.43	2.42
6. Real personal consumption per head	0.95	0.83	0.73	·	0.57
7. Private capital expenditures	2.17	3.36	1.85	·	13.52
8. Government expenditures, total[a]	1.43	.58	2.07	·	13.61
9. Government expenditures, military[a]	2.43	3.83	·	·	·
10. Money in circulation	1.27	3.17	2.18	4.66	2.78
11. Assets of financial institutions	1.29	2.47	2.70	6.51	8.61
12. Central government debt[a]	1.72	3.78	2.63	3.45	17.09
	II. Average annual rate of change (percent)				
1. National product, current prices	7.3	20.2	18.4	·	14.7
2. National product, constant prices	4.2	4.1	−1.4	·	2.9
3. National product deflator	3.0	15.7	10.0	·	11.5
4. Agricultural production	3.5	−3.7	−5.3	−10.2	−0.9
5. Manufacturing production	10.5	7.7	0.3	−19.0	7.0
6. Real personal consumption per head	1.1	−3.5	−10.0	·	−4.2
7. Private capital expenditures	16.8	27.4	22.8	·	22.2
8. Government expenditures, total[a]	7.4	35.6	27.4	·	22.2
9. Government expenditures, military[a]	19.4	30.8		·	·
10. Money in circulation	4.9	26.0	29.7	47.9	18.1
11. Assets of financial institutions	5.2	19.8	39.2	59.7	18.0
12. Central government debt[a]	11.5	30.5	38.0	36.3	24.4

[a]Fiscal years starting April 1.

SOURCES: Lines 1–2 and 6: Table 5-1.   Lines 4 and 5: *HYS*, pp. 92, 96.   Line 7: *JEG*, p. 290.   Line 8: *HYS*, pp. 49, 51; "government expenditures on goods and services" as shown in national product accounts.   Line 9: *HYS*, pp. 133, 141.   Line 10: Hoekendorf, for 1931–40 and col. 1 plus col. 3 for 1937–45.   Line 11: As for table 3-11. Line 12: *HYS*, p. 159.

and expenditures was due in part to the still rather limited expansion in money in circulation—by between 20 and 40 percent, according to most of the several estimates available—and in the resources of all financial institutions by not much more than one-fourth, although total government expenditures expanded by more than 40 percent and the central government's debt rose by more than 70 percent. These developments will be reviewed in sections 3 and 4.

i. During the second subperiod, that is, the years 1937 through 1941, the Japanese economy shifted from a predominantly civilian to a predominantly military pattern, both in the structure of production and employment and in the economic policy and control measures adopted. Late in 1941, even before Pearl Harbor, the country was practically on a war footing, the sphere of initiative and decision by private business having been drastically curtailed by the promulgation of the Total National Mobilization Law in the spring of 1938. In many respects the style of Japanese economic management in the subperiod, as well as to a lesser extent in the preceding subperiod of 1932–36, was closer to that of the autocratic and nationalistic Meiji period—witness Japan's withdrawal from the League of Nations in March 1933—than to the quasi-democratic 1910s and 1920s.

j. The fact that the Japanese economy was, with few exceptions, fully utilized in 1936 is

TABLE 5-3. Price Movements, 1931–1945

	National product deflator	Wholesale prices	Consumer prices	Wages	Stock prices	Interest rates (percent)	Rural land prices (1934-36 = 100)	Urban land prices (1936 = 100)	Foreign exchange (¥ per gold)
		1934-36 = 100							
	(1)	(2)	(3)	(4)	(5)	(6)	(7)	(8)	(9)
1931	90	74.8	92.4	101	44	9.4	100	·	2.05
1932	93	83.0	93.4	102	60	9.3	93	·	3.56
1933	98	95.1	96.3	103	85	8.9	93	·	5.03
1934	97	97.0	97.6	101	101	8.6	96	·	5.71
1935	101	99.4	100.1	100	96	8.2	100	·	5.92
1936	104	103.6	102.4	98	102	7.4	104	100	5.81
1937	110	125.8	110.4	101	119	7.0	113	102	5.85
1938	122	132.7	120.9	104	135	6.8	124	109	5.95
1939	150	146.6	135.5	111	115	6.4	139	114	6.49
1940	191	164.1	167.4	122	156	·	167	123	7.30
1941	215	175.8	159.2	134	120	·	165	129	7.30
1942	261	191.2	164.8	144	143	·	160	135	·
1943	303	204.6	173.9	169	168	·	169	155	·
1944	370	231.9	194.7	·	174	·	190	163	·
1945	·	350.3	286.2	·	177	·	220	210	·

SOURCES: **Col. 1:** 1931–40, *ELTESJ*, 1:233; *HYS*, p. 51, linked in 1940. **Col. 2:** Bank of Japan, 1934–36 basis; *HYS*, p. 76. **Col. 3:** *ELTESJ*, 8:136. 1939–45 extrapolated on basis of Tokyo retail price index (*HYS*, p. 80). **Col. 4:** *ELTESJ*, 8:247, col. 5; 1931–39 average daily male wage in manufacturing. 1940–43 extrapolated on basis of ibid., p. 246, col. 2. **Col. 5:** *HYS*, p. 253. **Col. 6:** Average rate on bank loans (Ministry of Finance, as cited by Ott, 1960, p. 302). **Col. 7:** Average of March prices of dry and paddy fields (*HYS*, pp. 88–89); March 1946 value 1,118. **Col. 8:** *HYS*, p. 87. **Col. 9:** *HYS*, p. 320.

reflected in the failure of the volume of output, measured by gross national product in constant prices, to rise by much more than one-fifth between 1936 and 1941—all of it in 1937—notwithstanding an increase in the labor force by 6 percent (excluding primary industries by 18 percent)[5] and in the net fixed capital stock by about one-third (excluding residences by about two-fifths).[6] Manufacturing production, however, increased by 45 percent and the shift toward heavy industry continued, but the rate of expansion was considerably slower than it had been in the preceding five-year period.

k. The concentration on military activities is evident in the rise of military expenditures by nearly 300 percent between 1936 and 1941 and in their rising share in total central government expenditures, which sharply increased from slightly less than one-fifth of gross national product in 1936, practically the same as in 1931, to one-third in 1941. It is also reflected in the fact that total agricultural production and real personal consumption per head decreased between 1936 and 1941 by 12 and 17 percent, respectively.

l. The forced-draft increase in output, particularly in the heavy industries, by means of government deficits and rapid credit expansion in an already fully employed economy resulted in a sharp inflation. Within the five years between 1936 and 1941 the general price level more than doubled and retail prices advanced by 55 percent, notwithstanding substantial price controls and subsidies. These movements are not astonishing in view of an increase of the central government's debt by 280 percent, the volume of money by something like 200 percent (table 5–4), and the assets of financial institutions by 170 percent.

m. The heavy demands for imported raw materials connected with the armaments program resulted in substantial deficits on current account in the balance of payments in 1937 and 1938.[7] At the same time, long-term capital exports to the dependent areas increased greatly. As a result, gold and foreign exchange reserves had to be reduced considerably and short-term foreign liabilities augmented sharply. According to the balance of payments statistics, gold reserves declined by nearly ¥ 3 bill. in 1937–40 (no figures available for 1941) and short-term debts (including errors and omissions) increased more than ¥ 2 bill., whereas long-term capital exports, most of which were lost as a result of World War II, grew by about ¥ 4 bill. For the entire period 1932–40, long-term capital exports of about ¥ 6 bill. or about 3 percent of the period's gross national product, were financed in about equal parts by the reduction of monetary reserves and increases in short-term foreign debt. As a result, Japan in 1940 had considerably larger foreign investments and debts than in 1931, but their importance, in relation, for example, to national product, was smaller.

n. From 1942 until the middle of 1945 the Japanese economy was, of course, dominated by the requirements of full-scale war. An ever-increasing proportion of resources was devoted to military and directly supporting activities and the entire economy became tightly, although not very efficiently, controlled. This was particularly true from 1943 on, when the country's critical position became clear to the government, and it became evident how far from a full mobilization for war the country was, in deed if not in words, an exact parallel to the approximately contemporary situation in Germany until Stalingrad.[8]

o. Between 1941 and 1944 the volume of real national product failed to increase and in 1944 is estimated to have been slightly lower than in 1937.[9] The value of munitions production rose sharply from ¥ 3.5 bill., or nearly one-tenth of gross national product in 1940–41, to more

5. *HYS*, p. 57.

6. *ELTESJ*, 3:151, assuming the increase in 1941 to have equaled that of 1940.

7. *ELTESJ*, vol. 1.

8. For developments during this period, cf. particularly the studies by USSBS and Cohen listed in footnote 1.

9. The much older USSBS estimate indicates an increase, in 1940 prices, from ¥ 40 bill. in fiscal years 1940–41 and 1941–42 to ¥ 49 bill. in 1944–45, whereas according to table 5–1, it was 6 percent lower. The notorious difficulties of measuring real national product in a war economy prevent a more definite statement, in view of these discrepancies, than that real gross national product increased only slightly, if at all, during the war.

TABLE 5-4. Money in Circulation, 1931–1945 (¥ Mill.)

	Currency			Bank deposits		
	HYS[a] (1)	Fujino (2)	A and N (3)	HYS (4)	Fujino (5)	A and N (6)
1931	1683	1055	1799	975	2959	3818
1932	1788	1091	1906	1043	2747	3990
1933	1932	1187	2051	1144	3015	4238
1934	2033	1310	2194	1249	3223	4437
1935	2189	1361	2311	1215	3228	4465
1936	2306	1388	2485	1346	3466	4834
1937	2788	1747	3155	1790	4295	5855
1938	3297	2265	3478	2362	5273	7293
1939	4425	2447	4654	3577	7058	10484
1940	5545	3290	6000	4119	9519	13157
1941	7086	·	7827	5018	·	15972
1942	8122	·	9274	5888	·	20254
1943	11268	·	13099	6263	·	23137
1944	18894	·	22856	7403	·	31801
1945	46386	·	56658	9899	·	46180

[a]Excluding notes of Banks of Taiwan and Chosen but including subsidiary coins.

SOURCES: As for table 4-3.

than ¥ 12 bill. (all in 1940 prices) in 1944–45, or one-fourth of gross national product,[10] and other war expenditures also increased sharply. All of this increased use of resources occurred at the expense of non-war consumption. As a result, real consumer expenditures per head declined by more than an additional one-fourth between 1941 and 1944, falling to only three-fifths of the 1934–38 level. In 1944, when the Japanese war effort reached its peak, war expenditures probably absorbed about one-half of gross national product (table 5–5).[11,12]

p. As only a small part of the increase in military expenditures was covered by taxes or sales of securities to savers, the growing deficits had to be largely financed by the Bank of Japan and other financial institutions. The effects of this policy are visible in a further increase between 1941 and 1944 in government debt by more than 160 percent, in money in circulation by 120 percent (or by more than 200 percent, according to another estimate), and in the assets of all financial institutions by 170 percent, involving annual rates of expansion of 30 to 40 percent.

q. Such a rate of inflation could not help producing a further sharp increase in prices, notwithstanding price controls and subsidies. Between 1941 and 1944 the national product deflator rose by 70 percent. Even though the increases in the official price indices were substantial—100 percent for wholesale prices between 1941 and 1945 and 80 percent for Tokyo retail prices—they lost contact with effective (black-market) prices for nonrationed transactions from 1943 on. As early as December 1943, black-market prices for important consumer goods were 5 to 20 times as high as official prices, and by mid-1945 they were in many cases 10 to more than

10. Although national product estimates do not exist for the year 1945 or parts of it, the volume of output during the first half of 1945 is likely to have been substantially below the 1944 level.

11. Munitions output reached its peak in September 1944 when it was nearly three times as large as it had been in December 1941 and four times as large as in April 1941. By July 1945 it had declined by more than one-half from the peak of ten months earlier (USSBS, pp. 203–04).

12. An indication of the speed of the armaments buildup is given by the fact that its gross value, in 1930 prices, has been estimated to have risen from ¥ 5.2 bill. in 1935 to ¥ 12.3 bill. in 1940, or by 19 percent a year, compared with the much smaller rate of growth of only 6 percent between 1900 and 1935 (Ishiwata, p. 5). These figures compare with growth rates of the gross nonmilitary fixed capital stock in 1934–36 prices by 3.8 percent a year from 1936–40 and an average of 2.9 percent between 1900 and 1935 (ELTESJ, 3:148–50).

TABLE 5-5. National Product and War Expenditures, 1941–1945

	1941–42	1942–43	1943–44	1944–45	1941–42 to 1944–45
	I. Amounts (¥ bill. of 1940)[a]				
Munitions	3.5	4.9	8.6	12.2	29.2
Pay, travel, subsistence	1.5	1.8	2.3	3.4	9.0
Plant and equipment in munitions industries	2.8	2.5	4.5	4.9	14.7
War expenditures at home	7.8	9.2	15.4	20.5	52.9
War expenditures abroad	2.2	2.5	3.4	7.1	15.2
Total central government expenditures	8.0	11.6	16.2	22.2	58.0
Gross national product[b]	40.3	40.6	45.1	49.3	175.3
	II. Percent of gross national product				
Munitions	8.7	12.1	19.1	24.7	16.7
Pay, travel, subsistence	3.7	4.4	5.1	6.9	5.1
Plant and equipment in munitions industries	6.9	6.2	10.0	9.9	8.4
War expenditures at home	19.4	22.7	34.1	41.6	30.2
War expenditures abroad	5.5	6.2	7.5	14.4	8.7
Total central government expenditures	19.9	28.6	35.9	45.0	33.1

[a]Fiscal years starting April 1.   [b]The more recent estimates of real national product (table 5-1, col. 2) do not show any increase in 1943 and 1944.

SOURCE: U.S. Strategic Bombing Survey, p. 15.

100 times as high. The black-market price for rice, for example, rose from 6 times the official price at the end of 1943 to 28 times in mid-1944, 44 times in late 1944, and 70 times in July 1945.[13] This partly repressed inflation was, of course, only a foretaste of the open hyperinflation of the immediate postwar years, which by 1951 was to lift the national product deflator to about 140 times its 1941 level.

r. Japan's balance of payments during the third subperiod, using one very rough estimate,[14] was approximately even on current account, the modest positive balance on commodities, services, and investment income being more than offset by net government expenditures, which did not include the bulk of military expenditures abroad. Continuing net Japanese investments abroad, presumably mostly in dependent and occupied areas, averaged about ¥ 1.3 bill. a year, or a little more than 2 percent of national product. How this substantial amount was financed does not seem to be known in detail. Virtually all of these foreign investments were lost at the end of the war.

s. During the 1930s and the war period the stock exchange lost much of the position in the country's financial structure that it had acquired in the preceding decades. The volume of trading showed no definite trend but for the period was on the average about one-third above the level of the 1920s, only one-half of the increase in the price level.[15] This increase, however, was considerably below the expansion in the number of shares listed and the capitalization of all corporations. Prices recovered sharply in 1932–34 from the depression trough but then showed no definite trend until the later part of the war. In 1941 the stock price index was about one-third above the average level of 1921–25, and stocks continued to lag behind inflation. In January 1945 stock prices were less than one-fourth higher than they had been when the war started, whereas the level of prices of commodities and services had multiplied several times.

t. Real estate prices showed a definite upward trend beginning with the mid-1930s. During

13. USSBS, p. 225.

14. USSBS, p. 91. The *ELTESJ* (vol. 1) estimate, shown in table 5–1, indicates a negative balance on current account equal to 1 1/2 percent of national product.

15. On stock exchange developments during this period, cf. Adams, 1964, chap. 4, pp. 2 and 3.

the remainder of the 1930s the rise was more rapid for farmland, but urban land prices caught up during the war. Early in 1945 both indices stood at about twice the 1936 level. Their rise, therefore, lagged considerably behind that of the general price level, which approximately quadrupled during that interval.

u. Interest rates lost much of whatever economic importance they had after Japan abandoned the gold standard and adopted an easy money policy, which was intended to facilitate and to reduce the cost to the government of, first, the reflation of the economy in the early 1930s; and then the financing of military production and operations. Thus the discount rate of the Bank of Japan for commercial bills was gradually reduced from 6.57 percent in 1931 to 3.65 percent in mid-1933 and from April 1936 until October 1946 remained unchanged at 3.29 percent, unaffected by a near-war, a full-scale war, economic collapse, and hyperinflation (1.80, 1.00, and 0.90 sen per ¥ 100 per day, the Japanese way of setting discount rates until the early 1970s). Other interest rates followed the downward trend, although generally more slowly. Thus the rates charged by banks were reduced between 1931 and 1945 from about 9.5 to 6.5 percent. Long-term government security yields were reduced from 5 to 3.5 percent, whereas those of industrial bonds were lowered to 4.25 percent. The reduction also affected rates paid on deposits, with those of the postal saving system declining from 4.2 percent in 1930 to 2.6 percent in 1945.[16]

2. CAPITAL FORMATION AND SAVING[17]

a. Capital Formation

Although the aggregate gross domestic capital formation ratio, averaging 25 percent for 1932–36, was already well above the level of the preceding three to four decades, a further sudden and sharp upward jump occurred in the second subperiod, lifting the average for 1937–41 to 37 percent, including military capital expenditures of 8 percent. In 1942–44 the ratio, now excluding military expenditures, averaged 27 percent, compared with ratios of 22 percent and 29 percent, respectively, in the two preceding subperiods, using the narrower concept of capital expenditures. The second subperiod, as well as the third, therefore, confronted the Japanese economy with a financing task of unprecedented magnitude. These developments can be followed in table 5–6.

For the 1930s, military capital expenditures represented about one-fifth of total domestic gross capital formation, rising from about one-tenth of the total in the first subperiod to more than one-fourth in the second. They probably became predominant during the third subperiod for which no comparable statistics exist.

Non-military capital formation grew rapidly, even after adjustment for price increases, throughout the 1930s. In 1940 it was two and a half times as large as it had been in 1931, although total gross national product had expanded by only two-thirds. It managed to keep at about that level for the following five years, partly because of the expansion of the privately owned facilities in war-related industries. As a result, the private capital formation ratio rose from one-sixth in 1932–36 to more than one-fifth in 1942–44.

Until the war, the main change in the structure of civilian capital formation had been the decline of the share of residential construction from the already low level of 9 percent in the first subperiod to 5 percent in the second, thus further reducing the demands for finance originating from that sector. The share of inventory investment averaged more than one-third), which was partly due to the upward trend in commodity prices. The proportion of the government's civilian capital expenditures declined sharply, with that of local governments being cut in half between the first and second subperiods. As a result, private nonresidential investment absorbed an

16. *HYS*, pp. 260 ff.
17. Because the setup of this and the following sections parallels that in chapter 4, some comments about sources, reliability of estimates, and similar matters offered there are not repeated.

TABLE 5-6. Capital Formation, 1932–1944

	Total (1)	Gross fixed capital formation				Inventory investment (6)	Capital consumption allowances (7)	Net capital formation (8)
		Total (2)	Private (3)	Government civilian (4)	Government military (5)			
				I. Amounts (¥ bill.)				
1932–36	19.26	14.10	7.79	4.23	2.08	5.16	8.02	11.24
1937–41	61.31[a]	43.92	25.88	5.46	12.58[b]	17.39	17.00[c]	44.31
1942–44	51.14[c]	41.74	33.40	8.34	·	9.40	13.20[c]	37.94[c]
1932–44	131.71[d]	99.76	67.07	18.03	14.66[e]	31.95	38.22[d]	93.49
				II. Distribution (percent)				
1932–36	100.0	73.2	40.4	22.0	10.8	26.8	41.6	58.4
1937–41	100.0	71.6	42.2	8.9	20.5	28.4	27.7	72.3
1942–44	100.0	81.6	65.3	16.3	—	18.4	25.8	74.2
1932–44	100.0	75.7	50.9	13.7	11.1	24.3	29.0	71.0
			III. Relation to gross national product (percent)					
1932–36	24.8	18.2	10.0	5.4	2.7	6.7	10.3	14.5
1937–41	36.6	26.2	15.4	3.3	7.5[f]	10.4	10.1	26.3
1942–44	26.7	21.7	17.3	4.3	·	4.9	6.9	19.7
1932–44	30.1	22.8	15.3	4.1	3.3[g]	7.3	8.7	21.4

[a]Excluding military expenditures in 1941.   [b]1937–40.   [c]Excluding military expenditures for 1941.   [d]Excluding military expenditures from 1941 on.   [e]1932–40.   [f]10.3 percent if national product of 1937–40 is used as divisor.
[g]7.3 percent if national product of 1932–40 is used as divisor.

SOURCES OF LINE I: *JEG,* pp. 290, 296, for cols. 2–5 and 7; Fujino, 1975, p. 191, to 1940, and *HYS,* p. 48, for 1941–44 for col. 6.

increasing share of total civilian capital expenditures, the rise particularly pronounced for equipment expenditures.

b. Saving

The total net saving rate averaged, as table 5–7 shows, one-eighth for the period as a whole and was highest in the boom years 1937–41 with one-sixth but below one-tenth in the first subperiod, which was still affected by the depression, and in the war years 1942–44. In view of the weakness of the statistics and the conceptual difficulties of measuring net saving in a war or near-war situation, this finding, as well as the other interpretations of the same set of statistics, must be treated with great caution.[18]

The war and the preparation for it produced radical changes in the trend of saving of the main sectors and in their contribution to total net national saving. Although both the absolute volume of net saving of the personal and corporate business sectors and their saving ratios increased sharply, in the case of the personal sector from about 8 percent of disposable income in 1932–36 to nearly one-fourth in 1937–41 and to more than one-third in 1942–44, most of the increase, and in the 1942–44 period all of it, was offset by the growing dissaving of the government civilian sector.

For personal saving it is again necessary to compare the results of the residual and the synthetic method. The relevant estimates are shown in table 5–8. The synthetic estimates are far

18. As in the preceding period, the sum of private and government saving (table 5–7) is below the conceptually equal sum of net fixed capital formation, inventory investment, and foreign balance (tables 5–6 and 5–1), but this time the difference is disturbingly large and the reason for it is not evident. The difference would disappear, at least for the 1930s, if it could be assumed that the estimates of saving do not include saving corresponding to inventory investment.

TABLE 5-7. Saving, 1932–1944

	Total net saving (1)	Private saving			Government saving		
		Total (2)	Corporate (3)	Other (4)	Total (5)	Civilian (6)	Military (7)
		I. Amounts (¥ bill.)					
1932–36	6.65	5.78	1.30	4.48	0.87	−1.21	2.08
1937–41	27.47ᵃ	31.74	4.80	26.94	−4.27	−15.35	11.08ᵇ
1942–44	18.04ᶜ	53.30	7.68	45.62	−35.26	−35.26	·
1932–44	52.16ᵈ	90.82	13.78	77.04	−38.66	−51.82	13.16ᵉ
		II. Distribution (percent)					
1932–36	100.0	86.9	19.5	67.4	13.1	−18.2	31.3
1937–41	100.0	115.5	17.5	98.1	−15.5	−55.9	40.3
1942–44	100.0	295.5	42.6	252.9	−195.5	−195.5	·
1932–44	100.0	174.1	26.4	147.7	−74.1	−99.3	25.2
		III. Relation to gross national product (percent)					
1932–36	8.6	7.5	1.7	5.8	1.1	−1.6	2.7
1937–41	16.4	18.9	2.9	16.1	−2.6	−9.2	6.6ᶠ
1942–44	9.4	27.7	4.0	23.7	−18.3	−18.3	·
1932–44	11.9	20.7	3.2	17.6	−8.8	−11.8	3.0ᵍ

ᵃExcluding military expenditures in 1941.   ᵇ1937–40.   ᶜExcluding military expenditures.   ᵈExcluding military expenditures from 1941 on.   ᵉ1932–40.   ᶠ9.0 percent if national product of 1937–40 is used as denominator.   ᵍ6.6 percent if national product of 1932–40 is used as denominator.
SOURCE OF LINE I: *JEG*, pp. 296–97, except col. 3 for 1932–41 (*HYS*, p. 50).

above the residual figures for all three subperiods, as they were in the 1920s, with the excess amounting to over 80 percent for the entire period and to nearly 70 percent for 1932–41.

Using the synthetic estimate, with great reservation, for the structure of household saving, it appears that for the decade preceding full-scale war activities, but strongly influenced by, first, reflation and then by rearmament and inflation, net real investment less debt increase absorbed only 6 percent of total personal saving. Claims against financial institutions dominated to the extent of three-fourths of the total, one-half thereof, and hence more than one-third of total personal saving, being in the form of deposits with thrift institutions. Currency and deposits (including a substantial proportion of savings deposits with commercial banks) accounted for another one-third of all claims against financial institutions and for nearly one-fourth of all personal saving, ratios substantially higher than those observed in the 1920s, which in part reflect the process of inflation. The importance of bonds and stocks was about the same in both subperiods and fairly similar to that in the 1920s, with government issues predominating among the bonds in contrast to the preceding decade.

There is even for this period no material from household sample surveys that sheds much light on the volume and structure of household saving. Small-scale surveys conducted annually throughout the 1930s indicate for urban worker households a "balance between income and expenditure," (a concept that should probably be interpreted as akin to total financial saving) of 12 percent from 1932 to 1936, with only very small annual changes. This figure lies between ratios of about 8 and 14 percent of disposable income of all households that can be derived from the residual and the synthetic estimates of table 5–8. The ratio then rose rapidly and reached 17 percent in 1937–39, the latest years for which the data are available. The increase in savings deposits alone accounted for slightly more than 6 percent of household income and thus for one-half of the total reported saving in 1934–36 and for 8½ percent, and again one-half of total reported saving of these households, in 1937–39.[19]

19. The absolute figures reported (*HYS*, pp. 356–57) can be compared with the available aggregative data on saving

TABLE 5-8. Residual and Synthetic Estimates of Household Saving, 1932–1944 (Percent)

	1932–36	1937–41	1942–44	1932–41	1932–44
I. Residual estimate, ¥ bill.	4.5	26.9	45.6	31.4	77.0
II. Synthetic estimate, ¥ bill.[a]	8.2	44.5	88.6	52.7	141.3
Synthetic estimate, percent	100	100	100	100	100
1. Net residential construction	7	2	1	3	2
2. Net agricultural investment	12	4	3	5	4
3. Claims against financial institutions	79	74	79	75	78
4. Securities					
a. Government bonds[b]	13	7	8	8	8
b. Corporate bonds[b]	1	3	3	3	3
c. Corporate stock	16	13	5	13	8
5. Home mortgage debt	4	1	1	2	1
6. Other consumer debt[c]	2	0	0	0	0
7. Farm debt	21	2	0	5	2

[a]Sum of lines 1–4 less sum of lines 5–7.   [b]Domestic securities only.   [c]Only policy loans.

SOURCES: Line I: Table 5-6.   Line II: As in table 4-6; line II-1, *HYS*, p. 48.

3. THE DEVELOPMENT OF FINANCIAL INSTITUTIONS

a. The Main Types of Institutions

(i) THE BANK OF JAPAN. Throughout this period the Bank of Japan expanded its assets and liabilities in the service of, first, the policy of reflation that followed the abandonment of the gold standard and then the financing of rearmament, quasi war, and full-scale war.

The tempo of expansion remained relatively slow from 1932 through 1936. In these five years total assets increased by 25 percent, or on the average of a little less than 5 percent a year, considerably below the expansion of national product, which proceeded at the rate of 8 percent a year. The share of the bank in the assets of all financial institutions remained virtually unchanged at about 5½ percent. The only component of assets that increased considerably were government securities, holdings of which rose from ¥ 260 to ¥ 830 mill., or by 26 percent a year, the bank's contribution to financing the government deficits resulting from reflation and rearmament. This increase was paralleled in amount by an expansion in the volume of bank notes issued from ¥ 1,330 to ¥ 1,865 mill., or by nearly 7 percent a year.[20]

Expansion accelerated rapidly in the following five years. The total assets of the bank increased from ¥ 2.5 bill. to ¥ 7.7 bill., or by 25 percent a year, slightly outstripping the expansion of national product at a rate of 20 percent a year. Similarly, the bank's assets

---

deposits. Assuming an average number of urban households of 10 million, the increase in saving deposits would be fully ¥ 3 bill. for the five years 1932 through 1936 and about another good ¥ 3 bill. for the three years 1937–39. The increase in deposits with savings banks and the Post Office Saving System during these two periods was about ¥ 1.1. bill. and ¥ 4.3 bill., respectively. However, because part of urban households saving deposits were kept with commercial banks, much of the increase in their time and saving deposits (¥ 2.2 bill. and ¥ 5.4 bill., respectively) should be taken into account. This would yield totals of at most ¥ 3.3 bill. and ¥ 9.7 bill. for the two periods, figures that would accommodate the blown-up sample figures for the 1932–36 period but would exceed them greatly for 1937–39. Another difficulty is that the aggregative figure for 1937–39 is about three times as large as that for 1932–36, whereas the sample total is about the same for the two periods. On the other hand, the ratio of the increase in saving deposits to total household surplus of about one-half is substantially higher than that of about one-third indicated for all households by the synthetic method, a relationship between the two measures that one would expect, given the greater likelihood of accurate reporting of saving deposits than most other forms of household saving.

20. *HYS*, pp. 192–93.

fully ¥ 5 bill. in the three years 1942 to 1944, whereas other lendings expanded by about ¥ 8 bill. As a result, the bank's share in total government debt declined from 13 to 7 percent.

All of the increase in assets, and indeed more than that, is attributable to the bank's purchases of government securities, holdings of which jumped from ¥ 0.8 bill. in 1936 to ¥ 5.3 bill. in 1941, when they constituted more than two-thirds of the bank's total assets against only one-third five years earlier and one-eighth in 1931, an indication of how completely the bank had become the engine that was directly financing the government's war-connected deficits. Notwithstanding the rapid expansion of its holdings, the bank in 1941 owned only one-eighth of the government's total debt, compared with 6 percent in 1936 and less than 4 percent in 1931. The expansion was reflected primarily in a rise in the note issue from ¥ 1.9 bill. to ¥ 6.0 bill., or by 26 percent a year, considerably more than the rise of national product.

Acceleration of expansion continued during the period of full-scale war. In the three years ending with 1944 the bank's assets rose by more than three times from below ¥ 8 bill. to ¥ 26 bill., or at an average of nearly 50 percent a year, which was far above the rate of increase in national product of 18 percent a year on the basis of annual figures. The bank again expanded much more rapidly than most other financial institutions so that its share in total institutional assets increased further, from 6½ percent in 1941 to more than 8 percent in 1944, the highest level since 1925. In this period, however, most of the expansion of assets took the form of lending to the banking system and business, all with the ultimate aim of financing war-connected activities. Thus holdings of government securities and loans to the government increased by only fully ¥ 5 bill. in the three years 1942 to 1944, whereas other lendings expanded by about ¥ 8 bill. As a result, the bank's share in total government debt declined from 13 to 7 percent.

Reflecting the passive attitude of the bank throughout this period, its discount rate on commercial loans remained at 3.3 percent from the spring of 1936 on, having been reduced in five steps from the high of 6.6 percent prevailing from November 1931 to March 1932.

During the 1930s the role of the Yokohama Specie Bank as the foreign arm of both the Bank of Japan and the Ministry of Finance appears to have declined. This changed as the area controlled militarily by Japan expanded and the Yokohama Specie Bank became the government's financial agent in the occupied areas. This new role probably explains the extraordinary expansion of the bank's loans and government deposits during the war. Thus lendings increased from ¥ 1.6 bill. in 1941 to ¥ 48 bill. in 1944 and ¥ 108 bill. in 1945, whereas government deposits and deposits with the bank's overseas branches shot up from ¥ 2.1 bill. in 1941 to ¥ 32 bill. in 1944 and to ¥ 261 bill. in 1945.[21] Practically all of these assets and liabilities were wiped out when the bank was liquidated by the occupation forces and reemerged on a more modest scale as the Bank of Tokyo, the only bank organized under the Foreign Exchange Bank Law.

ii COMMERCIAL BANKS. During this period the commercial banking system, like the Bank of Japan, became more and more an engine of inflation, fueled by increasing government deficits, first in an attempt to move the economy out of the state of depression and underemployment and then to finance military and supporting activities. In the process the banks increasingly lost the possibility of determining their own lending or liquidity policies and became executors of government instructions.

The expansion of the banking system's assets started in 1933, but through 1937 it remained moderate by Japanese standards, averaging only 6 percent a year. Expansion sharply accelerated in the following four years, until the start of full-scale war, to an average of 22 percent and continued at the same speed throughout 1942–44. At that time assets were more than four times as large as they had been in 1936. Notwithstanding the apparently rapid increase, the assets of the commercial banking system bore about the same relation to national product at the end of the period as at the beginning, being at the end of both 1931 and 1944 slightly in excess of one year's national product. Until 1941 the share of commercial banks in the assets of all

21. *HYS*, p. 207.

financial institutions remained in the neighborhood of two-fifths. The considerable decline shown in the statistics for 1942–45, resulting mainly from the extraordinary expansion of the assets of the Yokohama Specie Bank, is of little economic relevance for developments in Japan proper.

Although loans and discounts remained the largest category of assets, their share in total assets (excluding interoffice accounts) declined from about 55 percent in 1931 to 50 percent in 1937 and to 45 percent in 1941 to recover to 50 percent in 1944.[22] The character of the loans changed, of course, with the financing of war-connected production increasingly encroaching on the traditional financing of light industries and domestic and foreign trade. The effects of rearmament and war are most obvious in the increasing share of securities of the central government, from about one-tenth in 1931 to one-sixth in 1937, one-fourth in 1941, and one-third in 1944. The proportion of central government domestic securities held by the commercial banks, however, stayed in the neighborhood of fully one-fifth throughout the period. Other securities, mainly local government and corporate bonds, absorbed about 15 percent of assets during the 1930s, but their share declined to 10 percent by 1944. Among these, the securities of government-sponsored, war-connected issues predominated. The book value of corporate stock held kept its small share of fully 2 percent of assets as well as of the par value of total stock outstanding until 1941. The share of own funds continued to decline, as is to be expected in an inflationary expansion of assets, falling from more than one-fifth of deposits in 1931 and 1937 to less than one-tenth in 1941 and to about 5 percent in 1944.

The effect of the period's inflation is also evident in the change in the structure of deposits, although the main changes occurred during the war years and the statistics[23] may exaggerate the economically relevant changes that did occur. From 1932 through 1941 "current" deposits, which may be regarded as part of the money supply, rose slowly from 12 to 17 percent of total deposits but fell back to 12 percent in 1944. The share of "ordinary" deposits kept close to 20 percent until 1942 and rose to 26 percent in 1944. Although "notice" deposits increased from 6 percent of deposits in 1931–36 to 11 percent in 1942, they had almost disappeared by the end of the war. "Time" deposits, finally, accounted for nearly three-fifths of the total from 1931 to 1936 but then declined to one-half in 1941–42. They fell to one-third of the total at the end of the war, reflecting the rapid increase of "other" (mainly government) deposits to nearly 30 percent. What proportion of deposits represented part of advances retained in borrowers' deposit accounts (so-called *buzumi* deposits) and whether and how the proportion changed over the period does not seem to be known.

The process of concentration proceeded throughout the 1930s and accelerated during the war, being fostered by the government and becoming practically compulsory during the second half of the period, as the government felt that the financing of rearmament and war could be more efficiently handled by a smaller number of large banks, which could be more easily controlled by the government. Thus the number of commercial banks declined from nearly 700 in 1931 to not much more than 400 in 1936 and to less than 200 in 1941 to be reduced by 1944 to 72. At that point the number of banks had been cut by 85 percent in one decade and by about 95 percent within two decades, a speed of concentration in commercial banking probably unmatched anywhere. The shrinkage in the network of branches continued, although naturally at a much slower pace. From about 4,500 in 1931 the number of branches declined to about 3,600 in 1936, remained around that level through 1942, and was then only slightly reduced to not much more than 3,100 at the end of the war. Thus the total assets per bank doubled from ¥ 22 mill. in 1931 to ¥ 44 mill. in 1936, and then shot up to ¥ 236 mill. in 1941 and to ¥ 1,150 mill. in 1944. Assets per office rose less rapidly but still very substantially, from less than ¥ 3 mill. in 1931 to ¥ 4½ mill. in 1936, to more than ¥ 11 mill. in 1941, and to ¥ 24 mill. in 1944, all

22. *ESJ*, 1961, pp. 55 ff.
23. Cf. *ESJ*, 1961, pp. 60 and 66.

increases well ahead of the rise in the price level. In real terms the assets of the average office were more than three times as large in 1941 as a decade earlier.

As in the preceding period, the share of city banks increased at the expense of local banks, namely, from one-half in 1934 to nearly two-thirds in 1945. Similarly, the share of the Big Four (Mitsui and Dai Ichi having combined to form Teikoku) in total bank deposits rose from 37 percent in 1930 to nearly one-half of the total in 1945.[24]

(iii) THRIFT INSTITUTIONS. During the first half of the 1930s, thrift institutions (excluding the Deposit Bureau) grew slowly, from 1931 to 1936 at not much more than 5 percent a year, but the rate of growth accelerated sharply, as did that of other financial institutions and national product, during the second half of the decade and during World War II. From 1936 to 1941 the annual growth rate of assets averaged more than 20 percent, and for the war years 1942–44 it shot up to 40 percent.[25] Although hardly above the expansion rates of all financial institutions, near the end of the period they were much above the growth rate of national product. As a result, the share of thrift institutions in the assets of all financial institutions remained in the neighborhood of one-fourth, whereas the ratio of thrift institutions' assets to national product rose from 60 percent in 1931 to nearly 70 percent a decade later, after having dipped in 1936 to 60 percent, and increased further to more than 110 percent in 1944. There is no doubt that from the mid-1930s on the expansion of the assets of thrift institutions, essentially reflecting the inflow of household deposits, was extraordinarily large, in part as a result of the unavailability of consumer goods and forced saving. As a result, deposits in thrift institutions rose from 45 percent of personal disposable income in 1936 to about 140 percent in 1944.

Although all types of thrift institutions grew rapidly, if measured by assets in current prices, there were substantial differences among the various types. The slowest rates of growth between 1931 and 1944 were shown by trust accounts (11 percent) and savings banks (15 percent) because most of them were transformed into commercial banks in the early 1930s. Postal saving deposits, as well as the assets of the primary urban and rural credit cooperatives, grew at average rates of more than 20 percent. Expansion was most rapid for the central organizations of cooperatives, as the primary cooperatives to an increasing degree redeposited the funds they received with these institutions instead of investing them in loans or securities.

The funds of the thrift institutions were made available to an increasing extent to the government and to war-related production as the period proceeded. By 1944 central government securities accounted for nearly two-thirds of the assets of savings banks, more than one-fourth of those of urban credit cooperatives, and nearly one-half of those of the Central Bank of Agricultural Cooperatives, which administered most of the funds collected by local and prefectural agricultural credit cooperatives. Most of the remaining funds were made available indirectly to the government, mainly through the intermediation of the Deposit Bureau. The only important funds of thrift institutions that might be regarded as not being fairly closely related to the war effort were the loans made by rural credit cooperatives to farmers, which in 1944 represented only about 2 percent of the total assets of all primary thrift institutions, as well as some relatively small holdings of securities carried over from the early 1930s.

During this period the Deposit Bureau, which has not been included in the preceding statistics, became increasingly a conduit for investment in government securities of funds provided to the extent of between two-thirds and three-fourths by the postal saving system. Government securities accounted for at least four-fifths of the bureau's assets from the mid-1930s on, compared with less than one-half in 1931. Between 1931 and 1941 the bureau absorbed nearly one-fourth of the total net issues of government securities, and the proportion increased to nearly one-third in 1942–44.

24. Cf. table 3–9.

25. These rates overstate the growth in deposits because of the increasing layering within the cooperative credit system.

(iv) INSURANCE ORGANIZATIONS. Until the middle 1930s insurance organizations continued to expand more rapidly than either the entirety of financial organizations or the economy as a whole. As a result, the share of the assets of insurance organizations in total assets of all financial organizations increased between 1931 and 1936 from less than 8 to 10 percent, whereas the relation of their assets to gross national product advanced from 20 to 26 percent. From then on, however, life insurance organizations, accounting throughout the period for more than five-sixths of the firms in the entire insurance sector, lost in relative importance as is usual in inflationary periods. By 1944 the share of insurance organizations in the assets of all financial organizations had fallen below 6 percent, the relationship that had prevailed in the late 1920s, although the ratio of their assets to national product stayed at the level of one-fourth, which had been reached in the mid-1930s. The Post Office life insurance organization did slightly better in both respects than private life insurance companies, accounting in 1944 for slightly more than one-fourth of the assets of all life insurance organizations, compared with a little more than one-fifth in 1931.

Although private insurance companies, like most other financial institutions, had to increase the proportion of central government bonds in their assets, their share continued moderate, rising from 6 percent in 1931 to 20 percent in 1941 and fully 30 percent in 1944. Thus insurance companies throughout the period remained important buyers of corporate securities. Between 1931 and 1944 their holdings of corporate bonds and stocks increased by ¥ 0.6 bill. and ¥ 2.2 bill., respectively, which in the case of stocks represents a substantial fraction of the total public issues of the period. Even in 1944 corporate securities accounted for nearly one-third, and loans for another one-eighth, of the total assets of private insurance companies.

Although the Post Office life insurance organization continued to make the bulk of its funds available to the government directly or indirectly, it also acquired a substantial amount of corporate bonds, probably mainly of government-owned or -sponsored companies, which in 1944 accounted for nearly one-fifth of its total assets.

The concentration movement, which characterized many types of financial institutions during this period, is visible in a reduction of the number of life insurance companies in operation from 40 in 1931 to 21 in 1944 and of non-life companies from 51 to 17. The proportion of private insurance under zaibatsu control is likely to have increased substantially.

(v) LONG-TERM CREDIT BANKS. Throughout most of the 1930s long-term credit banks stagnated, their assets increasing only from ¥ 3.3 bill. in 1931 to ¥ 3.9 bill. in 1938 and their share in the assets of all financial institutions declined from 8½ to 6½ percent. The situation changed when the government used the banks, particularly the Industrial Bank, to participate in the financing of war-related industries in Japan and in the controlled areas. Assets then increased sharply to about ¥ 24 bill. in 1944, or 8 percent of the assets of all financial institutions.

b. Financial Institutions as a Whole

(i) CHANGES IN THE DISTRIBUTION OF ASSETS AMONG INSTITUTIONS. Table 5–9 shows the average growth rate of total reported assets of each of the fourteen groups of financial institutions for each of the three subperiods and for the period as a whole, as well as the share of each group in the total assets of all financial institutions, changes in the shares reflecting differences in the growth rates.

During the first subperiod the trends observed during the 1920s were still in force and the average rate of growth was not much more than that of the preceding decade. Thrift institutions and life insurance organizations grew considerably more rapidly than the banking system, and the shares of the banking system and the long-term credit banks declined slightly.

In the second subperiod and particularly in the third, the effects of rapid inflation became evident. Now thrift institutions and life insurance organizations grew only at about the same rate as the banking system, but the share of life insurance organizations declined rather sharply from

TABLE 5-9. Growth and Distribution of Assets of Financial Institutions, 1931–1944 (Percent)

	Annual growth rate				Distribution				Relation to national product			
	1932–36 (1)	1937–41 (2)	1942–44 (3)	1931–44 (4)	1931 (5)	1936 (6)	1941 (7)	1944 (8)	1931 (9)	1936 (10)	1941 (11)	1944 (12)
1. Bank of Japan	4.8	25.2	47.8	21.3	5.6	5.4	6.6	8.3	14.3	12.2	15.6	18.9
2. Yokohama Specie Bank	2.9	25.2	83.4	26.9	3.1	3.3	3.4	8.1	7.8	7.4	8.3	18.4
3. Commercial banks	4.6	18.7	23.4	14.1	42.2	40.4	37.6	27.4	107.9	90.7	88.6	62.5
4. Bank trust accounts	6.4	11.4	21.4	11.2	4.6	4.8	3.4	2.2	11.9	10.9	7.8	5.0
5. Savings banks	2.4	24.0	19.3	14.6	4.8	4.2	4.8	3.4	12.3	9.4	11.4	7.7
6. Post Office Saving System	6.1	23.4	44.6	20.8	7.5	7.7	8.8	10.3	19.2	17.4	20.6	23.4
7. Deposit Bureau	7.3	23.8	45.2	21.6	9.7	10.6	12.2	14.5	24.9	23.8	28.8	33.1
8. Mutual loan companies	7.4	41.0	26.2	23.8	0.4	0.4	1.0	0.8	1.1	1.0	2.4	1.7
9. Credit cooperatives	6.3	28.0	53.1	24.2	5.9	5.9	8.0	11.2	14.6	13.3	19.0	25.6
10. Long-term credit banks	0.4	17.5	47.8	16.6	8.5	7.2	6.3	8.0	23.4	16.1	14.9	18.1
11. Life insurance companies	10.7	15.6	23.2	15.4	4.8	6.1	5.0	3.6	12.2	13.7	11.8	8.3
12. Other insurance companies	5.1	12.2	28.7	13.0	1.1	1.1	0.8	0.7	3.0	2.5	1.9	1.5
13. Post Office life insurance	15.7	14.7	25.4	17.5	1.7	2.7	2.1	1.6	4.4	6.0	5.0	3.7
14. People's Bank	—	—	19.3	—	—	—	0.1	0.1	—	—	0.3	0.2
15. All financial institutions	5.5	20.4	37.1	17.9	100.0	100.0	100.0	100.0	256.9	224.5	236.3	219.8

SOURCE: As in table 3-11.

10 percent in 1936 to 6 percent in 1944. The extraordinarily rapid expansion of the assets of the Yokohama Specie Bank in the government's service in the occupied area casts some doubt on the relevance of the changes in shares between 1941 and 1944.

(ii) DISTRIBUTION BY TYPES OF ASSETS. Changes in the distribution of assets were fairly radical and reflected the increasing importance of military production and government deficits. The relevant figures, unfortunately limited to very broad asset categories, are shown for all financial institutions together in table 5–10.

Excluding interfinancial assets, which continued to account for approximately 30 percent of total reported assets (except in 1944 when the ratio fell to 15 percent), developments were characterized by the sharp and rapid decline in the share of loans and discounts from nearly two-thirds in 1930 to one-half in 1935 and to around two-fifths in 1940 and 1944. More striking, the increase in loans and discounts represented only a little more than one-third of the expansion of total assets (excluding interfinancial assets) from 1931 through 1944, compared with a share of about three-fifths in the 1920s.

Most of this decline is accounted for by the trebling of the share of central government securities from 15 percent in 1930 to 45 percent in 1944. For the period as a whole, nearly one-half of the total increase in assets of financial institutions was made available directly to the government in the form of net purchases of central government securities. The net purchases of other securities absorbed about one-seventh of the total increase in assets and came to constitute nearly one-third of total assets in 1940 (in both cases excluding interfinancial assets), compared with not much more than one-fifth in 1930. Although their share declined sharply in the years of full-scale war, most of them may be regarded as having indirectly financed government and military activities.

(iii) THE SHARE OF FINANCIAL INSTITUTIONS IN SECURITIES OUTSTANDING. Notwithstanding the sharp increase of the holdings of government securities by financial institutions in absolute amounts and in relation of their total assets, the share of these holdings in central government securities outstanding did not show a sharp or continuous trend, although it did remain dominant throughout the period. The share increased from less than two-thirds in 1930 to nearly four-fifths in 1940 but then declined to less than three-fifths in 1944 as the government managed during the war years to place large amounts of its bonds with private nonfinancial sectors, particularly

TABLE 5-10. Rate of Increase and Distribution of Main Types of Assets
of Financial Institutions, 1931–1944

	1931–35	1936–40	1931–40	1941–44
	I. Rate of increase (percent per year)			
Cash and deposits	−2.0	17.3	7.2	33.0
Loans and discounts	−1.0	13.4	5.8	29.5
Central government securities	14.7	27.9	21.1	39.2
Other securities	8.0	13.3	10.6	23.8
Other assets	6.6	17.3	11.8	−16.3
Total assets[a]	3.9	17.5	10.5	25.8
	II. Share in increase in total assets (percent)[a]			
Cash and deposits	−5.4	8.6	6.9	12.3
Loans and discounts	−10.6	24.2	19.9	34.3
Central government securities	47.5	32.7	34.5	46.6
Other securities	34.5	13.2	15.8	14.1
Other assets	34.0	21.3	22.9	−7.3
Total assets[a]	100.0	100.0	100.0	100.0

[a]Excluding interfinancial assets.

SOURCE OF BASIC DATA: Ott, 1960, passim.

households. As a result, financial institutions during the 1930s absorbed about seven-eighths of all net new issues of central government securities, whereas their share was not much in excess of one-half in the 1941–44 period.

In the case of other securities (mostly corporate bonds and bank debentures), the increase in the holdings of financial institutions resulted in a substantial sustained rise in the proportion of all such securities outstanding. Thus financial institutions in 1944 held about one-half of all Japanese securities other than those of the central government, compared with only one-fifth in 1930 and one-third in 1935. Although the proportion of corporate stocks in the portfolios of financial institutions almost doubled, assuming book values equal to par values, it did not substantially exceed one-tenth even in the 1940s. In the case of corporate bonds and bank debentures, the holdings of financial institutions seem to have been close to 100 percent by the end of the war.

(iv) THE ISSUE RATIO OF FINANCIAL INSTITUTIONS. In the period from the Great Depression to the mid-1930s, which can still be regarded as part of the peacetime economic history of Japan, the new issue ratio of financial institutions of 12 percent, roughly eliminating interfinancial issues, was, as table 4–15 shows, already considerably more than the 1920s ratio of less than 7 percent. Of the three main components, non-monetary deposits and life insurance equities, which appear to be attributable to households, were, with more than 7 percent of national product, considerably above the 1920s level of 5 percent. This is not incompatible with the fact that real personal consumption per head was only slightly higher in 1932–36 than it had been in 1922–31 but indicates, rather, an increase in the ratio of household saving through financial institutions to personal disposable income. The difference was even larger, relatively, for the two other components, the money issue ratio and the residual.

The figures for the 1937–41 period reflect the rapid inflation of the incomes and prices then prevailing in combination with a repression of consumption. Whether the available statistics, which put the adjusted net new issue ratio at one-third for 1937–41, exaggerate the increase over the early 1930s is difficult to determine in view of the absence of most of the statistics against which such an estimate would have to be evaluated. There is no reason for doubt, however, that this period's ratio was actually considerably higher than that of the preceding five years. The money issue ratio rose substantially, absolutely as well as in proportion to the total ratio, and the ratio of household non-monetary claims against financial institutions to national product increased from 7 to 17 percent, although its contribution to the total ratio declined from fully three-fifths to not much more than one-half. The "residual" increased from 3½ to 9 percent but stayed at nearly three-tenths of the aggregate ratio.

There is little doubt that the tendencies visible in the 1937–41 period were accentuated in the war years of 1942–44. The increase of currency in circulation alone in the three years 1942–44, as reported in the official statistics,[26] was equal to 6 percent of gross national product and the increase in non-monetary household claims against financial institutions to another 30 percent. However, many of the basic statistics for that period, including the estimates of national product, are very unreliable and affected by double counting, which cannot be satisfactorily eliminated. In such a confused situation, the calculations become problematical.

4. FINANCING THE MAIN NONFINANCIAL SECTORS

a. Nonfinancial Business Enterprises

From the mid-1930s, and at the latest from about 1937 on, Japanese business, particularly the manufacturing sector, became more and more closely tied to production for rearmament and war and progressively lost control over its operations, real and financial, to governmental

26. *HYS*, p. 167.

TABLE 5-11. New Issue Ratios of Main Types of Financial Institutions, 1932–1944
(Percent of Gross National Product)

	1932–36	1937–41	1942–44	1932–44
1. Bank of Japan	0.68	3.11	8.94	5.25
2. Yokohama Specie Bank	0.56	1.42	10.59	5.31
3. Commercial banks	4.82	15.10	20.08	15.47
4. Savings banks	0.28	2.22	2.32	1.92
5. Post Office Saving System	1.18	3.98	10.78	6.48
6. Trust banks	0.77	0.96	1.40	1.12
7. Mutual loan banks	0.08	0.56	0.60	0.49
8. Credit cooperatives	0.86	3.98	12.68	7.26
9. Deposit Bureau	1.88	5.58	15.28	9.19
10. Long-term credit banks	0.36	2.44	8.61	4.79
11. People's Bank	—	0.09	0.05	0.06
12. Life insurance companies	1.46	1.80	2.64	2.11
13. Other insurance companies	0.15	0.26	0.54	0.36
14. Post Office life insurance	0.82	0.73	1.24	0.97
15. All institutions	13.90	42.22	95.76	60.78

SOURCES OF BASIC DATA: Same as for tables 3-11 and 5-1.

bureaus and agencies. Because direct financing by the government was relatively rare, because the government was able to attain its objectives by directives to financial institutions, and because the statistics do not distinguish between nominally private capital formation and borrowing for civilian and military purposes, this radical change in the character of sources and uses of funds is not evident in the very condensed sources-and-uses-of-funds statement of large nonfinancial enterprises shown in table 5–12.

The first subperiod, 1932–36, was still showing signs of the depression in the relatively low level of capital expenditures of 1.6 percent of gross national product, the reduction of long-term indebtedness, and the high internal financing ratio, which is exaggerated because trade credit is omitted from sources and uses sides but understated because fixed capital expenditures are apparently entered on a net basis. Capital expenditures expanded rapidly after the mid-1930s not only in nominal terms but also after allowance for the rise in prices to reach 2 percent of national product. Although corporate saving increased substantially, it could not keep up with the increase in capital expenditures and inventory investment. The difference was made up primarily by borrowing from financial institutions, although external financing through the issuance of corporate stocks and bonds, the latter absorbed predominantly by financial institutions, increased sharply, from 2 to more than 3½ percent of national product.

Although the corporations covered by table 5–12 account for only about one-third of the universe of nonfinancial corporations, to judge by their capital (net worth plus bonds), the larger group of all nonfinancial enterprises shows a similar financing picture. In 1932–36, still under the influence of the depression, more than three-fifths of financing was internal, and all external funds came from sales of corporate stock, with net borrowings from the Deposit Bureau and nonbank financial institutions being offset by net reductions in bank debt and debentures outstanding. For the rest of the period, when total funds raised increased from less than one-tenth to considerably more than one-fourth of national product, own funds could satisfy less than one-third of needs and sales of corporate stock less than one-fourth. Banks provided four-fifths of all debt financing and two-fifths of all external funds (table 5–13).

Although comprehensive data are unavailable, the growth of the zaibatsu seems to have decelerated in the mid-1930s, more, however, as a result of conscious policy to meet increasing opposition from small business, left-wing political groups, and parts of the military than for

TABLE 5-12. Sources and Uses of Funds of (287 to 331) Large Industrial Corporations, 1932–1941

	Amounts (¥ bill.)		Distribution (percent)		Relation to gross national product (percent)	
	1932–36 (1)	1937–41 (2)	1932–36 (3)	1937–41 (4)	1932–36 (5)	1937–41 (6)
1. Paid-in capital	1.61	4.69	46	32	2.08	2.80
2. Reserves	0.95	2.54	27	17	1.22	1.52
3. Corporate bonds	−0.08	1.48	−2	10	−0.10	0.88
4. Other liabilities	1.05	6.16	30	41	1.35	3.68
5. Fixed assets	1.23	3.53	35	24	1.59	2.11
6. Inventories	0.76	4.36	22	29	0.98	2.60
7. Other current assets	1.45	8.60	41	58	1.87	5.13
8. Other items, net	0.09	−1.62	3	−10	0.12	−0.97
9. Total sources and uses	3.53	14.87	100	100	4.55	8.87

SOURCE OF COLS. 1 AND 2: *HYS*, pp. 336–37.

economic reasons.[27] The same considerations impelled some of the zaibatsu to offer shares in a few of the large enterprises that they controlled to the public. The sale of part of Mitsui's holdings in Oji Paper Company, the dominating firm in that industry, and of some of the shares in three large Mitsubishi companies were probably the outstanding cases of this aspect of the zaibatsu appeasement policy.

The situation was reversed, or more appropriately the previous trend continued and accelerated, when the government decided on a policy of far-reaching industrial mergers to create larger units. The zaibatsu, not only the four old combines but also a number of newer and smaller groups, were the main beneficiaries of this policy. As a result, at the end of the war ten combines controlled about one-third of Japanese business. The four big zaibatsu at the time owned almost one-fourth of the paid-in capital of all corporations, and six lesser zaibatsu owned another one-tenth.[28] Mitsui and Mitsubishi each accounted for about one-twelfth of the total. The share of the zaibatsu was particularly high in finance, shipping, and heavy industry. The Big Four owned about one-half of the capital of all banks and all insurance companies and nearly seven-eighths of that of all trust companies. The other six zaibatsu contributed another one-tenth in insurance but had hardly anything in banks and trust companies. In the heavy industries the Big Four controlled about one-third of the capital, with the other six combined adding another one-sixth. The interest of the zaibatsu was much smaller in light industries, about one-tenth for the leading four combines and one-sixth for all ten of them, and negligible in public utilities; they had substantial interest, however, in commerce and trade, about one-fifth for the ten combines, and dominated the shipping industry, the Big Four owning three-fifths of the capital. These developments are reflected in the movements of the ratio between the estimated assets of the Big Four zaibatsu and the fixed and current assets of all nonfinancial corporations, which declined from 8½ percent in 1930 to 7½ percent in 1936 but exceeded 12 percent in 1942.[29]

It is likely that the nonfinancial enterprises belonging to the Big Four received most of their external funds from or through the banks, trust companies, and insurance companies that belonged to the group and that they accounted for a substantial proportion of total funds made available by these financial institutions. Statistical material that would permit a quantification of

27. Cf. Tiedemann, particularly pp. 290 ff.

28. Hadley, p. 45.

29. Assets of big four zaibatsu from Cohen, 1949 (read off from chart, p. 508); fixed and current assets of all financial corporations from *HYS*, pp. 334–35. The level of the ratio appears low, but movements may be acceptable.

TABLE 5-13. Sources of Funds of Nonfinancial Enterprises, 1932–1944 (Percent)

	1932–36	1937–41	1942–44	1932–44
Corporate stock	38.3	29.1	17.5	23.8
Debentures	−1.2	6.5	8.3	6.8
Borrowing from				
Banks	−1.3	27.9	50.2	36.9
Deposit Bureau	1.2	0.3	1.7	1.1
Other financial institutions	4.2	5.2	−5.6	−0.5
All external funds	38.2	69.0	72.1	68.2
Own funds	61.8	31.0	27.9	31.8
All funds				
Percent	100.0	100.0	100.0	100.0
¥ bill.	8.9	44.8	58.1	111.9
Percent of national product	11.5	26.8	30.2	25.6

SOURCE OF BASIC DATA: *HYS*, p. 248.

these relationships, which are crucial to an evaluation of the role of closed-circuit financing in the prewar financial structure of Japan and for a judgment about changes over the 1920s and 1930s, apparently is not available.

b. The Government

Two aspects of the finances of the government in this period are of particular importance for financial development: The size of the deficit, essentially reflecting increasing military and related expenditures, and the methods of financing the deficit, particularly the proportion financed by the banking system. In view of the confused state of government financial statistics, particularly since the late 1930s, it seems best to limit discussion to the increase in the government's debt and its financing.

The absolute increases in government debt, their rate of growth, their relation to national product, and their absorption can be followed in table 5–14. In the reflation period of 1932–36 the average growth rate of the government's debt and its relation to national product were still moderate, with about 9 and 6 percent, respectively, and local governments still accounted for about one-fifth of the total increase. A runaway expansion of central government debt, which started with the China incident of 1937, resulted in an annual rate of 25 percent in 1937–41 and

TABLE 5-14. Government Debt and Its Financing, 1932–1944[a]

	1932–36	1937–41	1942–44	1932–44
1. Increase in debt (¥ bill.)				
a. Central government	4.3	30.4	110.2	144.9
b. Local government	1.1	0.5	0.8	2.4
c. Total	5.4	30.9	111.0	147.3
2. Rate of increase (percent per year)	9.3	25.2	50.5	24.0
3. Relation of increase to national product (percent)	7.0	18.4	57.6	33.6
4. Distribution of central government debt increase (percent)				
a. Banking system	32	36	29	30
b. Other financial institutions	38	44	50	47
c. Others	30	20	21	23

[a]Fiscal years beginning April 1.

SOURCES OF BASIC DATA: Lines 1a and 1b: *HYS*, pp. 159, 162.   Lines 4a–4c: Ott, 1960, passim.

more than 50 percent in the war years of 1942–44. The increase was equal to fully one-sixth of gross national product in 1937–41 and to nearly three-fifths in 1942–44 if the difference between fiscal year figures for debt and calendar year figures for national product are ignored.

Contrary to a common experience during war-connected inflations, the share of the banking system in absorbing the vast increases in government debt remained throughout the period in the neighborhood of one-third. On the other hand, other financial institutions, primarily thrift institutions, directly and through the Deposit Bureau, increased their share in the net new issues of government securities from less than two-fifths in 1932–36 to one-half in 1942–44. A large part of the government's deficit was thus financed in a not immediately inflationary manner by directing the thrift institutions, which were swamped with large amounts of otherwise uninvestable household surpluses, to put these savings at the government's disposal. The government thus had to place only between one-third and one-fifth of the increase in its debt outside the financial system. The absolute amounts involved were large, particularly since the late 1930s, and their ratio to national product was substantial (nearly 4 percent of national product in 1937–41 and about 12 percent in 1942–44), but purchases of government securities by households and to a lesser extent business enterprises had by that time become quasi-compulsory.

c. Agriculture

During the 1930s agriculture continued in the semidepressed condition of the 1920s. Output in 1938–42 was only 6 percent higher and the fixed capital stock 4 percent larger than they had been a decade earlier, whereas the number of gainful workers was 3 percent lower. The level of prices of agricultural products and land rose considerably from the mid-1930s on as did the cost of living of farm families.[30] To judge by the changes in the capital stock, gross and net capital expenditures were at extremely low levels, the latter even becoming negative during the war.[31]

It is not astonishing, therefore, that farm debt increased only moderately, between 1931 and 1937 by about two-fifths.[32] The ratio of agricultural debt to the value of farmland and reproducible assets appears to have remained on the order of one-fourth throughout the 1930s. Although financial institutions seem to have continued to furnish about two-fifths of the total, the loans by agricultural cooperatives stagnated at a level of slightly below ¥ 1 bill.,[33] and their share in total farm debt declined from about one-fifth in 1931 to about one-seventh in 1937 and may not have been above one-tenth in 1941.

The debt-asset ratio of a very small sample of farmers remained around one-tenth from 1931 to 1936 but then declined sharply to less than 4 percent in 1941 and to less than 2 percent in 1944, both the result of a decrease in the amount of debt per household from about ¥ 600 in 1931 to ¥ 300 in 1941 and to an increase in assets from less than ¥ 6,000 in 1931 to ¥ 8,300 in 1941.[34] Assuming a number of farm households of about 6 million, these sample figures correspond to nationwide aggregates of debt of somewhat below ¥ 4 bill. in 1931 and of less than ¥ 2 bill. in 1941. The first of these figures is about two-thirds as large as the overall estimate. The blown-up values of assets are far above the macroeconomic estimates. It is, therefore, doubtful whether much attention should be paid to these data.

d. Households

Residential construction, the main source of the household sector's demand for external funds, is estimated at only ¥ 5.2 bill. for 1932–44,[35] of which about two-thirds may be

---

30. *ELTESJ*, 8:135–36.
31. *ELTESJ*, 3:154–55.
32. Cf. estimates listed in Ott, 1960, p. 123.
33. *HYS*, p. 226.
34. Institute for Developing Economies, *One Hundred Years of Agricultural Statistics in Japan*, pp. 218–19.
35. *ELTESJ*, 1:187.

allocated to nonfarm households, thus equaling about 3½ percent of total gross domestic fixed capital formation and about 0.8 percent of gross national product. The resulting increase in mortgage debt may have been on the order of ¥ 1 bill. to ¥ 2 bill., a quantity entirely negligible, even when augmented by the small increase in policy loans[36] and in consumer credit other than interhousehold accommodations, compared with the fund requirements of the government and of business. This is not astonishing in a period when the household sector as a whole was awash with cash.

5. THE FINANCIAL SUPERSTRUCTURE AS A WHOLE

a. The New Issue Ratios of the Nonfinancial Sectors

Although the ratios (table 5–15) for the three subperiods are not too dissimilar from those observed in the 1920s during the first subperiod of reflation, the effects of rearmament and rapid inflation here too became dominant from the mid-1930s on.

Thus the new issue ratio of all nonfinancial domestic sectors rose from about 18 percent of national product in 1932–36 to nearly 50 percent in 1937–41 and in 1942–44 may have reached the extraordinary level of more than four-fifths, if the available figures are to be believed. This increase was, of course, mainly due to the rapid expansion of the issues of the central government, whose ratio to national product shot up from less than 5 percent in 1932–36 to 18 percent in 1937–41 and finally to nearly 60 percent during the war years. As a result, the central government in 1932–36 supplied only one-fourth of all issues of nonfinancial sectors but nearly two fifths in 1937–41 and as much as one-half in 1942–44.

Issues by the business sector, increasingly producing for the government, also rose sharply, from 10 percent of national product in 1932–36 to more than one-fourth, in 1937–41 and probably also in 1942–44. Among them, borrowings from financial institutions gained in importance, rising to nearly one fifth of total issues in 1937–41 and probably to about one-half in 1942–44. The share of stock declined to fully one-fourth of all issues of the private sectors in 1937–41 from a share of more than two-fifths in 1932–36, very high ratios in historical perspective.

b. The Financial Intermediation Ratio

The relation of the unadjusted new issue ratio of financial institutions to the new issue ratio of the nonfinancial sectors rose nearly three-fourths in 1932–36 to nearly nine-tenths in 1937–41. Although the level of the adjusted ratio is considerably lower, with adjustments for duplication in the ratio for financial institutions becoming increasingly difficult and uncertain from the mid-1930s on, the upward trend is likely to have persisted. For the decade 1932–41 the adjusted ratio may have been in the 70 to 80 percent range, compared with an adjusted ratio for the preceding decade of 60 to 65 percent. This increase in the ratio, which indicates a larger role of financial institutions in the provision of funds to the nonfinancial sectors, is to be expected in an inflationary situation fueled by government deficits.

6. THE NATIONAL BALANCE SHEET

During the 1930s basic national balance sheet relationships derivable from table 4–19 did not change greatly. The financial interrelations ratio advanced from 1.20 to 1.41, whereas the ratio of financial institutions' assets to tangible wealth rose from 0.51 to 0.55. The ratio of the issues of nonfinancial sectors advanced substantially, from below 0.69 to 0.85, partly because of the

36. Policy loans of the Post Office life insurance system increased by only ¥ 14 mill. between 1931 and 1944, although they rose ¥ 82 mill. between 1931 and 1938 to lose practically the entire increase in the following six years. Assuming the same ratio of policy loans to assets to prevail in life insurance companies, the increase in all policy loans between 1931 and 1944 would have been only about ¥ 50 mill.

TABLE 5-15. New Issue Ratios, 1932–1944 (Percent of Gross National Product)

	1932–36	1937–41	1942–44	1932–44
I. Financial institutions				
a. Including interfinancial issues	13.9	42.2	95.8	60.8
b. Excluding interfinancial issues	12.0	33.0	·	·
II. Nonfinancial sectors	18.3	47.6	·	·
1. Central government[a]	4.9	17.6	57.0	32.2
2. Local governments[a]	1.3	0.3	1.8	1.2
3. Business	9.5	28.4	·	·
a. Corporate bonds[a]	−0.1	1.7	3.7	2.2
b. Corporate stock[b]	4.1	7.6	5.3	5.9
c. Other borrowings	0.4	8.8	15.4	10.1
d. Trade credit	5.1	10.3	·	·
4. Others[c]	2.6	1.2	·	·
III. Foreign issues	−0.4	−0.1	·	·
IV. All sectors[d]	29.9	80.5	·	·

[a]Domestic issues only.   [b]Including stock of financial institutions.   [c]Home mortgages and farm debt not supplied by financial institutions.   [d]Ib + II–III.

SOURCES OF BASIC DATA: Line I: Table 5-10.   Line II-1 to 3c: As for table 4-22, lines II-2a, 2b, 2c, and 2g.   Line II-3d: As for table 4-22, line II-2d.   Line II-4: Rough estimates.   Line III: Based on current balance in balance of payments (*ELTESJ*, 1:191).

expansion of government debt, which increased their share in total financial assets from one-tenth to one-seventh; because of the rise in the ratio of financial assets of the nonfinancial sectors from one-sixth to more than one-fifth; and because of the increase in the excess of market over par value of corporate stock. Stocks came to constitute about one-third of the total value of instruments issued by nonfinancial sectors, considerably above the ratio of at least one-fifth or one-fourth obtaining in 1930, 1920, and 1913. For all sectors the market value of stocks represented about one-fifth of all financial instruments in 1940, compared with about one-eighth in 1930, about one-sixth in 1920, and one-eighth in 1913. Equity securities thus constituted in 1940 a considerably larger proportion of the portfolios than a decade earlier in the depths of the depression or a generation earlier in 1913. Both relationships are not unexpected in an inflationary economy that is growing rapidly in real terms. The expansion of financial assets also kept approximately in step with that of national product, the ratio remaining in the neighborhood of six years' income. Details of the distribution of national assets and in their relation to national product in 1930 and of changes in these relationships between 1930 and 1940 can be followed in table 4–20.

No attempt has been made to develop a national balance sheet for 1944 or 1945, when the volume of financial assets was bloated by inflation and the stock of reproducible assets was severely reduced by war damage, making its replacement cost very difficult to calculate.

6 Paradise Regained, 1946–1953

In absolute terms, the basket of commodities and services at the disposal of the average Japanese in 1953—¥ 81,000, or $225 at the exchange rate—although worth considerably more in purchasing power, cannot be regarded as paradisiacal. But it must have seemed so to the average Japanese. The return to a reasonably satisfactory standard of living, only slightly below the previous high point of the mid-1930s, after the terrors of the later phases of the Pacific war and the physical and moral deprivations of the first postwar years, must have appeared to him, indeed, like paradise regained.

In contrast to the other chapters, very little will be said here about the institutional changes in the financial superstructure. Such changes that were important and enduring will be discussed in chapter 7. This chapter, therefore, is limited to a brief description of the changes in the infrastructure from 1946 through 1953 and to an equally brief discussion of the transition from the hyperinflation of the late 1940s to the establishment, via the Dodge and Shoup reforms, of the financial fundaments of the monetary stability and the spectacular growth of the following two decades.

1. THE INFRASTRUCTURE

At the end of 1953 Japan's population was nearly one-fourth larger than it had been in 1936 or 1945, partly the result of the forcible repatriation of several million people who had lived in the former dependencies. The total labor force had grown slightly more rapidly and the work force

TABLE 6-1. Development of Infrastructure, 1945–1953 (1936 = 100)

	1945	1949	1953
1. Population	102.9	116.5	124.0
2. Labor force total	94.5[a]	110.3	126.2
3. Labor force excluding agriculture	104.7[a]	102.7	133.5
4. Cultivated area[b]	93.1[c]	84.5[d]	.
5. Net fixed capital stock before destruction	160.0	—	—
6. Net fixed capital stock after destruction	120.0	140.0	160.0

[a]1944.   [b]Paddy and ordinary fields; 1936 assumed equal to average of 1930 and 1940.   [c]Average of 1940 and 1950.   [d]1950.

Sources of basic data: Lines 1–3: *JEG*, pp. 310–11.   Line 4: *HYS*, p. 18.   Lines 5 and 6: Rough estimates obtained by combination of estimates of net capital stock for 1936 and 1940 in 1934–36 prices (*ELTESJ*, 3:151), capital formation in 1934–36 (*JEG*, p. 293); assumption of net/gross ratio of two-thirds in 1941–45 and three-fifths in 1946–53; and estimate of destruction of one-fourth of structures and equipment (*HYS*, p. 27). Fujino's estimate, according to which stock in 1953 was equal to only 64 percent of 1938 and 52 percent of that of 1940 (1975, pp. 191–92), is difficult to accept.

TABLE 6-2. National Product, Consumption, and Capital Formation, 1934–1936 and 1945–1953

Fiscal year beginning April 1	Current prices (¥ bill.) (1)	Gross national product		Personal consumption per head 1934–36 prices (yen) (4)	Gross capital formation ratio (percent) (5)	Current balance of payments (¥ bill.) (6)
		Constant (1934–36) prices				
		Amount (¥ bill.) (2)	Change (percent) (3)			
1934/36	167	16.67	—	158	19.0	0.16
1945	190	14.80[a]	−11.2	103[b]	.	.
1946	475	10.87	−26.6	90	22.1	−6
1947	1309	11.97	+10.1	95	26.4	7
1948	2665	13.92	+16.3	105	28.2	21
1949	3376	14.47	+4.0	114	24.6	75
1950	3946	16.24	+12.2	121	25.5	171
1951	5442	18.43	+13.5	131	30.6	157
1952	6263	20.45	+11.0	150	26.6	81
1953	7055	21.60	+5.6	167	24.0	−74

[a]Geometric average of values for 1944 and 1946.   [b]Estimated on basis of 50 percent of gross national product, the geometric average of the values for 1944 and 1946.

SOURCES: Col. 1: *ELTESJ*, 1:179, except 1945, which is a very rough estimate based on price and output movements. Cols. 2, 4, and 5: Ibid., pp. 179 and 214.   Col. 6: *HYS*, p. 50, for 1946–51; *ARNIS*, 1976, p. 90 for 1952 and 1953.

TABLE 6-3. Capital Formation and Saving, 1946–1953 (Percent of Gross National Product)

	1946	1948	1953	1946–53
I. Gross capital formation	22.1	18.3	24.0	26.5
1. Residential	2.3	1.8	2.9	2.0
2. Other fixed private	7.8	8.0	12.2	10.6
3. Inventories	6.7	1.6	2.0	7.3
4. Government	5.5	6.9	6.9	6.6
II. Capital consumption allowances	5.1	4.1	7.8	6.0
III. Net capital formation	17.0	14.2	16.1	20.5
IV. Net saving	16.0	11.9	15.1	21.9
1. Personal[a]	1.7	−0.3	5.6	6.2
2. Corporate	−0.2	0.1	3.0	2.7
3. Government	−4.8	11.9	5.7	8.7
4. Net foreign lending	−1.3	0.2	−1.1	1.4
V. Statistical discrepancy	1.0	2.3	1.0	1.4

[a]Residual (line IV minus the sum of lines IV-2, 3, and 4).

SOURCE OF BASIC DATA: *ELTESJ*, 1:187.

outside agriculture considerably more. The net fixed capital stock had grown by more than one-third since the end of the war and thus had made good the destruction of about one-fourth of the stock during the war. Even the capital stock per head or per member of the labor force was about one-fourth above the level of 1936. Only the cultivated area was still substantially below the prewar level. The reconstruction of the infrastructure may thus be regarded as having been completed.

The same conclusion is reached by examining the level of production and consumption. In 1953 real gross national product was nearly one-third above the 1934–36 level, and product per head just passed that level in 1953 as did real consumption per head. An important factor in this rapid recovery was the increase in the gross capital formation ratio from less than one-fifth in 1934–36 to more than one-fourth in 1951–53. The great Japanese inflation of 1945–49 thus apparently had not seriously interfered with the country's recovery from the physical damage and the economic and social disorganization caused by its participation in World War II, or the Pacific war as it is called in Japan. Tables 6–1 through 6–3 provide the basic data for following the reconstitution of the infrastructure between 1945 and 1953.

2. CAUSES AND COURSE OF THE GREAT INFLATION

As in most, if not all, hyperinflations[1]—and that term should be applicable to a 35-fold increase in the national product deflator in four years, or at an average of more than 140 percent per year, and an almost 80-fold increase, or nearly 200 percent a year, in reported consumer prices—the causal chain is fairly clear. The inflation originated in the large government deficits, largely financed by the banking system, and was aggravated in its initial phases by sharp reductions in the volume of output and by economic disorganization. It sharply decelerated or stopped when these bank-financed deficits were brought under control following the financial reforms initiated by the Dodge and Shoup missions in 1949 and 1950.[2] The crucial figures will be found in table 6–4. From 1946 to 1948, the deficit of the central government equaled 14, 7, and 6 percent of gross national product, whereas the credits of the banking system to the government amounted to more than 8, 13½ and 5½ percent of national product. Bank credits to the government became significantly negative in 1949 and 1950, to the extent of nearly 2½ percent of national product, and remained small, averaging about 1½ percent of national product from 1951 to 1953. The banking system in the crucial years 1946 to 1948 absorbed more than 110 percent of the total increase in the central government's debt of 7 percent of national product. In the 1949–53 period, the banking system accounted for only one-third of a total increase in government debt of 1¼ percent of national product.

The large deficits of the central government, which equaled more than one-third of its expenditures in 1945 and 1946 and still about one-fifth in 1947 to 1949, were due, particularly in the first few years, in part to very large, and apparently very liberal expenditures for compensation for war damages, repatriation, and reconstruction. The fact that final decisions rested not with the Japanese government but with the occupation authorities may have contributed to the large deficits until the Dodge-Shoup fiscal reforms.

Differing from most hyperinflations, the rate of price rise soon decelerated from the maximum of nearly 100 percent per quarter, measured by the Tokyo retail price index, in the fourth quarter of 1945 and the first quarter of 1946, immediately after the surrender on August 15, 1945. For the following year, it averaged 16 percent per quarter, still 80 percent a year. After another flare-up to 60 percent per quarter in the second half of 1947 and another of more than 70 percent in the third quarter of 1948, price rises subsided to an average of 2 percent per quarter from 1949 to 1953. Retail prices actually fell or rose by less than 1 percent in half of the twenty

1. For a comparative analysis of seven European hyperinflations, cf. Cagan. Strangely enough, no detailed analysis of the Japanese Great Inflation appears to exist in Western languages and possibly not even in Japanese.

2. Cf. Cohen, 1949, pp. 447 ff., and 1958, chap. 6, and Shiomi, pp. 77 ff.

TABLE 6-4. Central Government Domestic Borrowing, 1945–1953 (Percent of Gross National Product)

| | | Securities | | | Absorption | | | | | |
	Total (1)	Long (2)	Short (3)	Borrowings (4)	Bank of Japan (5)	Commercial banks (6)	Deposit Bureau (7)	Other financial institutions (8)	All financial institutions (9)	Other (10)
1945	25.00	17.40	0.70	6.90	4.15	6.40	3.90	4.80	19.25	5.75
1946	13.90	6.81	5.86	1.20	7.17	1.16	2.17	-0.94	9.56	4.34
1947	7.28	2.77	1.18	3.33	11.97	1.57	-0.30	0.01	13.25	-5.97
1948	6.14	2.66	2.79	0.69	4.96	0.53	0.16	0.51	6.16	-0.02
1949	3.35	3.29	-0.05	0.11	-1.26	-0.43	0.42	-0.23	-1.50	4.85
1950	-2.11	-1.27	-0.02	-0.82	-2.25	-0.68	0.25	-0.43	-3.11	1.00
1951	1.68	0.39	1.40	-0.11	0.61	-0.01	0.40	-1.14	-0.14	1.82
1952	2.96	1.22	1.39	0.35	2.59	0.01	-0.35	0.09	2.34	0.62
1953	0.34	1.50	-0.55	-0.60	0.36	0.90	-0.57	0.09	-0.03	0.37
1946-49	5.60	3.20	1.48	0.91	3.58	1.09	0.32	0.76	4.25	1.37
1950-53	0.95	0.67	0.54	-0.26	0.26	-0.09	-0.13	0.01	0.05	0.90
1946-53	2.14	1.32	0.78	0.04	1.12	0.21	-0.02	-0.19	1.12	1.02

SOURCES OF BASIC DATA: Cols. 1–5: HYS, pp. 158 and 193.   Cols. 6 and 7: Ott, 1960, pp. 131 and 133.   Col. 8: Ibid., p. 131, plus borrowings from Bank of Japan (HYS, p. 193).

quarters of this period and exceeded 4 percent in only four quarters, all in 1949 or 1950, in the latter year as a result of the fillip given the Japanese economy by American purchases connected with the Korean War.

As in most hyperinflations, the dispersion of prices was, as table 6–5 shows, very great in the short run but small among commodity prices and wages if the entire inflation period is considered. Thus, the general price level, wholesale prices, consumer prices, and wages in 1953 were fully 300 times as high as in 1934–36, and the multiplier ranged only from 307 for wages to 352 for wholesale prices. The two most important asset prices, for land and corporate stock, lagged behind, that for urban land moderately, that for rural land substantially, and that for corporate stock catastrophically, if the stock price index can be trusted. The price of the dollar in 1953 was only 105 times its 1934–36 level, but the discrepancy is explained to a large extent by the full doubling of the United States price level.

The relationships between money supply and price level for the period from the middle 1930s, when the Japanese economy began to be subject to a forced draft for rearmament and later for war, to 1953 satisfy even a naïve quantity theory—both the main price indices and the volume of currency as well as of money supply (M-1) were about 300 times as high at the end as at the beginning of the period. The correspondence, however, leaves much to be derived for shorter intervals, not to speak of annual or quarterly variations. This is not astonishing in view of the large changes in monetary policy, the extent of price control, the velocity of circulation, and, last but not least, the movements in real output that occurred during these two decades.

The main difference is that from the mid-thirties to 1944, the price level rose much less than the money supply, whereas for most of the following decade, the rise in the price level far exceeded the expansion of the money supply, whose components are shown in table 6–6, indicating a substantial decrease in the income velocity of circulation in the first part of the period and an increase in the second. Thus, the official price level in 1945, before the onset of the hyperinflation, and partly the result of price controls was only slightly above three times its 1934–36 value (though nearly seven times if the national product deflator is used), whereas the money supply (M-1) was fifteen times as large as it had been a decade earlier. Between 1945 and 1953, on the other hand, the money supply expanded less than 20 times, but prices rose 100-fold and wages more than 130-fold.

The correspondence between the inflation in the money supply and in the price level,

TABLE 6-5. Annual Price Movements, 1945–1953 (1934–36 = 1.00)

| | National product deflator (1) | Wholesale prices (2) | Consumer prices (3) | Wages (4) | Stock prices (5) | Land prices | | Foreign exchange (8) | Interest rates (9) |
						Rural (6)	Urban (7)		
1945	12.8	3.5	3.1	2.3	1.8	1.5	2.1	—	.79
1946	43.7	16.3	18.9	10.0	1.2	3.7	5.0	—	.95
1947	109.4	48.2	51.0	32.9	1.3	8.9	13.6	—	1.23
1948	191.4	127.9	149.6	91.9	2.6	16.5	36.5	—	1.61
1949	233.3	208.8	243.4	157.1	5.5	23.7	52.4	104.7	1.73
1950	243.0	246.8	239.1	187.9	3.1	32.1	65.8	104.7	1.60
1951	295.3	342.5	307.5	235.2	3.8	47.6	88.2	104.7	1.58
1952	302.3	349.2	300.5	272.2	6.6	69.2	130.9	104.7	1.58
1953	322.6	351.6	311.0	307.0	9.2	99.1	219.3	104.7	1.52

SOURCES: **Col. 1:** *ELTESJ*, 1:233, except 1945, which is the implicit deflator derived from table 3-2, cols. 1 and 2, and 1952, which is from *HYS*, p. 57.   **Col. 2:** *HYS*, p. 77.   **Col. 3:** *HYS*, p. 80; Tokyo consumer price index.   **Col. 4:** *Fujino*, 1975, p. 192, linked to *HYS*, p. 70.   **Col. 5:** *HYS*, p. 253.   **Col. 6:** *HYS*, pp. 88–89; average of index for March of current and following years; for description see *HYSE*, pp. 60–62.   **Col. 7:** *HYS*, p. 87; figures generally refer to September.   **Col. 8:** *HYS*, p. 322.   **Col. 9:** *HSJE*, p. 82; Tokyo rate for loans on bills.

TABLE 6-6. Changes in Money Supply, 1945–1953 (1934–36 = 1.00)

			1945	1946	1947	1948	1949	1950	1951	1952	1953
1. Currency			24.3	40.7	94.8	135.6	153.6	182.6	219.0	249.3	276.1
2. Demand deposits	All banks	B.J.[a]	10.7	24.7	43.0	91.4	121.0	142.5	199.9	276.8	310.9
3.		Asakura	58.9[d]	21.2	38.6	46.6	93.8	135.8	189.7	267.5	310.9
4.	Ordinary banks	Asakura	10.1	22.2	40.2	84.8	112.8	148.2	204.4	254.5	294.7
5.		B.J.[a]	5.1	4.9	7.2	15.3	33.7	51.7	84.3	134.3	173.2
6. Time and saving deposits	All banks	Asakura	9.4	6.4	7.4	8.5	23.2	51.6	80.6	133.1	178.2
7.	Ordinary banks	Asakura	8.5	4.2	4.7	9.7	26.1	46.2	71.0	106.0	142.9
8.		B.J.[a]	15.8	30.7	62.3	114.6	133.2	157.5	205.8	266.5	297.9
9. M-1[b]	All banks	Asakura	48.5[d]	27.1	55.5	78.8	118.8	149.9	198.5	262.0	300.4
10.	Ordinary banks	Asakura	14.9	28.4	58.6	108.0	126.6	159.8	211.7	252.7	288.4
11.		B.J.[a]	8.7	17.2	32.0	60.0	74.1	95.0	130.0	180.8	216.0
12. M-2[c]	All banks	Asakura	27.7[d]	16.1	30.1	41.5	64.9	97.9	136.0	193.7	235.6
13.	Ordinary banks	Asakura	11.6	15.9	30.6	57.0	74.4	100.8	137.5	176.5	212.9

[a] Bank of Japan. [b] Currency and demand deposits. [c] M-1 plus time and saving deposits. [d] Reflects the extraordinary expansion of the deposits of the Yokohama Specie Bank in connection with operations in the occupied territories.

SOURCES OF BASIC DATA: Line 1: *HYS*, p. 167. Lines 2, 5, 8, and 11: *ESA*, 1974, p. 72, plus line 1; line 11 includes deposits not classified as to maturity. Lines 3, 4, 6, 7, 9, 10, 12, and 13: Asakura and Nishiyama, pp. 822–23.

TABLE 6-7. Quarterly Price and Currency Movements, 1945–1954
(Percent per Quarter Changes)

	Wholesale prices (1)	Retail prices (Tokyo) (2)	Currency in circulation (3)		Wholesale prices (4)	Retail prices (Tokyo) (5)	Currency in circulation (6)
1945M	+9.3	+10.5	−2.9	1950M	+3.8	−7.0	−12.2
J	+18.2	+12.0	+26.0	J	+1.2	+0.9	−0.0
S	+15.7	+11.0	+55.8	S	+13.3	+10.8	+5.7
D	+83.4	+97.8	+32.9	D	+9.0	+5.8	+28.2
1946M	+77.2	+96.1	−1.9	1951M	+17.7	+19.8	−6.0
J	+36.5	+70.7	+79.1	J	+2.7	+0.6	+2.8
S	+21.4	+8.8	+49.3	S	+2.6	−1.0	+2.1
D	+13.5	+26.4	+44.1	D	+1.0	−1.8	+21.5
1947M	+7.7	+10.3	+23.6	1952M	−1.0	+0.4	−1.0
J	+35.7	+18.3	+17.6	J	−1.5	−0.5	+0.8
S	+102.6	+54.8	+14.6	S	+0.2	+1.3	+0.6
D	+25.2	+65.6	+39.7	D	−1.7	−1.0	+24.3
1948M	+4.0	+11.5	−0.2	1953M	+1.0	+4.0	+10.0
J	+8.2	+6.8	+5.3	J	+1.0	+1.3	+0.5
S	+78.3	+72.8	+13.5	S	+3.5	+3.2	+1.1
D	+9.9	+12.8	+25.4	D	+0.2	+2.1	+21.1
1949M	+5.2	+4.5	−4.3	1954M	+0.2	+2.4	−14.8
J	+6.2	+1.9	+11.3	J	−5.0	+0.3	+0.1
S	+3.6	+5.9	−0.8	S	+0.4	+0.3	−3.5
D	+1.0	−5.9	+19.2	D	+0.1	−1.8	+20.4

SOURCES OF BASIC DATA: **Cols. 1, 2, 4, 5:** *Japan Statistical Yearbook*, 1961, pp. 322–24.   **Cols. 3, 6:** Ibid., passim, e.g., 1949, pp. 576–77.

unadjusted for factors like changes in the volume of output, the extent and efficiency of price control, and the velocity of circulation, is quite poor on an annual basis and even poorer for quarterly movements.

Thus, the price level more than quintupled between 1945 and 1946 (annual averages), partly reflecting the disappearance of the repressed inflation through price controls, whereas the money supply hardly doubled. Price inflation continued to be well ahead of monetary inflation from 1947 to 1949, although to a much lesser extent than in 1946. When the economy had returned to a more nearly normal situation in the early 1950s, the increase in the money supply continued at relatively high rates, at an average of more than 20 percent M-1, but this now did not, except in 1951, affect the price level, partly because the volume of output increased very rapidly at an average rate of 10½ percent.

The quarterly relations between changes in the price level and of currency in circulation, which can be followed in table 6–7, are extremely erratic and do not show obvious lags. In seven quarters prices increased, sometimes very sharply, as in the first quarter of 1946, when currency in circulation decreased. In five quarters prices declined, although the volume of currency expanded, sometimes very substantially, as in the fourth quarters of 1949, 1951, and 1952. Even when both indicators moved up, as they did in most of the thirty-six quarters, the rate of increase in prices was not rarely more than twice as high (seven quarters) or less than one-half as high (nine quarters) as the rate of expansion of currency in circulation.

A less inadequate picture of the relationships between monetary and price inflation is provided in table 6–8, in which an attempt is made to show the quantity equation in Marshallian form for each of the years 1944 to 1953, using relatives to the fairly normal period of 1934–36 rather than absolute values; and distinguishing the three components of the money supply, currency, and demand and time deposits of ordinary banks.

TABLE 6-8. Quantity Equation (Marshallian Form),
1944–1953 (1934–36 = 1.00)

End of	Gross national product (1)	Currency (2)	k_c (3)	M-1[a] (4)	k_1 (5)	M-2[b] (6)	k_2 (7)
1944	7.2	9.8	1.38	7.9	1.11	6.5	0.92
1945	17.9	24.3	1.36	14.9	0.83	11.6	0.65
1946	47.3	40.7	0.86	28.4	0.60	15.9	0.34
1947	111.9	94.8	0.85	58.6	0.52	30.6	0.27
1948	176.6	135.6	0.77	108.0	0.61	57.0	0.32
1949	219.4	153.6	0.70	126.6	0.58	74.4	0.34
1950	278.6	182.6	0.66	159.8	0.57	100.8	0.53
1951	349.5	219.0	0.63	211.7	0.61	137.5	0.39
1952	397.9	249.3	0.63	252.7	0.64	176.5	0.44
1953	445.2	276.1	0.62	288.4	0.65	212.9	0.48
1934–36[c]	16.7	2.33	0.14	6.91	0.41	14.37	0.86

[a]Col. 2 plus demand deposits.   [b]Col. 4 plus time and saving deposits.
[c]¥ bill. for cols. 1, 2, 4, and 6.

SOURCES: **Col. 1:** Table 6-2, averaging figures for year and following year to approximate year-end rate.   **Cols. 2, 4, and 6:** Asakura and Nishiyama, p. 822; data in cols. 4 and 6 refer to ordinary banks.   **Cols. 3, 5, and 7:** Gross national product divided by cols. 2, 4, and 6.

The excess of the price over the monetary inflation rate, already noted, is reflected in the declines of the k-ratio, the reciprocal of income velocities. These declines were particularly sharp in 1946, the first full year of high inflation, but continued at a slower rate throughout the period in the case of currency, but only through 1947 for M-1 and M-2. For time deposits, and hence M-2, the ratio increased substantially from 1949 or 1950 on. As a result, the ratio in 1953 was at about two-thirds the 1934–36 level for currency and M-1, that is, income velocity of circulation was one and a half times as large, and at one-half that level for M-2.

As in most inflations, the purchasing power of the money supply declined (table 6–9), although very much less than in the European hyperinflations.[3] In 1945 the purchasing power of both currency and M-1 and M-2 was considerably higher than it had been in 1934–36, partly because the price indices used understate the effective rise in the price level. The ratio declined precipitously in 1946, particularly for M-2, but exhibited different movements over the following years. The value of currency in circulation showed an irregular upward trend and in 1953 was about 15 percent below the 1934–36 level, although real national product was 30 percent higher. The recovery from the trough of 1948, when their purchasing power had fallen to not much more than one-third and one-fifth, respectively, of their 1934–36 level, was much more rapid for M-1 and M-2, but both were still below their 1934–36 level in 1953, very slightly for M-1 but still by more than one-fourth for M-2. In all three cases, the ratio to national product was thus still well below what it had been in the mid-1930s.

3. FINANCIAL INSTITUTIONS

In the early phases of the inflation the growth of the assets of financial institutions lagged seriously behind the rise in prices or the expansion in current prices of national product. In 1946 to 1948, their growth rate of 55 percent per year was less than half as large as that of national

3. In six of the seven cases of hyperinflation studies by Cagan, the real value of currency of deposits fell to less than 5 percent of its level at the start of the hyperinflation (pp. 28 ff.).

TABLE 6-9. Purchasing Power of Money in Circulation,
1945–1953 (1934–36 = 100)

End of year	National product deflator basis			Retail price basis			Exchange rate basis		
	C (1)	M_1 (2)	M_2 (3)	C (4)	M_1 (5)	M_2 (6)	C (7)	M_1 (8)	M_2 (9)
1945	1.09	2.18	1.25	3.94	7.86[a]	4.50[a]			
1946	0.62	0.41	0.25	1.43	0.95	0.57			
1947	0.68	0.40	0.21	1.00	0.58	0.32			
1948	0.73	0.38	0.20	0.69	0.36	0.19	1.46	0.75	0.40
1949	0.64	0.47	0.27	0.63	0.46	0.27	1.46	1.07	0.62
1950	0.67	0.55	0.36	0.69	0.57	0.37	1.74	1.43	0.93
1951	0.73	0.66	0.45	0.71	0.64	0.44	2.09	1.89	1.30
1952	0.79	0.83	0.62	0.82	0.87	0.64	2.39	2.50	1.85
1953	0.84	0.91	0.71	0.85	0.93	0.73	2.63	2.86	2.25

NOTE: C = currency; M_1 = currency + demand deposits; M_2 = currency + demand deposits + time and savings deposits.

[a]Distorted by inclusion of Yokohama Specie Bank.

SOURCES: For numerator, Asakura and Nishiyama, p. 822. For denominator, table 6-5; year-end values for national product deflator estimated as geometric average of values for current and following year.   Cols. 1–3: National product deflator estimated as geometric average of values for current and following fiscal year, except 1944 and 1945, which are for calendar years. Figures, therefore, refer to February 15 of following year rather than to December 31.
Cols. 4–6: December value of Tokyo retail price index (*Japan Statistical Yearbook*, 1961, p. 322).   Cols. 7–9: Yen-dollar rate of 360; no quotations available for 1944–47.

product, with the result that their ratio to national product declined from 130 percent at the end of 1945 to not much more than 50 percent in 1948, compared with 260 percent in 1936, and that the real value of their assets, adjusted by the national product deflator, which had already been halved by the end of 1945, declined by an additional three-fifths, falling to one-fifth of its value in the mid-1930s.

The movement was reversed in the second part of the period when inflation abated. From 1949 through 1953, the assets of financial institutions increased at an average annual rate of nearly 40 percent, almost twice as rapidly as nominal national product expanded and about three times as fast as the price level rose. The price-adjusted value of the assets of financial institutions at the end of 1953 was about three times as high as it had been five years earlier and stood at 120 percent of national product, compared with not much more than 50 percent in 1948. The reconstitution of the country's financial superstructure thus made very considerable progress between 1948 and 1953, but even at the end of the period, the real value of the assets of financial institutions was not much more than one-half of what it had been in the mid-1930s, and its relation to national product was slightly below the level of two decades earlier.

As often happens in inflations, the net issue ratios of financial institutions, that is, the ratio of the increase in their liabilities to national product, was very high in the first two years of the period, averaging 70 percent in 1945 and 1946, and for 1947 to 1953 averaged as much as 24 percent, with a range from 16 to 30 percent. These high rates are compatible with a decrease in the real value and in the relation to national product of the assets of financial institutions because the rapid rise of prices continuously reduced the real value of the accumulated assets.

During an inflation, the differences in the rates of growth of the assets of the different

TABLE 6-10. Financial Institutions, 1945, 1948, and 1953 (Percent)

	New issue ratio			Distribution of assets			Relation to gross national product[a]		
	1946	1948	1953	1945	1948	1953	1945	1948	1953
Bank of Japan	7.6	5.6	0.9	18.3	25.0	10.2	23.9	13.4	12.1
Commercial banks	22.3	9.7	13.5	34.2	35.0	45.4	44.7	19.3	54.1
Post Office Saving System	1.2	1.0	1.2	11.2	5.1	4.4	14.6	2.7	5.3
Bank trust accounts	0.1	0.0	0.9	1.3	0.7	2.3	1.7	0.4	2.8
Deposit Bureau	2.8	1.3	2.0	12.2	6.3	7.3	15.9	3.4	8.6
Long-term credit banks	6.4	0.2	-2.8	9.4	4.6	3.1	12.2	2.4	3.6
Mutual loan and savings banks	0.3	0.4	1.4	0.6	1.1	4.2	0.8	0.6	5.0
Agricultural credit cooperatives	2.8	1.3	0.9	5.4	5.3	3.3	7.1	2.8	3.9
Other credit cooperatives	8.7	1.2	3.0	2.9	6.4	8.9	3.8	3.4	10.6
Government financial institutions[b]	0.3	2.6	3.3	0.1	8.2	7.2	0.1	3.8	8.6
Life insurance companies	0.5	0.1	0.4	2.4	1.1	1.2	3.1	0.6	1.4
Other insurance companies	0.0	0.1	0.3	0.6	0.6	0.8	0.8	0.4	1.0
Post Office life insurance	0.4	0.0	0.7	1.5	0.7	1.7	2.0	0.4	2.0
All financial institutions	53.9	23.7	25.7	100.0	100.0	100.0	130.5[c]	53.6	119.0

[a]Average of national product for year and year following; roughly estimated for 1945.   [b]In 1948 mainly Reconversion Finance Bank; in 1953 Japan Development Bank.   [c]In 1944, 219.8 (table 5-9).

SOURCES OF DATA ON ASSETS: *HYS*, pp. 193, 217, 238 ff.; Ott, 1960, pp. 192, 202, 226, 230, 253; *ESA*, 1969, p. 88; 1975, p. 140.

types of financial institutions, and hence the distribution of total assets among them, are usually much greater than in normal times. The results of these differences are evident in table 6–10. The share of the banking system, which is closest to the origin of inflation, increased from 53 percent in 1945 to 60 percent in 1948 but fell back to 56 percent in 1953 when inflation decelerated. The movement was most pronounced in the case of the Bank of Japan, whose share rose to one-fourth in 1947 and 1948, compared with 18 percent in 1945 and 8 percent in 1944, but declined to 10 percent in 1953, which was still nearly twice its share in the mid-1930s. The share of commercial banks, on the other hand, began to rise only when inflation slowed down, increasing from fully one-third from 1945 to 1948 to 45 percent in 1953, somewhat above their share of two-fifths in 1936. The real value of the assets of the banking system in 1948 was only one-half of what it had been in 1945, but by 1953 it had surpassed the earlier level by two-fifths, which was entirely due to a near doubling of the real assets of commercial banks. In contrast, the share of long-term credit, saving, and insurance organizations declined sharply in the first part of the period and failed to recover substantially in the second part. Thus, the share of the Post Office Saving System fell from 11 percent in 1945 to 4 percent in 1953, that of insurance organizations declined from 4.5 to 3.7 percent, and that of long-term credit organizations was cut from 9½ to 3 percent. Similar declines occurred in the real value of assets and the relation to national assets of these three types of organizations. In 1953, the real value of their assets was still more than two-fifths below the level of 1945, although it was three times as large as at the nadir of 1948. The relations to national product were even less favorable, falling from one-third in 1945 to 6 percent in 1948 and recovering to only one-eighth in 1953.

Of the full dozen groups of financial institutions, only three require attention, the Bank of Japan, the commercial banks, and the Reconversion Finance Bank.

Changes in the structure of the assets of the Bank of Japan can be followed in table 6–11. The bank, rather astonishingly, at the end of 1945 made less than one-fourth of its resources available to the government. This share, however, increased sharply in the period of high inflation, rising to a peak of more than four-fifths in 1948. It declined substantially, beginning in

TABLE 6-11. Bank of Japan during the Inflation, 1944–1953

End of	Total assets (¥ bill.)	Percent					
		Lendings to nongovernment	Lendings to government	Government securities	Bank notes	Government deposits	Other deposits
1944	25.0	35.8	3.8	38.5	71.1	18.1	7.7
1945	79.1	47.2	14.2	9.0	70.0	22.5	5.3
1946	115.0	43.8	6.6	30.2	81.1	5.6	9.5
1947	254.7	12.7	20.9	57.2	86.0	2.6	8.2
1948	405.0	12.8	20.6	61.2	87.7	3.5	5.6
1949	400.0	22.2	25.0	47.2	88.8	3.0	1.7
1950	510.5	52.7	12.3	26.8	82.7	9.3	1.4
1951	594.7	59.1	6.7	21.2	85.1	5.3	1.2
1952	766.3	42.6	5.0	37.3	75.2	12.0	3.9
1953	831.8	47.0	1.4	37.8	75.7	7.2	6.4

SOURCE: *HYS*, p. 193.

1950, and by the end of 1953 had fallen to below two-fifths. This movement was paralleled by a decline in the share of lending to the private sector in 1947 and 1948 and a sharp recovery from 1950 on, restoring the share of the private sector to nearly one-half.

Changes in the structure of the assets of commercial banks, shown in table 6–12, were dominated by the decline in the share of securities, mostly those issued by the central government, from nearly one-third in 1945 to slightly below one-tenth from 1950 on. They were offset by an increase in the share of loans and discounts, from not much more than two-fifths in 1946 and 1947 to fully three-fifths from 1949 on, well above the share of the 1930s.

The Reconversion Finance Bank, set up by the government in January 1947 to assist business enterprises squeezed by inflation, which included an apparently liberal granting of loans to cover current deficits, financed itself partly by Treasury funds but mostly by debentures bought primarily by the banking system and thus contributed directly or indirectly to monetary inflation. In 1947 and 1948 the bank's net loans amounted to 3½ and 2½ percent of national product, and for the two years together they were equal to one-tenth of all lendings to the private economy by the banking system. The gradual liquidation of the bank was a main point of the anti-inflationary Dodge program. From 1949 on the bank's outstanding loans were gradually reduced or written off, and it was eliminated in 1952.

4. THE NONFINANCIAL SECTORS

a. The Government

Notwithstanding its large deficit on current account, the government undertook capital expenditures on a large scale, partly for reconstruction. These expenditures accounted, on a gross basis, for 6½ percent of national product, ranging only from 5½ to 8 percent, and represented one-fourth of total gross capital expenditures during the 1946–53 period.[4] They were, in real terms, considerably heavier in the period of high inflation of 1946–48 than in the following five years and were, on an annual basis, about 75 percent in excess of the government's non-military capital expenditures in the 1930s. As gross capital expenditures were about four times as large as the government's net borrowing, most of both its gross and net capital expenditures during the inflation were financed by government saving.

During the period of high inflation, more than the entire increase in government debt was

4. Cohen, p. 85, and *HYS*, p. 231.

TABLE 6-12. Structure of Assets of Commercial Banks, 1945–1953 (Percent)

	1945	1946	1947	1948	1949	1950	1951	1952	1953
Liquid assets[a]	6.7	8.3	12.2	17.0	16.8	11.8	10.8	13.4	11.7
Foreign exchange	0.0	0.0	0.0	0.0	0.1	8.6	6.9	3.9	3.4
Securities	31.0	19.4	22.9	18.9	11.4	8.5	8.1	8.0	8.1
Loans and discounts	52.2	43.6	43.5	56.9	66.9	58.0	63.9	62.2	62.9
Interoffice accounts	—	2.4	5.1	4.6	2.7	1.4	1.5	1.7	1.7
Other assets	10.1	26.4	16.2	2.6	2.0	11.9	8.9	10.9	12.2
Total assets, percent	100.0	100.0	100.0	100.0	100.0	100.0	100.0	100.0	100.0
Total assets, ¥ bill.	138	247	312	583	880	1503	2015	2720	3706

[a]Cash, deposits with others, due from correspondents and agencies, and call loans.

SOURCE OF BASIC DATA: Ott, 1960, pp. 192, 194.

absorbed by financial institutions, particularly the Bank of Japan, with the result that their share in total government debt increased, as table 6–13 shows, from nearly three-fifths at the end of the war to more than nine-tenths three years later. The situation changed radically during the first years of abating inflation. Now financial institutions actually decreased their holdings of government debt by nearly one-fifth, as nonfinancial sectors, presumably mainly households, resumed their large-scale purchases of government securities. At the end of 1953 the government's debt was held in about equal proportions by financial and nonfinancial sectors, compared to a share of financial institutions in the government's domestic debt of nearly two-thirds in 1935.

b. Nonfinancial Corporations

During the eight years from 1946 through 1953, real corporate gross fixed capital expenditures were, on an annual basis, about one-tenth higher than in 1934–36, if it is assumed that in both periods about one-half of total private nonresidential capital expenditures were attributable to corporations,[5] although real national product was still one-sixth lower than in the mid-1930s. Real corporate gross fixed capital expenditures amounted to fully 5 percent of national product, rising moderately from hardly 4 percent in 1946–48 to nearly 5½ percent in 1949–53. Corporate saving, on the other hand, has been estimated at practically zero for 1946–48, fully 3 percent of national product for 1949–53 and 2½ percent for the period as a whole,[6] although such calculations are very hazardous in a period when rapid inflation is likely substantially to distort corporate accounts. Accepting the figures, they indicate a large need for external financing, particularly in the period of high inflation.

This deduction is confirmed by the statistics of the supply of industrial, presumably mainly corporate, funds of table 6–14. For the entire period, external funds accounted for two-thirds of total funds, compared with one-half in the mid-1930s, although the share declined from nearly four-fifths in the period of high inflation to slightly less than two-thirds from 1949 to 1953. Within external funds, stocks supplied one-eighth and debentures less than 4 percent, leaving five-sixths to loans and discounts, presumably supplied by financial institutions, primarily commercial banks, for the period as a whole as well as for both subperiods. The sale of stocks contributed considerably more, and debentures much less, of external funds in the more inflationary first subperiod. Retained profits provided a negligible share of internal funds in the first subperiod but in the second subperiod contributed one-sixth of total funds, almost as much as capital consumption allowances. All these shares would be somewhat reduced if trade credit were included in the statistics. In comparison to the mid-1930s, the period of inflation is

5. ELTESJ, 1:187; *JEG*, p. 293. Assumes that corporate fixed capital expenditures may be equated to total private expenditures less those in agriculture, construction, and services and those on dwellings (*JEG*, pp. 294–95 for 1951–53).
6. *JEG*, p. 297.

TABLE 6-13. Distribution of Holdings
of Government Securities, 1945, 1948, and 1953[a]

	1945	1948	1953
Bank of Japan	9.2	63.2	38.3
Commercial banks	17.5	14.2	5.2
Deposit Bureau	20.0	9.6	4.2
Other financial institutions	12.4	5.0	0.7
All financial institutions	59.2	92.0	48.4
Other sectors	40.8	8.0	51.6
All sectors, percent	100.0	100.0	100.0
All sectors, ¥ bill.	199	524	851

[a]Percent of amounts outstanding.

SOURCE OF BASIC DATA: *HYS*, pp. 159, 193, 272 ff.

characterized by a much higher degree of reliance on external funds, particularly loans and discounts, which provided considerably more than one-half of total funds against less than one-tenth in 1934–36; a sharp decline in the use of stock financing, from two-fifths to less than one-tenth of total funds; a halving of the share of capital consumption allowances; and a contribution of retained earnings of one-seventh in both periods.

c. Households

Almost no reliable information is available regarding the saving and investment behavior of households in the Great Inflation. Capital expenditures on dwellings, most of which may be attributed to households, amounted to 2 percent of national product and one-tenth of total gross capital formation for the period as a whole, with little difference between its two parts, compared with less than 1½ percent in the mid-1930s, and hence was unaffected by the inflation. Personal saving is put at 10 percent of personal disposable income for the entire period, compared with 15 percent in 1934–36, although it is estimated to have been slightly negative for 1946–49.[7] The latter result is difficult to accept, as households obviously saved in every year considerable amounts in the form of currency and demand and saving deposits, even though the real value of the amounts so accumulated was virtually wiped out by the rise in prices, and households seem to have reduced their holdings of government securities to the extent of about 1 percent of national product.

d. Issues of Nonfinancial Sectors

For the period as a whole the ascertainable issues of nonfinancial sectors were equal to nearly 15 percent of national product. The inclusion of trade credit,[8] mortgages, and a few other smaller types of issues, for which no statistics are available, probably would increase the new issue ratio to more than 20 percent.[9]

7. *HYS*, pp. 38 ff.

8. Fujino's estimate of inventory investment in 1952 and 1953 (1975, p. 192; not available for 1946–51) is equal to 5.4 percent of gross national product.

9. This figure raises a problem as it is below the new issue ratio of financial institutions of about 25 percent, although conceptually it should be above it, unless the nonfinancial sectors reduced their holdings of financial instruments so that financial institutions could absorb more than the entire amount of net issues. Part of the difference is explained by duplications within the reported total liabilities of all financial institutions, which have been used here to measure their net issues. The elimination of these duplications, particularly the liabilities of the Deposit Bureau and the interbank and intercooperative liabilities, would substantially reduce the net issue ratio of financial institutions below the calculated 25 percent but probably not much below 20 percent. There is no doubt, however, that the financial intermediation (the issues of financial institutions divided by those of nonfinancial sectors) was very high during the inflation as it also was in the 1930s.

TABLE 6-14. Supply of Industrial Funds, 1934–1936 and 1946–1953 (Percent)

	Distribution				Relation to gross national product			
	1934–36	1946–49	1950–53	1946–53	1934–36	1946–49	1950–53	1946–53
External funds	49.1	78.2	64.3	67.2	7.4	14.4	15.2	15.0
Stocks	39.5	12.5	7.2	8.4	6.0	2.3	1.7	1.9
Debentures	0.2	1.0	2.9	2.5	0.0	0.2	0.7	0.6
Loans and discounts	9.4	64.6	54.1	56.3	1.4	11.9	12.8	12.6
Internal funds	50.9	21.8	35.7	32.9	7.7	4.0	8.5	7.4
Depreciation	37.3	19.4	18.4	18.6	5.6	3.6	4.4	4.2
Retained profits	13.4	2.4	17.3	14.3	2.0	0.4	4.1	3.2
Total, percent	100.0	100.0	100.0	100.0	15.1	18.4	23.7	22.3
Total, ¥ bill.	7.59	1437	5383	6820	—	—	—	—

SOURCE OF BASIC DATA: Cohen, 1958, p. 93 (Bank of Japan data).

Annual variations, which can be followed in table 6–15, were substantial, ranging for ascertainable issues from 10 to 25 percent. With the exception of 1946, years in which real national product rose more than the average for the period usually showed relatively high new issue ratios, but the relationship was not a close one.

For the period as a whole bank loans accounted for considerably more than one-half of total ascertainable issues, but the ratio was considerably higher in 1950–51 and much lower in 1946 and particularly in 1947 when central government issues were still very large. For the entire period government issues represented nearly one-fourth of the total, split in the ratio of nearly two-to-one between central and local governments. Corporate stock issues were equal to one-sixth of the total, only a part of them representing open-market offerings, whereas the share of corporate debentures, with 4 percent, remained small.

As in the case of financial instruments issued by financial institutions, most of those issued by nonfinancial sectors increased much less in volume than either prices rose or nominal national product expanded. Thus, at the end of 1953 domestic government debt was about 93 times as high as it had been in 1934–36, local government debt 113 times, industrial debentures 68 times, and bank borrowings 260 times, compared with an increase of the price level by more than 300

TABLE 6-15. Issue Ratios of Nonfinancial Sectors, 1946–1953
(Percent of Gross National Product)

	Central government debt	Local government debt	Industrial bonds	Corporate stocks[b]	Bank borrowing	Total[c]
1946	13.85	−0.02	−0.27	0.95	10.27	24.78
1947	7.28	1.04	0.01	0.70	1.67	10.70
1948	6.15	0.66	0.01	2.22	8.00	17.04
1949	2.99	0.89	0.39	2.88	7.88	15.03
1950	−2.11	1.00	1.10	2.47	8.00	10.46
1951	1.68	1.06	0.66	1.76	9.61	14.77
1952	2.89	2.96	0.59	3.30	9.74	19.48
1953	0.35	1.82	0.58	2.58	7.70	13.03
1946–53	2.11	1.22	0.55	2.47	8.32	14.67

[a]Change in amount outstanding divided by national product.   [b]Paid-up value; includes financial corporations.
[c]Excluding trade credit.

SOURCE OF BASIC DATA: *HYS*, pp. 159, 162, 195, 251, 331.

times and of national product by about 420 times. The most pronounced lag in the expansion of the volume of financial instruments occurred during the high inflation. At the end of 1948, when national product was about 180 times as high as in 1934–36 and the price level about 200 times as high, the multiplier was less than 60 for government domestic debt, not much more than 10 for local government debt, less than 4 for industrial debentures, less than 40 for bank debt, and less than 50 for corporate stock. Hence, the price-adjusted value of their instruments, as well as their relation to national product, had fallen to less than one-third for even government debt and corporate stock and to a small fraction for the typically long-term local government and industrial bonds. At the end of 1945 the size of the financial superstructure was probably still about three times as large a national product, well below the ratio of about 5 in the mid-1930s, a reflection of the effects of the sharp acceleration of inflation after the end of the war. By the end of 1948 the ratio had fallen precipitiously to probably not much above unity. Five years later, as inflation decelerated, it had climbed back to about 2, still far below the value of two decades earlier. A somewhat more reliable estimate, which is available only for a few benchmark dates,[10] indicates that financial assets in 1940 were equal to nearly seven times national product and nearly one and a half times national wealth. By 1955, half a decade after the end of the high inflation, these ratios, although considerably above the trough of 1948, were still not much above twice national product and not much more than one-half of national wealth. Even in 1975 both ratios were still below their values of the mid-1930s. This was, in part, the result of the radical shrinkage of Japan's financial superstructure during the Great Inflation.

10. Cf. tables 4-19 and 7-39.

7   The Japanese Miracle? 1954–1975

Dating the turning point in the postwar period that separates the relatively short period of reconstruction—characterized in its first half by a rapid and heavy inflation—from the long upward swing ending, as now seems fairly evident, in 1973, is to some extent arbitrary. The end of 1953 has been selected because by that time the main indicators of economic growth, particularly gross national product, had reached or slightly exceeded the prewar level. The choice of 1954 as the beginning of the two decades that witnessed a rise of real national product by more than 530 percent, or an average of nearly 10 percent per year, and consequently changed Japan's position in the world economy, is also motivated by an accidental consideration. The flow-of-funds statistics, which provide the basic quantitative framework for much of the discussion of financial development, start with 1954. The years 1974 and 1975, the third watershed, experienced the first serious postwar recession, which terminated the upward phase of a long swing that started in the mid-1950s, presumably to be followed by a long downswing, characterized by, on the average, substantially lower rates of growth. The discussion in this chapter, therefore, will concentrate on the period of reconstruction, 1946 through 1953, some aspects of which have already been covered in chapter 6, the extraordinary two decades from 1954 through 1973, and the first four years of the following period, which will be treated in less detail, although the relevant statistical data will be found in either chapter 6 or in the tables of this chapter for 1974–77.

1. BASIC CHANGES IN THE INFRASTRUCTURE

a. Although the quantitative changes in the Japanese economy and in its financial system between 1945 and 1977 have been spectacular, the qualitative structural changes have been more limited. They are nevertheless important, both in the infrastructure of product, income, and wealth and in the financial superstructure.

b. Structural changes were probably most far reaching in the political field. Internationally, Japan was reduced from being the dominant power in Eastern Asia, exploiting a vast colonial empire, to a demilitarized country comprising only the home islands, that is, limited to the area it had controlled at the restoration of 1868. Domestically, a parliamentary democracy, dominated throughout the postwar period by the same political party, which was more an agglomeration of a half dozen cliques than a homogeneous political organization, replaced a monarchy that had again become nearly absolute and had been closely associated with the military during the decade preceding World War II. Thus two of the prewar elites—the military and the imperial court—disappeared.

c. In the equally important though more problematic field of personality traits and social relations, changes appear to have been moderate. They certainly appear so in relation to the immense quantitative expansion of the Japanese economy and to the far-reaching modifications in the country's political structure or to the changes in Japanese society during the first two decades of the Meiji era. In particular, the features of national cohesion and the symbiosis of the elites, to a degree far exceeding that in contemporary Western societies, were preserved.[1]

d. Economically, the main effects of the war were the destruction of a substantial fraction, possibly as much as one-fourth,[2] of the country's reproducible capital stock and the loss of all foreign investments. The losses of the labor force through war casualties were more than offset by the forcible repatriation of the Japanese who had lived abroad. As a result of the war, real national product per head in 1947,[3] two years after the end of hostilities, was only one-half as large as it had been in 1939, and it did not reach the prewar level until the mid-1950s.

e. Of the main factors of production, the labor force expanded by fully one-third, or at an average annual rate of 1.5 percent per year, between 1953 and 1973. Because the average hours worked per year declined slightly and the quality of the labor force increased considerably, effective labor input is estimated to have increased at an annual rate of one-half in excess of that of employment.[4]

f. The growth of the capital stock was spectacular, as may already be inferred from the level and movement of the capital formation ratios. For the two decades 1954–77 gross capital formation averaged more than one-third of national product, rising from a ratio of about one-fourth at the beginning of the period to an average of 37 percent from 1967 to 1973, excluding consumer durables, which would add another 3 to 4 percentage points to the ratio. The absolute volume of real gross capital formation increased at the extraordinary rate of nearly 14 percent a year between 1953 and 1973. Such rates of growth in the presence of a mild secular inflation produce a low ratio of capital consumption allowances, for the period as a whole only about one-third, according to the official estimates, which use original cost depreciation, yielding a net capital formation at the extraordinarily high rate of nearly one-fourth of national product. As a result, in 1973 the gross business capital stock, which may be more relevant than the total net stock in the analysis of economic growth, was almost seven times as large as it had been twenty years earlier, having grown at an average rate of 10 percent per year.[5] The financing task thus imposed on the Japanese economy, and in particular on its financial institutions, was immense. How it was handled will be discussed in the following sections.

g. Using appropriate weights for labor (adjusted for quality changes) and for capital inputs, the input of these two basic factors would have increased national income at an annual rate of more than 5 percent.[6] The rise in output, however, was further and considerably aided by the massive importation of Western technology, mainly from the United States. The effect of this importation was strengthened and accelerated by the rapid increase and the consequent very low average age of the capital stock and the cost-reducing effects of large-scale economies of scale.

h. The effects of increases in inputs, particularly those of technology, and changes in industrial structure, are visible in the average growth rate of aggregate real gross national product of 10 percent and of real product per head by 9 percent, both ratios unequaled in Japan's previous history or in any other country for a period as long as two decades. As a result, real national product per head, which had fallen to below one-half of the 1938 level immediately after the war, regained the prewar level in the mid-1950s and in 1973 was about four times as high as it

1. This is an admittedly subjective impression, necessarily based on the study of only a small part of the rich literature in this field and relying much on Nakane's *Japanese Society*.

2. The official estimate (*HYS*, p. 27) puts the losses at ¥ 65 bill. compared to an actual national wealth at the end of the war of ¥ 189 bill.

3. Maddison, 1969, p. 154, for relation of aggregate real national product in 1939 and 1947 (56 percent).

4. Denison and Chung, 1976, p. 94.

5. According to another estimate (Fujino, 1975, p. 192), the real net fixed capital stock increased at a rate of 13 percent per year between 1953 and 1970. Inclusion of less rapidly growing inventories would reduce the rate by less than 1 percentage point. In a period of rapid growth, the net/gross ratio would be expected to decline and the growth rate of the net stock would be expected to be above that of the gross stock.

6. Ibid.

had been three and a half decades earlier. This implies an average annual growth rate of slightly more than 4 percent between 1938, the prewar peak, and 1973, that is, a rate considerably above the rate of 2 to 2½ percent observed between 1885 and 1938.

i. To put the situation in sharper relief, if Japan had continued to grow after 1938 at the rate of the preceding half century, the hypothetical growth curve of real national product per head would have met the actual curve in the early 1960s, the year of coincidence depending on the exact prewar growth rate assumed. From then on, the actual curve lies above the extrapolated hypothetical curve. By 1973 Japan's actual real national product per head was about two-thirds higher than it would have been if it had continued to grow after 1938 at an annual rate of 2½ percent, probably the highest defensible estimate; and it would have been twice as high if the prewar growth rate is put at only 2 percent. Thus, if a Japanese economic miracle has occurred, it occurred in the two decades between the recovery of the prewar level in the mid-1950s and the end of the long postwar swing in 1973.

j. As a result of the sharp increase in the capital formation ratio, the share of private consumption expenditures in gross national product declined substantially from about two-thirds in the mid-1950s to not much more than one-half in the early 1970s, even though that of general government consumption expenditures also fell from about 11 to 8 percent. Consequently, real personal consumption expenditures per head increased considerably more slowly than national product. The annual average rate of increase of more than 7 percent between 1953 and 1973, however, was still very high, in comparison to both previous Japanese and Western experience, and permitted a tripling of real consumption per head in two decades. By 1973 average real consumption should have been about three and a half times as high as the highest prewar level, when personal consumption was held down by high military expenditures. However, even in 1973 Japanese consumption per head of about ¥ 520,000, or about $1,850 at the exchange rate ¥ 280 per dollar, which slightly understates the purchasing power of the yen over consumption goods,[7] was only at one-half of the U.S. level.

k. Although cyclical fluctuations, primarily resulting from changes in business capital expenditures, are clearly visible, the increase in aggregate real national product between 1954 and 1973 never fell below 5 percent. The rhythm of the postwar expansion is evident in the movements of the percentage rate of growth in national product shown in table 7–1, although annual data smooth extreme movements. The peak years, by cyclical dating,[8] of 1954, 1957, 1961, 1964, 1970, and 1973 are generally visible in the movements of real gross national product, which advanced by 7 (1955), 14, 13, 12, and 10 percent a year, respectively. Movements also are evident in the trough years of 1958 (5½ percent), 1962 (7 percent), 1965 (6 percent), and 1971 (5 percent), all rates that would be regarded as very good in other countries, most of which, except 1971, reflected temporary balance-of-payments difficulties and the credit restrictions that were applied to overcome them. As a result, no less than every second year showed a growth rate of 10 percent or more. It is still too early to define and date long cyclical swings during the postwar period. Although one swing is supposed to have lasted from 1954 to 1965 (trough to trough),[9] it may well be found to have extended through 1973 once the evidence of the late 1970s and early 1980s becomes available.

l. Compared to the immense expansion of the volume of real national product, a more than sixfold increase between 1953 and 1973, structural changes among major sectors measured by their contribution to net national product were moderate and were in the same direction and of similar dimensions as in countries experiencing a much lower rate of growth. The most pronounced change, of course, was the decline of the share of agriculture from more than one-fifth in the early 1950s to only 7 percent in 1973. Next to it stands the rise in the share of manufactur-

7. According to Kravis, et al., the purchasing power of the yen over consumption goods in 1973 was 49 percent above the exchange rate. By 1977 the difference was smaller, probably about 25 percent.

8. *Japanese Economic Indicators,* January 1976.

9. Ohkawa and Rosovsky.

TABLE 7-1. Basic Characteristics of Development of Real Infrastructure
on Annual Basis, 1953–1978

	Gross national product			Real private consumption per head (1955 = 100) (4)	Gross capital formation ratio (percent) (5)	Labor force (mill.) (6)	Gross business capital stock (¥ trill. of 1965) (7)	Current balance of payments (¥ trill.) (8)
	Current prices (¥ trill.) (1)	1970 prices (¥ trill.) (2)	Annual increase (percent) (3)					
1953	7.06	14.75	5.4	90.7	24.0	39.36	17.50	−0.01
1954	7.83	15.53	5.3	93.8	23.5	39.89	18.73	−0.02
1955	8.62	16.90	8.8	100.0	24.7	41.19	19.37	0.08
1956	9.73	18.13	7.3	106.8	28.7	41.97	20.43	−0.01
1957	11.08	19.48	7.4	112.5	33.3	43.03	21.94	−0.22
1958	11.52	20.58	5.6	119.5	27.7	43.24	23.35	0.10
1959	12.93	22.40	8.9	127.7	29.8	43.68	25.00	0.13
1960	15.50	25.41	13.4	139.5	33.8	45.41	27.50	0.05
1961	19.13	29.07	14.4	150.2	40.5	45.62	30.89	−0.35
1962	21.20	31.10	7.0	162.9	35.9	46.14	34.51	−0.02
1963	24.46	34.25	10.1	177.1	35.8	46.52	38.17	−0.28
1964	28.93	38.89	13.5	194.7	36.2	47.10	42.54	−0.17
1965	32.07	41.18	5.9	202.4	32.3	47.87	45.40	0.34
1966	37.36	45.67	10.9	217.1	32.9	48.91	49.67	0.45
1967	44.09	51.36	12.5	235.0	36.0	49.83	55.42	−0.07
1968	52.60	58.56	14.0	254.6	37.2	50.61	62.95	0.38
1969	61.61	65.70	12.2	280.8	37.3	50.98	71.96	0.76
1970	73.50	73.44	11.8	299.0	38.9	51.53	82.63	0.71
1971	80.92	77.25	5.2	316.8	35.7	51.86	93.75	2.00
1972	92.75	84.58	9.5	338.4	35.4	51.99	105.88	2.00
1973	113.09	93.01	10.0	361.7	38.2	53.26	118.77	−0.03
1974	135.06	92.50	−0.5	362.4	37.4	53.10	130.10	−1.33
1975	148.80	93.84	1.4	366.3	29.0	53.23	140.44	−0.20
1976	167.29	99.92	6.5	378.5	31.6	53.78	149.68	1.08
1977	186.35	105.36	5.4	390.7	30.6	54.52	159.01	2.84
1978[a]	205.00	111.50	5.8	406.2	32.0	55.40	·	3.00

[a]Preliminary estimates.

Sources: **Cols. 1 and 2:** 1953–64, ARNIS, 1976, pp. 192 ff.; 1965–77, ARNA, pp. 76 ff.   **Col. 4:** 1953–74, ESA, various issues; 1975–77, ARNA, p. 81.   **Col. 5:** 1953–74, ARNIS, 1976, pp. 70 ff., does not include consumer durables; 1965–77, ARNA, pp. 8–9.   **Col. 6:** 1954–59, HYS, p. 56; 1960–70, ESA, 1970, p. 269; 1975, p. 265; 1971–77, ESM, November 1978, p. 1955.   **Col. 7:** 1953–64, Economic Planning Agency estimates (mimeographed); 1975–77, extrapolated on basis of gross capital stock of all industries excluding agriculture and finance (ARNA, pp. 612–13); 1965–77, ARNA, 1979, pp. 610 ff.   **Col. 8:** 1953–71, ARNIS, 1976, pp. 90 ff.; 1972–77, ARNA, pp. 10–11.

ing from not much more than 20 to nearly 30 percent of net national product. (The broader group of manufacturing, mining, and construction rose from almost 30 to close to 40 percent.) All other sectors increased their combined share from about one-half to fully 55 percent. Within the other sectors, the trade, services, and finance sectors gained, substantially so only in the case of finance.

m. As the postwar period proceeded, the rapid increase in Japan's foreign trade, in particular the sharp expansion of its manufacturing exports, created serious domestic and international problems. During most of the period these showed themselves chiefly in current account deficits during boom years, for example, in 1953–54, 1957, and 1961–64, when imports spurted, deficits that necessitated sometimes sharp monetary contractions. From the middle of the 1960s, however, the situation reversed itself and resulted in increasingly large current

TABLE 7-2. Comparison of Growth Rates between
1954–1973 and 1974–1977 Periods (Percent per Year)

	1954–73	1974–77
I. Infrastructure		
Population	1.1	1.2
Labor force, total	1.5	0.6
Labor force, nonagricultural	3.4	1.0
Real gross business capital stock	10.0	7.6
Real gross national product	9.6	3.1
Real consumption per head	7.2	2.0
Real gross capital formation	13.8	−1.2
Export volume	16.9	12.3
Terms of trade	0.1	−9.6
II. Financial superstructure		
Money supply—M1	16.4	10.8
Money supply—M2	17.4	13.9
Current gross national product	14.9	13.3
National product deflator	4.5	9.8
Wholesale prices	1.4	9.7
Consumer prices	4.6	13.2
Wages	6.4	16.0
Stock prices	11.9	1.0
Rural land prices	10.5	15.2[a]
Urban land prices	18.8	4.9

[a]1974 and 1975.

SOURCES: Tables 7-1, 7-3, 7-4; *ESA*, 1979.

account surpluses, which are partly reflected in the stability of export prices in the face of an increase in wholesale prices by more than 30 percent and in the general price level by 140 percent.[10] This was possibly due to economies of scale in manufacture for exports, aided by marginal-cost or even less than marginal-cost pricing. These surpluses, rising from less than ¥ 400 bill. in 1968 to ¥ 2,000 bill. in 1971 and 1972, equal to about 2¼ percent of national product in the latter two years, provided a powerful inflationary force and finally forced a substantial appreciation of the yen in terms of most foreign currencies.

n. The extraordinary tempo of forced growth during the postwar period has to some extent taken place at the expense of the future, namely, by neglecting important sectors of the infrastructure, particularly housing, the road system, and many welfare activities, and by disregarding or failing to make good the damage to the environment, particularly the air, stream, and sea pollution caused by practically uncontrolled industrial activities.[11] The importance of these acts of omission and commission is difficult to assess in quantitative terms, but their existence and significance for the country's future economic growth are admitted by both Japanese and foreign economists and by the government itself.[12]

o. The extraordinary growth of the Japanese economy in the two decades ending with 1973 had, of course, political and social as well as economic causes. Although a quantitative allocation is almost impossible, at least four mainsprings can be identified. The first is the

10. Cf. *IFS*, May 1978, pp. 226 ff.

11. An indication of the relative neglect of certain sectors is the fact that housing and capital expenditures by the central government each accounted for only about one-sixth of total gross capital formation. Similarly, the per head "social capital" stock in Japan in 1970 was hardly in excess of one-half of that in Great Britain and one-fourth of that in the United States (Economic Planning Agency, *Economic Survey of Japan 1970–1971*, p. 79).

12. For a fairly detailed discussion, cf. ibid., pp. 113 ff.

extremely high rate of capital formation, which in turn depended to a good extent on an astonishingly high rate of personal saving in fixed-value claims subject to an erosion, a result of continuous increases in the level of consumer prices, at an average annual rate of 4½ percent. The second mainspring is the wholehearted adoption, without much regard for social and environmental consequences, of technological progress, imported or increasingly domestically developed. The third mainspring is marked by the remarkably light liquidity constraints and the near-absence of the fear of debt by Japanese business enterprises in a rapid expansion of investment and output, aided, except during short cyclical intervals, by the authorities' conscious policy of easy money and low interest rates—in real terms often not much above zero. And the fourth, but not least, mainspring is the single-minded and cooperative concentration of business and government, without substantial opposition, on rapid economic growth, exactly as in the Meiji period, motivated, as then, at least in the first part of the period, by the resolve to lift Japan from a position of economic and political inferiority.

p. These two decades of *croissance à outrance* came to an end in 1973, to some extent as a result of the oil crisis but primarily for more basic domestic and international economic, social, and political reasons. In 1974 and 1975, real gross national product failed to grow at all, for the first time since the late 1930s. Even during the first two years of the recovery the rate of growth averaged only 6 percent, still a very respectable figure in international comparison but only approximately one-half of the growth rates in the corresponding two-year periods following the troughs of 1958, 1962, 1965, and 1971. The periods of double-digit growth are, one may be fairly sure, over. The annual movements of the most important indicators for the years 1974 to 1977 (or 1978) may be followed in table 7–1. The figures in the upper half of table 7–2 illustrate the sharp difference between the growth rates (percent) for the four years since 1973 and those of the long upward swing of the preceding two decades.

2. MONEY, PRICES, AND INTEREST RATES[13]

a. In the seven years 1945 to 1951, Japan, used to a slow secular rise in prices, experienced a hyperinflation that multiplied the price level by about one hundred times on the basis of wholesale as well as retail prices. After an interval of a few years, slow secular inflation resumed in 1956, the general price level (national product deflator) more than doubling between 1953 and 1973 and rising at an annual average rate of 4½ percent. The rate of increase was very small from 1956 to 1959 but accelerated from 1961 on, doubling between 1960 and 1973 at an annual average of 5½ percent, compared with a rate of only 3½ percent for the half century between 1885 and 1938 before the onset of the high inflation. More important for financial developments was the failure of the accelerated secular inflation to affect seriously the obviously prevailing money illusion, the persistence of which is evidenced, for example, by the continued practice of keeping most household saving in the form of fixed money claims when the real interest rates on such claims were often close to or below zero. The main price indices are shown on an annual basis in table 7–3.

b. Through most of the postwar period the Bank of Japan followed an accommodating monetary policy, which permitted a rapid increase in the money supply to facilitate fast economic growth. As a result, the money supply (M-1) increased twenty-one times from 1953 to 1973, that is, at an annual rate of 16 percent. This was slightly less rapidly than the expansion of national product in current prices, which proceeded at an annual rate of nearly 15 percent. Consequently, the income velocity of money showed a downward trend, declining from an only slightly fluctuating value of a little below 4 in 1953–58 to a level, again with only moderate fluctuations, around 3½ from 1964–70 and falling further to an average of slightly more than 3

---

13. The two most detailed descriptions, in Western languages, of monetary and financial institutions are Adams and Hoshii and Pressnell, whereas the two most important analytical treatments are those of Suzuki and Wallich, and Wallich.

TABLE 7-3. Price Movements, 1953–1978 (1965 = 100)[a]

	Gross national product deflator (1)	Wholesale prices (2)	Consumer prices (3)	Wages; manufacturing (4)	Stock prices (5)	Rural land prices (6)	Urban land prices (7)
1953	65.4	97.8	65.9	41.6	41.5	32.0	9.5
1954	66.5	97.1	68.1	44.3	32.0	45.6	12.3
1955	67.1	95.4	67.1	45.9	36.1	56.2	14.0
1956	70.0	99.6	67.7	50.1	49.0	65.9	16.5
1957	73.9	102.6	69.7	51.8	53.7	74.6	20.0
1958	72.9	95.9	70.4	53.2	56.5	80.6	24.4
1959	74.9	96.9	71.4	57.2	82.3	86.3	30.9
1960	78.7	97.9	74.0	61.8	106.1	91.3	41.2
1961	84.0	98.9	77.9	69.1	122.4	94.5	58.3
1962	87.5	97.3	83.0	75.4	107.5	94.9	69.2
1963	91.3	99.0	90.1	83.2	118.0	95.2	80.0
1964	95.0	99.2	93.7	92.2	104.4	97.4	91.6
1965	100.0	100.0	100.0	100.0	100.0	100.0	100.0
1966	105.0	102.4	105.2	111.8	120.1	105.5	105.2
1967	110.1	104.3	109.2	126.3	120.4	117.0	113.9
1968	115.3	105.1	115.1	145.0	129.9	135.5	129.4
1969	120.4	107.4	121.1	169.1	165.0	143.8	151.7
1970	128.5	111.3	130.3	198.7	178.6	157.0	181.6
1971	134.5	110.4	138.2	226.3	195.9	165.9	210.2
1972	140.8	111.3	144.5	261.8	308.2	184.0	237.9
1973	156.1	129.0	161.6	323.2	395.6	234.3	297.7
1974	187.4	169.4	200.9	407.7	335.3	283.3	366.2
1975	203.4	174.5	224.7	454.5	340.1	310.9	350.4
1976	214.9	183.2	245.6	511.8	379.3	·	353.1
1977	227.1	186.7	265.4	560.5	411.2	·	360.7
1978	236.5	182.0	275.0	600.0	450.0	·	368.0

[a]Annual averages.

SOURCES: **Col. 1:** 1954–64, *ARNIS*, 1970, pp. 90–91; 1965–77, *ARNA*, pp. 84–85.   **Cols. 2 and 3:** 1954–62, *ESA*, 1970, p. 4; Tokyo for col. 3; 1963–77, *ESA*, 1977, p. 6; all Japan for col. 3; 1978, *IFS*, June 1979, p. 212.   **Col. 4:** 1954–77, *ESA*, 1977, p. 5; 1978, *IFS*, June 1979, p. 214.   **Col. 5:** 1954–78, *ESA*, 1970, p. 1; 1974, p. 1; 1977, p. 187; *IFS*, May 1978, pp. 226–27; June 1979, p. 212.   **Col. 6:** 1950–65, *HYS*, pp. 88–89; average of indices for paddy and dry fields; figures refer to prices in March; 1966–75, Japan Real Estate Institute.   **Col. 7:** 1950–54, *HYS*, p. 87; prices refer to September; indices of Japan Real Estate Institute. 1955–77; *ESA*, 1970, p. 264; 1977, p. 303; prices refer to March.

percent in 1972–78. Throughout most of the period, currency issued by the Bank of Japan constituted about one-fourth of the total money supply, and check deposit money about three-fourths.

c. The total increase in currency issued by the Bank of Japan between 1953 and 1973 of ¥ 11.6 bill. was based primarily on loans and discounts to banks of ¥ 5.8 trill., mainly the large city banks, and secondarily on government securities (¥ 1.4 trill.). Foreign, mostly dollar, assets became important as a basis of currency expansion only near the end of the period, increasing by ¥ 3.5 trill. over the period, seven-eighths of which were acquired in 1968–73. Even in 1973, however, foreign assets were equal to only one-third of bank notes issued, compared to ratios of about one-seventh for government securities and one-half for loans and discounts to deposit banks.[14] Monetary policy, therefore, operated mainly through the Bank of Japan's direct ac-

14. The position changed radically in 1971 as a result of an unprecedented surplus in the balance of payments; during this one year foreign assets of the Bank of Japan increased by ¥ 3.0 trill. and claims on the government were reduced by

quisition or redemption of government securities from the Treasury or the banks, as there was no broad open market, or through the bank's readiness or reluctance to accommodate the city banks, which was only partly reflected in the official discount and loan rates and mainly evidenced by credit ceilings or expressed in moral suasion (so-called window guidance). Reserve requirements exist and apply not only to commercial banks but also to trust banks, long-term credit banks, and the larger cooperative credit organizations, but they are so low (since September 1969 between 0.25 and 0.50 percent for time deposits and between 0.75 and 1.50 percent for other deposits, depending on the size of the bank) that they are not likely to have considerably influenced the behavior of the affected institutions or to have been used as a major means of monetary policy.

d. Money supply, which can be followed on an annual basis in table 7–4, increased more rapidly during periods of ease than during periods of restraint, with the exception of the expansion period of 1965–67; but even during periods of restraint the money supply expanded at a rate of slightly more than 1 percent per month. The periods of monetary restraint occurred during the later part of the expansionary phases of the business cycle or during contractions, whereas the periods of monetary ease took place during the early phases of expansion or during sidewise movements.[15]

e. Whereas the general movement of prices was upward and markedly so from the 1960s on, variations among different types of commodities and services or assets were pronounced. Thus the general price level (national product deflator) and consumer prices approximately doubled from 1960 to 1973. Prices of investment goods, however, rose by only one-third, although the cost of residential construction nearly doubled; and export prices, particularly important for Japan's economic growth, as well as the prices of consumer durables, hardly rose at all.[16]

f. Asset prices advanced for the period as a whole, and throughout most of it, considerably more rapidly than the prices of commodities and services. Thus agricultural land prices rose seven times between 1953 and 1973, that is, at an average annual rate of more than 10 percent, more than twice the rise in the general price level, which may be explained to only a minor extent by the fact that they had risen by only about 125 times between 1938 and 1953, compared with an advance in the consumer price index by about 240 times.[17] The rise was even more spectacular in urban land prices, aided by an ever-increasing demand as cities expanded. The index of urban land prices multiplied by no less than 31 times from 1953 to 1973, or at an average annual rate of 19 percent, or more than four times the rise in the general price level. The prices of corporate stock, representing the equity in larger business enterprises, rose during the same period nearly ten times, an annual rate of growth of 12 percent or nearly three times the rise in the general price level. Such rises necessarily generated immense capital gains, mostly as yet unrealized at the end of the period. They must have greatly accentuated inequalities in the distribution of wealth, because most corporate stock and nonresidential real estate is owned by a relatively small proportion of the population.[18]

g. The level of nominal interest rates showed, as table 7–5 indicates, no definite trend during the period. Because most interest rates are formally or informally controlled by the Bank

---

more than ¥ 1.1 trill. and claims on deposit banks by ¥ 1.6 trill. Thus at the end of 1971 foreign assets were equal to more than two-thirds of reserve money against not much more than one-fourth one year earlier. Part of these changes were reversed in 1973 when the balance of payments surplus disappeared.

15. The average monthly rate of expansion of the money supply was 1.1 percent for the four periods of restraint within the period from the middle of 1961 to the end of 1971 compared with an average of 1.9 percent for the three periods of monetary ease. The rate for the period of neutral-monetary policy, from August 1968 to September 1969, with 1.7 percent falls between them. These figures are derived from classification of periods as to restraint in OECD EDS/MPS (17) 12a and monthly changes in money supply in *IFS*.

16. *ESA*, 1975, pp. 273 ff.

17. *HYS*, pp. 80 and 88–89.

18. The problem will be taken up in section 6c. It is astonishing that it apparently has not attracted any detailed quantitative research by Japanese economists, including their numerous Marxist wing.

TABLE 7-4. Money Supply (M$_1$), 1953–1978

	Outstanding, end of year			Change during year		
	Amount (¥ trill.) (1)	Rate of change (percent) (2)	Percent of gross national product (3)	Amount (¥ trill.) (4)	Percent of gross national product (5)	Income velocity (6)
1953	1.94	15.9	26.1	0.25	3.54	4.00
1954	2.01	3.6	24.4	0.08	1.02	3.94
1955	2.33	15.8	25.4	0.32	3.71	3.97
1956	2.71	16.4	26.0	0.38	3.91	3.86
1957	2.82	4.1	25.0	0.11	0.99	4.01
1958	3.19	13.1	26.1	0.36	3.13	3.83
1959	3.04	−4.7	21.4	−0.15	−1.16	4.15
1960	4.15	36.6	24.0	1.11	7.16	4.31
1961	4.91	18.4	24.3	0.76	3.97	4.22
1962	5.73	16.6	25.1	0.82	3.87	3.98
1963	7.70	34.5	28.8	1.98	8.09	3.65
1964	8.70	13.0	28.5	1.00	3.47	3.52
1965	10.29	18.3	29.6	1.59	4.94	3.39
1966	11.72	13.9	28.8	1.44	3.84	3.40
1967	13.37	14.1	27.7	1.65	3.73	3.53
1968	15.16	13.4	26.5	1.79	3.39	3.70
1969	18.28	20.6	27.1	3.13	5.07	3.69
1970	21.36	16.8	27.7	3.08	4.18	3.72
1971	27.69	29.6	31.9	6.33	7.81	3.30
1972	34.53	24.7	33.6	6.83	7.36	2.98
1973	40.31	16.7	34.5	5.79	5.12	3.02
1974	44.95	11.5	31.7	4.64	3.44	3.15
1975	49.95	11.1	31.6	5.00	3.36	3.14
1976	56.18	12.5	31.8	6.23	3.72	3.15
1977	60.79	8.2	31.1	4.61	2.47	3.19
1978	68.93	13.4	32.3	8.14	3.97	3.16

SOURCES: **Col. 1:** *IFS*, May 1978, pp. 226–27; January 1979, p. 212.   **Col. 6:** Gross national product (table 7-1, col. 1) divided by average of current and preceding year.

of Japan, short-term fluctuations have little significance except for the two fairly free rates, at the short-term end of the range the rate for call money and at the long end the yield of Telephone Company bonds.

The call money rate exhibited very sharp short-term movements, reflecting its function of establishing equilibrium in the interbank money market. It ranged during the period between 5 and 22 percent, the latter during the credit squeeze of 1957, but mostly kept within the range of 6 to 9 percent. The yield of Telephone Company bonds varied between a low of 7½ percent, reached in mid-1956, late 1966, and late 1971, and a high of 14 percent in 1961, but for most of the period moved between 8 and 10 percent with the exception of a bulge from mid-1961 to late 1962.

Institutional debit rates, which are cartelized and supervised by the Bank of Japan, naturally show much smaller fluctuations. Thus the average rate charged on bank loans and discounts, on the basis of annual averages, stayed until 1978 between 7½ and little more than 9 percent, showing a slightly declining tendency over the period. The effective rate is higher because of the requirement that a substantial proportion of the proceeds, apparently something like one-fourth to one-third, varying according to the quality of borrower, be kept generally on current account, which yields virtually no interest (so-called buzumi deposits).

All these rates have been held during most of the period below what may be regarded as their equilibrium levels. As a result, an unsatisfied fringe of borrowers has existed, except

TABLE 7-5. Interest Rates, 1954–1978 (Percent)

	Bank of Japan discount (1)	Call money (2)	Bank loans (3)	Bond yield (4)	Telephone bond yield (5)	Bank three-month deposits (6)	Trust Bank five-year deposits (7)	Postal Saving ordinary deposits (8)	Yield on listed stocks (9)
1954	5.84	7.67	9.08			4.00	9.00	3.96	9.44
1955	7.30	6.94	8.98			4.00	9.00	3.96	7.96
1956	7.30	6.76	8.44	7.44		4.00	7.10	3.96	6.68
1957	8.40	11.78	8.41	7.79		4.00	7.50	3.96	7.14
1958	7.30	9.69	8.51	7.98		4.00	7.50	3.96	6.66
1959	7.30	8.36	8.12	7.98		4.00	7.50	3.96	4.54
1960	6.94	8.40	8.77	8.07		4.00	7.50	3.96	3.93
1961	7.30	11.44	8.00	8.06	14.03	4.00	7.07	3.60	3.24
1962	6.57	10.31	8.21	8.71	12.50	4.00	7.07	3.60	3.86
1963	5.84	7.54	7.79	.	8.79	4.00	7.07	3.60	4.24
1964	6.57	10.03	7.90	.	9.21	4.00	7.07	3.60	5.69
1965	5.48	6.97	7.80	.	8.19	4.00	7.07	3.60	5.92
1966	5.48	5.84	7.48	7.43	7.70	4.00	6.98	3.60	4.44
1967	5.84	6.39	7.32	7.51	7.96	4.00	6.98	3.60	4.74
1968	5.84	7.88	7.46	7.84	8.53	4.00	7.03	3.60	4.36
1969	6.25	7.70	7.41	8.13	8.90	4.00	7.03	3.60	3.37
1970	6.00	8.29	7.66	8.25	9.17	4.00	7.23	3.60	3.47
1971	4.75	6.42	7.59	7.58	7.91	4.00	7.03	3.60	3.41
1972	4.25	4.72	7.05	6.72	6.64	3.75	6.63	3.36	2.24
1973	9.00	7.16	7.19	7.64	8.52	4.25	7.70	3.84	2.09
1974	9.00	12.54	9.11	9.91	11.66	5.50	8.83	4.32	2.53
1975	6.50	10.67	9.10	9.44	9.60	4.50	8.13	3.84	2.31
1976	6.50	6.98	8.26	8.89	8.88[a]	4.50	8.13	3.84	1.82
1977	4.25	5.68	7.56	7.27	6.58[a]	3.25	6.53	2.88	1.78
1978	3.50	4.36	6.31	6.37	6.65[a]	2.50	6.22	.	1.59

[a]December.

SOURCES: **Cols. 1 and 2:** *IFS*, May 1978, pp. 226–27; January 1979, p. 211; col. 1 refers to rate at end of year.   **Col. 3:** *ESA*, 1975, pp. 57 ff.; 1977, pp. 67 ff. Ministry of Finance, *Monthly Finance Review*, February 1979, p. 20.   **Cols. 4 and 5:** Tokyo Stock Exchange, *Annual Statistics Report*, 1970, p. 103; *Monthly Statistics Report*, January 1976, p. 85. Col. 4 is based on 11 issues from 1956 to 1960 and between 32 and 75 issues thereafter. Data for 1976 to 1978 in col. 4 refer to averages of yields of public corporation and industrial bonds and bank debentures (Ministry of Finance, *Quarterly Bulletin of Financial Statistics*, March 1979); those in col. 5 come from *ESM*, various issues.   **Cols. 6–8:** *ESA*, 1975, pp. 57 ff.; 1977, pp. 61–62.   **Col. 9:** Ministry of Finance, *Monthly Finance Review*, February 1979.

possibly during the relatively brief periods of contraction, that is, of slow growth of the economy, and financial institutions have resorted to some form of credit rationing. For the same reasons, effective interest rates have in many cases been increased above official rates by various devices in a "gray market."[19] The rates paid by institutions similarly showed no trend. Thus the rate on ordinary postal saving deposits stayed until 1971 between 3.6 and 4.0 percent and the rate on three-month time deposits in banks remained fixed at 4 percent, but the rate of five-year deposits with trust banks declined from 9 to 7 percent.

Because the general price level, measured by the national product deflator or the consumer price index, advanced on the average by 4½ percent a year, the level of real interest rates was low, a factor that probably contributed to the rapid growth in investment. From the middle 1960s, when the price level rose by about 6 percent a year, the rates received by savers from institutions were in fact negative for short-term deposits and even for long-term deposits were

19. The "disequilibrium" character of the Japanese credit market and interest.

not above 2 percent. This, however, does not seem to have deterred households from continuing to put most of their financial saving into deposits of this type. Similarly, the real yields of bonds as well as the real cost of bank loans were moderate, well below 5 percent throughout the period.

The current dividend yield on corporate stocks was quite high early in the period, averaging 7½ percent for 1954–58, then fell precipitously to a low of not much more than 3 percent in 1961 as stock prices advanced sharply, but recovered to nearly 6 percent in 1965 as stocks receded from their high. In 1969–70 yields again declined sharply, to not much more than 2 percent in 1972 and 1973. However, allowance for the realized and unrealized capital gains over the period would increase these figures substantially. For the entire period the annual average rate of appreciation of stock prices of 12 percent added to the average dividend yield of 5 percent produces an average total yield for stockholders of 17 percent per year, fluctuating, for five-year periods, between a low 7 percent in 1964–68 and a high of 28 percent in 1969–74.[20]

As in the case of the country's infrastructure, the four years following the peak of the long swing in 1973 showed a very different, and generally less favorable, picture from that of the preceding two decades. This is evident from the comparison in the lower half of table 7–2 of the rates of change (percent) in money and prices in 1974–77 with those in the 1954–73 period.

The main difference between the two periods is the acceleration of the rate of inflation after 1973, which more than doubled the rate of increase in the prices of commodities and services and was accompanied by a marked slowdown in the surge of asset prices. This acceleration occurred in the face of a substantial reduction in the rate of expansion of the money supply. The rate of expansion of national product in current prices was slightly below that of the preceding two decades as the decline in the growth rate of real product was somewhat larger than the increase in the rate of inflation. Reflecting the recession of 1974–75 and the slow recovery by Japanese standards of the following two years, interest rates fell to the lowest levels of the postwar period and often of the last century. By 1978, however, the rate of inflation, at about 4 percent for the national product deflator and for consumer prices, had returned to the average of the postwar period.

3. CAPITAL FORMATION, SAVING, AND SECTORAL FINANCIAL SURPLUSES AND DEFICITS[21]

The outstanding characteristic in the development of Japan's real infrastructure during the postwar period, next to and partly responsible for the rapid growth in national product, is the high and rising level of the capital formation ratio.

During the two decades from 1954 through 1973 Japan devoted nearly two-fifths of its

20. Tokyo Stock Exchange, *Annual Statistics Report*, 1970, p. 79, for yields that are unweighted averages for dividend-paying issues. The weighted averages for all issues in the first section (the majority of all stock listed) for 1959–70, not available earlier, is 5.0 percent compared to 4.3 percent for the unweighted average of dividend-paying issues.

21. The flow-of-funds figures used in this chapter are generally taken from the Bank of Japan's publications, primarily *BJFFA, 1954–63, 1964–71*, and *1970–77* editions. However, the staff of the Flow-of-Funds Section of the Economic Research Department of the Bank of Japan, then headed by Sadao Ishida, kindly made available some additional breakdowns within the financial and the government sectors and some revised figures for the years before 1970. The tables shown in this chapter are in some cases on a grosser basis than those published, i.e., they try to avoid netting claims and liabilities among sectors and subsectors, although the nature of the basic documents did not always permit this. Finally, four subsectors of the financial sector as defined for the purposes of this chapter—the Foreign Exchange Fund, the Trust Fund Bureau, government financial institutions, and securities companies—are included in the Bank of Japan's publications until the early 1970s in the government and corporate business sectors. The figures for another subsector ("other financial institutions," which includes call money dealers, security finance companies, and branches of foreign banks) are not shown separately in the Bank of Japan's publication although the figures for the subsector are included in the (net) total for all financial institutions, but because of the netting process cannot be obtained as residuals between the sector totals and the published data for subsectors. The figures used for the years 1970 to 1977 are taken unchanged from the Banks' publications, and hence are not fully comparable to those before 1970.

total gross national product to capital formation. The ratio rose from not much more than one-fourth in 1954–55 to one-third in 1956–60 and to more than two-fifths in 1966–73. Because of the rapid rate of increase in the volume of capital expenditures, and in part also because of their calculation in the national accounts on the basis of original rather than of replacement cost, capital consumption expenditures offset only about one-third of the total and two-fifths of fixed gross capital expenditures. The net capital formation ratio, therefore, averaged about one-fourth of national product, a very high ratio from almost every point of view.

The three outstanding characteristics of the structure of capital formation in postwar Japan were, the order of enumeration not necessarily indicating relative importance for economic growth or for finance, first, the high share of machinery and equipment (in 1971–73, on a gross basis, one-fourth of total gross capital expenditures including consumer durables and one-seventh of national product); second, the low share of dwellings and consumer durables (together not much more than one-fourth of total gross capital formation and not much more than one-tenth of national product); and, third, the substantial share of the public sector of approximately one-seventh of gross capital formation by general government and nearly one-tenth by government enterprises.

Because net capital imports and exports have been small, averaging only about 1 percent of domestic capital formation, these capital formation ratios can be regarded as practically equal to the domestic saving ratios. Here the outstanding characteristics, which will be discussed in some detail in section 5, are, first, the very high saving ratio of the personal sector (including unincorporated farm and nonfarm enterprises), which averaged for the period as a whole with little fluctuation slightly more than one-half of total net national saving except in 1974–77 when its share rose to more than two-thirds, more than one-fourth of personal disposable income, and about one-fifth of gross national product; second, the high gross but relatively low net saving ratio of nonfinancial corporations, averaging for the entire period less than one-tenth of total net saving (although more than one-sixth for 1956–73) and less than 2 (about 4) percent of national product; and third, the very high saving ratio of the public sector, particularly on a net basis, which is due in part, however, to the astonishingly low capital allowances of the public sector as calculated in the national accounts; such saving represents for the entire period with little fluctuation until 1974 about one-fourth of total net saving and more than 6 percent of national product.

From the point of view of financial analysis, the most interesting figures are the sectoral financial surpluses and deficits (the differences between the sector's saving and its capital expenditures), which indicate the extent to which individual sectors make funds available to or absorb them from other sectors. Table 7–6 shows annual surpluses and deficits, expressed as a percentage of gross national product to eliminate the effect of the rapid growth in all absolute figures over the postwar period. Separate ratios are shown only for the three main nonfinancial sectors because no further breakdown is available for the very large and heterogeneous personal sector or for the corporate business sector. Financial institutions have been omitted for most of the period as differences between their capital expenditures and saving are generally small.[22]

For the period as a whole the personal sector had a large financial surplus, which, calculated from the national accounts, averaged about 7 percent of gross national product and does not show large fluctuations when five-year periods are considered. This was the result of a

---

22. The financial surpluses and deficits derived from national accounts as the difference between capital expenditures and saving, which underlie the following paragraph in the text, differ from those shown in the flow-of-funds accounts as the difference between the acquisition of financial assets and the incurrence of liabilities on which table 7–6 is based. These differences are not astonishing, as the two sets of figures are taken from two independent sources of data. Although these differences are regrettable, they are in general not large enough to affect the conclusions drawn in this section from the figures. Except for table 7–5 and the discussion based on it, this chapter uses the figures from the flow-of-funds accounts, because only this set permits the breakdowns of the totals among groups of financial institutions and among types of financial instruments that are essential for financial analysis.

TABLE 7-6. Sectoral Financial Surpluses and Deficits, 1954–1977
(Percent of Gross National Product)

	Public (1)	Personal (2)	Corporate business (3)	Financial institutions[a] (4)	Rest of the world (5)	All sectors[b] (percent) (6)	All sectors[b] (¥ trill.) (7)
1954	−2.2	5.9	−3.9	—	0.2	12.2	0.95
1955	−2.2	7.4	−4.3	—	−1.0	14.9	1.29
1956	0.0	8.9	−9.0	—	0.1	18.0	1.76
1957	0.8	6.9	−9.7	—	2.0	19.4	2.15
1958	−0.3	6.2	−4.5	—	−1.4	12.4	1.43
1959	−0.8	9.1	−7.3	—	−1.0	18.2	2.35
1960	0.6	8.9	−9.1	—	−0.3	18.9	2.92
1961	0.9	10.0	−12.7	—	1.9	25.4	4.86
1962	−1.0	8.9	−8.0	—	0.1	17.9	3.80
1963	−1.3	7.6	−7.5	—	1.1	17.6	4.30
1964	−2.3	9.2	−7.5	—	0.6	19.6	5.65
1965	−2.8	7.9	−4.0	—	−1.1	15.8	5.03
1966	−3.9	8.9	−3.8	—	−1.2	17.6	6.63
1967	−3.1	9.3	−6.4	—	0.2	19.0	8.36
1968	−2.7	8.8	−5.5	—	−0.7	17.8	9.34
1969	−1.6	8.3	−5.5	—	−1.3	16.8	10.36
1970	−0.9	7.9	−6.9	0.9	−1.0	17.6	12.86
1971	−1.9	9.4	−6.2	1.2	−2.5	21.2	17.10
1972	−2.7	11.5	−7.9	1.3	−2.2	25.6	23.76
1973	−2.9	8.8	−7.6	1.6	0.0	20.9	23.64
1974	−3.7	10.3	−8.5	1.0	1.0	24.5	33.04
1975	−7.3	10.5	−4.1	0.8	0.1	22.8	34.08
1976	−7.4	11.4	−3.9	0.6	−0.6	23.9	40.13
1977	−7.2	11.0	−2.6	0.3	−1.5	22.6	42.14

[a]For 1954–69 no surplus or deficit is shown in flow-of-funds accounts.   [b]Absolute sum of sectoral surpluses and deficits.

SOURCE OF BASIC DATA: *BJFFA*, 1970–77, 1964–71, and 1954–63.

gross investment ratio of about 12 percent and a gross saving ratio of nearly 19 percent. On the basis of the figures for the sector's nonresidential capital expenditures, excluding consumer durables, and scattered information from household income and expenditure samples, to be discussed in section 5, one may venture the guess that all three main subsectors—farmers, nonfarm unincorporated entrepreneurs, and other, mainly employee, households—had a substantial financial surplus. The financial deficit of the public sector was small, except in 1974–77, with the sector's saving covering most of its capital expenditures. The corporate business sector shows a large financial deficit, averaging 7½ percent of national product and reaching a peak of more than 9 percent in the boom of 1971–73. This is the result of the fact that the sector's gross saving, although exceeding one-eighth of national product, has covered less than two-thirds of its very large gross capital expenditures, the ratio being on the order of one-third on a net basis.

The absolute values of the financial surpluses and deficits of the three broad sectors have, of course, increased considerably, but their relations to each other and their ratios to national product as shown in table 7–6 on the basis of flow-of-funds accounts, values that are not identical with those derived from the national income and product accounts, have exhibited hardly any trends, although they have experienced considerable cyclical variations over the period.

One immediately evident feature is the regularity of the sign of the series for each of the sectors. Thus all the twenty annual values for nonfinancial corporations are negative, that is, they indicate a financial deficit or an excess of capital expenditures over saving. Similarly, all twenty values for the personal sector are positive. In the case of the public sector sixteen values are negative and only four, all in years of sharp upswings and before 1962, are positive. It is only for the rest of the world that years of surpluses and deficits are about equal in number, the deficit years, which indicate balance of payments surpluses, predominating since 1965.

The surplus of the personal sector in relation to national product shows an upward trend, rising from fully 7 percent in 1954–56 to 10 percent in 1971–73. The relation of the annual values to the phases of the business cycle is weak. Some peak years are associated with high values of the ratio (1961 and 1964), but others are not (1957, 1970, and 1973). Of the four troughs, three (1954, 1958, and 1965) are accompanied by low values of the ratio, but two (1962 and 1974) do not show such an association. The relation is not more pronounced for nonfinancial corporations. Thus the cyclical peaks of 1957 and 1961, and to a lesser extent that of 1970, are evident in high values of the financial deficit, whereas those of 1964 and 1973 are not. Two of the four troughs, those of 1954 and 1958, are reflected in a low financial deficit, whereas the situation at the 1962 and 1965 trough, is unclear, and the 1974 trough shows a large deficit. The relation is considerably more pronounced for the public sector. Here the position changes from a surplus to a deficit, involving net borrowing from other sectors, as a peak is succeeded by a trough (1957–58, 1961–69, 1970–71) or at least the deficit ratio increases (1964–65). The connection is clearest for the rest of the world sector, at least until 1970, a change from cyclical peak to trough being accompanied by a sharp improvement in the balance of payments, which is evidenced by a shift from a financial surplus to a deficit (1954–55, 1957–58, 1964–65), by a sharp reduction in surplus (1961–62), or by an increase in the deficits. Indeed, this shift, brought about or strongly aided by monetary stringency, is an important characteristic of Japanese postwar business cycles.

In most years the financial surplus of the personal sector has been about equal to the combined deficits of the other sectors. It is only at strong cyclical peaks, such as in 1957 and in 1961, although not in all of them, that the adverse balance of international payments has offset a substantial part of the financial deficit of the corporate business sector. This did not happen at the 1969–70 peak, but by that time the structural changes in Japanese foreign trade, creating massive export surpluses, had become so strong as to override the previously prevailing cyclical movements in the balance of payments.

The ratio of the absolute sum of sectoral financial surpluses and deficits to the gross national product of the nonfinancial sectors, which is probably the best measure of the intensity of financial activity, is shown in table 7–6, column 6, for each year from 1954 to 1973. The setup of the flow-of-funds accounts unfortunately makes it necessary to derive this ratio from the absolute sum of the financial surpluses and deficits of only five sectors (public, personal, corporate business, financial institutions, and the rest of the world), figures that are derived by netting the financial surpluses of surplus units within one sector against the deficits of the deficit units within the same sector, rather than as is theoretically preferable, that is, as the absolute sum of financial surpluses and deficits of all individual economic units.[23]

This ratio shows a slight upward trend from about 15 percent in 1954–56 to 23 percent in 1975–77, averaging about 18 percent over the two decades (excluding financial institutions). Cyclical fluctuations, however, are pronounced. Up to the late 1960s, business cycle peaks (1957, 1961, 1964) are reflected in ratios above the period average and well above surrounding years. Similarly, the ratio is well below the period average and below surrounding years in cyclical trough years (1958, 1962–63, and 1965).

The effects of the 1974–75 recession and the much slower rates of growth in the recovery of 1976–77 are reflected in changes in the level and structure of saving and investment. The national saving and investment ratios were considerably lower in 1974–77 than they had been since the 1960s, but they remained very high in international comparison. The decline was

---

23. Cf. Goldsmith, 1969, Appendix 1.

particularly pronounced in the corporate business sector, whose gross investment ratio fell to 17 percent of national product in 1974–77 compared with nearly 25 percent in the boom of 1971–73 and to 20 percent in the 1960s. The investment ratios of the personal and public sectors stayed at their levels of the 1960s. The decline was much more pronounced in the saving ratios of the corporate business and public sectors, becoming negative in the corporate sector for the first time in the postwar period. In contrast, the net saving ratio of the household sector increased to more than 18 percent of national product, or one-fourth of personal disposable income, the highest ever reached for a period of this length.[24,25]

4. FINANCIAL INSTITUTIONS[26,27]

a. Overview

Structural changes were also relatively small in financial institutions compared to the immense expansion of the scale of operation as measured by total assets, which increased from less than ¥ 9 trill. in 1953 to nearly ¥ 290 trill. in 1973, or at the extremely rapid rate of 19 percent in nominal and of 14 percent in real terms. The most important change was the increasing importance, partly through the creation of new institutions, of financial institutions specializing in the financing of agriculture and small business, most of which were in cooperative form or operated by the government. Thus the share of these cooperative or public institutions increased from less than one-eighth of the assets of all financial institutions in 1950 to nearly one-fourth a quarter century later, with most of the increase occurring in the 1950s. A second structural change of importance was the creation of several types of private institutions connected with the stock market, security companies, similar to stock brokerage and investment banking firms in Western countries; security finance companies, which specialized in financing stock market activities; and investment trusts. However, these three types of institutions in 1975 accounted for not much more than 1½ percent of the assets of all financial institutions, having reached a peak with a share of 4 percent in 1960.

b. Structure of Assets and Liabilities

The essential features of the Japanese system of financial institutions are visible in tables 7–7 to 7–12. Tables 7–7 and 7–9 reflect the situation at the end of the period, with table 7–7 showing the structure of the financial assets and liabilities of a dozen groups of financial institutions and table 7–9 showing the share of each group of institutions in the total financial assets and liabilities of all institutions. Table 7–8 makes it possible to follow the changes in the structure of assets and liabilities of the two most important groups, the Bank of Japan and deposit

24. These ratios do not make allowances for net purchases and sales of land, which affect the sectoral saving and investment accounts, although they wash out in the national accounts. These transactions were negative and large for the personal sector, amounting to a reduction of gross and net saving and investment of 4.9 percent of national product in 1971–73 and of 1.4 percent in 1974–77. They were positive to the extent of 4.0 and 0.6 percent of national product in the case of corporations, and of 0.8 and 0.7 percent, respectively, in that of the public sector (ARNA, pp. 60 ff.).

25. These figures are taken from the national accounts. The estimates of sectoral financial surpluses and deficits that can be derived from them differ, and sometimes substantially, from those of table 7–6, which come from the flow-of-funds accounts.

26. The description of the operations and postwar development of the individual types of financial institutions has been kept to a minimum because several official and unofficial publications exist in English that provide it in detail, e.g., the Bank of Japan's Money and Banking in Japan (1964), The Japanese Financial System (1970), The Bank of Japan (3rd ed. 1971), and Money and Banking in Japan (1973), edited by L. S. Pressnell; the Fuji Bank's Banking in Modern Japan (2nd ed., 1967); and Adams and Hoshii's, A Financial History of the New Japan (1972).

27. A brief description of the Bank of Japan's flow-of-funds accounts, which provide the statistical basis for much of the discussion in this section, will be found in chapter 4 of A Study on Flow-of-Funds in Japan (Bank of Japan). Figures for security investment companies and for securities companies are not identified in the English version of the accounts for all years—they are included with "trust accounts" and "corporate business," respectively—and therefore cannot be separately shown in some tables, but they are small enough not to affect the picture.

TABLE 7-7. Structure of Financial Assets and Liabilities of Financial Institutions, 1977 (Percent)

	All financial institutions (1)	Bank of Japan (2)	City banks (3)	Other banks (4)	Trust accounts (5)	Small business institutions (6)	Agricultural institutions (7)	Investment companies (8)	Securities companies (9)	Insurance companies (10)	Postal Saving and life insurance (11)	Trust Fund Bureau (12)	Other government institutions (13)
					I. Financial assets								
Currency and demand deposits	1.8	—	2.9	1.0	—	4.0	4.2	—	12.3	3.3	1.2	—	0.1
Other deposits	9.4	—	0.3	0.1	—	1.5	2.0	—	5.0	4.0	80.6[c]	—	0.1
Government securities	9.7	46.2	9.6	11.2	5.6	4.3	12.7	13.6	2.6	4.2	0.8	15.4	0.9
Other debt securities	6.7	0.6	4.1	7.2	11.0	7.7	12.2	37.0	10.7	8.4	7.0	5.8	0.2
Corporate stock[a]	2.6	—	3.4	2.8	2.3	0.5	0.5	30.3	17.2	18.7	—	—	0.1
Loans	68.6	29.8	79.1	77.7	77.9	82.1	68.4	18.7	52.3	61.5	10.4	78.9	98.6
Other financial assets	1.3	23.5	0.6	—	3.2	—	—	0.4	—	—	—	—	—
All financial assets													
Percent	100.0	100.0	100.0	100.0	100.0	100.0	100.0	100.0	100.0	100.0	100.0	100.0	100.0
Trill. ¥	420.2	17.6	71.9	66.0	19.0	60.2	24.8	4.7	2.0	22.7	45.7	60.0	25.6
					II. Liabilities and corporate stock								
Currency and demand deposits	18.1	100.0	27.5	27.3	—	23.3	26.7	—	—	—	0.2	—	—
Other deposits	57.0	—	56.2	43.3	100.0	64.9	65.5	—	—	—	79.5	99.8	11.0
Debt securities	5.5	—	1.6	21.6	—	5.5	6.1	—	11.4	0.9	—	—	—
Corporate stock[a]	1.6	—	1.2	1.2	—	0.2	—	100.0	43.3	0.0	—	—	84.7
Loans	7.9	—	13.5	1.0	—	0.4	0.1	—	45.3	—	—	—	—
Other liabilities	9.8[b]	—	—	5.5	—	5.7	1.6	—	—	99.1[b]	20.3[b]	0.2	4.3
All	100.0	100.0	100.0	100.0	100.0	100.0	100.0	100.0	100.0	100.0	100.0	100.0	100.0

[a]Book value.   [b]Of which, insurance liabilities account for 7.0 percent in col. 1: 88.8 percent in col. 10, and 20.2 percent in col. 11.   [c]Deposits with the Trust Fund Bureau.

SOURCE OF BASIC DATA: *BJFFA*, 1970–77, pp. 79 ff.

money banks, throughout the postwar period. Similar information for the specialized credit institutions is readily available only since 1970. The three sets of statistics are not entirely comparable, because they differ in the degree of consolidation and in the grouping of institutions; tables 7–7 and 7–9 are derived from the flow-of-funds accounts and eliminate many more interinstitutional claims and liabilities than does table 7–10, the deposit money banks of table 7–8, for example, excluding the long-term credit banks included in the "other banks" category of tables 7–7 and 7–9.

The most important characteristics of the portfolio structure of Japanese financial institutions are:

(i) The low degree of primary and secondary liquidity. This is not fully evident in the tables because of extensive netting within cash and demand deposits.

(ii) The relatively small importance of holdings of securities.

(iii) The predominance of loans to business and the concomitant small share of consumer credit, including home mortgages, a characteristic not visible in the tables because of the absence of a breakdown of loans in the flow-of-funds accounts.

(iv) The predominance of time and savings deposits among sources of funds.

(v) The very low ratio of equity to liabilities.

Primary liquidity (cash, deposits with others, and call loans) is relatively low. For city and regional banks, it amounted in 1977 to 7 percent of assets, having declined from 12 percent for city banks and 10 percent for regional banks in 1955. However, in the case of city banks, borrowed money in 1977 amounted to 4½ percent, the same ratio as in 1955, coming in about equal parts from the Bank of Japan and from the call market, that is, mainly the regional banks.[28] In fact, in their relations with the Bank of Japan, the city banks were usually net debtors to a considerable extent until the period of balance of payments surpluses in the early 1970s. This situation, known as overloan, has been one of the main distinctive traits of the Japanese banking structure both in the prewar and postwar periods.[29,30]

Government securities now make up one-tenth of the assets of all financial institutions, a sharp increase from the 5 percent in 1970, which reflects the heavy deficit financing of the central government since 1973. The share, however, differs greatly among institutions, ranging among major groups from 4 percent for insurance companies and small business finance institutions, 10 percent for deposit banks, and 15 percent for the Trust Fund Bureau to nearly one-half for the Bank of Japan.

Other debt securities account for 7 percent of total assets and are in that order of magnitude for banks, financial institutions, small business, insurance companies, the Postal Saving System, and the Trust Fund Bureau. They bulk much more heavily only in the case of investment companies.

Corporate stocks absorb at book value only 2½ percent of all financial institutions' assets, although at market about three times as high a share.[31] They are of considerable importance only

28. *ESA*, 1978, pp. 81 ff.

29. Probably no feature of the monetary mechanism of Japan has been more written about than "overloans"; cf. particularly Suzuki, chap. 1, and Wallich and Wallich, pp. 284 ff.

30. Total assets and liabilities as reported in the banks' balance sheets (e.g., *ESA*, 1978, pp. 81 ff.) are much higher, usually by 25 to 30 percent, than shown in the flow-of-funds accounts. The main discrepancies are on the asset side: the omission in the flow-of-funds accounts of real estate, foreign exchange, customers' liabilities for acceptances and guarantees and interoffice accounts, as well as a reduction of cash presumably because of netting of interbank accounts. The same items plus reserves explain the difference on the liabilities side.

31. Flow-of-funds statistics provide estimates for the market value of corporate stock holdings for only the corporate and personal sectors. It has been assumed that the ratio of market to book value for financial institutions is the same as for the combined holdings of the corporate and personal sectors, i.e., about 2.30 in 1970 and 3.10 in 1977. This procedure has not been applied to the stock of investment companies, which is apparently entered at market value.

in the portfolios of insurance and securities companies, with a share of nearly one-fifth, and particularly among investment companies with a share of nearly one-third.

Loans constitute the dominating asset, usually accounting for more than three-fourths of the total, for all groups except investment trusts, the Postal Saving System, and the Bank of Japan, because of its large accumulation of foreign assets in the 1970s. Loans are extended by the deposit and trust banks mainly to large business enterprises; by financial institutions to small business and agriculture; and less exclusively by the Trust Fund Bureau and other government financial institutions, which together extend about one-half of all loans made by financial institutions, to smaller enterprises and households.

Time and saving deposits, including insurance funds, are the main source of funds for most financial institutions. Their share is close to two-thirds for all financial institutions taken together and is below three-fifths only for the banking system. Currency and demand deposits account for less than one-fifth of total sources and even in commercial banks and financial institutions for agriculture and small business for only around one-fourth. Time and saving deposits and currency are provided primarily by households, demand deposits by business. For the banking system, persons in 1977 accounted for one-fourth of demand deposits and 55 percent of time deposits. Corporations furnished most of the remainder. For all financial institutions, the share of the personal sector is higher: one-half for demand deposits and currency, three-fourths for time and saving deposits, and fully two-thirds for all deposits. Both categories are considerably increased in the statistics by the requirement of keeping a substantial fraction of loans as buzumi deposits.

The raising of substantial funds by medium-term debentures is a peculiarity of the Japanese financial system. Although they furnished in 1977 only 5½ percent of the total funds of all financial institutions, they were of considerable importance for long-term credit banks with more than two-thirds of their total funds, for government financial institutions with fully one-tenth, and for financial institutions dealing with small business and agriculture with 6 percent. They are mostly held by other financial institutions.

Own funds account for less than 2 percent of the total, according to the flow-of-funds statistics. Actually, the ratio is considerably higher, because these statistics value corporate stock at book value and do not include reserves; own funds may actually account for close to 10 percent.

Table 7–8 shows the changes in the balance sheet structure of the Bank of Japan and deposit money (commercial) banks for six benchmark dates between 1955 and 1977 and for specialized credit institutions for 1970, 1975, and 1977.

The changes in the asset structure of the Bank of Japan largely reflect developments in the balance of payments. Foreign assets fluctuated between one-fourth and one-half of total assets, whereas most of the remainder had the form of claims on government except in the mid-1960s when, reflecting an easy money policy, claims against deposit money banks absorbed more than two-fifths of the bank's funds. Their share fell to not much more than one-fourth in the 1970s when the banks became less dependent on borrowing from the Bank of Japan as a result of large balance of payments surpluses and a slower rate of growth. Note issues have since 1960 accounted for considerably more than four-fifths of all sources of funds, the share of government deposits falling from more than 15 to 5 percent.

The changes in the balance sheet structure of deposit money banks over the past decades were remarkably small, given the extraordinary growth rates of the economy and its financial superstructure. The only two substantial, though not radical, changes in the 1970s were on the asset side, the sharp increase in the share of claims on the government and the small decline in that of claims on the private sector, reflecting, on the one hand, the central government's deficit financing and, on the other, the sharp reduction in the rate of economic growth. On the liabilities side, a fairly sharp decline occurred in the share of demand deposits, along with a corresponding

TABLE 7-8. Balance Sheet Structure of Credit Institutions, 1955–1977
(Percent of Total Assets)

	1955 (1)	1960 (2)	1965 (3)	1970 (4)	1975 (5)	1977 (6)
I. Bank of Japan (trill. ¥)	1.09	1.55	3.02	6.98	15.78	19.12
Foreign assets	45.6	42.3	25.7	25.0	25.0	36.7
Claims on government	41.7	28.4	32.1	42.9	49.4	36.5
Claims on deposit money banks	12.7	29.3	42.2	32.2	25.5	26.8
Reserve money	64.0	85.8	92.3	88.7	94.1	91.0
Government deposits	5.6	16.7	9.0	3.3	4.2	5.3
Other liabilities (net)	30.4	−2.5	−1.3	8.0	1.6	3.7
II. Deposit money banks (trill. ¥)	3.62	11.14	29.58	63.62	148.77	188.97
Reserves	1.3	1.9	1.8	1.7	2.2	1.8
Foreign assets	1.3	2.6	3.1	3.7	2.7	2.4
Claims on government	3.0	2.4	2.6	2.9	4.3	8.7
Claims on private sector	94.4	93.1	92.5	91.6	90.8	87.2
Demand deposits	35.5	25.7	27.1	25.6	25.8	24.7
Time deposits	45.0	52.2	51.1	51.7	50.6	51.5
Bonds	—	—	4.7	6.2	7.3	8.1
Foreign liabilities	1.6	3.6	4.2	3.1	5.5	4.1
Credit from monetary authorities	3.8	3.8	4.3	3.5	2.7	2.7
Other liabilities (net)	14.0	14.7	8.6	9.9	8.2	8.7
III. Specialized credit institutions (trill. ¥)	·	·	·	27.83	81.11	114.87
Claims on government	·	·	·	14.7	13.0	15.4
Claims on private sector	·	·	·	76.2	80.3	77.2
Claims on deposit money banks	·	·	·	9.1	6.7	7.3
Time and savings deposits	·	·	·	50.9	50.1	50.8
Certificates	·	·	·	24.2	21.0	20.3
Government deposits	·	·	·	22.1	20.7	20.0
Credit from monetary system	·	·	·	2.5	7.7	8.2
Other liabilities (net)	·	·	·	0.3	0.4	0.7

SOURCE: *IFS*, May 1978, pp. 226–27; January 1979, p. 220.

increase in the share of time deposits, between 1955 and 1960, and a new source of funds, bank debentures, which had come to furnish nearly one-tenth of the total by 1977. Foreign liabilities increased substantially but even at the end of the period supplied less than 5 percent of total funds.

The seven years of the 1970s are too short a period to have led to noticeable changes in the balance sheet structure of specialized credit institutions.

In 1977 the banking system accounted as table 7–9 shows, for about two-fifths of the resources of all financial institutions; financial institutions for small business and agriculture for one-fifth; government financial institutions, including considerable intragroup claims and liabilities, for about 30 percent; and insurance companies for 5 percent. (Changes in these relationships over the postwar period will be discussed later.) Differences in the share of the various groups in the several financial instruments were, as table 7–9 shows for 1977, quite pronounced. Thus, on the asset side, the Bank of Japan held one-fifth of the government securities in the portfolios of all financial institutions compared to its asset share of only 4 percent; the private banks more than one-third, about in line with their asset share; institutions for small business and agriculture one-seventh, compared to an asset share of one-fifth; and government financial institutions one-fourth, slightly less than their share in the assets of all financial institutions. Holdings of private debt securities were fairly well in line with asset shares for most groups. In the case of corporate stock, the holdings of insurance, investment, and securities companies

TABLE 7-9. Distribution of Financial Assets and Liabilities among Financial Institutions, 1977 (Percent)

	All institutions (trill. ¥) (1)	All institutions (percent) (2)	Bank of Japan (3)	City banks (4)	Other banks (5)	Trust accounts (6)	Small business institutions (7)	Agricultural institutions (8)	Investment companies (9)	Securities companies (10)	Insurance companies (11)	Postal Saving and insurance (12)	Trust Fund Bureau (13)	Other government institutions (14)
I. Financial assets														
Currency and demand deposits	7.9	100.0	—	26.7	8.9	—	30.8	13.5	—	3.2	9.6	7.0	—	0.2
Other deposits	39.6	100.0	—	0.6	0.2	—	2.3	1.3	—	0.3	2.3	93.0c	—	0.1
Government securities	40.6	100.0	20.0	17.0	18.3	2.6	6.3	7.7	1.6	0.1	2.3	0.9	22.7	0.6
Other debt securities	28.1	100.0	0.4	10.5	17.1	7.4	16.4	10.7	6.2	0.8	6.7	11.3	12.3	0.2
Corporate stock[a]	11.1	100.0	—	21.9	16.5	3.9	2.7	1.2	12.7	3.1	37.8	—	—	0.3
Loans	288.1	100.0	1.8	19.7	17.9	5.1	17.2	5.9	0.3	0.4	4.8	1.6	16.4	8.8
Other financial assets	4.7	100.0	86.8	—	0.0	12.9	—	—	0.4	—	—	—	—	—
All financial assets	420.1	100.0	4.2	17.1	15.7	4.5	14.3	5.9	1.1	0.5	5.4	10.9	14.3	6.1
II. Liabilities and corporate stock														
Currency and demand deposits	76.1	100.0	23.1	26.0	23.7	—	18.4	8.7	—	—	—	0.1	—	—
Other deposits	239.5	100.0	—	16.9	11.9	7.9	16.3	6.8	—	—	—	15.2	25.0	—
Debt securities	23.1	100.0	—	5.0	61.9	—	14.3	6.6	—	—	—	—	—	12.2
Corporate stock	6.9	100.0	—	12.0	11.7	—	2.1	—	68.0	3.3	2.9	—	—	—
Loans	33.2	100.0	—	29.3	2.0	—	0.7	0.0	—	2.6	0.0	—	—	65.4
Other liabilities	41.3	100.0b	—	—	8.7	—	8.3	0.9	—	2.2	54.4b	22.5b	0.3	2.7
All liabilities	420.1	100.0	4.2	17.1	15.7	4.5	14.3	5.9	1.1	0.5	5.4	10.9	14.3	6.1

aBook value.   bOf which, insurance accounts for 71.2 percent in col. 2, 48.8 percent in col. 11, and 22.4 percent in col. 12.   cDeposits with the Trust Fund Bureau.

SOURCE OF BASIC DATA: *BJFFA, 1970–77* (1978), pp. 77 ff.

TABLE 7-10. Assets of Main Types of Financial Institutions, 1950–1977 (Trill. ¥)

	1950 (1)	1955 (2)	1960 (3)	1965 (4)	1970 (5)	1975 (6)	1977 (7)
Bank of Japan	0.51	0.86	1.44	3.15	6.43	15.62	18.55
Commercial banks[a]	1.54	4.72	11.80	28.03	56.62	127.62	154.17
Commercial bank trust accounts	0.02	0.32	1.47	3.66	7.72	20.98	30.04
Post Office Saving System	0.16	0.54	1.14	2.72	7.77	24.64	36.70[c]
Long-term credit banks	0.21	0.38	1.15	2.99	6.55	16.81	20.87
Mutual loan and savings banks	0.06	0.46	1.21	3.65	7.63	19.53	21.31
Cooperative nonagricultural banks[b]	0.12	0.91	2.57	8.77	18.53	41.78	54.90
Cooperative agricultural banks[b]	0.24	0.84	1.82	5.98	12.41	29.94	39.16
Trust Fund Bureau	0.26	0.90	2.08	5.05	14.63	42.81	59.84
Government development banks[b]	0.01	0.70	1.54	3.41	7.69	18.60	29.00
Life insurance companies	0.04	0.19	0.75	2.24	5.86	12.89	16.39
Other insurance companies	0.02	0.10	0.22	0.48	1.43	3.88	4.98
Post Office life insurance	0.03	0.24	0.70	1.20	2.41	6.37	9.23
Securities companies	—	—	0.36	0.51	1.30	2.21	3.03
Securities finance companies	—	0.01	0.08	0.44	0.27	0.44	0.46
Investment companies	—	0.06	0.69	1.13	1.32	3.35	4.69
Total	3.22	11.23	29.02	73.41	158.57	387.47	503.32

[a]Includes banking accounts of trust banks.   [b]Sum of deposits, borrowed funds, and capital.   [c]Estimated.

SOURCE: ESA, various issues, e.g., 1977, pp. 32, 80 ff.

were far ahead, and those of cooperative and government financial institutions were far behind. Loans again were distributed fairly in accordance with asset shares.

c. Differences in Expansion and in the Position of the Main Types of Financial Institutions

From 1953 to 1973 the total combined assets of all financial institutions expanded at an average annual rate of 19 percent.[32] Because the price level advanced at an average rate of only 4 ½ percent, the growth of financial institutions' deflated assets proceeded at an average rate of more than 14 percent, well ahead of the rate of expansion of real national product of 9½ percent, an extraordinary performance for an economically and financially developed country. It is astonishing that the tempo of expansion did not decrease during the period. In nominal terms the average growth rate of assets was 19 percent in 1953–60; 18½ percent in the 1960s, and 22 percent in the boom of 1971–73. The process, however, slackened in real terms, the expansion of the assets of financial institutions falling from 15½ percent in 1953–65 to 12 percent in 1966–70, rates still ahead of the growth rate of real national product but by a margin declining from 6½ percent per year in the 1953–65 period to 1½ percent in 1966–73. The 1974–75 recession reduced the growth rate of assets in nominal terms to 15 percent but for the first time in the postwar period stopped expansion in real terms altogether, in line with the halt of growth in real national product. During the first two years of the 1976–77 recovery, the assets of financial institutions grew at a rate of 14 percent in nominal and 8 percent in real terms, both substantially below those of the two decades ending in 1973, and the excess of their growth over that of national product, 2 percent, was not much above that of the 1974–75 recession and far below that of the postwar period.

The momentum of expansion was so pervasive that, as tables 7–10 and 7–11 show, it carried practically all types of financial institutions with it. With rates of growth as high as those that prevailed in postwar Japan, however, even seemingly small differences in the average

32. This figure is derived from the combined assets of table 7–10. The rate obtained from the consolidated balance sheets of the flow-of-funds accounts should be only fractionally different.

TABLE 7-11. Growth of Assets of Main Types of Financial Institutions, 1951–1977
(Percent per Year)

	1951–55 (1)	1956–60 (2)	1961–65 (3)	1966–70 (4)	1971–75 (5)	1976–77 (6)
Bank of Japan	11.0	10.9	16.9	15.3	19.4	9.0
Commercial banks	25.1	20.1	18.9	15.1	17.6	9.9
Commercial bank trust accounts	74.1	35.7	20.0	16.1	22.1	19.6
Post Office Saving System	27.5	16.1	19.0	23.4	26.0	22.0
Long-term credit banks	12.6	24.8	21.1	17.0	20.7	11.4
Mutual loan and savings banks	50.3	21.3	24.7	15.9	20.7	11.6
Cooperative nonagricultural banks	50.0	23.1	27.8	16.1	17.7	14.6
Cooperative agricultural banks	28.5	16.7	26.9	15.7	19.3	14.4
Trust Fund Bureau	28.2	18.2	19.4	23.7	24.0	18.2
Government development banks	·	17.1	17.2	17.7	19.3	24.9
Life insurance companies	36.6	31.6	24.5	21.2	17.1	12.8
Other insurance companies	38.0	17.1	16.9	24.4	22.1	13.3
Post Office life insurance	51.6	23.9	11.4	15.0	21.5	20.4
Securities companies	—	—	7.2	20.6	11.2	17.1
Securities finance companies	—	51.6	40.6	−9.3	10.3	2.2
Investment companies	—	63.0	10.4	3.2	20.5	18.3
Total	28.4	20.9	20.4	16.6	19.6	14.0

SOURCE: Table 7-10.

annual rate of expansion will cumulate over two decades into large absolute differences. Thus, whereas the assets of all financial institutions increased 45-fold between 1955 and 1977, the multiplier ranged from 22 for the Bank of Japan, 33 for deposit banks, and 41 for government financial institutions to 54 for the cooperative credit institutions, whose expansion was aided by the government, and 86 for life insurance companies, which had experienced slow growth before World War II and, in addition, were particularly hard hit by the inflation of the early postwar period.

As a result of these differences in their growth rates substantial changes occurred in the relative position of the main groups of financial institutions, which can be followed in table 7–12. The most important change is the declining share of the banking system, from 50 percent of the total in 1955 to 34 percent in 1977. This was due to the halving of the share of the Bank of Japan from 8 to 4 percent and a decline of the share of the commercial banks from 42 to 30 percent which was more pronounced for the city banks (from 29 to 19 percent) than for the local banks (from 12 to 10 percent), whereas the share of the trust banks doubled from 3 to 6 percent. Those movements are in the direction observed in the postwar period in most developed countries.[33] This, of course, does not necessarily mean that the importance of banks within the country's financial system declined proportionately, because their influence within the system is not solely determined by the relative size of their assets. A second significant movement is the increase in the share of the cooperative credit organizations for small business and agriculture from 16 to 19 percent and a third the rise in the share of insurance companies from 2½ to 5 percent, which is still a very low ratio for developed countries. The share of all government financial institutions increased from 21 to 26 percent, a result primarily of the increased share of the postal saving system, which is reflected in that of the Trust Fund Bureau.

Although the degree of concentration within the main groups of financial intermediaries, is high, it does not seem to have increased since it was considerably reduced immediately after the war by the occupation authorities. Thus the share of the five largest commercial banks

33. Goldsmith, 1971, table 15.

TABLE 7-12. Distribution of Assets among Financial Institutions, 1950–1977 (Percent)

	1950 (1)	1955 (2)	1960 (3)	1965 (4)	1970 (5)	1975 (6)	1977 (7)
Bank of Japan	15.8	7.7	5.0	4.3	4.1	4.0	3.7
Commercial banks	47.8	42.2	40.7	38.2	35.7	33.0	30.5
Commercial bank trust accounts	0.6	2.9	5.1	5.0	4.9	5.4	5.9
Post Office Saving System	5.0	4.8	3.9	3.7	4.9	6.4	7.2
Long-term credit banks	6.5	3.4	4.0	4.1	4.1	4.3	4.7
Mutual loan and savings banks	1.9	3.9	4.1	4.9	4.8	5.0	4.8
Cooperative nonagricultural banks	3.7	8.1	8.9	11.9	11.7	10.8	10.8
Cooperative agricultural banks	7.5	7.5	6.3	8.1	7.8	7.7	7.7
Trust Fund Bureau	8.1	8.0	7.2	6.9	9.2	11.0	11.8
Government development banks	0.3	6.2	5.3	4.7	4.9	4.8	5.7
Life insurance companies	1.2	1.7	2.6	3.1	3.7	3.3	3.2
Other insurance companies	0.6	0.9	0.8	0.7	0.9	1.0	1.0
Post Office life insurance	0.9	2.1	2.4	1.6	1.5	1.6	1.8
Securities companies	—	—	1.2	0.7	0.8	0.6	0.6
Securities finance companies	—	0.1	0.3	0.6	0.2	0.1	0.1
Investment companies	—	0.5	2.4	1.6	0.8	0.9	0.9
Total	100.0	100.0	100.0	100.0	100.0	100.0	100.0

SOURCE: Table 7-10.

dropped sharply from nearly 50 percent in 1945 to 34 percent in 1956 and further declined to 30 percent in 1970.[34] Trust and long-term credit banking, however, continued to be in the hands of a very small number of institutions, six to seven trust banks and three long-term credit banks. Concentration remained higher in life insurance, the five largest of twenty companies accounting in 1970 for about two-thirds of the total assets of the industry.[35]

d. The Network of Financial Institution Offices

Because Japan was fully developed financially before World War II, the network of offices of financial institutions in the postwar period has generally expanded only slightly more than corresponds to the increase in population, a little more than one-fourth between 1955 and 1977. Thus the number of branches of commercial banks rose by about 45 percent, to one branch per 7,200 inhabitants. The Post Office Saving System expanded the number of offices by less than 40 percent, to one branch per 2,200 persons.

The concentration of offices, and still more of activities, in large cities, particularly Tokyo and secondarily Osaka, is heavy (table 7–14). The most important financial institutions have their main offices in one of these two cities. In the case of the commercial banks, Tokyo alone accounts for more than two-fifths of loans and discounts and more than one-third of deposits, probably including those of most corporations operating on a nationwide basis, although the share in population is only about one-tenth and the share in national income about one-sixth. The degree of concentration has not changed at all during the past decade in the case of Tokyo, although the share of Osaka has declined.

e. The New Issue Ratios of Financial Institutions

Possibly the best simple measure of the changes in the position of financial institutions in the economy is their net new issue ratio, that is, the ratio of net changes in liabilities (including the issuance of equity securities by financial institutions) to gross national product, a ratio that already has been presented and discussed in chapters 2 through 6 for the period from 1868–1945.

34. For 1945 and 1956: Ehrlich, p. 268; for 1970: Federation of Bankers' Associations of Japan, p. 69.
35. Adams and Hoshii, p. 207.

TABLE 7-13. Assets of Main Types of Banks, 1955–1977

	1955 (1)	1960 (2)	1965 (3)	1970 (4)	1975 (5)	1977 (6)
I. Amounts (¥ trill.)						
City banks	3.20	7.94	18.87	36.89	80.87	95.32
Regional banks	1.39	3.45	8.33	17.22	39.61	50.10
Trust banks[a]	0.13	0.40	1.13	2.51	7.14	8.75
Long-term credit banks	0.38	1.15	2.99	6.55	16.81	20.87
All banks, combined	5.10	12.94	31.32	63.17	144.43	175.04
All banks, consolidated[b]	3.88	10.06	23.93	48.25	108.74	134.94
II. Distribution (percent)						
City banks	62.7	61.3	60.2	58.3	56.0	54.5
Regional banks	27.3	26.7	26.6	27.3	27.5	28.6
Trust banks[a]	2.5	3.1	3.6	4.0	4.9	5.0
Long-term credit banks	7.5	8.9	9.5	10.4	11.6	11.9
All banks	100.0	100.0	100.0	100.0	100.0	100.0
III. Rate of growth (percent per year)[c]						
City banks	23.6	19.9	18.9	14.3	17.0	8.6
Regional banks	28.9	19.9	19.3	15.6	18.1	12.5
Trust banks[a]	30.5	25.4	23.3	17.3	23.3	10.7
Long-term credit banks	12.5	24.7	21.1	17.0	20.7	11.4
All banks, combined	23.4	20.5	19.3	15.1	18.0	10.1
All banks, consolidated[b]	—	21.0	18.9	15.1	17.6	11.4
IV. Relation to gross national product (percent)						
City banks	34.8	45.9	54.4	47.8	51.2	48.7
Regional banks	15.1	19.9	24.0	22.3	25.1	25.6
Trust banks[a]	1.4	2.3	3.3	3.3	4.5	4.5
Long-term credit banks	4.1	6.6	8.6	8.5	10.6	10.7
All banks, combined	55.6	74.7	90.2	81.8	91.4	89.5
All banks, consolidated[b]	42.3	58.1	68.9	62.5	68.8	69.5
V. Net issue ratio (percent of gross national product)[c]						
City banks	5.94	7.80	8.70	6.69	7.71	4.09
Regional banks	2.84	3.39	3.88	3.30	3.92	2.97
Trust banks[a]	0.27	0.44	0.58	0.51	0.81	0.46
Long-term credit banks	0.48	1.27	1.46	1.32	1.80	1.15
All banks, combined	9.53	12.90	14.62	11.83	14.24	8.65
All banks, consolidated[b]	—	10.17	11.04	9.04	10.66	8.26

[a]Banking accounts only.   [b]As shown in *BJFFA*.   [c]Five (or two) years ending with year indicated.

Source of I: *ESA*, 1977, pp. 79 ff.

The discussion is continued in this section for the postwar period, but it is limited in detailed form to the years 1954–77 for which now available flow-of-funds statistics permit a much more reliable and disaggregated analysis than was possible for the preceding decades. Because the financial situation was extremely confused and reliable figures are scarce for the first years between 1945 and 1953 and because the later part was essentially concerned with rebuilding the financial structure disorganized by the aftermath of war and hyperinflation, the omission of the eight-year period is not too serious.

The new issue ratio of financial institutions, reported annually for 1954 through 1977 in table 7–15, has shown an upward trend from 24 percent in 1956–60 and much lower values for the preceding years to 28 percent in the 1960s. It then jumped sharply upward to 38 percent in the boom of 1971–73 and fell back to a still fairly high average of 30 percent both in the 1974–75 recession and the early part of the following recovery. Compared to its trend, the ratio

TABLE 7-14. Regional Distribution of Bank Loans and Deposits, 1968, 1973, and 1977
(Percent)

	Loans and discounts			Deposits			Population[a]	National income
Prefecture	1968 (1)	1973 (2)	1977 (3)	1968 (4)	1973 (5)	1977 (6)	1973 (7)	1971 (8)
Tokyo	42.4	42.6	43.2	34.2	34.5	34.0	10.6	16.7
Osaka	17.2	16.7	15.5	15.1	14.7	13.2	7.4	9.7
Other 45	40.4	40.7	41.3	50.7	50.8	52.8	82.0	73.6

[a]For greater Tokyo and Osaka "areas," the percentages are 24.0 and 14.1 (*MSJ*, January 1979, p. 7).

SOURCE OF BASIC DATA: **Cols. 1–6:** *ESA*, 1977, pp. 131–32.   **Cols. 7 and 8:** *Japan Statistical Yearbook*, 1973–74, pp. 14, 490, 492.

was highest in, or more commonly one year before, the peak year of a business cycle, as in 1956, 1961, 1963, 1969, and 1972. It was relatively low in the short recession periods, for example, in 1957–58, 1962, 1965, and 1974. There thus exists a fairly clear, but not perfect, association between the value of the net issue ratio of financial institutions and hence the intensity of financial activity and the business cycle.

As table 7–15 shows, the trends and variability of the ratio, as well as its responsiveness to cyclical fluctuation in the economy, differ considerably among institutions. There is no need to dwell on differences in trend as they correspond to the differences in the growth rates of assets of the different types of institutions, which have already been discussed. The variability is highest, as might be expected, for the central bank. Compared to an average ratio (including until 1969 the separately reported Foreign Exchange Fund) of 1¼ percent for the entire period of 1954–77, the range extends from 0.4 in the trough year 1975 and 0.8 in that of 1958 to 2.0 and 2.8 in the cyclical peak years 1961 and 1973. The issue ratio of the private banking system, which on the average accounts for about one-half of the overall ratio, also shows considerable variations, although no trend from 1956 on is indicated. It is definitely higher in the upswing than in the recession phases of the cycle. After 1955 the ratio moved between 8 and 12 percent with the exception of the peaks of more than 15 percent in 1963, the first year of a strong boom; 14 percent in 1971, classified as a recession year; and 17 percent in 1972, again the first year of an upswing. Trust deposits, the postal saving system, the cooperative credit organizations for small business and agriculture, and the insurance organizations showed relatively small short-term fluctuations around a substantially rising trend, nearly 14 percent in 1977 against less than 7 percent in 1956. Variations were also small for government credit institutions. The sharpest fluctuations were shown for the institutions associated with the stock market—security companies, investment trusts (responsible for most of the fluctuations in table 7–15, column 5, in which they are included), and call money dealers and security finance companies, which are not shown in table 7–15. In this case, the values reached in 1956–61, at the top of the stock market boom, were never again duplicated.

To understand the factors behind the movements of the new issue ratio of financial institutions, it is necessary to go beyond the formal breakdown into ratios for the different types of institutions. One of several possible approaches is to start from the fact that the issues of financial institutions can be divided into three parts according to their economic character. The first is the issuance of money in the form of currency and current deposits. The second consists of the non-monetary claims of the personal sector against financial institutions, primarily in the form of time and saving deposits and insurance contracts. In Japan the bank debentures held by the personal sector should be included, as should the personal sector's holdings of investment company shares and the stock of other financial institutions, all relatively small, although they

TABLE 7-15. New Issue Ratios of Financial Institutions, 1954–1977 (Percent of Gross National Product)[a]

	Total (1)	Bank of Japan (2)	Foreign Exchange Fund (3)	Banks[b] (4)	Trust accounts[c] (5)	Trust Fund Bureau (6)	Small business financial institutions (7)	Agricultural financial institutions (8)	Government financial institutions (9)	Insurance companies (10)	Securities companies (11)	Postal saving and life (12)
1954	13.59	0.42	0.96	3.43	0.57	2.43	1.48	0.48	1.40	0.53	·	1.90
1955	12.76	1.75	−0.07	5.66	0.98	2.13	1.90	0.78	0.90	0.62	·	1.61
1956	23.28	1.34	0.38	11.26	0.81	2.54	2.23	0.99	1.04	0.76	·	1.91
1957	20.88	1.89	−1.07	9.67	1.20	2.58	2.42	0.63	1.16	0.83	0.40	1.63
1958	20.82	−0.21	1.00	8.72	1.41	2.67	2.57	0.71	1.54	0.91	0.46	1.11
1959	26.51	0.52	0.61	11.34	2.09	2.33	3.24	1.18	1.48	0.98	0.55	2.27
1960	28.67	0.56	0.38	12.22	3.04	2.87	3.54	1.41	1.45	1.03	0.65	1.63
1961	31.24	2.63	−0.61	12.47	3.96	2.50	4.20	1.40	1.33	1.02	0.47	1.67
1962	26.47	0.90	0.35	9.96	1.39	2.67	5.00	1.51	1.46	1.05	0.05	1.73
1963	31.74	1.00	0.10	15.32	1.64	3.02	4.88	1.74	1.26	1.12	−0.21	1.63
1964	26.49	1.11	0.15	11.32	1.17	2.37	3.91	2.28	1.64	1.22	0.09	1.52
1965	25.70	1.22	−0.11	11.20	0.71	2.84	3.80	1.35	1.65	1.22	−0.23	1.74
1966	26.12	0.67	0.08	9.84	0.71	3.44	3.96	2.46	1.75	1.36	−0.17	2.07
1967	27.46	1.29	—	9.76	1.10	3.68	4.39	2.19	1.71	1.37	0.33	2.18
1968	26.11	0.82	0.13	9.73	1.22	3.85	2.75	1.97	1.77	1.35	0.25	2.19
1969	29.79	1.04	0.16	10.09	1.65	3.99	4.51	2.42	1.76	1.49	−0.18	2.43
1970	27.42	1.19	—	9.74	1.42	3.48	4.17	1.68	1.67	1.89	0.34	2.36
1971	33.93	1.18	—	13.81	1.93	4.05	4.41	1.54	1.81	2.01	0.51	2.85
1972	43.09	2.19	—	17.15	2.69	4.82	6.29	2.50	1.66	1.89	−0.98	3.39
1973	36.56	2.79	—	12.13	1.79	4.62	5.71	2.39	2.05	1.73	−0.05	3.43
1974	28.91	1.47	—	8.61	1.50	4.37	4.48	1.40	2.21	1.55	0.13	3.37
1975	30.58	0.39	—	8.29	1.55	5.32	4.40	2.42	2.31	1.64	0.19	4.13
1976	31.07	0.77	—	9.04	1.80	5.26	4.06	1.79	2.21	1.67	0.06	4.28
1977	29.77	0.73	—	7.47	2.50	5.63	3.46	1.50	2.18	1.61		4.63

[a]Figures up to and after 1970 are not fully comparable. [b]Includes commercial banks, trust banks, and long-term credit banks. [c]Includes investment trusts.

SOURCES OF BASIC DATA: *BJFFA*, 1970–77; 1964–71, 1954–63, except for column 12 (*ESA*, 1977, pp. 173–74; 1975, pp. 167–68).

cannot be ascertained. The third part is more heterogeneous and includes claims among financial institutions. The bulk of this part, however, is made up of the non-monetary claims of the nonfinancial corporate and government sectors and of the rest of the world. It also includes the part of net issues of equity securities not purchased by the personal sector, as well as errors of estimation.

Expressing the absolute figures as percentages of gross national product to remove scale incomparabilities, the following basic expression is obtained for the new issue ratio of financial institutions (ϕ):

$$\phi = \zeta + \alpha + \omega + \beta$$

where ζ is the ratio of net money issues to national product, α the ratio of non-monetary claims of the personal sector against financial institutions, ω the similar ratio for all other non-monetary issues of financial institutions, and β a residual. Whereas ζ will be broken down into two components, money absorbed by the personal sector (μ_1) and money absorbed by other sectors (μ_2), and ω will be subdivided according to the claimant sector (using subscripts c, e, f, and g to identify claims of nonfinancial corporations, the rest of the world, domestic financial institutions, and the government, respectively), α will be factored to identify some of its important components. To that end, the ratio of these claims to national product will be related to the personal saving ratio (σ), that is, the ratio of personal total net saving (PS) to personal disposable income (PDY); to the share of gross personal financial saving ($GPFS$); to net total personal saving (χ); and to the share of the acquisition of claims against financial institutions ($PCFI$) to the personal sector's acquisition of all financial assets (v), which is a measure of the sector's preference for these indirect financial assets. In order to restore the relation to gross national product as the denominator one more factor is needed, the ratio of personal disposable income to gross national product (ρ). The net new issue ratio of financial institutions then becomes:

$$\phi = (\mu_1 + \mu_2) + \rho\sigma\chi v + (\omega_f + \omega_c + \omega_g + \omega_e) + \beta$$

where β is a residual, and the second component is derived as:

$$\frac{PCFI}{GNP} = \frac{PDY}{GNP} \times \frac{NPS}{PDY} \times \frac{GFS}{NPS} \times \frac{PCFI}{GFS}$$

The breakdown of the new issue ratio of financial institutions into these components is shown annually for the period 1956 through 1977 in table 7–16.

For the period as a whole, the first of the three major components, the money issue ratio, amounted to about 5 percent of gross national product (unweighted average of annual values), a fairly high ratio for developed countries, and accounted for fully one-sixth of the entire new issue ratio. The second part, personal sector claims against financial institutions (in Japan including the claims of the considerable mass of farm and nonfarm unincorporated enterprises), averaged more than 11 percent, or somewhat above two-fifths of the total issue ratio, whereas the third part of other identified claims with 7 percent contributed one-fourth of the total, leaving an average residual of nearly 5 percent, or one-sixth of the total.

Year-to-year changes in the ratio were considerably more pronounced in the money issue ratio and in the rather heterogeneous third component than in the ratio for personal sector claims against financial institutions. The latter ratio fluctuated over the entire period between 8 and 16 percent, showing a rising trend from 7 percent in 1954–56 to 14½ percent in 1975–77. In contrast, the money issue ratio, averaging slightly less than 5 percent for the period, fluctuated between less than 1 and as much as 9 percent, although it moved within the narrow range of 4 to 6 percent in fifteen years of the twenty-four-year period. The third component showed the widest fluctuations, from less than 2 to more than 12 percent, but kept within 2 percentage points of its

TABLE 7-16. Components of New Issue Ratio of Financial Institutions, 1954–1977[a,b]

		Money			Personal sector claims					Other claims					
	Total (1)	Total (μ) (2)	Personal sector (μ_1) (3)	Other sectors (μ_2) (4)	Total (α) (5)	$\frac{PDY}{GNP}$ (ρ) (6)	$\frac{PS}{PDY}$ (σ) (7)	$\frac{GPFS}{PS}$ (χ) (8)	$\frac{PCFI}{GPFS}$ (ν) (9)	Total (ω) (10)	Interfinancial (ω_f) (11)	Corporate (ω_c) (12)	Government (ω_g) (13)	Foreign (ω_e) (14)	Residual (β) (15)
1954	13.59	0.47	0.50	-0.03	6.41	72.9	9.61	144.3	63.4	1.65	0.11	1.42	0.15	-0.03	5.06
1955	12.76	3.79	1.87	1.92	6.91	74.0	13.37	91.6	76.3	1.68	0.01	1.76	-0.09	0.32	-0.38
1956	23.28	5.19	2.55	2.64	8.00	71.6	13.67	118.2	69.2	8.59	3.55	2.63	1.82	0.59	1.24
1957	20.88	1.52	0.71	0.81	7.95	70.5	15.60	96.9	74.6	6.42	4.28	2.41	0.05	-0.32	7.13
1958	20.82	3.15	1.31	1.84	9.01	72.1	15.03	100.2	83.0	5.19	1.82	2.94	0.28	0.15	3.47
1959	26.51	4.43	2.43	2.00	10.31	71.7	16.69	114.4	75.3	7.72	3.56	3.56	-0.19	0.79	4.05
1960	28.67	5.23	2.85	2.52	10.44	69.0	17.44	116.6	74.5	8.91	4.43	2.84	0.12	1.52	3.95
1961	31.24	4.53	2.93	1.60	10.49	65.4	19.20	120.0	69.6	12.29	7.17	3.18	0.32	1.62	3.93
1962	26.47	4.94	2.51	2.43	9.08	68.1	18.64	122.9	58.2	8.41	3.42	4.71	0.09	0.19	4.04
1963	31.74	9.09	2.82	6.27	9.47	68.6	18.00	113.5	67.5	8.95	2.04	5.51	0.13	1.27	4.23
1964	26.49	4.31	2.50	1.81	9.55	66.4	16.72	118.3	72.3	9.04	4.83	3.25	0.09	0.87	3.59
1965	25.70	5.45	2.18	3.27	10.61	68.7	17.15	109.5	79.1	7.89	4.22	3.39	0.18	0.10	1.75
1966	26.12	4.81	2.80	2.01	11.74	67.8	17.97	128.3	75.1	5.18	1.93	3.32	0.23	-0.30	4.39
1967	27.46	4.49	2.76	1.73	11.79	66.9	19.81	120.2	74.0	6.46	2.59	2.75	0.34	0.78	4.72
1968	26.11	4.50	2.58	1.92	11.34	65.6	20.48	109.5	77.1	6.45	3.09	2.80	0.23	0.33	3.82
1969	29.79	6.31	3.43	2.88	12.50	64.4	20.45	123.1	77.1	7.22	4.14	2.92	0.23	-0.07	3.76
1970	27.42	4.51	2.27	2.24	10.67	63.4	18.06	124.1	74.8	6.97	1.75	3.08	0.23	0.38	5.27
1971	33.93	7.17	2.99	4.18	11.59	64.6	17.48	134.9	76.1	9.94	-2.17	5.46	1.76	4.67	5.23
1972	43.09	7.99	4.88	3.11	14.78	65.4	17.98	165.2	76.1	12.60	3.93	5.56	1.98	0.99	7.72
1973	36.56	5.75	3.99	1.76	13.71	66.6	20.48	135.9	74.0	8.21	4.96	2.64	2.12	-1.46	8.89
1974	28.91	4.46	2.09	2.37	12.48	70.7	23.72	88.0	84.6	4.65	2.20	0.29	2.07	0.26	7.32
1975	30.58	3.67	1.60	2.06	15.74	73.4	22.50	106.6	85.6	3.80	-0.31	2.27	1.90	-0.14	7.37
1976	31.07	4.33	2.23	2.10	14.30	73.8	22.37	107.2	80.8	5.41	0.54	2.24	1.98	0.68	7.03
1977	29.77	2.72	1.46	1.26	13.44	72.9	21.18	106.1	82.1	6.21	1.33	1.72	2.31	0.85	7.40

[a]Figures up to and from 1970 are not fully comparable.   [b]Percent of gross national product, except for cols. 6–9, which are percent.

SOURCE OF BASIC DATA: Tables 2–4, 6–14; *BJFFA*, various issues.

average of 7 percent in fifteen years. The residual fluctuated widely and irregularly from less than 1 to 9 percent.

The money issue ratio for the period as a whole is made up in about equal parts of the ratios for money absorbed by the personal sector and that absorbed by all other essentially nonfinancial sectors. The relationship of near equality is also observed for most of the years of the period. The two ratios are apart by more than 1 percentage point in only 7 years (1961, 1963, 1965, 1967, 1971, 1972, and 1973), the ratio of the personal sector varying much less from year to year than the combined ratio of the other sectors.

Turning to the second main component, personal sector claims against financial institutions, its first factor, the ratio of personal disposable income to gross national product, which is nonfinancial in character, fell from an average of 71½ percent in 1956–58 to one of less than 65 percent in 1969–71, reflecting an increase in the capital formation ratio, but returned to a level of 73 percent in the four years following the 1973 turning point.

The second factor, the net personal saving ratio derived from the national income accounts and not including saving in the form of consumer durables, has shown a definite upward trend, which will be discussed in section 6. It has increased from an average of 12 percent in the mid-1950s to one of more than 22 percent in 1975–77. These ratios would increase near the end of the period by about 3 percentage points if consumer durables were included but by only about 1 point during the mid-1950s.

The ratio (χ) of gross personal financial saving to total net personal saving, which depends on the ratio of indebtedness and of depreciation to gross saving, was nearly 1.20 for the period as a whole, indicating the extent to which these forms of indirect financial saving have dominated total net household saving, a situation that will have to be examined more closely in section 5c. The inclusion of consumer durables would reduce the ratio by about one-tenth. This was the result of a ratio of nearly 1.20 of gross personal financial saving to total net personal saving, which would be reduced by virtue of a net/gross financial saving ratio of about two-thirds to a ratio of net financial to total net personal saving of about 0.80. The ratio of the acquisition of non-monetary claims against financial institutions to total gross financial saving of the personal sector (ν), finally, averaged 0.75.

There is no marked trend in the ratio of gross personal financial saving to net total personal saving (χ); but there is an upward movement in the ratio of personal sector non-monetary claims against financial institutions to gross personal financial saving (ν) from 0.76 in 1956–58 to 0.83 in 1975–77. There is a general, but not very tight, tendency for high ratios of χ to be associated with low ratios of ν and vice versa, a tendency that results in the product of χ and ν, that is, the ratio of the personal sector's non-monetary claims against financial institutions to the sector's total net saving, deviating less from its average than either of its components from their averages.

The ratios ρ, α, χ, and ν, as they are derived from flow-of-funds accounts, unfortunately apply not only to the household sector but also include the unincorporated farm and nonfarm sectors as well as nonprofit institutions, all of which may be assumed to behave differently from households, at least in some respects. There is no way at the present time to overcome this shortcoming, which makes any analysis of the figures less informative than it otherwise could be. Considerable additional information on consumer households and their various types, as well as on households of farm and nonfarm entrepreneurs, can be extracted from sample surveys, which are available in Japan for the postwar period more often, indeed annually since the mid-1950s, and are based on larger samples than in any other country. Some of this information will be utilized in the discussion of household saving in section 6c, but the well-known difficulties of blowing up household samples, as well as the limitation of resources, made it impossible to integrate them into the flow-of-funds universe.

Of the four components of the third part of the new issue ratio, the claims of the rest of the world (ω_e) is of small importance, accounting on the average for only 0.6 percentage points, or

TABLE 7-17. New Issue Ratios of Financial Instruments, 1954–1977
(Percent of Gross National Product)[a]

	1954 and 1955 (1)	1956 to 1960 (2)	1961 to 1965 (3)	1966 to 1970 (4)	1971 to 1973 (5)	1974 to 1977 (6)
Currency and demand deposits	2.18	3.88	5.68	4.93	8.52	4.10
Currency	0.30	0.96	1.15	1.20	1.67	0.83
Deposits	1.88	2.92	4.53	3.73	6.85	3.27
Time deposits	6.18	8.26	9.62	10.09	13.53	11.12
Trust deposits	0.72	0.70	1.16	1.19	1.58	1.37
Insurance	1.01	1.43	1.43	2.05	2.25	2.22
Debt securities	2.94	2.88	4.05	5.40	6.10	8.30
Short term government	1.56	0.40	0.28	0.45	0.20	0.62
Central government bonds	−0.04	−0.03	−0.04	1.18	1.62	3.35
Local government bonds	0.16	0.19	0.25	0.42	0.69	1.14
Public corporation bonds	0.30	0.50	1.26	1.58	1.23	1.25
Industrial bonds	0.30	0.74	0.90	0.50	0.64	0.51
Bank debentures	0.68	1.08	1.42	1.29	1.76	1.44
Loans	6.14	15.58	19.31	17.52	24.38	16.52
By Bank of Japan	−2.15	0.78	1.00	0.22	−0.13	−0.03
By private financial institutions	5.58	12.17	15.64	14.40	20.70	11.72
By government	2.66	2.36	2.64	2.82	3.68	4.77
By securities companies	—	0.16	0.07	0.04	0.12	0.01
Call loans	0.55	0.11	−0.05	0.03	0.00	0.05
Trade credit[b]	2.75	7.64	9.77	10.16	10.85	4.45
Corporate stock	1.74	3.77	3.73	1.06	1.76	1.04
Excluding investment trusts	1.84	2.96	3.09	1.07	1.36	0.75
Investment trusts	−0.10	0.81	0.64	−0.01	0.40	0.29
Equities other than stock	0.37	0.46	0.29	0.22	0.23	0.12
Gold and foreign exchange	−0.14	0.52	0.01	0.26	1.43	0.41
Others	−0.57	0.81	0.98	0.90	−0.29	2.06
All instruments	23.32	45.94	56.04	53.79	70.34	51.70

[a]Unweighted averages of annual values.   [b]Does not include trade credit among unincorporated enterprises.

SOURCE OF BASIC DATA: *BJFFA*, 1970–77; 1964–71; 1954–63.

less than one-tenth of the total ratio, and has moved quite erratically. Claims by the government (ω_g) have averaged another 0.9 percent, considerably more from 1970 on than before, possibly because of changes in the methods of calculation. The remaining two components, interfinancial claims and loans (ω_f) and domestic corporate deposits (ω_c), were of about equal size, averaging 2.6 and 3.3 percentage points, respectively, and together account for four-fifths of the total ω ratio.

Corporate deposits reached their peak ratios in the upswing of 1962–64, when they averaged 5 percentage points, and again in the 1971–72 upswing with 5½ percentage points and accounted for three-fifths and one-half of the total ω ratio compared to an average of not much more than two-fifths. Year-to-year fluctuations in the ratio were substantial. There seems to be some negative association between the phases of the business cycle and the movements of the ω_e ratio, but it is not a tight one.

The last component (β) includes those interfinancial claims, particularly within government financial institutions, that are not identified as such in the flow-of-funds accounts but are eliminated in consolidation and also absorbs all inconsistencies and errors. It has averaged nearly 5 percentage points, after 1955 has never been below 3 percentage points, and has increased from close to 4 from 1959 to 1969 to more than 7 percentage points since 1972. For some purposes it is preferable to eliminate explicit as well as implicit interfinancial claims. This would reduce the net issue ratio of financial institutions from 28 to well below 25 and possibly not much more than 20 percent.[36]

f. The Relation of Financial Institutions' Assets to National Product

The new issue ratio, which is a relation between two flows, may usefully be supplemented by three other ratios, a hybrid stock-flow ratio, that between the assets of financial institutions and national product, and two stock ratios, those between the assets of financial institutions and all financial assets and national wealth. The first ratio is shown in table 7–18 for seven benchmark years between 1950 and 1977. The other ratio will be discussed in section 8.

The outstanding feature is the sharp increase in the ratio to national product from 1950 to 1965, which continues a similar movement that began during the preceding decade, and a much smaller further increase in the early 1970s. Thus the assets of financial institutions increased considerably more rapidly than national product during the postwar period up to the mid-1960s but have been broadly in step with national product since then. This movement was hardly affected by valuation changes because corporate stocks constitute only a very small fraction of the total assets of financial institutions, in 1977 less than 2 percent of book value and probably about 5 percent at market value. As a result, the ratio of the assets of financial institutions to gross national product increased from an estimated fully 80 percent in 1950 and 130 percent in 1955 to nearly 230 percent in 1965 and 270 percent in 1977.

The differences in the movements of the ratios for the various types of financial institutions are, of course, the same as those already observed in the growth rates of their assets. Thus the increases in the ratios for trust accounts, the cooperative financial institutions for small business and agriculture, and insurance companies were proportionately much larger than that for all financial institutions, whereas the increase in the ratio for commercial banks was substantially lower, and the ratio for the Bank of Japan did not increase at all.

5. THE MARKETS FOR THE MAIN FINANCIAL INSTRUMENTS

In Japan a market, in the sense of regular trading in substantial amounts that results in freely established prices, exists only for corporate stock and for the bonds of the Telephone Company. There are relatively few transactions in private, long-term debt securities, which in Japan commonly have a maturity of seven years from their original issuance. Even government securities have only a narrow market, which in the case of short-term securities is essentially limited to direct transactions between the Ministry of Finance, the Bank of Japan, some government financial institutions, and the large commercial banks. Other debt instruments, such as loans, accounts receivable, and mortgages, hardly ever change hands.

a. An Overview of the Issues of the Nonfinancial Sectors

Limitations of space and time prevent a discussion of the course of the issues of all financial instruments issued during the postwar period by the nonfinancial sectors, except for the main types of marketable issues, corporate stock and public and corporate debt securities, which will be dealt with in subsections b and c. For the sake of completeness, however, a few comments will be made on the issue ratios of all financial instruments issued by the nonfinancial sectors. Whereas tables 7–18 to 7–20 classify the issues by type of instrument rather than by issuer, two of the three types of instruments involved, loans and trade credit, are almost

---

36. The flow-of-funds makes it possible to develop a similar breakdown for the new issue ratio for each of the dozen types of financial institutions for which separate figures are given, in which case the relationships between the components—μ, χ, ν, and ω—might, of course, be different. Such a breakdown would undoubtedly improve our understanding of the determinants of the new issue ratio of financial institutions, but I admit to not having had the time, the clerical resources, and the energy to undertake the substantial amount of calculations involved.

TABLE 7-18. Relation of Assets of Main Types of Financial Institutions
to Gross National Product, 1950–1977 (Percent)

	1950 (1)	1955 (2)	1960 (3)	1965 (4)	1970 (5)	1975 (6)	1977 (7)
Bank of Japan	10.9	9.4	8.3	9.1	8.3	10.0	9.5
Commercial banks	32.8	51.4	68.1	80.7	73.3	80.7	78.8
Commercial bank trust accounts	0.4	3.5	8.5	10.5	10.0	13.3	15.4
Post Office Saving System	3.4	5.9	6.6	7.8	10.1	15.6	18.8
Long-term credit banks	4.5	4.1	6.6	8.6	8.5	10.6	10.7
Mutual loan and savings banks	1.3	5.0	7.0	10.5	10.0	12.4	10.9
Cooperative nonagricultural banks	2.6	10.0	14.8	25.3	24.0	26.4	28.1
Cooperative agricultural banks	5.1	9.2	10.5	17.2	16.1	18.9	20.0
Trust Fund Bureau	5.6	9.8	12.0	14.5	18.9	27.1	30.6
Government banks	0.2	7.6	8.9	9.8	10.0	11.8	14.8
Life insurance companies	0.9	2.1	4.3	6.5	7.6	8.2	8.4
Other insurance companies	0.4	1.1	1.3	1.4	1.9	2.5	2.5
Post Office life insurance	0.6	2.6	4.4	3.5	3.1	4.0	4.7
Securities companies	—	—	2.1	1.5	1.7	1.4	1.5
Securities finance companies	—	0.1	0.5	1.3	0.3	0.3	0.2
Investment trusts	—	0.7	4.0	3.3	1.7	2.1	2.4
Total	66.8	122.4	168.6	211.5	205.4	245.2	258.7

SOURCE: Table 7-10.

exclusively issued by nonfinancial corporations or by unincorporated business enterprises and may therefore be treated as belonging to the business sector, in the economic though not in the flow-of-funds sense. The third small item, equities other than stock, is attributed in the flow-of-funds accounts in about equal parts to corporate and public financial institutions and to nonfinancial corporations.

For the period as a whole, the issues by nonfinancial domestic sectors averaged 30 percent of gross national product. They reached nearly 40 percent in the boom of 1971–73 but in the four following years averaged less than 25 percent. Loans, mostly by financial institutions, accounted for nearly three-fifths of the total and trade credit for fully one-fourth, corporate stocks and bonds contributing only 8 and 6 percent, respectively.

The distribution of total issues of nonfinancial sectors among instruments over the period did not show substantial changes before the turning point of 1973, except for the decline in the share of corporate stock from 15 percent in 1956–60 to 11 percent in 1966–70 with a further sharp drop to about 3 percent in the 1970s.

There were, of course, considerable annual fluctuations in the absolute ratios as well as in their share in the total issues of the nonfinancial sectors, many of them connected with business cycle developments.

The cyclical sensitivity is most pronounced for trade credit. Thus the ratio of the change in trade credit outstanding, which in the flow-of-funds accounts does not include trade credit among unincorporated enterprises, to national product was above 10 percent in 1959, 1961–63, 1967, 1969–70, and 1972–73, when most of these years were in the later phases of an upswing, but remained below 6 percent in 1954–55, 1957–58, 1964–65, 1971, 1974–75, and 1977, mostly late upswing or trough years. The extremely high average of the ratio of more than 10 percent of national product for the 1961–73 period, as well as the fact that from 1956 on it fell below 4 percent in only three years (1965, 1971, and 1977), not to speak of its never showing a negative value, is an indication of the very intensive use, in international comparison, of trade credit, which in part reflects the widespread practice of subcontracting from large to medium-sized and small enterprises.

The ratio of increases in loans to national product moves at an even higher level, averaging

TABLE 7-19. Distribution of New Issues of Financial Instruments, 1954–1977 (Percent)

	1954 and 1955 (1)	1956 to 1960 (2)	1961 to 1965 (3)	1966 to 1970 (4)	1971 to 1973 (5)	1974 to 1977 (6)
Currency and demand deposits	9.4	8.4	10.1	9.2	12.1	7.9
Currency	1.3	2.1	2.1	2.2	2.4	1.6
Deposits	8.1	6.3	8.0	7.0	9.7	6.3
Time deposits	26.5	18.0	17.2	18.8	19.2	21.5
Trust deposits	3.1	1.5	2.1	2.2	2.2	2.6
Insurance	4.3	3.1	2.6	3.8	3.2	4.3
Debt securities	12.6	6.3	7.2	10.0	8.7	16.1
Short-term government	6.7	0.9	0.5	0.8	0.3	1.2
Central government bonds	−0.2	−0.1	−0.1	2.2	2.3	6.5
Local government bonds	0.7	0.4	0.4	0.8	1.0	2.2
Public corporation bonds	1.3	1.1	2.2	2.9	1.7	2.4
Industrial bonds	1.3	1.6	1.6	0.9	0.9	1.0
Bank debentures	2.9	2.4	2.5	2.4	2.5	2.9
Loans	26.3	33.9	34.5	32.6	34.7	32.0
By Bank of Japan	−9.2	1.7	1.8	0.4	−0.2	−0.1
By private financial institutions	23.9	26.5	27.9	26.8	29.4	22.7
By government	11.4	5.1	4.7	5.2	5.2	9.2
By securities companies	—	0.3	0.1	0.1	0.2	0.0
Call loans	0.2	0.2	−0.1	0.1	0.0	0.1
Trade credit	11.8	16.6	17.4	18.9	15.4	8.6
Corporate stocks	7.5	8.2	6.7	2.0	2.5	2.0
Excluding investment trusts	7.9	6.4	5.5	2.0	1.9	1.5
Investment trusts	−0.4	1.8	1.2	−0.0	0.6	0.5
Equities other than stock	1.6	1.0	0.5	0.4	0.3	0.2
Gold and foreign exchange	−0.6	1.1	0.0	0.5	2.0	0.8
Other instruments	−2.4	1.8	1.7	1.7	−0.4	4.0
All instruments	100.0	100.0	100.0	100.0	100.0	100.0

SOURCE OF BASIC DATA: *BJFFA*, 1970–77; 1964–71; 1954–63.

19 percent with only a very slight upward trend until 1973, but shows cyclical fluctuations not quite as sharp as trade credit. Thus the range of the annual values after 1955 extends from 12 percent in the trough year 1958 to 21 percent in 1961 and 1963, the first a peak year, the second close to it, and to an average of nearly 24 percent in the upswing of 1971–73. Thirteen of the twenty-two values lie within the range of 16 to 20 percent. Loans by private financial institutions were the dominating factor in loan financing. For the period as a whole they accounted for about four-fifths of the total, the government contributing the remaining one-fifth mostly through its financial institutions, including the Bank of Japan. Whereas the ratio for Bank of Japan loans, which remain largely within the financial sector, fluctuated widely around its average of only 0.2 percent of national product and was negative in one year out of three, the ratio of loans of other government financial institutions was quite steady, ranging until 1972 only between 2.2 and 3.1 percent of national product and within that range followed a countercyclical pattern. It increased sharply to an average of nearly 5 percent in 1973–77 as part of the government's effort to support and reexpand the economy in and after the recession of 1974–75. This set of ratios is possibly the best evidence of the relentless push or pull of business credit by financial institutions to rapidly expand the Japanese economy in the postwar period.

An attempt can be made to break down the new issue ratio for all financial instruments emitted by the nonfinancial sectors or for the issues of certain types of instruments, although the data available permit the separation of only two components, the capital formation ratio and the external financing ratio, that is, the quotient of funds raised externally to gross (or net) capital

TABLE 7-20. Determinants of New Issue Ratios of Nonfinancial Sectors, 1954–1977[a]

	1954 and 1955 (1)	1956 to 1960 (2)	1961 to 1965 (3)	1966 to 1970 (4)	1971 to 1973 (5)	1974 to 1977 (6)
Corporate business						
Gross capital formation ratio	0.092	0.172	0.204	0.196	0.205	0.167
External financing ratio	1.035	1.272	1.274	1.122	1.317	0.800
Net new issue ratio	0.095	0.219	0.261	0.220	0.269	0.134
Personal sector						
Gross capital formation ratio	0.080	0.081	0.103	0.131	0.136	0.138
External financing ratio	0.370	0.648	0.548	0.512	0.573	0.425
Net new issue ratio	0.030	0.052	0.056	0.067	0.079	0.058
Government						
Gross capital formation ratio	0.080	0.072	0.089	0.092	0.054	0.053
External financing ratio	0.305	0.246	0.294	0.572	1.060	1.990
Net new issue ratio	0.024	0.018	0.027	0.053	0.057	1.055
All nonfinancial sectors						
Gross capital formation ratio	0.251	0.326	0.396	0.418	0.394	0.359
External financing ratio	0.640	0.900	0.902	0.832	1.023	0.795
Net new issue ratio	0.161	0.293	0.357	0.348	0.403	0.285

[a]Unweighted averages of annual values.

Sources of basic data: *BJFFA, ARNIS,* and *ARNA*.

formation. The rationale of these ratios, shown in table 7–20, is the fact that external financing serves primarily, although not exclusively, to defray part of capital expenditure.

For the period 1954–77 as a whole, the ratio for all nonfinancial sectors taken together, of slightly more than 30 percent, resulted from a gross capital formation ratio of 37 percent and an external financing ratio of 86 percent, indicating that all nonfinancial sectors' net borrowing (including the issuance of equity securities) was equal to seven-eighths of their gross capital expenditures including expenditures on consumer durables. The external financing ratio for all nonfinancial sectors, which is of main interest for financial analysis, showed considerable cyclical fluctuations. Net issues exceeded gross capital expenditures in 1959, 1963, and 1972–73, all years within a cyclical upswing. On the other hand, the ratio was below two-thirds in the trough year 1954 and in 1957 (beginning of downturn) and around three-fourths in 1964–65 (before and after the peak of October 1964), 1968 (monetary restraint), 1974 (recession) and 1977. In addition to the cyclical movements, a slight downward trend can be detected in the ratio. Thus the average for 1956–63 of 0.94 compares with a ratio of slightly more than 0.80 for the period beginning with 1964, with the exception of an average of more than 1.10 in the boom of 1972–73.

The issue ratio, as well as its two components, naturally differs considerably, in level and less so in movement, among the three broad nonfinancial sectors. The external financing ratio, which is of chief interest here, was lowest for the personal sector (including unincorporated business), declining from nearly 70 percent in 1956–58 to not much more than 45 percent in 1975–77. The ratio for the more narrowly defined household sector would be considerably lower. As it stands, the ratios show only moderate fluctuations after 1956, sixteen of the twenty-one values keeping within the range of 0.45 and 0.60, and are not closely associated with the business cycle. The corporate business sector shows the highest ratio, 1.15 for the period as a whole, which reflects substantial requirements to finance increases in trade receivables and liquid assets in addition to capital expenditures. The ratio showed no trend from 1956 to 1973. Cyclical movements were only faintly evident. The ratio was highest in 1959, 1963, 1967, and

1972, one to three years before cyclical peaks. It was lowest in 1957, 1964–65, 1968, 1971, and 1974–75, of which only the last three coincide with recession years. The external financing ratio of the government sector showed a sharp break in 1971. Whereas it averaged a little more than one-third, with a substantial upward trend, from 1956 to 1970, it stayed continuously above nine-tenths from 1971 on, averaging 170 percent for the 1971–77 period and reaching a peak of more than 200 percent in 1976, which reflects heavy deficit financing by the central government.

b. Stock Market Developments[37]

The Japanese stock market of the postwar period has been characterized by about a half-dozen main features, some of them reflected in table 7–21.

(i) New issues of stock, although substantial in absolute amounts, have provided only a small part of the total funds raised by the corporate business sector and have financed only a small proportion of their capital expenditures.

(ii) The great majority of new stocks have been offered until recently at par to old shareholders.

(iii) A substantial redistribution of stockholdings occurred in the early part of the postwar period as a result of the sale, ordered by the government at the behest of the American occupation authorities, to the general public of the large blocks of stock of numerous large corporations held by the zaibatsu.

(iv) Notwithstanding the zaibatsu dissolution, the majority of all stock outstanding has remained in the hands of other corporations and financial institutions. Since the late 1950s not much more than two-fifths of all corporate stock has been held by individual owners, and their share has declined sharply in the 1970s to not much more than one-fourth. Between 1955 and 1970, financial institutions have increased their share from less than one-fourth to one-third and have sharply raised it in the 1970s to nearly one-half. At the same time, the proportion of intercorporate holdings has increased from less than one-fifth to more than one-fourth.

(v) Throughout much of the period the market has been very active and quite speculative, making extensive use of credit for the purpose of carrying positions.

(vi) Reflecting in the early part of the period the prevailing high inflation and in the later part the rise of corporate profits as the Japanese economy rapidly expanded, stock prices have shown a sharp upward trend.

(vii) Reopened in May 1949 after an interruption of four years, the market experienced a boom in the late 1950s and early 1960s, which quadrupled stock prices between 1954 and 1961. The boom could not be sustained, however, and in the mid-1960s some of the largest brokerage firms were in serious financial difficulties, which required the intervention of the Bank of Japan.[38] Prices moved sideways from 1961 to 1968, and value of trading showed no upward trend. The upward movement of prices and of trading activity resumed in 1969 and continued with only minor interruptions into 1973, by which time stock prices were three times as high as they had been in 1968 and twelve times as high as in 1954, compared with an increase in the price level by only 135 percent. After a setback in the recession of 1974–75, stock prices, although not the volume of trading, resumed their upward trend, but even in 1978 they were only 14 percent above their 1973 level, compared with an increase in the price level of more than 50 percent.

From 1956 to 1977, according to the flow-of-funds accounts, the total value of corporate stock issued amounted to nearly ¥ 17 trill., excluding issues of investment trusts of ¥ 3.3 trill. (table 7–22).[39] This was equal to 1.2 percent of the period's national product. The ratio

---

37. The most detailed description (in English) of developments connected with the stock market is provided by Adams and Hoshii, particularly pt. 2, chaps. 2 and 3 and pt. 3, chap. 3.

38. For a description, cf. Adams and Hoshii, pt. 2, chaps. 1, 2, and 3.

39. These are book values. Because almost all stocks were offered at par, the amount paid by investors or received by issuers would be only slightly higher.

TABLE 7-21. Stock Market Developments, 1954-1977

	Stock issues excluding col. 2 (bill. ¥) (1)	Investment trust stock issues (bill. ¥) (2)	Stock outstanding (bill. ¥) (3)	Trading value (bill. ¥) (4)	Trading velocity (5)	Prices (1965 = 100) (6)	Yield (percent) (7)	Price-earnings ratio (8)	Stock-holdings (mill.) (9)
1954	175	2	782	375	0.48	32	9.44	.	8.31
1955	116	−19	1102	442	0.40	36	7.96	.	8.61
1956	267	8	1705	1340	0.79	49	6.68	.	8.65
1957	352	69	1746	1577	0.90	54	7.14	7.56	9.28
1958	283	73	2409	2390	0.99	57	6.66	15.81	9.89
1959	331	122	3929	5589	1.42	82	4.54	16.88	10.67
1960	599	275	5644	9334	1.65	106	3.93	17.98	11.90
1961	996	579	6429	9807	1.53	122	3.24	15.00	15.09
1962	785	81	8003	9893	1.24	108	3.86	15.68	17.03
1963	654	67	7718	8234	1.07	118	4.24	13.80	18.30
1964	866	31	7694	4830	0.63	104	5.69	12.35	18.36
1965	255	−185	8804	5783	0.66	100	5.92	14.47	18.07
1966	421	−147	9737	7571	0.78	120	4.44	13.76	17.72
1967	409	−86	9639	6281	0.65	120	4.74	10.27	17.12
1968	565	−53	13134	11723	0.89	130	4.36	11.89	17.15
1969	805	161	19030	18674	0.98	165	3.37	12.98	17.38
1970	1070	257	16825	12030	0.72	179	3.47	9.59	17.85
1971	950	289	23520	18851	0.80	196	3.41	14.33	17.60
1972	1428	457	49548	28814	0.58	308	2.24	26.08	16.66
1973	1438	374	40034	20139	0.50	396	2.09	14.57	17.58
1974	917	455	37469	15933	0.43	335	2.53	14.95	18.49
1975	1331	357	44780	18976	0.42	340	2.31	.	19.18
1976	1099	491	54923	27930	0.51	379	1.82	.	.
1977	1355	851	53638	25527	0.48	411	1.78	.	.

SOURCES: **Cols. 1 and 2:** 1954–77, *BJFFA*, 1970–77 and earlier issues. Slightly different figures are given in Ministry of Finance, *Monthly Finance Review*, e.g., March 1979. **Col. 3:** 1954–77, Tokyo Stock Exchange, *Annual Statistics Report*, 1977, p. 138. Market value of stocks listed on all exchanges at end of year. **Col. 4:** 1954–77, col. 4 divided by col. 3. **Col. 6:** 1954–77, table 7-2, col. 5; annual average. **Col. 7:** 1954–77, table 7-4, col. 9; annual average. **Cols. 8, 9:** 1954–75, Tokyo Stock Exchange, op. cit., various issues, e.g., 1977, pp. 118–19.

TABLE 7-22. Issuance and Acquisition of Corporate Stock, 1956–1977 (Percent)[a]

	1956–60 (1)	1961–65 (2)	1966–70 (3)	1971–75 (4)	1976–77 (5)
	I. Issuance				
Financial institutions	8.6	6.6	13.1	15.0	18.0
Nonfinancial corporations	91.4	93.4	86.9	86.2	82.0
All sectors, percent	100.0	100.0	100.0	100.0	100.0
All sectors, ¥ trill.	1.83	3.57	2.87	6.06	2.45
	II. Net acquisitions				
Financial institutions	39.8	24.2	46.0	54.4	63.8
Banks	8.7	9.6	25.3	22.9	19.5
Small business financial institutions	0.6	0.8	0.8	1.2	1.9
Agricultural financial institutions	0.3	0.1	0.8	0.0	0.6
Insurance companies	7.5	9.1	26.0	20.3	24.7
Trust accounts[b]	22.7	7.7	−7.1	8.3	15.5
Security companies	.	.	.	1.6	1.4
Government financial institutions	0.0	0.0	0.1	0.1	0.3
Government	2.2	0.3	0.3	1.4	0.7
Nonfinancial corporations	22.7	34.1	21.5	32.5	21.3
Personal sector	35.3	38.4	32.2	11.8	19.7
Rest of the world	.	.	.	−0.2	−5.5
All sectors, percent	100.0	100.0	100.0	100.0	100.0
All sectors, ¥ trill.	2.02	3.97	3.42	8.29	4.20

[a]Excluding shares of investment trusts.   [b]Mostly investment trusts.

SOURCES OF BASIC DATA: *BJFFA*, 1970–77, and earlier issues.

averaged 3 percent from 1956 to 1960 and 2 percent in 1961–65 but declined sharply to not much more than 1 percent in 1966–70, probably reflecting the dullness of the stock market in the mid-1960s. The ratio continued at a low level of less than 1 percent of national product in the 1970s, notwithstanding the resumed sharp upward movement in stock prices.

The upward trend in the amounts of stock issued by nonfinancial corporations is therefore much less pronounced than that of most other financial instruments. Thus stock issued just doubled between 1956–60 and 1961–65 and actually declined by about one-fifth between 1961–65 and 1966–70. The average level of the 1970s of stock issued, ¥ 1.2 trill., was only twice that of the 1960s. Financial institutions, mainly banks, accounted for less than one-eighth of total new issues. However, if investment trust stocks are included, their share increases to about one-fourth. When the proceeds of stock issues of nonfinancial corporations of less than ¥ 14 trill. are compared with either total funds raised by these corporations or with their capital expenditures, the resulting proportions are rather low. Thus for the period from 1956 to 1977, stock issues represented only about 3½ percent of all sources of funds, the proportion declining sharply from 8 percent from 1956 to 1965 to 2½ percent during the last decade.

Similarly, the ratio of stock issues to gross and net capital expenditure declined over the period, first slowly and then more sharply. The low was reached in 1965–67 and the ratios recovered somewhat in the last years of the 1960s. If the comparison is made with gross capital expenditures, the ratio declines from one-eighth in 1956–65 to about 5 percent from 1966 to 1977 for a period average of about 6 percent. The level is, of course, higher in relation to net capital expenditures, namely, on the order of 15 percent. These ratios overstate the importance of corporate stock issues in financing capital expenditures because a part of the proceeds of stock issues, although probably only a small part, was used for other purposes. On the other hand, stock issues have been more important than the averages indicate for some industries and, of course, for many individual firms. The fact, however, remains that stock issues have only been a secondary source of funds for nonfinancial corporations, far behind borrowings from financial institutions, as will become evident in the discussion of the sources of funds of corporate business in section 6b.[40]

The distribution of the holdings of corporate stock among sectors (always excluding investment trust stock, about nine-tenths of which are held by the personal sector) is shown in table 7–23 on the basis of flow-of-funds statistics, which cover all nonfinancial corporations for the period 1955–77, and in table 7–24 for stocks listed on the Tokyo Stock Exchange, a group that measured by nominal capital covers fully two-thirds of all corporations, including virtually all large corporations for which statistics are available.

The effect of the dissolution of the conglomerates and the distribution of the stocks they and the controlling families held is clearly seen in table 7–24. The proportion of shares in listed corporations held by domestic individuals (the statistics are based on numbers of shares held rather than on their value) increased from 53 percent in 1945 to 61 percent in 1950 (from 57 to 73 percent if security dealers are included), and the proportion held by corporations declined from 25 to 11 percent. Apparently, however, this change was largely reversed in the following quinquennium because the share of individuals was back to 53 percent in 1955 whereas that of corporations had recovered moderately to 13 percent and that of financial institutions had advanced sharply from 13 to 24 percent, partly because of the advent of investment companies, which held 4 percent of all stock outstanding.[41]

From 1955 on it is preferable to use flow-of-funds data, which are more comprehensive in coverage and distinguish a larger number of holder groups. Considerable additional changes in the distribution of the corporate stock outstanding occurred between 1955 and 1960 and are evident in table 7–23. The share of the personal sector declined further, from 54 percent to 43 percent, although the value (at issue prices) of the stocks they held more than doubled. This decline, however, was almost offset by individuals' acquisition of substantial amounts of investment company stock. Financial institutions continued the sharp increase in the proportion of all stock held, raising it from 23 to 34 percent, the result mostly of the increase in investment trusts' holdings from 5 to more than 15 percent.

Changes in distribution were much smaller in the 1960s. The share of the personal sector was unchanged if investment trust stocks are excluded. Although the share of all financial institutions together remained at just above one-third of the total, changes within the sector were considerable. Thus the proportion of stock held by investment trusts and securities companies was quartered from nearly 20 to 4½ percent, that is, reduced below one-half of the level of 1955, whereas that of commercial banks and insurance companies doubled from 7 to 14 percent each. The proportion of intercorporate holdings rose only moderately, reaching in 1970 nearly one-fourth of all stock outstanding.

The reduction of the share of individuals resumed and accelerated in the 1970s. As a result, the personal sector in 1977 owned only one-fourth of all shares, excluding those of investment trusts, less than one-half of the proportion they had held two decades earlier. On the other hand, intercorporate holdings stayed at one-fourth and those of financial institutions advanced sharply to nearly one-half, banks and insurance companies each accounting for nearly one-fifth of all stocks outstanding. Foreign holdings, negligible until the mid-1950s, partly because of obstacles put in their way by the government, accounted even at the end of the period for only 3 percent of the total.

Because the financial household surveys do not, as everywhere, cover the upper-income and -wealth groups adequately, not much is known about the distribution of the shareholdings of

40. For a discussion of the reasons for the relatively small importance of stock financing, cf. Wallich and Wallich, pp. 300 ff.

41. This set of figures exaggerates the changes in the first postwar decade because it does not include the numerous smaller and often closely held corporations in which fewer changes in ownership presumably occurred and which, in particular, were not affected by the zaibatsu dissolutions.

TABLE 7-23. Distribution of Holdings of Corporate Stock, 1955–1977 (Percent)

		1955 (1)	1960 (2)	1965 (3)	1970 (4)	1975 (5)	1977 (6)
I.	Financial institutions[a]	23.3	34.3	29.1	33.7	42.7	47.4
	1. Banks	5.1	7.0	8.5	13.8	17.9	18.2
	a. City	3.3	4.6	5.4	8.4	10.6	10.4
	b. Local	1.3	1.4	1.4	1.6	2.0	2.2
	c. Trust	0.2	0.3	0.6	1.6	2.5	2.8
	d. Long-term credit	0.4	0.7	1.1	2.1	2.8	2.8
	2. Trust accounts	0.2	0.2	0.4	0.5	0.4	1.6
	3. Cooperative credit organizations	0.3	0.6	0.7	1.1	1.1	1.4
	4. Government financial institutions	—	—	0.0	0.1	0.1	0.1
	5. Insurance companies	7.2	7.0	8.8	13.8	16.9	18.4
	6. Investment trusts	5.3	15.5	9.3	3.7	4.9	6.2
	7. Securities companies	5.2	3.9	1.4	0.7	1.4	1.4
II.	Government[a]	3.5	2.5	1.3	1.0	1.3	1.2
III.	Corporate business[a]	19.2	20.2	24.7	24.0	27.3	25.7
IV.	Personal sector[a]	54.1	42.5	45.0	41.3	28.7	25.7
V.	Total, book value[a]	100.0	100.0	100.0	100.0	100.0	100.0
VI.	Total, estimated market value (trill. ¥)[a,b]	2.2	8.5	13.9	21.8	67.6	75.9
VII.	Investment trust shares	100.0	100.0	100.0	100.0	100.0	100.0
	1. Financial institutions	3.3	6.6	5.5	5.2	10.6	7.6
	2. Personal sector	86.7	90.6	91.1	93.3	88.5	90.9
	3. Other sectors	10.0	2.0	3.5	1.5	0.9	1.5

[a]Excludes stocks of investment trusts.   [b]Assuming the ratio of market to book value to be the same as for the corporate and personal sectors as shown in flow-of-funds accounts.

SOURCES OF BASIC DATA: *BJFFA*, various issues, except for lines I-1a to 1d, which are based on *ESA*, 1977, pp. 77 ff. and for line VI (table 7-39).

the personal sector among different income, wealth, occupational, and age groups or their geographical distribution. The number of stockholdings (not stockholders) in listed corporations (table 7–21) increased from fully 8 million in 1954 to 19 million in 1975, but almost all of the increase occurred in the 1950s and early 1960s. Since then the increase has been considerably less than the growth in population. This trend is confirmed by the fact that the proportion of households reporting ownership of stock had declined from about one-fourth in 1960, a very high ratio, to 18 percent in 1974, investment trust shares accounting for about 7 and 2½ percent of the total (table 7–36).

A further indication of development in the stock market is provided by the growth of the securities companies, which combine the activities of stock brokerage, stock market credit, and investment banking on the limited scale that it is practiced in Japan. The assets of securities companies reached a peak of ¥ 540 bill. in 1962 and then declined to ¥ 450 bill. two years later, whereas the volume of stock trading was cut in half. Some of the largest companies got into serious financial difficulties as a result of the decline in stock prices and the withdrawal of deposits and had to be reorganized by a consortium formed by the Bank of Japan.[42] Securities finance companies, which primarily provide funds to securities companies, grew from about ¥ 25 bill. in 1957 (principal assets) to ¥ 120 bill. in 1962. Here, however, the shrinkage was less pronounced and briefer, namely, to about ¥ 95 bill. in 1963. Since the mid-1960s the securities

42. The difficulties of the securities' companies in 1964–65 were primarily the result of their practice of borrowing various securities from customers to use as collateral for their own borrowing. When confidence in these companies began to crumble, customers rapidly withdrew their securities, and the companies, not being able to repay the banks for the amounts they had borrowed on these securities, had to apply for emergency credits. This episode is discussed in detail in Kotake.

TABLE 7-24. Distribution of Ownership of Listed Corporate Stock, 1945–1975 (Percent)[a]

	1945 (1)	1950 (2)	1955 (3)	1960 (4)	1965 (5)	1970 (6)	1975 (7)
Number of companies	631	713	787	785	1578	1587	1710
1. Public sector	8.3	3.1	0.4	0.2	0.2	0.2	0.2
2. Financial institutions (excluding 3 and 4)	11.2	12.6	19.5	23.2	23.3	31.0	34.5
3. Investment trusts	—	—	4.1	7.5	5.6	1.4	1.6
4. Security dealers	2.8	11.9	8.0	3.7	5.8	1.2	1.4
5. Nonfinancial domestic corporations	24.6	11.0	13.2	17.7	18.4	22.1	26.3
6. Nonfinancial foreign corporations	—	—	1.5	1.1	1.4	3.0	2.5
7. Other domestic holders	53.1	61.3	53.2	46.3	44.8	39.9	33.5
8. Other foreign holders	—	—	0.2	0.3	0.4	0.2	0.1
9. Total	100.0	100.0	100.0	100.0	100.0	100.0	100.0

[a]Based on number of shares, not value.

SOURCES: *ESA*, 1961, p. 183; Tokyo Stock Exchange, *Annual Statistics Report*, various issues, e.g., 1972, p. 180 (includes nonlisted stocks).

companies have again expanded in line with stock market activities, their assets rising by about 500 percent between 1965 and 1977 and maintaining a ratio of slightly above one-half of 1 percent of those of all financial institutions. Securities finance companies, on the other hand, have stagnated, and their share in the assets of all financial institutions declined from 0.6 to 0.1 percent. Throughout the period, larger securities companies have absorbed smaller ones or merged with the result that the number of firms in 1971, 234, was only one-fourth as large as it had been twenty-five years earlier. In addition, about one-half of the total business was concentrated in the four largest firms, Daiwa, Nikko, Nomura, and Yamaichi[43], and the eighty-three firms that were members of the Tokyo stock exchange accounted for two-thirds of the number of offices, seven-eighths of the number of employees, and 95 percent of the capital.[44]

c. The Market for Debt Securities

The market for debt securities is characterized by four peculiarities. First, it deals mostly in medium-term securities, because short-term securities are issued only by the central government and the Foreign Exchange Fund and debentures commonly have a seven-year life; second, it is predominately a market among financial institutions; and third, it is essentially a controlled rather than a free market, with issuance and original distribution being arranged by the Ministry of Finance, the Bank of Japan, and a group of leading private, cooperative, and government credit institutions.[45]

Debt securities play a relatively minor role in the Japanese financial system. Net issues from 1956 to 1977, totaling more than ¥ 90 trill (table 7–25), were equal to 6 percent of national product, the net issue ratio rising from 3 percent in 1954–60 to nearly 5 percent in 1960 and to more than 8 percent in 1974–77. The total amount outstanding at the end of 1977, ¥ 92 trill., represented slightly more than one-tenth of all financial instruments, compared with a share of not much more than 7 percent in 1955, all of the increase having occurred in the 1970s. Annual fluctuations in the volume of net issues and in the issue ratio were substantial. The net issue ratio fluctuated between 0.3 percent in 1957 and 9.7 percent in 1977. The exclusion of central

43. Jefferies and Co., Inc., p. 234.
44. Tokyo Stock Exchange, *Annual Statistics Report*, e.g., 1977, pp. 130–31.
45. This feature is particularly marked for bonds. There are only about 200 corporations "entitled to issue bonds," which have been "deliberately selected" by the authorities "with the aim to make the most of the available funds" (Hisamizu, in Jefferies and Co., Inc., pp. 221).

TABLE 7-25. Distribution of Outstandings and Issuance of Debt Securities, 1953–1977 (Percent)

	1953 (1)	1960 (2)	1970 (3)	1977 (4)
	I. Outstandings			
Central government, short	29.4	21.3	10.7	7.4
Central government, long			14.4	32.1
Local government	2.3	5.2	6.7	11.5
Public corporations	2.7	11.5	26.9	18.8
Nonfinancial enterprises	27.6	24.6	13.7	8.6
Financial institutions	37.9	37.4	27.7	21.7
Total, percent	100.0	100.0	100.0	100.0
Total, trill. ¥	0.66	2.82	22.22	92.35
	II. Issues[a]			
Central government, short		18.9	26.6	6.3
Central government, long	·			37.7
Local government	·	6.2	6.9	13.1
Public corporations	·	14.2	29.1	16.2
Nonfinancial enterprises	·	23.6	12.1	7.0
Financial institutions	·	37.2	25.4	19.7
Total, percent	·	100.0	100.0	100.0
Total, trill. ¥	·	2.16	19.40	70.13

[a]Derived from change in outstandings during period ending with benchmark date.

SOURCE OF BASIC DATA: *BJFFA*, 1970–77 and 1954–63.

government securities reduces fluctuations considerably but shows only a faint relation to the business cycle.

At the end of 1977 the issues of the central government, about one-fifth of which were short-term, accounted for nearly two-fifths of all debt securities outstanding. Local government and public corporation bonds made up another three-tenths. There was thus only less than one-third left for the debt securities of private issuers, among which the debentures of long-term credit banks, some of which may be regarded as semiofficial institutions, predominated. Bonds issued by private nonfinancial corporations accounted for less than one-tenth of the total. The relation between public and private debt securities changed considerably over the period, with that of the public sector, (including public corporations), increasing from less than two-fifths to nearly three-fifths in 1970 and to more than two-thirds in 1977. Although public corporations were responsible for most of the increase during the 1960s, it was the jump of the mainly long-term securities of the central government by 550 percent that accounted for most of the increase during the 1970s.

Throughout the postwar period, as before World War II, the bulk of the outstanding debt securities has been acquired at issuance and held until maturity by the financial sector as table 7–26 shows. The share of all financial institutions in net new issues of debt securities remained close to three-fourths throughout the period. Within the financial sector, however, the share of the main groups changed considerably. For the period as a whole the commercial banking system was the largest buyer, absorbing fully one-fourth of total net issues of debt securities. Its share, however, declined sharply from nearly one-half in 1956–60 to less than one-fourth in the 1970s. The Bank of Japan, as a part of its expansionary monetary policy, absorbed since the mid-1960s fully one-tenth of all net issues of debt securities. Another one-sixth was acquired by the Trust Fund Bureau and the postal saving and life insurance systems. Cooperative credit institutions were fairly steady buyers, acquiring since the mid-1960s nearly 15 percent of all net issues.

Debt securities are naturally of quite different importance in the portfolios of the various

TABLE 7-26. Distribution of Holdings of Debt Securities, 1955–1977

	1955 (1)	1960 (2)	1965 (3)	1970 (4)	1975 (5)	1977 (6)
Financial institutions						
Bank of Japan	37.9	17.5	12.6	12.7	13.0	8.9
Banks	31.4	39.3	36.9	24.8	22.7	24.0
City	17.5	23.0	21.5	13.3	10.4	10.6
Local	12.8	13.6	10.8	8.0	8.1	8.5
Trust	0.4	1.0	2.2	1.4	1.4	1.7
Long-term credit	0.7	1.7	2.4	2.1	2.8	3.2
Trust accounts	0.3	0.3	0.3	1.1	2.7	3.4
Trust Fund Bureau	11.6	14.7	10.4	15.6	13.6	13.7
Postal Saving and life insurance				3.0	4.0	3.9
Small business financial institutions	1.9	3.1	5.9	6.0	7.9	7.8
Agricultural financial institutions	4.6	4.9	6.8	6.7	5.5	6.7
Government financial institutions	0.9	0.4	0.4	0.2	0.1	0.3
Insurance companies	0.5	0.6	0.8	2.1	2.1	3.1
Investment trusts	·	1.5	3.2	2.9	3.2	2.6
Securities companies	·	·	0.2	0.3	0.4	0.3
Total	89.1	82.3	78.3	75.4	75.2	74.7
Central government	—	0.9	0.7	0.6	0.7	1.2
Public corporations and local government	0.1	0.1	0.2	0.1	0.1	0.1
Nonfinancial corporations	2.9	5.9	7.0	5.3	4.1	3.8
Personal	7.9	10.9	13.8	18.5	19.9	20.2
All domestic sectors, percent	100.0	100.0	100.0	100.0	100.0	100.0
All domestic sectors, ¥ trill.	1.46	3.26	8.62	22.17	59.08	92.13

SOURCE OF BASIC DATA: *BJFFA*, 1970–77, pp. 50 ff., and earlier issues.

groups of financial institutions. At the end of the period they constituted nearly one-half of the total financial assets of the Bank of Japan and nearly one-third of those of investment trusts, which resulted from the trusts' poor experience with stocks in the early 1960s. Debt securities were the second most important asset of government financial institutions, mainly the Trust Fund Bureau, and of the agricultural cooperative credit organizations with a share of total assets of about one-fourth. They constituted about one-sixth of total assets in the case of insurance companies and private banks, the proportion ranging from only 11 percent for city banks and trust accounts to 18 percent for local banks and 19 percent for trust banks. For the other institutions, the importance of debt securities was secondary.

Although the nonfinancial sectors together absorbed about one-fourth of the total net issues of debt securities throughout the period, the share of nonfinancial corporations declined from 5 percent in the 1960s to 3 percent in the 1970s, whereas that of the personal sector remained at one-fifth. Even in 1977 debt securities represented less than 8 percent of total financial assets of the personal sector, which was a considerable increase over the share of 2 percent in 1955. However, the structure of the personal sector's portfolio of debt securities changed substantially over this quarter century. Although central government securities accounted for three-fifths of the total in 1955, their share had declined in the 1970s to one-fifth from a trough of less than one-tenth in 1960. On the other hand, the share of bank debentures increased sharply, from about one-fourth to more than one-half. As a result, the personal sector in 1977 held nearly one-half of all bank debentures outstanding, nearly one-fourth of industrial bonds, and one-sixth of public corporation bonds, whereas its share in central government securities stood at one-tenth and that in local government bonds, more than nine-tenths of which were held by financial institutions, was negligible.

The importance of debt securities among the assets of the household sector does not seem to vary greatly. It was minor throughout the income range in 1974, rising from 1.3 percent in the lowest income quintile to 3.0 percent in the highest (table 7–35), although it was probably higher at the top income levels, which are not adequately covered by the household financial surveys.[46]

Some evidence of the near absence of a market for debt securities is provided by the fact that from 1956 to 1970 the volume of trading in such securities amounted to only approximately 2 percent of the amount outstanding, the ratio rising from about 1½ percent in 1956–65 to 3 percent in 1966–70. The rise, however, was entirely due to increasing activity in the coupon and discount bonds of the Telephone Company, which telephone subscribers are bound to acquire to obtain service, the only debt security for which something like a free and broad market exists. The extent of over-the-counter trading in debt securities is not known but is believed to be small, as such securities are treated by the financial institutions that acquire them at issuance more like term loans than like marketable assets.

6. FINANCING AND PORTFOLIO STRUCTURE OF THE MAIN NONFINANCIAL SECTORS

The uses and sources of funds of the three main nonfinancial sectors of the economy will be surveyed briefly in order to indicate the portfolio policies they followed, that is, the changes in their asset structure, and to show the ways in which they financed their capital expenditures or their acquisition of financial assets, that is, the changes in their liabilities and net worth.

In each case the sector is first surveyed on an aggregative uniform basis, that is, for the sector as a whole, for the period 1956–77 and then for the period's five three- to five-year subperiods, on the basis of the Economic Planning Agency's national accounts and the Bank of Japan's flow-of-funds accounts. This presentation is supplemented for the corporate business sector by evidence on the sources and uses of funds of some broad groups of corporations characterized by industry and size and by a very brief discussion of two problems that are of particular importance for this sector, the degree of concentration and the relationship between business enterprises and financial institutions. No similar disaggregation is possible for the personal sector. Here the macroeconomic data derived from the flow-of-funds accounts are supplemented by the microeconomic information derived from sample surveys of household finances. Resources and space have limited the microeconomic data, which for the household and corporate sectors are available in profusion, to the minimum regarded as essential to put the macroeconomic picture into proper perspective.

a. The Public Sector[47]

The importance of the public sector is evident from the facts that from 1954 through 1977 the sector, which includes central and local general government activities as well as those of public nonfinancial enterprises, accounted for nearly one-fourth of capital formation and nearly one-fifth of saving. Changes in the ratios over the period, apart from short-term fluctuations, were relatively small until the mid-1970s.

For the entire period 1956–73, the public sector covered about four-fifths of its very substantial and multifarious capital expenditures by its saving (table 7–27), so that its financial deficit totaled less than 2 percent of national product. In 1974–77, however, the ratio rose sharply to more than 6 percent. The small size of the financial deficit of the public sector as a

---

46. The average share of bonds in total financial assets for all households in 1974 was 2.4 percent on the basis of household financial surveys (table 7–36), whereas the corresponding share in the macroeconomic flow-of-funds accounts was 6.5 percent, possibly because of an underestimation of holdings among the usually insufficiently covered highest income groups. These are the tribulation of financial statistics. If the household surveys, rather than the flow-of-funds statistics, are used, households would in 1974 have held about ¥ 3 trill. of debt securities, or 6.5 percent of the total outstanding, rather than the 19.4 percent shown in the flow-of-funds accounts.

47. For a more detailed discussion of developments until 1965, cf. Patrick, 1968.

TABLE 7-27. Uses and Sources of Funds of Public Sector, 1956–1977[a]

	1956–60 (1)	1961–65 (2)	1966–70 (3)	1971–73 (4)	1974–77 (5)
			A. Uses (percent)		
Tangible assets					
Gross investment	82.6	85.5	79.7	76.8[b]	77.7[b]
Capital consumption allowances	10.0	8.6	9.8	11.5	11.9
Net investment	72.6	76.9	69.9	65.3	65.8
Financial assets					
Cash	1.6	1.3	1.0	1.0	1.1
Time deposits	1.9	1.3	2.2	1.4	1.8
Loans	0.2	0.0	−0.1	0.0	0.0
Securities	0.6	0.3	0.3	0.2	1.0
Corporate stock	0.8	0.1	0.0	0.2	0.1
Others	12.3	11.6	16.8	20.4	18.3
Total	17.4	14.5	20.3	23.2	22.3
			B. Sources (percent)		
Saving					
Gross saving	80.9	70.8	63.0	47.5	26.4
Net saving	70.7	62.9	53.9	46.0	14.5
Liabilities					
Loans	10.5	12.3	10.3	16.0	23.8
Securities	7.2	15.7	25.5	26.5	49.0
Short-term government securities	0.9	3.4	2.5	1.1	4.9
Government bonds	−0.6	0.0	9.1	12.2	27.3
Local government securities	2.0	2.5	3.0	5.1	8.9
Public corporation bonds	4.9	9.9	10.9	7.9	7.9
Others	1.4	1.2	1.2	0.2	0.8
Total	19.1	29.2	37.0	42.5	73.6

[a]Central and local governments and public enterprises.   [b]Includes land (1971–73, 5.9 percent; 1974–77, 5.7 percent) not previously included.

SOURCES OF BASIC DATA: *ARNIS*, 1975; *ARNA*; *BJFFA* (for financial assets and liabilities).

whole until 1973 was the result of a large financial surplus of the central government combined with large financial deficits of local governments and public corporations.

Total calls on external funds rose from fully 2 percent of gross national product in 1956–65 to 3½ percent in 1966–70 but shot up to 6½ percent in 1974–77. About two-thirds of total net borrowing took the form of debt securities—one-tenth in the form of local government bonds and nearly one-sixth in that of public corporation securities—whereas loans accounted for about one-third. The net issues of the central government fluctuated considerably more than those of local governments and public corporations.

Borrowing by the central government remained small until 1964 in accordance with the budget balancing policies originally imposed by the occupation authorities, which involved abstention from the issuance of medium- or long-term government bonds. As a result, the net issues of the central government totaled not much more than ¥ 500 bill. from 1956 to 1965, all short-term obligations, equal to only 0.3 percent of national product. The central government's new issue ratio rose to 1.4 percent of national product from 1966 to 1970, four-fifths of which represented the first long-term issues in the postwar period and were an instrument of the government's incipient countercyclical deficit financing. Long-term issues of the central government rose to 1.6 percent of national product in 1971–73 and jumped to 3½ percent in 1974–77, short-term issues remaining slightly above one-half of 1 percent, because stemming the 1974–75 recession and supporting the 1974–77 upswing called for large-scale deficit financing.

The issue ratio of local governments and the more important public corporations showed a strong upward trend, rising from 0.6 percent of national product in 1956–60 to nearly 1 percent in 1961–65, to nearly 1½ percent in 1966–73, and to more than 2 percent in 1974–77.

The securities of the central government even now, after the sharp increase in the 1970s, account for only 9 percent of the financial assets of financial institutions (the ratio was below 5 percent as recently as 1973), for only 1½ percent of those of the personal sector (0.6 percent in 1973), and are virtually absent from the portfolios of nonfinancial business enterprises. Such figures show that these securities do not play the same role, either as a balancing item or a permanent investment in the portfolios of the financial and nonfinancial sectors, that they do in many other developed countries. The holdings of local government and public corporation bonds, accounting in 1977 for less than 7 percent of the assets of financial institutions and less than 1½ percent of the assets of the personal sector, also have only a very minor position in the portfolios of these sectors.

Both main sources of public sector funds, securities and loans, are, as has already been pointed out, essentially the result of arrangements regarding amounts, timing, and terms among the Ministry of Finance, the Bank of Japan, and the main private, public, and cooperative financial institutions, rather than of the operation of market forces. It was relatively easy to work out these arrangements during the postwar period until the early 1970s because the public sector's needs for external funds were moderate. The relatively low level of these requirements in turn has reflected a rapid rise in government revenues, even at tax rates that were reduced almost every year because of the expansion of the economy. In the 1960s the ratio of government current revenue to gross national product was, as a matter of policy, kept below one-fifth, and general government consumption expenditures absorbed less than one-tenth of national product. Consequently, during much of the period, public expenditures on welfare, on some parts of the economic infrastructure, and on the environment were neglected. These conditions have been changing since the early 1970s. Thus the ratio of public expenditures to national product rose to nearly one-fourth in 1974–77.

b. The Business Sector

The importance of the business sector within Japan's financial system is probably best indicated by the fact that in the period from 1956 to 1977 it absorbed about three-fourths of all (net) funds raised by nonfinancial sectors.

(i) THE STATISTICAL PICTURE. Comprehensive information on financial assets and liabilities and on sources and uses of funds is available only for the corporate segment of the business sector. This, however, is not too serious a limitation because corporations account for more than four-fifths of the assets of all business enterprises.

The uses and sources of funds of nonfinancial corporations in the five standard periods from 1956 through 1977 are shown in table 7–28. For the twenty-two year period nonfinancial corporations undertook capital expenditures of more than ¥ 250 trill. (17 percent of national product), divided between ¥ 225 trill. (15½ percent) of expenditures on structures and equipment and ¥ 25 trill. (nearly 2 percent) on additions to inventories. In addition, nonfinancial corporations increased their financial assets by nearly ¥ 200 trill. (14 percent), but nearly one-half of this represented trade credit among corporations and about ¥ 6 trill. (less than one-half of 1 percent) were used for the acquisition of stock of other corporations, so that the increase in claims against other sectors amounted to about ¥ 100 trill. (7 percent of national product). These increases in claims consisted to the extent of ¥ 22 bill. (1½ percent) of trade credit to unincorporated businesses and of about ¥ 65 trill. (4½ percent) of bank deposits.

The two main financial uses of funds are rather remarkable for their size. Trade credit outstanding at the end of 1977 was well over twice as large as inventories, even excluding trade credit among unincorporated enterprises, an extraordinarily high ratio in international comparison, and accounted until 1973 for considerably more than one-fourth of all uses and more than

TABLE 7-28. Uses and Sources of Funds of Nonfinancial Corporate Business, 1956–1977

	1956–60	1961–65	1966–70	1971–73	1974–77
Uses (percent)					
Tangible assets					
Gross capital expenditures	54.6	51.4	53.8	51.1[a]	61.4[a]
Capital consumption					
allowances	18.7	21.2	23.6	20.9	32.5
Net capital expenditures	36.0	30.1	30.3	30.2	28.9
Financial assets					
Cash	5.0	7.3	5.3	7.4	8.0
Time deposits	8.7	10.1	8.0	10.6	7.6
Loans	0.7	0.2	0.1	0.0	0.0
Debt securities	0.8	0.9	0.6	0.5	0.9
Corporate stock	2.7	2.3	0.8	1.8	1.1
Trade credit	24.6	28.8	31.0	28.0	19.5
Others	2.9	−1.0	0.5	0.6	1.5
Total	45.4	48.6	46.2	48.9	38.6
Total Uses	100.0	100.0	100.0	100.0	100.0
Sources (percent)					
Saving					
Gross saving	32.4	32.1	38.6	33.4	40.8
Net saving	13.9	10.6	15.3	12.5	8.3
Incurrence of liabilities					
Loans	34.9	35.6	32.5	37.6	38.7
Industrial bonds	2.4	2.2	1.3	1.4	2.8
Corporate stock	9.6	7.4	2.6	2.7	2.8
Trade credit	19.2	22.1	25.0	23.4	14.4
Others	1.6	0.6	0.0	1.3	0.5
Total	67.6	67.9	61.4	66.6	59.2
Total sources	100.0	100.0	100.0	100.0	100.0

[a]Includes land (1971–73, 9.0 percent; 1974–77, 2.2 percent) not previously included.

SOURCES OF BASIC DATA: *ARNIS,* 1976; *ARNA; BJFFA* (for financial assets and incurrence of liabilities).

one-fifth of all sources of funds. This may be explained in part by the large extent of subcontracting in Japan.

Liquid assets, predominantly bank deposits, absorbed about one-sixth of all uses of funds. Part of this amount, however, represents the deposits (buzumi) that are required to be held against bank loans. If the proportion of such deposits is put at about one-fourth of commercial bank borrowings, the ratio would be reduced to below one-tenth.

The high proportion of external financing among sources of funds is one of the characteristics of business finance in Japan. From 1965 to 1977 external financing accounted for considerably more than three-fifths of all funds, including the contribution of corporate stock, which declined from 10 to 3 percent. The fully one-third remaining represented retained earnings. On a net basis the share of external funds predominated to the extent of four-fifths. Here again, however, the picture looks somewhat different if trade credit among nonfinancial corporations is omitted and attention is limited to the external funds provided by other sectors. In that case, external funds supplied about 55 percent on a gross basis and more than two-thirds of the total on a net basis.

If attention is focused on only the five subperiods of three to five years each, rather than on year-to-year fluctuations, changes in the distribution of uses of sources, although not negligible, are not very marked. Thus financial uses accounted in all four periods through 1973 for between 45 and 49 percent of all uses, and the share of external financing in all sources of funds remained between 61 and 68 percent. In the 1974–75 recession and the weak recovery of 1976–77 the shares of both financial uses and external sources of funds were lower by nearly 10 percentage points. It remains to be seen whether this marks a permanent downward shift in the propensity of nonfinancial corporations for external financing.

Borrowings from financial institutions maintained their share of slightly more than one-half of total external sources in all subperiods through 1973 and increased it to nearly two-thirds in 1974–77, whereas that of trade credit rose from fully one-fourth in 1956–60 to two-fifths in 1966–70 but fell back to below one-fourth in 1974–77. The share of corporate stock in external financing declined sharply, from 12 percent in the first two subperiods to less than 5 percent since the late 1960s, whereas the share of industrial bonds fell until 1973 from 3½ percent to 2 percent. Borrowing from financial institutions among sources outside the business sector thus rose from less than three-fourths in 1956–60 to seven-eighths since the second half of the 1960s. Nonfinancial corporations thus became increasingly dependent on borrowing from financial institutions as the postwar period progressed. In Japan, as in the United States,[48] "business enterprises exploit fully the availability of trade credit and then bond issues, borrowing from financial institutions and lastly stock issues."[49]

Another set of statistics, summarized in table 7–29, which also covers, to judge by the size of funds reported, unincorporated enterprises and is available back to 1946, provides more information on sources of funds, particularly loans from financial institutions. It shows that the share of banks (excluding their trust accounts) in total loans and discounts to business declined steadily from two-thirds in 1956–60 to not much more than two-fifths in 1974–77, whereas that of other private financial institutions declined from 18 to 12 percent. The share of government financial institutions and of government-assisted cooperative credit organizations rapidly increased in importance, supplying in 1974–77 over one-tenth and one-third, respectively, of all business credit by financial institutions compared to not much more than 5 and less than 15 percent in 1956–60.

The annual fluctuations in the level and pattern of financing nonfinancial corporations generally show the expected cyclical pattern. Thus borrowings rise sharply in relation to national product in the later parts of an upswing, for example, in 1956–57, 1960–61, 1969–70, and 1972–73; whereas the increase in institutional credit used is relatively small near a trough or shortly after, for example, in 1956–59, 1962, and 1974–75. Trade credit shows a similar pattern, as does the issuance of corporate stock, which was relatively high in all peak years and low in all trough years except 1962.

The material available (in Western languages) on the financing of business enterprises of different size is not sufficient to determine whether or not some features of the financing process are systematically related to enterprise size, particularly when the effects of industrial and other nonfinancial differences are eliminated. The figures do show, however, some apparently size-related differences, such as the higher profit margins (profit to sales) but lower profitability (profits to total assets) of the larger enterprises, and a higher ratio of fixed to total assets and a more rapid rate of inventory turnover for the smaller enterprises.[50]

There exists, of course, a fairly clear connection between the size of the firm and its main sources of credit. Thus in the late 1950s the smallest size classes of manufacturing firms borrowed about one-fourth of their requirements from "business acquaintances, usurers, relatives, and friends" and another 30 percent from financial institutions for small business, whereas city banks provided only about one-tenth of the total. At the other end of the scale in the case of large manufacturing enterprises, city, trust, and long-term credit banks together accounted for

48. "Nonfinancial corporations seem to turn to equity financing only when all other sources of capital have been exhausted" (McGowan, p. 203, in R. W. Goldsmith, ed., 1973).

49. Mikitani, p. 108.

50. Bank of Japan, *Financial Statements of Main Industrial Corporations in Japan, Analysis of Financial Statistics by Size of Corporation,* annually.

TABLE 7-29. Supply of Funds to Industry, 1946–1977 (Total External Funds = 100)[a]

	1946–50	1951–55	1956–60	1961–65	1966–70	1971–73	1974–77
External funds[a]	100.0	100.0	100.0	100.0	100.0	100.0	100.0
Shares	13.5	13.9	14.2	13.9	6.8	5.4	5.6
Industrial bonds	3.6	3.7	4.7	4.4	3.1	3.1	4.6
Loans and discounts	82.9	82.3	81.1	81.7	90.2	91.7	89.8
Private financial institutions	69.8	59.8	63.1	60.8	58.1	56.4	50.0
Banks	55.2	48.5	48.0	42.4	42.0	45.9	39.1
Others	14.6	11.3	15.1	18.4	16.1	10.4	10.9
Cooperative financial institutions	5.1	12.6	11.0	14.6	23.1	28.2	28.3
Mutual loan and savings banks	3.2	7.0	5.4	6.6	6.5	6.0 ⎫	6.1 ⎫
Credit associations	1.8	4.4	4.5	6.2	7.8	7.8 ⎬ = 23.6	7.9 ⎬ 22.0
Other cooperatives	—	1.2	1.1	1.9	8.8	9.8 ⎭	8.0 ⎭
Government financial institutions	5.8	5.8	4.9	4.9	7.8	6.2	10.0
Special accounts	2.2	4.1	2.2	1.4	1.2	1.3	1.5
Internal funds							
Total	42.0	74.9	74.6	69.4	96.9	68.3	81.9
Depreciation	27.7[b]	47.6	47.2	48.5	60.9	48.6	71.7
Retained profits	14.3[b]	27.3	27.4	20.9	36.0	19.7	10.2
Total external funds, trill. ¥	1.58	4.27	9.87	24.17	43.03	59.15	55.36
Total external funds, percent of GNP	13.4	12.1	16.3	13.0	16.0	20.6	12.3

[a]Excluding trade credit.   [b]Fiscal year.

SOURCES: Derived from *ESA*, 1971, pp. 31–34; 1975, pp. 43–44; 1977, p. 48.

more than two-thirds of total borrowings, whereas the share of "business acquaintances" had become negligible.[51]

Whether smaller business enterprises, in corporate or unincorporated form, have particular difficulties in obtaining funds, that is, difficulties exceeding those that simply reflect their financial situation and riskiness, cannot be decided on the basis of available statistics, although a preference of the banking system, supposedly not rationally motivated, for large borrowers has been asserted.[52] In 1976 smaller and medium-sized enterprises (defined as those capitalized at below ¥ 100 mill., i.e., $300,000) accounted for nearly one-third of total loans of the private banking system,[53] whereas fully two-fifths went to larger enterprises (capitalization of more than ¥ 1 bill.). The share of smaller enterprises would be considerably higher if the cooperative and government credit institutions were included. City and local banks both provided smaller enterprises with about the same absolute amount of credit, but the relative importance of small enterprises as borrowers was nearly twice as high in the case of local banks, with one-half of the total, than for city banks. Trust banks and long-term credit banks were only a minor source of financing for smaller enterprises and allocated only about one-eighth of their total loans to them.

There exist, finally, as in other countries, considerable differences in the structure of assets and liabilities among enterprises in different industries, which can be followed for 1974 in table 7–30. In particular, the share of financial assets varies, compared to an average of nearly one-half, from not much more than one-tenth in electricity and one-fifth in real estate to three-fourths in trade. If notes and accounts receivable are excluded, the range is much narrower, from 4 percent in electricity to 22 percent in trade. The share of liquid assets, on the other hand, varies only, excluding electricity, from 8 to 14 percent. The share of net worth is generally low, 15 percent for all industries, ranging from 5 percent in trade to nearly 30 percent in services. Whereas current liabilities account on the average for nearly two-thirds of all obligations, the share is below one-fourth in electricity and one-third in real estate but close to seven-eighths in trade and construction.

(ii) FROM ZAIBATSU TO KEIRETSU.[54] After the concentration of Japanese business and private finance had reached a peak both in the 1930s and during World War II, at least insofar as larger enterprises are concerned, it was suddenly and sharply reduced during the late 1940s by the government at the behest of the American occupation authorities. This was accomplished by, first, the dissolution of the topholding companies that controlled through stock ownership the numerous and diversified corporations making up the large conglomerates, which, in turn, were owned by the members of one group, for example, the Mitsui, Sumitomo, Yasuda, and Iwasaki (for the Mitsubishi zaibatsu) families and in some cases by a small number of their close associates. The second means of reducing concentration was the sale of the stocks held by the top holding companies, and sometimes directly by members of the controlling group, to employees and directly or indirectly to the general public.[55] This period of effective deconcentration,

51. These figures have been taken from a chart by Shinohara, 1968, p. 53. The chart is based on data in a book (in Japanese) by K. Miyazawa (1961). Although Shinohara does not indicate the date to which the figures refer, it has been assumed that the date is close to the publication date of Miyazawa's book. The sources shown in the graph do not add to 100 percent, because creditors, such as local banks, government financial institutions, and insurance companies, are not shown.

52. This charge has been made with particular emphasis and in a spirit of criticism by Ehrlich, e.g., in the conclusions for both the postwar and prewar periods on p. 523 ff.

53. ESM, January 1977, p. 190 ff.

54. The most detailed description in English of the dissolution of the zaibatsu and the formation of the keiretsu will be found in Hadley. Almost all books dealing with Japan's economic and financial development in the postwar period provide briefer treatments, e.g., Adams and Hoshii, chap. I: 1, 3; II: 3, 2, and III: 1, section i; Cohen, 1949 and 1958; and Yamamura, 1967, chap. 7. Cf. also Caves and Uekusa, 1976, pp. 494 ff. I have not been able to use the more recent statistics on the development of conglomerates, which are provided by an apparently annual publication (Keiretsu no Kenkūyu) by the Japanese Economic Organizations' Association (Keidanren), because it is only available in Japanese.

55. Sales from June 1947 to March 1950 totaled ¥ 6.75 bill., of which ¥ 1.78 bill. were sold to employees, ¥ 2.54 bill. directly to the general public, and ¥ 2.43 bill. to security dealers who redistributed them (Yamamura, 1967, p. 7). This compares with a market value of all shares listed on the Tokyo Stock Exchange of ¥ 122 bill. in 1949 (HYS, p. 253).

TABLE 7-30. Structure of Assets and Liabilities of Principal Enterprises, 1974

	All industries	Manufacturing	Mining	Construction	Trade	Real estate	Transportation	Electricity	Service
Assets	100.0	100.0	100.0	100.0	100.0	100.0	100.0	100.0	100.0
Tangible	45.6	48.9	45.5	56.6	13.1	70.2	61.1	85.4	54.2
Financial	48.4	46.9	47.8	40.1	75.5	22.1	32.2	11.3	38.0
Cash	9.2	10.5	10.1	9.7	8.2	8.8	9.1	3.6	13.9
Notes receivable	11.2	9.2	5.2	7.7	25.5	1.5	0.3	—	0.7
Accounts receivable	14.5	12.9	10.3	12.4	27.9	1.6	4.9	2.2	2.7
Securities	1.7	2.1	1.4	0.1	0.8	2.3	3.5	0.9	0.3
Investments	11.8	12.3	20.8	10.1	13.0	7.9	14.3	4.6	20.4
Other	6.0	4.3	6.7	3.3	11.5	7.7	6.6	3.3	7.8
Liabilities	84.8	81.8	77.8	83.0	94.7	82.0	85.8	81.0	71.5
Current	55.0	54.2	39.9	70.3	79.7	27.3	28.6	18.6	33.8
Other	29.7	27.5	37.9	12.6	15.0	54.7	57.2	62.4	37.7
Net Worth	15.2	18.3	22.1	17.1	5.3	18.0	14.2	19.0	28.7

SOURCE: Bank of Japan, *Financial Statements of Principal Enterprises in Japan*, 1974.

however, was of short duration. Most of the groups were soon reestablished, in most cases even without a change of name, although new top holding companies were not created and the enterprises did not include exactly the same enterprises that had constituted the prewar conglomerates. However, the new groups, called *keiretsu* (a vague term literally meaning something like "lineage group") instead of zaibatsu (literally "money clique"), differed in three important aspects from the old family combines. First, they were much more loosely organized—ownership of a controlling proportion of the capital of the corporations belonging to the keiretsu was replaced by cross ownership of smaller blocks of stock within the group, cross directorships were established, and an informal coordination was maintained through regular meetings of the top officials and the chief members and by similar means. Second, whereas the zaibatsu had included a large commercial bank, which was owned and controlled by the top holding company, as an important member of the group, the key position in the keiretsu apparently is actually held by a large commercial bank (Mitsui, Mitsubishi, Sumitomo, Fuji, formerly Yasuda, and Dai Ichi) and is strengthened by, although not dependent on, the banks' ownership of a moderate proportion of the shares of some of the other companies in the group. Third, although the importance of the groups in the Japanese economy is, as table 7–31 shows, still very large, it is smaller than it was at the end of World War II.

In 1946, before the dissolution, the four largest zaibatsu accounted for 25 percent of the capital of all corporations and the next six largest zaibatsu for another 11 percent. The Mitsui and Mitsubishi combines alone controlled 9 and 8 percent, respectively, of all corporate capital and in 1939 (when their share of total corporate capital was under 4 percent each) included twelve of the one hundred largest Japanese corporations. By 1955 the share of the four largest combines, now measured by assets rather than capital, was still 16 percent and by 1970 it had risen to a little more than one-fifth and exceeded one-fourth if the three other bank-led keiretsu are included. The main changes in the postwar period, apart from the recovery in importance of the keiretsu, are the increase in the share of independent, large industrial corporations, mostly new enterprises in high-technology industries, and even more so in other companies outside the affiliate system, and the substantial reduction in the share of government companies, which operate mainly in the public utility industries. From the point of view of finance, the most important problem raised by the existence of the conglomerates, which include financial as well as nonfinancial enterprises, is the extent to which they constitute closed financial circuits, that is, the proportion of funds

TABLE 7-31. Distribution of Assets of Large Corporations by
Group Affiliation, 1955–1970 (Percent)[a]

Affiliate group	1955	1962	1970
Government	62.2	50.1	38.3
Long-term credit banks	2.1	3.3	4.3
Private financial institutions	23.3	28.4	29.2
Mitsui	6.1	3.8	5.0
Mitsubishi	5.0	6.4	7.2
Sumitomo	3.2	5.9	5.4
Fuji Bank (Yasuda)	2.9	3.6	3.8
Dai Ichi Bank	3.1	3.5	3.2
Sanwa Bank	1.4	2.2	2.6
Other banks	1.6	3.0	2.0
Giant industrial corporations	5.6	9.5	8.8
Foreign-owned enterprises	1.0	1.4	1.4
Companies outside the affiliate system	5.8	7.3	18.0

[a]Corporations with tangible assets of more than ¥ 5 bill.

SOURCE: Caves and Uekusa, p. 499.

required by the nonfinancial members of a group that is furnished by the financial institutions, in particular the banks, that belong to the group, and the proportion of the resources of the group's financial institutions that is made available to its nonfinancial enterprises. By this test, the postwar conglomerates are only partly closed. A very substantial part of the funds of financial enterprises in the group is made available to group nonfinancial enterprises. On the other hand, the nonfinancial enterprises draw only a moderate proportion of their external funds from financial enterprises within the group and rely for much or most of their needs on sources outside the group. The degree of intergroup financing, of course, varies considerably among conglomerates.

Thus in 1966 eighteen nonfinancial core corporations belonging to the Mitsui group received on the (weighted) average 30 percent of their total bank borrowing from institutions within the group, the ratio of intergroup borrowing ranging from 3 to 60 percent. For seventeen nonfinancial corporations in the Mitsubishi conglomerate, intergroup borrowing averaged 38 percent with a range of 5 to 74 percent. Intergroup borrowing was most important in the Sumitomo combine, the group that was the first to be reconstituted after the zaibatsu dissolution. Twelve companies within the group received on the average one-half of their bank credit from institutions within the group, the share ranging from 36 to 60 percent.[56]

Looking at the situation from the point of view of the lending financial institutions, it appears that in the early 1960s nearly one-half of their total loans was made to group (keiretsu) corporations, the ratio varying between nearly two-fifths and three-fifths. The corresponding ratio was much lower, less than one-tenth for the long-term credit banks.[57]

When the same relations are observed from the borrowers' perspective, nonfinancial corporations affiliated with financial institutions are shown to rely on this link to a considerably smaller extent in their loan financing. On the average, they drew only one-sixth of their total borrowing from the large city bank with which they are affiliated, and the proportion varied only between 13 and 18 percent for the six groups. That the principle of *chasse gardée* does not prevail is evident from the fact that these corporations receive, on the average, nearly one-tenth of their total loans from the other five big city banks, that is, more than half as much as they draw from their keiretsu banks, although without concentration on any one of them. These figures are put in focus by the fact that seventeen large corporations (mainly public utilities but also Yawata Steel) not affiliated with any of the six big city banks, as well as nearly one thousand smaller unaffiliated corporations, nevertheless received about 15 percent of their loans from those banks. Hence, the reliance of affiliated corporations on the six big city banks was not much more pronounced than it was in the case of nonaffiliated corporations. Both groups of corporations relied to a considerably larger extent, namely, to about two-thirds, on not specifically identified "other financial institutions," that is, chiefly on the half dozen city banks not belonging to one of the six keiretsu, local banks, trust banks, the trust accounts of banks, insurance companies, and cooperative and public credit institutions.[58]

Less significant as a use or source of funds, but much more important from the point of view of coherence, are intergroup shareholdings. The proportion of intergroup shareholdings

56. Hadley, p. 160.

57. The data on the credit and stock interrelations within the keiretsu that can be found in the literature, at least that part available in English, are not easy to reconcile, which is due partly to the fact that they refer to different dates and cover somewhat different collections of corporations. Thus the statistics in the report of the Committee on the Monetary System (available only in Japanese), which underlie the discussion in this paragraph, show a considerably lower degree of dependence of the nonfinancial keiretsu members on the main bank in the group than do Hadley's statistics. This difference is partly explained by the fact that Hadley's figures include borrowings from trust banks, insurance companies, and other nonfinancial core companies within the keiretsu.

58. These relationships are not very astonishing if it is kept in mind that in 1965 the six big city banks may have accounted for about one-sixth of the loans and discounts made by all financial institutions; other city banks, trust banks and trust accounts, long-term credit banks, and life insurance companies for more than two-fifths; and cooperative and public credit organizations each for about one-sixth (*ESA*, 1972, pp. 27–28 and 67 ff.).

increased considerably from the middle 1950s, when the groups began to be reconstituted, to the early 1960s. At that point intergroup holdings in the three largest conglomerates ranged, as table 7–32 shows, from 16 percent (according to another source 24 percent) in the Mitsui group to 22 percent (31 percent) in the Mitsubishi group and to 27 percent (32 percent) in the Sumitomo group. Changes during the 1960s appear to have been small, with a tendency toward a very slight decline in the percentage of intergroup holdings. Whatever the exact figures, the level of the intergroup holdings is large enough to lodge voting control, on the average, firmly within the group.

(iii) THE PUZZLE OF THE FINANCES OF UNINCORPORATED BUSINESS ENTERPRISES. Because the flow-of-funds accounts of the Bank of Japan do not have a separate sector for unincorporated business enterprises, any discussion of their financing must remain fragmentary. Some estimates are provided in the national income accounts for the main nonfinancial uses of funds, namely, the capital expenditures of unincorporated business. Similarly, some of the liability items shown in the flow-of-funds accounts can be roughly allocated to unincorporated enterprises, namely, the net trade debt shown in the personal sector of the accounts, and a proportion of total loans of the sector can be attributed, but only very roughly, to unincorporated business. On the other hand, there is no way of allocating part of the accumulation of financial assets by the personal sector to unincorporated business except cash and this again only with a good deal of arbitrariness. The resulting picture, rough as it must remain, is not without interest even if it raises more questions than it answers.

The outstanding and puzzling feature of this tentative uses-and-sources statement is that the gross capital expenditures by farm and nonfarm unincorporated enterprises are measured nationally as ¥ 57 trill. but are shown in the flow-of-funds accounts by only ¥ 30 trill. Borrowings of financial institutions by unincorporated enterprises are not known. If they bore the same proportion of slightly above one-half to capital expenditures as in the case of corporations, they would have totaled ¥ 32 trill. This is not an unreasonable figure, although probably on the low side, given that the total borrowings of the household sector, including unincorporated enterprises, were put in the flow-of-funds accounts at ¥ 66 trill. Even if borrowings by unincorporated enterprises did not exceed ¥ 32 trill., their two main sources of funds of ¥ 59 trill. would be slightly in excess of their gross capital expenditures and, of course, far above their net capital expenditures of not much more than ¥ 30 trill. Account, however, must also be taken of a third source of funds, net sales of land, which seem to have been substantial. Net sales of land by the household sector alone in 1970–77 are estimated in the national accounts at ¥ 25 trill., much if not most of which must have come from agricultural enterprises. On a gross basis, these three sources of funds may have exceeded capital expenditures by something like ¥ 20 trill., whereas on a net basis they may have done so to the extent of ¥ 50 trill. It is difficult to find counterparts to their large amounts among uses of funds, let alone to accommodate business saving, which, to judge from the evidence of household sample accounts, were quite high

TABLE 7-32. Intergroup Shareholdings in Three Large Groups, 1954–1966

	Mitsui	Mitsubishi	Sumitomo
1. September 1954	9.9	17.1	16.4
2. March 1958	12.2	20.2	19.8
3. September 1960	15.6	21.7	27.2
4. 1961	24	31	32
5. 1966	23	28	30

SOURCES: Lines 1–3: *Oriental Economist*, February 1961 (cited in Brochier, p. 79). Lines 4–5: Hadley, pp. 214 ff.

compared to income. Unincorporated business enterprises undoubtedly accumulated some financial assets, but it is difficult to see how they could have reached the sums necessary to square their sources-and-uses-of-funds accounts. Thus the amounts in buzumi deposits could hardly have reached ¥ 10 trill. Even if unincorporated enterprises accounted for one-half of the currency and non-buzumi demand deposits of the entire household sector, they would have amounted to not much more than ¥ 10 trill. Large accumulations of time deposits and securities by unincorporated enterprises are unlikely. The problem, therefore, remains, and its solution is better left to Japanese experts in financial statistics and business management.

c. The Personal Sector

Whereas the business sector is the main determinant of the level and tempo of capital expenditures, the personal sector (which in the national and flow-of-funds accounts includes, without separation, unincorporated farm and nonfarm enterprises and the minor nonprofit institutions)[59] is the main supplier of saving, accounting during the period 1956–77 for more than one-half of gross and more than two-thirds of net national saving, hence the necessity of understanding the structure of personal saving for any analysis of the investment and saving process and the economic growth of postwar Japan.

Both the primary microeconomic data on personal saving[60] and the literature, often rather complex econometrically, that analyze these data, although they by no means exhaust them, are voluminous. They do not agree, however, on even some of the essentials of the process, let alone on the societal and psychological forces behind it.[61] Hence, a discussion as brief as this one, which essentially has to rely on that part of the secondary literature that is available in Western languages, must be limited to the main features of the personal saving process. It also must avoid taking a stand on matters on which the specialists still disagree. The most important disagreement probably concerns the question, not unknown in other countries, of the extent—as only extreme partisans will still insist on a monocausal explanation—to which the high and rising level of the personal saving ratio in postwar Japan is simply the result of the rapid increase in real income, which then becomes the explanandum, and to what extent it is the result of specific features of the saving behavior of Japanese employee and entrepreneurial households.[62]

The brief discussion in this section will start with a look at the information on personal sector saving and investment that can be derived from the national and the flow-of-funds accounts. Unfortunately, this information suffers from the failure of both accounts to disaggregate the very large and heterogeneous personal sector, particularly the failure to segregate the unincorporated farm and nonfarm enterprise sectors. This discussion will be followed by the

59. In the 1970s, nonprofit institutions accounted for only 0.8 percent of the disposable income of the personal sector and 1.1 percent of its capital consumption allowances (ARNA, pp. 188–89).

60. For the postwar period Japan has produced more numerous and larger household sample surveys of consumer finances than any other country, including the United States. Fortunately published in bilingual form, the surveys include fairly detailed information on household saving and financial assets and liabilities. The two main sources of this type, both published by the Bureau of Statistics of the Office of the Prime Minister, are the annual Family Saving Survey, available since 1960, and the quinquennial National Survey of Family Incomes and Expenditures, which is based on a larger sample and hence can classify households in more detail. Vol. 7 of the Third Survey (1969) and the results of the 1974 annual survey have been used in this chapter. Similar publications exist for farm households.

61. For a partial listing of literature in both Japanese and English, cf. Blumenthal, pp. 109–13. In this chapter the following English-language publications have been used: T. Blumenthal, Saving in Post-war Japan, 1970; R. Komiya, "The Supply of Personal Savings," in R. Komiya, ed., Post-war Economic Growth in Japan, 1966; T. Mizoguchi, Personal Savings and Consumption in Post-war Japan, 1970, and "High Personal Saving Rate and Changes in the Consumption Pattern in Post-war Japan," Developing Economies, 1970; T. Noda, "Savings of Farm Households," in K. Ohkawa, ed., Agriculture and Economic Growth: Japan's Experience, 1970; S. Okita, "Saving and Economic Growth in Post-war Japan," Asian Studies 2 (1964), and M. Shinohara, Growth and Cycles in the Japanese Economy, 1962, chaps. 9 and 10.

62. The protagonists of the first view ("no need to consider specific characteristics of Japanese personal saving behavior") are probably Ohkawa and Rosovsky in J. E. G. The opposing view is strongly espoused by Blumenthal (e.g., p. 91) and is also held by a number of Japanese specialists, e.g., Shinohara.

presentation of a few summary figures from the large store of microeconomic data collected by the sample surveys. The first set of figures does not break down saving by forms but is limited to aggregate saving ratios, that is, the relation between total saving and disposable income of groups of households. The second set deals only with the situation prevailing near the end of the period but distinguishes five income groups and two types of nonfarm households (workers and proprietors) and provides separate information on more than a dozen forms of total financial assets and liabilities.

(i) THE MACROECONOMIC PICTURE. Table 7–33 shows for the twenty-two-year period 1956–77, as well as for its five three- to five-year subperiods, the main sources and uses of funds of the personal sector, not in absolute figures but, to facilitate an analysis of their structure, as percentages of total uses or sources. It provides at the same time a picture of the main components of the personal sector's saving and investment. Table 7–34 expresses the same absolute figures as percent of personal disposable income.

During these twenty-two years, the personal sector's gross and net saving represented on the average nearly 30 percent and slightly more than 20 percent, respectively, of personal disposable income. In comparison, the personal sector's borrowings came to less than one-tenth

TABLE 7-33. Uses and Sources of Funds of Personal Sector, 1956–1977[a]

	1956–60	1961–65	1966–70	1971–73	1974–77
Uses					
Tangible assets					
Gross capital expenditures					
Business	4.5	4.4	5.5	5.9	5.4
Residences	4.2	6.2	8.9	9.7	9.1
Consumer durables	3.1	4.9	5.8	5.2	4.4
Total	12.0	15.5	20.2	20.8	18.9
Net capital expenditures					
Business	4.5	6.7	2.8	3.6	3.1
Residences			6.6	6.8	5.8
Consumer durables[b]	1.8	3.0	3.5	3.1	2.6
Total	6.3	9.7	12.9	13.5	11.5
Financial assets					
Cash	2.8	3.7	4.3	6.1	2.5
Time and trust deposits	8.6	9.9	12.4	15.6	14.5
Debt securities	0.6	1.0	1.7	2.0	2.1
Insurance	2.0	2.8	3.2	3.3	3.0
Corporate stock	2.0	2.2	0.6	0.1	0.4
Investment company stock	1.1	0.6	0.2	0.4	0.5
Others	0.6	1.0	0.0	−0.3	−0.0
Total	17.6	21.3	22.2	27.3	22.9
All uses (gross)	29.6	36.9	42.4	48.1	41.8
Sources					
Saving					
Gross	23.3	26.8	30.9	28.3	32.9
Net	17.6	20.8	23.6	21.0	25.5
Sale of land	·	·	·	7.5	1.9
Incurrence of liabilities					
Loans	3.9	4.9	6.6	9.4	6.5
Trade credit	2.4	4.0	3.2	2.9	1.5
Total	6.3	9.0	9.8	12.3	8.0
All sources	29.6	35.8	40.7	48.1	41.8

[a]Percent of personal disposable income.   [b]Assumed to amount to 60 percent of gross expenditures.

SOURCES OF BASIC DATA: *ARNIS* and *BJFFA* for 1956–70; *ARNA*, 1970–77, for 1971–77.

TABLE 7-34. Structure of Uses and Sources of Funds of Personal Sector, 1956–1977
(Percent)

	1956–60	1961–65	1966–70	1971–73	1974–77
Uses					
Tangible assets					
Gross capital expenditures	40.3	42.0	47.7	43.3	45.3
Business	15.3	12.1	13.1	12.3	13.0
Residences	14.4	16.9	20.8	20.2	21.8
Consumer durables	10.7	13.1	13.7	10.7	10.5
Net capital expenditures	21.5	25.8	30.1	28.0	31.6
Business	} 15.1	} 17.9	6.2	7.3	11.4
Residences			15.7	14.3	13.9
Consumer durables[a]	6.4	7.8	8.2	6.4	6.3
Financial Assets					
Cash	9.7	10.0	9.9	12.6	6.0
Time and trust deposits	29.2	27.1	29.2	32.4	34.6
Debt securities	1.9	2.7	4.0	4.1	5.0
Corporate stock	6.4	6.1	1.5	0.2	0.8
Investment trust stock	3.9	1.7	0.2	0.9	1.1
Insurance	6.9	7.6	7.4	6.9	7.2
Others	1.7	2.9	0.1	−0.6	−0.0
Total	59.7	58.0	52.3	56.7	54.7
All uses	100.0	100.0	100.0	100.0	100.0
Sources					
Saving					
Gross	78.6	74.9	76.0	59.9	76.4
Net	59.5	58.1	57.8	44.7	58.6
Sales of land	·	·	·	15.6	4.5
Liabilities					
Loans	13.5	13.9	16.2	19.5	15.4
Trade credit	7.9	11.2	7.8	6.0	3.7
Total	21.4	25.1	24.0	25.5	19.1
All Sources	100.0	100.0	100.0	100.0	100.0

[a]Estimated at 60 percent of gross expenditures.

SOURCE OF BASIC DATA: *ARNA*, pp. 62–63, 195, 207.

of disposable income and one-third of gross and more than two-fifths of net saving. At least one-half of the personal sector's borrowing, or fully 5 percent of disposable income, may be attributed to farm and nonfarm unincorporated enterprises, namely, net trade credit from corporations and a substantial part of the increase in loans. Most of the borrowing by households took the form of home mortgages (which will be discussed later); second in importance was consumer and security credit. In the 1970s net sales of land, probably mostly by the farm subsector, reflecting the extremely high land prices then prevailing, are estimated to have provided funds equal to about 4 percent of disposable income or about one-tenth of total sources. They probably were less important, but not negligible, in the preceding two decades.

Nearly one-fifth of disposable income was used for capital expenditures. In this case it is possible to separate the capital expenditures by unincorporated business enterprises on structures, equipment, and inventories from household expenditures on residences and consumer durables, with the result that the share of the former averaged slightly more than 5 percent of disposable income, whereas expenditures on residences absorbed nearly 9 and those on consumer durables about 5 percent.

The net acquisition of financial assets for the period as a whole accounted for nearly one-fourth of personal disposable income, an extraordinarily high ratio both in international comparison and in relation to Japan's earlier experience and a main characteristic of the saving and investment process in postwar Japan. Time deposits alone were equal to more than 13 percent of total disposable income, with currency and demand deposits adding another 4 percent. On the other hand, debt securities absorbed less than 2 percent, insurance claims 3 percent, and corporate stock not much more than 1 percent of disposable income. Only a small proportion of these amounts may be attributed to unincorporated business enterprises.

Most uses and sources of funds showed an upward trend compared to disposable income. Thus the total increased from 30 percent in 1956–60 to more than 40 percent from the late 1960s on, the ratio even climbing to nearly one-half in the 1971–73 boom to fall back to not much more than two-fifths in 1974–77. The increase was slightly more pronounced in the acquisition of tangible assets, particularly residences, than of financial assets. Among financial assets the rise was largest in the case of time deposits, whose relation to disposable income rose from less than 9 percent in 1956–60 to 15 percent in the 1970s, and thus accounted for the entire increase in the ratio of the acquisition of all financial assets to disposable income. Most of this increase occurred after the mid-1960s. The only instrument whose relation to disposable income declined was corporate stock, the ratio falling from 1.1 to 0.5 percent for investment company and still more steeply, from 2.0 to 0.4 percent, for other corporate stock, again mostly since the early 1960s, when the first, longest, and strongest postwar stock price boom came to an end. The resumption of the sharp upward thrust in stock prices in the 1970s apparently did not reverse the movement.

The structure of uses and sources of personal sector funds failed to show substantial changes if only the three- to five-year subperiods are considered. Thus the proportion of financial assets remained close to 58 percent. Within financial assets, however, the share of time deposits increased from 29 to 38 percent of total uses and that of debt securities from 2 to 5 percent, whereas that of corporate stock fell precipitously from more than 10 to 2 percent. The share of residences rose from one-seventh to more than one-fifth of total uses and from not much more than one-third to nearly one-half of total tangible assets, still a low ratio in international comparison. The shares of unincorporated business investment and consumer durables declined, the latter, in part, because of their relative price decline.

The strong upward trend in the saving ratio may be partly responsible for the fact that cyclical movements are not pronounced. Nevertheless, the five peaks of 1957, 1961, 1964, 1970, and 1973 can be recognized, although in three cases with only one year's lead or lag. There is no evidence of the troughs of 1962 and 1974 in the series, although those of 1958, 1965 (with one year's delay), and 1971 are visible.

Another characteristic of the saving process of the personal sector is its marked seasonality. From 1954 through 1977, the saving ratio, excluding consumer durables, reached its peak in every year in the fourth quarter, when it averaged nearly twice the annual rate. In contrast, the rate was very small, and until the mid-1960s often slightly negative, for the first quarter, whereas the second and third quarters were close to the annual average.[63] This extraordinary behavior is due, in part, to the custom of paying a substantial, but varying, part of the total annual income of workers and employees in the form of two variable bonuses, a larger one in December and a smaller one in June. Obviously, an above average proportion of these bonuses is saved rather than spent, a behavior in accordance with the generally accepted hypothesis that the saving rate tends to be higher for unexpected, or not exactly foreseeable, and irregular income.[64]

At the end of 1977 the total borrowings of the personal sector were put at ¥ 66 trill., or fully one-third of disposable income, a considerable increase from one-fourth in 1970 and one-fifth in 1964. Part of this, possibly as much as one-half, consists of the liabilities of unincorpo-

---

63. *ARNIS*, 1976; *ARNA*.

64. The relative importance of these bonuses had a tendency to rise over the postwar period as evidenced by the decline in the ratio of the regular income of the head of the household to total workers' household income from about 70 percent in 1953–58 to 65 percent in 1963–68 (Mizoguchi, 1970, 1:409).

rated farm and nonfarm enterprises to financial institutions. The rest is made up primarily of home mortgages, consumer debt, and the security debt of households.

Housing and housing finance have been stepchildren in Japanese economic and financial development since the Meiji era, but the situation has been rapidly changing in the last decade. It is only recently that serious efforts have been made to trace in any detail the sources of finance of residential construction and residential land acquisition. The fragmentary data now available do permit, however, a visualization of the essential features of the process.

The cost of construction of private dwellings acquired by owner-occupier households—according to the 1974 household sample survey, nearly two-thirds of nonfarm households owned their homes—or by noncorporate landlords included in the personal sector has risen steadily from 4 percent of disposable income in 1956–60 to nearly 10 percent in the 1970s, in part to rectify the earlier neglect of this sector. Land costs must have involved heavy additional expenditures for the owner-occupiers or landlords, because land prices rose very rapidly during the period and at its end seem to have been higher than construction costs.[65] Because the land was essentially acquired from owners belonging to the personal sector, no investment was involved for the sector as a whole.

Although our knowledge of housing finance is incomplete, there is no doubt that only a small fraction of the construction expenditures and land costs on new residential facilities, which are still overwhelmingly one-family homes, was financed by borrowing from financial institutions.[66] The figures assembled in table 7–35 suggest that the increase in credit to individuals for housing made by financial institutions during the twelve years 1966 to 1977 was in excess of ¥ 23 trill., which represented about one-fifth of the cost of construction of private residential structures and probably less than one-tenth of construction plus land cost. Some credit, but apparently only limited amounts, was supplied by other lenders—for example, corporate and government employers—but the bulk of the requirements of owner-occupiers or landlords of residential rental properties were self-financed. As a result, the ratio of institutional home mortgage debt to the value of the stock of dwellings is extraordinarily low, although rising, and is now probably on the order of one-tenth compared with possibly as little as 3 percent in 1956.[67]

The role of home mortgages in consumer finances has sharply increased since the mid-1960s. Thus the share of institutional home mortgage credit increased from 7 percent of the personal sector's total debt in 1965 to 25 percent in 1970 and to more than 35 percent in 1977.

Although the aggregate volume of home mortgage debt is relatively small, a considerable and rising proportion of households carries some indebtedness of this type. In the 1974 household sample surveys about one-fifth of all households reported liabilities for the purchase of house or land, and the proportion rose from one-eighth for low-income groups to one-third for middle-income groups (table 7–36).[68]

Until recently, the dominating outside source of residential financing was the government's Housing Loan Corporation, which obtains most of its funds directly or indirectly from the Ministry of Finance.[69] In 1977 the corporation still accounted for nearly one-fifth of all financial

65. Cf. discussion in Goldsmith, 1975, pp. 7 ff.

66. Some of the information on which the discussion of housing finance is based was supplied by the economic staff of the Housing Loan Corporation.

67. Based on the value of residential structures (table 7–39) and a land-structure ratio of approximately 2.

68. The household sample inquiries, which will be summarized in subsection b, give some clue to the identity of the borrowers. They indicate that in 1969 only 21 percent of all sampled urban households had any debt ''for purchase of houses and land'' and that the debt exceeded ¥ 600,000 (about $1,700) in only 8 percent of households. With an average debt of ¥ 165,000 for about 20 million urban households (about ¥ 800,000 for those households having debts of this type), the total debt on homes in urban Japan would be in the neighborhood of ¥ 3.3 trill. This estimate is quite compatible with the figures obtained from lenders' balance sheets (table 7–35). Real estate debt tends to increase in relation to income or assets among employees but not among individual entrepreneurial households. Debt is highest in relation to income in households whose head is between 30 and 50 years old (*1969 National Survey of Family Incomes and Expenditures,* vol. 7).

69. For balance sheets of the Housing Loan Corporation, cf. *ESA,* 1977, p. 163.

TABLE 7-35. Housing Credit of Financial Institutions to Individuals, 1965, 1970, and 1977

Lender	Amount outstanding (¥ bill.)			Distribution (percent)		
	1965	1970	1977	1965	1970	1977
City banks	8	225	3911	1.7	9.2	16.5
Local banks	19	220	3519	4.0	8.8	14.9
Trust banks and accounts	} 6	} 178	1715	} 1.3	} 7.9	7.2
Long-term credit banks			287			1.2
Mutual loan and savings banks	12	92	1784	2.5	3.6	7.5
Credit associations	—	259	2597	—	9.5	11.0
Labor credit associations	·	185	860	·	6.8	3.6
Agricultural cooperatives	·	332	1507	·	12.2	6.4
Life insurance companies	·	12	926	·	0.4	3.9
Housing loan companies	·	·	1317	·	·	5.6
Housing Loan Corporation	433[a,b]	1133[d]	4677	90.5	41.6	19.7
Total	487[c]	2720	23692[e]	100.0	100.0	97.5

[a]All housing loans.   [b]1955, ¥ 57 bill.; 1960, ¥ 144 bill. (*ESA*, 1961, p. 139).   [c]Only institutions for which amount of loans is known.   [d]March 31, 1971.   [e]Includes 592 (2.5 percent) institutions not separately listed.

SOURCES: Housing Loan Corporation; *ESA*, 1971; 1977, pp. 51 ff.

institutions' housing loans to individuals, sharply down from more than two-fifths seven years earlier and close to nine-tenths in 1965. For most other financial associations, housing loans were a secondary, although rapidly rising, use of funds. Thus, in 1977 they accounted for 7 percent of total loans and discounts of city banks; 9 percent of life insurance companies; about 11 percent of those of local banks, trust accounts, and mutual savings banks; 13 percent of credit associations; 16 percent of agricultural cooperatives; and, solitary peak, 60 percent of labor credit associations.

Reflecting the relatively backward status of housing finance, terms and procedures are far from standardized, and terms are, by American standards, rather harsh. Thus maturity is often less than ten years, although recently loans up to twenty-five years were instituted; the loan to value ratio generally does not exceed 70 percent; and interest rates were in the early 1970s in the neighborhood of 10 percent, although up to 12 percent for long maturities.

Organized consumer credit other than home mortgage and security credit is still of very small importance.[70] Even in 1977 the amount of such credit granted by all banks was reported as outstanding to the extent of only a little more than ¥ 500 bill.[71] As it equaled only about one-tenth of their annual expenditures on consumer durables and less than one-half of 1 percent of their disposable income, this amount is fairly negligible from the point of view of the consumers, as well as from that of the lenders, for whom it also represented less than one-half of 1 percent of their total loans. Astonishingly, the volume of consumer credit by banks has increased by less than 50 percent in the 1970s, or considerably less than consumers' disposable income. The volume of consumer credit extended by unorganized lenders, often at extremely high rates, is apparently much higher.[72] Consumer credit thus is one field in which the Japanese financial system is still very backward, although it is not likely that this situation will be perpetuated.

(ii) SAVING BEHAVIOR OF DIFFERENT TYPES OF HOUSEHOLDS. There is good reason to expect that households of different size, age, income, wealth, occupation, and location, to mention only the most obvious independent variables, differ both in the aggregate saving ratio

70. Cf. Adams and Hoshii, pp. 419–29.
71. *ESA*, 1977, p. 53.
72. Cf. *Business Week*, May 7, 1979, p. 117.

TABLE 7-36. Financial Assets and Liabilities of Households by Income Quintiles, 1974

		Income Quintile				
	Average	I	II	III	IV	V
1. Income (thou. yen)	2598	1084	1733	2251	2945	4979
2. Selected assets (thou. yen)	2704	1346	1699	2045	2863	5625
	I. Relation to total financial assets (percent)					
3. Demand deposits	15.42	20.66	18.60	17.40	14.38	12.95
4. Time deposits	42.94	41.45	43.47	43.97	40.63	43.94
5. Life insurance	19.94	23.45	23.71	22.61	20.51	16.63
6. Stocks	8.57	5.75	3.32	4.53	8.78	12.39
7. Bonds	2.41	1.34	2.64	1.64	2.04	3.04
8. Unit and open-end stock trust	0.70	0.40	0.28	0.22	0.85	0.97
9. Open-end bond trust	1.04	1.41	0.61	0.51	1.06	1.19
10. Loan trust	4.24	3.86	2.85	2.83	5.47	4.61
11. Nonfinancial institution deposits	4.74	1.68	4.52	6.30	6.23	4.23
12. Total liabilities	27.94	20.01	24.73	31.89	28.42	29.31
13. Financial institutions	19.64	15.30	15.91	22.46	18.63	21.42
14. Nonfinancial lenders	8.30	4.71	8.82	9.43	9.79	7.89
15. Real-estate debt (included in 12 to 14)	18.74	8.00	15.29	22.22	21.36	19.92
	II. Relation to income (percent)					
16. All selected assets	104.10	124.32	98.02	90.84	97.29	112.99
17. Demand deposits	16.05	26.51	18.23	15.81	13.99	14.63
18. Time deposits	44.70	51.54	42.61	39.44	39.53	49.65
19. Life insurance	20.76	29.16	23.24	20.54	19.95	18.79
20. Stocks	8.92	7.15	3.25	4.11	8.54	14.00
21. Bonds	2.51	1.66	2.59	1.49	1.98	3.46
22. Unit and open-end trust	0.73	0.50	0.27	0.20	0.83	1.09
23. Open-end bond trust	1.08	1.75	0.59	0.46	1.03	1.35
24. Loan trust	4.41	4.80	2.79	2.56	5.33	5.21
25. Nonfinancial institution deposits	4.93	2.09	4.43	5.72	6.11	4.80
26. Total liabilities	29.09	24.88	23.20	28.97	27.65	33.11
27. Financial institutions	20.44	19.02	15.60	20.40	18.13	24.21
28. Nonfinancial institutions	8.64	5.86	8.64	8.56	9.53	8.90
29. Real estate debt (included in 26 to 28)	19.51	9.95	14.99	20.18	20.78	22.51

SOURCE: Japan Bureau of Statistics, *1974 Family Saving Survey*, p. 28.

and in the structure of saving, as reflected in the relation of the accumulation of assets to the change in indebtedness and the distribution of asset accumulation among the main types of assets. The results of the sample surveys of household saving, assets, and liabilities bear out this expectation in Japan, as they do for other countries; and they have shown, as might also be expected, that the interrelationships among these numerous factors that differentiate one household type from another are very complicated. As a result, we are unable to explain many of the aspects of the level and structure of the saving of different groups of households; where such explanation is possible, rather complex econometric techniques are required. Nothing as ambitious and yet inconclusive is attempted here. Rather, the discussion will be limited to the annual aggregate saving ratio for a few broad types of households throughout the postwar period and the structure of financial assets and liabilities in 1974 for households of different income level and occupation, two factors that might be expected to have an influence on the level and structure of saving.

In postwar Japan the aggregate saving ratio, as ascertained by household sample surveys but not necessarily in actuality, has generally been higher for urban workers and employees than for farmers. The difference, however, was rather small, averaging less than 2 percent of disposable income in 1966–70.[73] Within the predominating group of urban workers and employees, the ratio has been slightly but consistently higher for white-collar than for other workers. No comparable series seems to be available for entrepreneurial households for the entire postwar period or most of it, but it is known from some of these inquiries that their aggregate saving ratio is considerably higher, partly because their average income is higher. These differences, of course, cannot be attributed without further analysis to the different occupations of the three groups, as the observed ratios may be influenced, or even primarily determined, by differences in age, income, or other characteristics of these broad groups of households.

Turning to differences in the structure of saving, it is necessary in a summary such as this to limit attention to the cumulated result of intergroup differences in the structure of financial assets and liabilities as they appear at a point in time rather than to follow them year by year, that is, to look at balance sheets rather than at income accounts. This means ignoring short-term changes but has the advantage of being less influenced by the errors in the annual flows.

Income is generally assumed to be a major factor in determining the level and structure of saving and asset accumulation. Table 7–36 shows, at least in the lower- and middle-income groups, the influence of income in postwar Japan.

The absolute amount of accumulated financial assets, and hence by inference also saving in the form of financial assets, tends, of course, to increase with income. Thus in 1974 selected financial assets, including the bulk of them other than currency, which according to flow-of-funds statistics averaged ¥ 0.34 mill. per household, increased from ¥ 1.35 mill. ($4,500) per household for the lowest fifth nonfarm households, arrayed by income, to more than ¥ 5.60 mill. ($19,000), compared to an average of ¥ 2.70 mill. ($9,000). The flow-of-funds accounts, on the other hand, indicate an average for all households, including unincorporated business enterprises and nonprofit organizations, of ¥ 5.40 mill., or nearly twice the amount shown in the household sample survey adjusted for differences in coverage. When assets are related to income, however, the ratio shows no relation to income, ranging only between 0.90 and 1.24 and being higher in the lowest and highest quintile than in the second to fourth quintiles.[74]

The differences in the structure of the portfolio of financial assets are also astonishingly small. Time deposits are the favorite vehicle of financial saving for all income groups, their share in total financial assets varying only between 41 and 44 percent, the significance of the differences being doubtful, given the relatively small number of households reporting (5,180).

73. Noda, 1970, p. 534, for 1951 to 1965; figures for 1966 to 1970 were kindly supplied by Mr. Noda. Cf *1969 National Survey of Family Incomes and Expenditures,* vol. 7, p. 122.

74. In Japan, as in other countries, the blown-up figures from household sample surveys, i.e., the result of the multiplication of the mean values obtained from the household inquiries by the number of households in the appropriate universe, fails to come up to the supposedly comparable figures derived for the personal sector, usually as a residual, from the macroeconomic flow-of-funds accounts. The differences between the two sets of figures are, however, disturbingly large in Japan. The blown-up sample figures from the *1974 Family Saving Survey* (p. 28) equaled only one-half (in 1969 only two-fifths) of the figures for the same financial assets shown in the Bank of Japan's flow-of-funds accounts. Even this low ratio is reached only as a result of the high ratio of more than four-fifths for life insurance, which is probably spuriously high because the household inquiries were most likely based on the face value of the contracts rather than on the much lower, but more appropriate, actuarial value embodied in the flow-of-funds accounts. As a result, the blown-up figures are on the order of one-half of the flow-of-funds data for deposit-type savings and for corporate stock and only one-fifth for bond and investment trust stock. More astonishing, in comparison to experience in other countries, is the fact that the understatement seems to be equally pronounced for liabilities, as liabilities to financial institutions reported in the household sample survey were not much above one-third of the flow-of-funds estimates. This may be explained in part by the fact that the surveys do not include the substantial borrowings of unincorporated enterprises.

The understatement of the blown-up household inquiry figures is due in part, as one may assume on the basis of the experience in the United States and Europe, to the failure of the sample to include an appropriate proportion of upper-income and wealthy households, who are notoriously averse to answering inquiries of this type. The difference between the blown-up household inquiry and the flow-of-funds figures is, however, so large in Japan that one must also suspect substantial underreporting in the lower- and middle-income and wealth groups, and, consequently, one must use the figures for even these groups only with great caution. This, again, is a problem that I must leave to the Japanese specialists, who, strange to say, do not seem to have been bothered by these blatant discrepancies, at least, to my knowledge, not in English print.

Similarly, the share of life insurance declines only from 23 percent in the two bottom quintiles to 17 percent in the top quintile. There is a substantial relation to income in only two important financial assets. The share of demand deposits, and presumably also that of currency, declines with increasing income, whereas the share of corporate stock increases from fully 3 percent in the second quintile to more than 12 percent in the top quintile.

The relation of income is slightly more pronounced for liabilities than for financial assets, the ratio rising from below one-fourth in the two lowest quintiles to less than three-tenths in the two top quintiles. This is due chiefly to a marked increase in the ratio of liabilities to own company, whereas that of liabilities to financial institutions moves irregularly without pronounced trend.

Differences are larger if workers' and industrial proprietors' households as reported in the *1969 National Survey of Family Incomes and Expenditures,* are compared. The ratio of liabilities to assets or to income is, not unexpectedly, considerably higher for entrepreneurial than for employee households. The difference is due mainly to higher other than real estate debt, which presumably finances business activities, but the size of this type of debt does not show a marked relation to entrepreneurs' income of financial assets. Real estate debt is also considerably higher for entrepreneurial than for employee households in the first three income quintiles, probably because the home or shop is used as collateral for loans, the proceeds of which are employed in business. This may also be the reason why the ratio of real estate debt to financial assets or to income increases with income among employee but not among entrepreneurial households.

Among financial assets, the increase in the share of corporate stock is more marked for employee households, for which the share rises from 3 to more than 20 percent, than for entrepreneurial households, where it advances only from 6 to 16 percent, although the average income is higher in each quintile in entrepreneurial than in employee households and substantially so in the top quintile. The reason may be that entrepreneurial households have a substantial equity in business-type tangible assets not covered in the sample inquiries, which in their portfolio are regarded as a substitute for the ownership of corporate stock.

The closest the household samples come to providing information on the portfolio structure of upper-income and wealthy households is provided by tabulations of the reports for the highest income and financial assets groups of employee and individual proprietor households. As the averages in these top groups are ¥ 4 mill. and less than ¥ 6 mill. for income and ¥ 5 mill. and ¥ 7 mill. for financial assets (between $11,000 and $19,000 at the then rate of exchange), the four groups, which together include a little more than 3,000 households, a quite respectable figure for inquiries of this type, seem to consist mostly of upper-middle-class households and are probably dominated by them, given the unlikelihood of adequate representation of the wealthy. It may be for this reason that the portfolio structure of these top groups, which apparently account for between 2 percent (employee households classified by income) and 12 percent (individual proprietors' households classified by size of financial assets) of the relevant universe of households, differs but little from those for households in the top quintile of income recipients.[75] The only significant difference is in the expected direction, that is, the higher share of stocks in the portfolios of employee households in the top income or wealth bracket, separately tabulated, of about one-third of total financial assets, compared to a ratio of one-fifth in the top quintile of income recipients in 1969 and one-eighth in 1974.[76]

75. This supposition cannot be verified because the surveys do not indicate the income or wealth distribution of households in the top groups. The fact that the group averages are only 33 to 95 percent above the lower-class boundaries does, however, cast strong doubt on the adequate representation of wealthy households.

76. The similarity in portfolio structure is not astonishing in view of the relatively small differences between the two samples in average income and financial asset holdings as shown below:

	Income	Wealth
	(¥ mill. per household)	
Employee households		
Top income quintile	2.07	2.24

Differences also exist in the structure of financial assets and liabilities among the different types of households (four types of employee households and six types of other households) distinguished in the 1969 survey.[77] Here again, apparent differences in the ratios cannot be attributed unequivocally to differences in occupation. To isolate the effect of occupation on the level and structure of asset holding and saving would require either cross tabulations, which would soon become unmanageable, or multivariate regression analysis. Nevertheless, the differences that can be observed in the basic tabulations provide some indications of the possible or probable effects of occupational factors. Because the ratios for all employee and proprietor households have already been discussed briefly, attention may now be concentrated on some smaller groups. Among these unincorporated entrepreneurs other than merchants and artisans, corporate administrators are of particular interest because they have the highest average income and asset holdings, and thus are probably nearest to the higher income groups, which, in general, are poorly represented in the surveys.

The first characteristic of these two groups is that their financial asset/income ratios are high, 1.3 and 2.0 compared to an average for all occupations of 1.1 and 0.9 for the most numerous group of employees. This, of course, reflects their relatively high saving ratios and possibly also their capital gains and inheritances of the past. Second, for both groups the ratio of corporate stocks to total financial assets is well above the average, as might be expected in view of their relatively high income. What is more interesting, however, is the fact that the ratio is much higher for corporate administrators (33 percent) than for unincorporated business proprietors (12 percent). Although this difference may be explained, in part, by the higher average income and financial assets of corporate administrators, it more likely reflects that their participation in the enterprise in which they work takes the form of stock ownership.

Assuming that the household sample surveys, although seriously understating the aggregate holdings of financial instruments by the personal sector, correctly reflect their relative holdings, except for the understatement of those of the upper-income groups, it is possible to derive from them the distribution of total or individual financial instruments among groups of households. In 1974 the lower half of income recipients held slightly less than one-third of all financial assets, whereas the top quintile held somewhat more than two-fifths, the shares being virtually the same for liabilities. These figures should be regarded as minimal for the top quintile, whose actual share may well have been in the neighborhood of one-half. The distribution undoubtedly differed among financial instruments, although the similarity of the holding/income ratios indicates that the differences are not likely to have been large in the most important type of financial assets, deposits with financial institutions. However, the lower half of income recipients owned only about one-sixth of all corporate stock held by the personal sector, in turn not much more than one-third of all stock outstanding, whereas the top quintile owned, if their holdings were not relatively, as well as absolutely, underreported, about three-fifths and could have owned as much as two-thirds even if relative underreporting was moderate.

Finally, a related aspect of the portfolios of the household sector, the penetration of the different types of financial instruments among them, as measured by the proportion of households who report ownership or debtor status of a given instrument, can be followed in table 7–37 for four benchmark dates between 1960 and 1974, except for currency, which is not covered by

---

¥ 3 mill. income	4.00	5.08
¥ 4 mill. financial assets	2.04	5.20
Individual proprietors' households		
Top income quintile	3.58	4.02
¥ 3 mill. income	5.75	5.87
¥ 4 mill. financial assets	3.16	7.15

77. *National Survey of Family Incomes and Expenditures,* vol. 7, table 8.

TABLE 7-37. Penetration of Selected Financial Instruments, 1960–1974 (Percent of Households Reporting Asset or Liability)

| | | | | 1974 | | |
| | | | | | Income (thou. ¥) | |
	1960	1965	1970	All house-holds	400–600	Over 5,000
Demand deposits	68.4	79.5	89.5	91.7	63.0	95.1
Post Office	42.4	46.4	51.6	45.1	35.3	47.0
Banks	31.9	42.5	57.9	64.1	30.7	80.0
Others	19.7	25.8	33.0	40.0	17.5	45.4
Time deposits	58.6	65.9	77.4	82.1	47.6	91.7
Post Office	31.1	32.5	39.3	41.9	28.2	47.0
Banks	28.9	35.1	46.6	51.1	15.9	73.7
Others	21.5	26.0	34.3	40.3	15.2	49.9
Life insurance	80.5	88.3	90.4	89.4	54.5	94.4
Post Office	·	61.2	57.2	54.0	44.1	62.9
Life insurance companies	·	73.6	79.4	79.9	37.8	90.0
Public and corporate bonds	5.6	8.8	12.1	10.5	6.8	23.9
Stocks and shares[a]	18.0	19.9	18.7	15.3	3.7	36.4
Stock of investment trust	} 10.0	10.0	3.7	2.6	0.0	8.7
Bond trust		4.0	3.2	4.1	0.0	8.6
Loan trust	3.2	6.8	8.2	7.7	3.4	15.7
Deposits in own company	11.6	21.5	17.1	18.3	0.0	21.0
Borrowing	27.7	19.6	40.6	44.4	25.6	54.7
From private financial institutions	·	10.3	11.0	17.3	4.4	33.2
From Housing Loan Corporation	3.9	4.3	4.9	6.0	4.7	7.7
From other government financial institutions	4.3	4.7	3.8	4.5	5.2	6.6
From life insurance organizations	6.8	7.7	3.5	3.0	0.0	5.4
From nonfinancial institutions	·	23.9	29.5	29.5	14.6	28.7
Installment debt	(13.8)	15.4	18.7	19.0	5.5	16.4
Liabilities for purchase of house or land	·	·	15.8	20.7	12.5	32.7

[a]Excluding stock of investment trusts.

SOURCE: Japan Bureau of Statistics, *1974 Family Saving Survey*, pp. 20–21, 90–91.

the household sample surveys but is held by all of them. In the fourteen years spanned by the table, the degree of penetration increased for practically all debt instruments, whereas it declined for corporate stock (excluding investment trust stock) from 18 to 15 percent. Increases in penetration were particularly pronounced for demand deposits, where the ratio doubled, and for bonds, for which it almost doubled. They were small in the case of life insurance and Post Office deposits. The increase was equally pronounced for liabilities, particularly borrowings from private financial institutions. In all cases, the participation rates are considerably higher in the upper-income groups, particularly for bank deposits and bonds and especially for corporate stock, where a ratio of more than one-third in the highest income group contrasts with one of 4 percent in the lowest group.

Because the household sample surveys do not cover tangible assets, it is not possible to investigate the structure of, and changes in, total assets, liabilities, and net worth of different groups of households during the postwar period. It seems, however, fairly safe to assume that the share of tangible assets, particularly owned homes and consumer durables, declines with increasing income, except possibly in the lowest income groups, and that the share of net worth increases. The inequality in the distribution of total assets should therefore be smaller than that of financial assets.

7. AN OVERVIEW OF FINANCIAL ASSETS AND LIABILITIES

To provide an overview of the distribution of the ownership of the various financial instruments among the five main domestic sectors and eight subsectors of financial institutions, table 7–38 expresses the holdings of a given instrument by a given sector or subsector as of March 31, 1978, as a percent of the total of all financial instruments then outstanding of ¥ 877 trill., or four times the national product at that time, eliminating duplications among different groups of financial institutions. Primarily presented for reference purposes, this table does not require extensive discussion. It shows that the largest three cells in the matrix are time deposits held by the personal sector and trade credit granted by corporations with one-seventh each, and commercial bank loans with one-eighth of all financial instruments outstanding, accounting together for two-fifths of the total. None of the other cells, except in the summary columns 1 and 2 or lines 5, 7, and 10, exceeds 7 percent of the total; and there are altogether eighteen cells (excluding in summary columns and lines) exceeding 1 percent.[78]

Table 7–39, which distinguishes only the four main domestic sectors, although it includes the rest of the world, and fewer types of financial instruments, shows the distribution of both financial assets and liabilities among sectors and within sectors. It thus permits an easy but very aggregative comparison of the portfolio structure of the five main sectors and of the distribution of the nine types of financial instruments being distinguished among them.

The differences in the uses and sources of financial funds among the sectors are large and have already been discussed in section 4 for financial institutions and in section 6 for the other sectors. They reflect the different functions of the main sectors in the country's financial superstructure. Thus loans to, and long-term bonds of, other sectors predominate among the assets of financial institutions, whereas deposit liabilities to other sectors represent more than two-thirds of their sources of funds. Deposits with financial institutions account for three-fourths of the financial assets of the household sector and for one-third of those of nonfinancial corporations, with trade credit constituting nearly three-fifths of the latters' financial assets. More than half of the household sector's liabilities consist of loans from financial institutions, whereas those of nonfinancial corporations amount to more than three-fourths, with trade credit contributing nearly one-third for corporations and nearly one-fourth for the personal sector as it includes unincorporated business enterprises.

The liabilities side of table 7–39 brings together formerly scattered information about the position of each of the five sectors as the holder or the issuer of the main types of financial instruments, again reflecting their position in the financial superstructure. Thus households hold about two-thirds of all deposits with financial institutions (including currency) and more than one-fifth of bonds and shares, accounting for fully one-fourth of all financial instruments outstanding. The share of nonfinancial corporations, which is similar for total financial assets, is about equally large in the case of demand deposits and corporate stock but much smaller for time deposits and bonds. Financial institutions furnish almost all loans and hold about three-fourths of debt securities and nearly one-half of all corporate stock, giving them a share in total financial assets of more than two-fifths. The distribution of the main types of liabilities is more concentrated. Although financial institutions are naturally responsible for all deposits and insurance

---

78. The figures are expressed as a percent of the consolidated total of ¥ 877 as shown in the flow-of-funds accounts, using market rather than book value of corporate stock and assuming that the ratio of market to book value is the same for financial institutions (3.10) as for the corporate and personal sectors, as it is indicated in the source. Investment company stocks are assumed to be shown at market value in the accounts. The unconsolidated figure, derived as the sum of cols. 3 through 16 of table 7–38, is about one-sixth higher, namely, close to ¥ 1,000 trill.; consequently, all ratios would be fully 10 percent lower if expressed as a percent of the unconsolidated total.

TABLE 7-38. Matrix of Financial Instruments, 1977 (Percent)

	All sectors^a (1)	Financial institutions — All^a (2)	Bank of Japan (3)	City banks (4)	Other banks (5)	Trust accounts (6)	Small business (7)	Agri- culture (8)	Govern- ment^b (9)	Insur- ance (10)	Invest- ment (11)	Securi- ties (12)	Central govern- ment (13)	Public corpo- rations and local govern- ment (14)	Corporate business (15)	Personal sector (16)
Currency and demand deposits^c	10.83	0.15		0.18	0.07		0.28	0.12	0.07	0.09		0.03	2.69	0.22	3.54	4.23
Time deposits	18.15			0.03	-0.03		0.08	0.04		0.10		0.01		0.33	4.07	13.75
Trust deposits	2.13				0.03		0.03			0.00				0.02	0.40	1.72
Insurance	3.43					0.37					0.28					3.43
Debt securities	10.77	8.05		1.16	1.43		0.84	0.72	1.93	0.33		0.03	0.13	0.02	0.41	2.17
Short-term government	0.79	0.68	0.96		0.00				0.14			0.08	0.08	0.00		
Central government bonds	3.43	2.92	0.53	0.64	0.58	0.00	0.17	0.10	0.95	0.06	0.01	0.00	0.05	0.00	.	0.43
Local government bonds	1.24	1.16	0.42	0.17	0.29	0.12	0.13	0.27	0.06	0.05	0.07	0.00			.	0.04
Public corporation bonds	2.02	1.53		0.10	0.22	0.18	0.14	0.14	0.59	0.08	0.06	0.01			.	0.33
Industrial bonds	0.93	0.70		0.09	0.13	0.02	0.25	0.11	0.04	0.04	0.10	0.01		0.01		0.21
Bank debentures	2.34	1.06	0.01	0.16	0.22	0.04	0.14	0.10	0.15	0.11	0.05	0.04				1.15
Stocks^d																
Excluding investment trust	8.32	3.94		0.87	0.65	0.66	0.09	0.02	0.01	1.53	0.52	0.12	0.04	2.10	2.68	2.18
Investment trust	0.55	0.04		0.01	0.01	0.01	0.01	0.01		0.00		0.00		0.06	0.01	0.50
Loans	30.49			6.67	6.02	1.72	5.65	1.86		1.63						
By Bank of Japan	0.26	0.26	0.26													
By private financial institutions	23.36	23.36		6.65	5.90	1.69	5.54	1.84		1.61		0.12				
By public financial institutions	6.50	6.50							6.50							
Call loans	0.37	0.37		0.02	0.12	0.03	0.11	0.02		0.02	0.05	0.00				
Trade credit	13.73	—													13.73	
Other instruments	1.58	0.71	0.83	0.06	-0.03	0.08	0.12	0.12		0.01	0.05		0.35		0.35	0.16
All instruments	100.00^f	43.39	2.05	9.00	8.16	2.83	7.10	2.91	8.51	3.69	0.90	0.31	3.20	0.66	24.60	28.14

^aLess than the sum of cols. 3–16 and 3–12, respectively, because of consolidation.   ^bConsolidation of postal saving and life insurance, Trust Fund Bureau, and other government financial institutions.   ^cIncludes deposits with Bank of Japan, the Trust Fund Bureau, and government current deposits.   ^dMarket value. The average ratio of market to book value indicated in the source was applied to all book value entries in cols. 4–12. Investment company stock shown in source is assumed to be at market value.   ^eDoes not include trade credit among unincorporated enterprises.   ^fAbsolute figure ¥ 855 trill.

SOURCE OF BASIC DATA: BJFFA, 1970–77, pp. 77–78.

TABLE 7-39. Distribution of Financial Assets and Liabilities within and among Main Sectors, March 31, 1978 (Percent)

	Within sectors						Among sectors					
	All sectors	Financial institutions[a]	Corporations	Government	Households	Rest of the world	Financial institutions	Corporations	Government	Households	Rest of the world	All sectors
Assets												
Currency and demand deposits	7.9	0.5	14.2	6.9	14.9	—	2.8	42.9	5.6	48.6	—	100.0
Other deposits	20.2	—	18.5	9.2	59.4	—	—	21.8	2.9	75.3	—	100.0
Short-term securities	0.8	1.7	0.1	1.2	—	1.0	84.9	3.5	9.0	—	2.5	100.0
Long-term securities	11.1	16.8	1.2	6.6	9.1	24.1	68.1	2.7	3.8	21.1	4.3	100.0
Corporate shares[b]	2.8	3.1	2.9	0.1	2.6	6.9	46.4	24.7	0.2	23.8	4.9	100.0
Loans	31.8	73.1	0.0	14.1	—	—	97.2	0.0	2.8	—	—	100.0
Life insurance	3.3	—	—	0.9	12.7	—	—	—	—	100.0	—	100.0
Trade credit	13.9	—	58.6	—	—	—	—	100.0	—	—	—	100.0
Other financial assets	8.2	4.8	4.4	61.0	1.3	68.0	19.6	12.5	47.3	4.1	16.5	100.0
All financial assets	100.0[c]	100.0	100.0	100.0	100.0	100.0	42.3	23.7	6.4[d]	25.6	2.0	100.0
Liabilities												
Currency and demand deposits	7.9	19.0	—	—	—	1.8	99.4	—	—	—	0.6	100.0
Other deposits	20.7	49.9	—	—	—	—	100.0	—	—	—	—	100.0
Short-term securities	0.8	—	0.6	8.2	—	—	—	25.5	74.5	—	—	100.0
Long-term securities	11.1	7.9	8.2	62.3	—	—	29.5	27.8	42.7	—	—	100.0
Corporate shares[b]	2.1	0.6	4.9	—	—	—	12.4	87.6	—	—	—	100.0
Loans	31.8	3.0	54.4	26.6	76.0	—	3.9	64.4	6.4	25.4	—	100.0
Life insurance	3.3	8.0	—	—	—	—	100.0	—	—	—	—	100.0
Trade credit	13.9	0.0	30.2	0.2	23.8	—	0.0	81.7	0.1	18.2	—	100.0
Other liabilities	8.3	11.6	1.7	2.7	0.2	98.2	57.5	7.7	2.4	0.1	32.2	100.0
All liabilities	100.0[c]	100.0	100.0	100.0	100.0	100.0	41.4	37.6	7.6[d]	10.6	2.8	100.0

[a]Consolidated. [b]Book value equal to about one-third of market value. [c]Absolute value ¥ 877.4 trill. [d]Includes 3.7 percent social security funds.

SOURCES OF BASIC DATA: *ARNA*, 1979, pp. 490–93, 582.

claims, they are also responsible for nearly one-third of long-term debt securities and one-eighth of corporate stock. Nonfinancial corporations issue more than one-fourth of all bonds, two-thirds of loans, four-fifths of trade credit, and seven-eighths of corporate stock. The government is responsible for nearly one-half of all debt securities but has only a minor share in other types of debt, resulting in a share of total liabilities of less than 8 percent. The household sector's share in total liabilities of one-tenth is limited to loans, where it amounts to one-fourth, and to trade credit with nearly one-fifth. Although the share of financial institutions and the government is about the same in financial assets and liabilities, corporations are substantial net debtors and the personal sector is a relatively even larger net creditor.

8. THE NATIONAL BALANCE SHEET

The analysis of financial developments in postwar Japan may be completed and summarized by the examination of the national balance sheet for six benchmark years between 1955 and 1977—

TABLE 7-40. National Balance Sheet, 1955–1977 (¥ trill.)

	1955 (1)	1960 (2)	1965 (3)	1970 (4)	1975 (5)	1977 (6)
			I. Tangible assets			
1. Land	24.10	54.70	100.60	189.57	401.34	451.16
a. Agricultural	14.80	23.70	29.60	45.77	89.96	97.67
b. Other	9.30	31.00	71.00	143.80	311.38	353.48
2. Fixed assets	8.80	17.80	41.90	107.84	307.72	386.29
a. Dwellings	2.00	3.30	8.70	20.68	69.32	90.11
b. Consumer durables	0.80	1.60	3.80	9.76	21.96	25.54
c. Other	6.00	12.90	29.40	77.40	216.44	270.64
3. Inventories	4.00	6.30	10.90	22.82	47.85	53.01
4. Domestic tangible assets	36.90	78.80	153.40	320.23	756.91	890.46
5. Net foreign assets	0.20	0.37	−0.41	1.68	2.16	6.77
6. National wealth	37.10	79.17	153.00	321.91	759.07	897.23
			II. Financial assets			
1. Currency and deposits	5.82	14.05	34.47	76.08	186.23	243.31
2. Loans	6.36	16.79	39.44	90.09	216.92	274.89
a. By government	1.46	3.58	6.08	16.13	44.96	63.51
b. By private institutions	4.90	13.21	33.36	73.96	171.96	211.38
3. Fixed interest securities	1.46	3.25	8.84	23.47	62.24	95.90
a. Government	0.77	0.98	1.46	7.04	24.47	47.06
b. Private	0.70	2.28	7.38	16.43	37.77	48.84
4. Insurance	0.37	1.25	3.62	8.71	20.41	27.83
5. Trade credit[a]	2.57	7.31	21.26	53.89	106.27	123.04
6. Corporate stock[b]	2.23	8.50	13.85	21.80	67.60	75.90
7. Other	1.06	2.38	1.84	17.03	44.25	59.53
8. Total financial assets	19.87	53.54	123.32	291.07	703.92	900.40
			III. National assets			
1. National assets	56.97	132.71	276.72	612.98	1462.99	1797.63

[a]Does not include trade credit among unincorporated business enterprises.   [b]Market value.

SOURCES: Line I-1: 1955–65, linked to estimate for 1970 of Economic Planning Agency (col. 5) by index derived from Goldsmith, 1975, pp. 142–44; agricultural land includes timber land and standing timber; 1970–77, ARNA, p. 440 ff. (for all lines). Lines I-2, 3: 1955–65, as for line I-1, linked to Goldsmith, 1975, p. 145 ff. Line I-2c: 1955–65, linked to Fujino, 1975, p. 192. Line I-2a, 2b: 1955–65, as for line I-1, linked to Goldsmith, 1975, p. 145 ff. Line I-2c: 1955–65, line 2 less lines 2a and 2b. Line I-5: 1955–65, Goldsmith, 1975, p. 150. Lines II: 1955–65, BJFFA, various issues. 1970–77, ARNA, p. 440 ff., except for lines II-3a and 3b; line 3a from BJFFA, 1970–77, and line 3b derived as residual. Line II-6: 1965–70, market value of corporate stock other than investment companies derived from data in BJFFA, assuming that ratio indicated for corporate and personal sectors is applicable to all sectors and that investment company stocks are entered at market value.

its structure, its relation to national product, its sectoral distribution in 1977, and the level and movement of a few important balance sheet ratios.

The absolute figures of table 7–40 indicate a 32-fold increase in national assets between 1955 and 1977, implying an annual rate of growth of 17 percent. The value of tangible assets increased 24-fold, or at 16 percent per year; land, 19-fold, or 14 percent; and reproducible tangible assets and financial assets, 45-fold, or 19 percent. These increases are due to a considerable extent to a continuous rise in the price level, which averaged nearly 6 percent per year for the national product deflator, although considerably less for capital goods. It is, therefore, preferable to concentrate on changes in the structure of the balance sheet, which reflect differences in the rate of growth of the value of the various components in current, although not in constant, prices, and on the relation of the value of tangible and financial assets to national product. It hardly needs to be stressed that the estimates that have to be used to construct the national balance sheets involve substantial margins of error, which are considerably wider, both for conceptual and statistical reasons, in the case of tangible than in that of financial assets. These reservations, however, do not cast doubt on the main conclusions that can be drawn from the balance sheets.

The first main change in the structure of the national balance sheet is the continuous increase in the share of financial assets, which rose from not much more than one-third in 1955 to one-half in 1977. The increase, however, was much more pronounced between 1955 and 1965 than in the following twelve years (table 7–41).

Within tangible assets the share of land declined steadily, notwithstanding extremely sharp

TABLE 7-41. Structure of National Balance Sheet, 1955–1977 (Percent of National Assets)

	1955 (1)	1960 (2)	1965 (3)	1970 (4)	1975 (5)	1977 (6)
			I. Tangible assets			
1. Land	42.3	41.2	36.4	30.9	27.5	25.1
a. Agricultural	26.0	17.9	10.7	7.5	6.2	5.4
b. Other	16.3	23.4	28.7	23.4	21.3	19.7
2. Fixed assets	15.4	13.5	15.1	17.6	21.0	21.5
a. Dwellings	3.5	2.5	3.1	3.4	4.7	5.0
b. Consumer durables	1.4	1.2	1.4	1.6	1.5	1.4
c. Other	10.5	9.7	10.6	12.6	14.8	15.1
3. Inventories	7.0	4.8	3.9	3.7	3.3	3.0
4. Domestic tangible assets	64.7	59.5	55.4	52.2	51.8	49.5
5. Net foreign assets	0.4	0.3	−0.1	0.3	0.1	0.4
6. National wealth	65.1	59.7	55.3	52.5	51.9	49.9
			II. Financial assets			
1. Currency and deposits	10.2	10.5	12.5	12.4	12.7	13.6
2. Loans	11.2	12.7	14.3	14.7	14.8	15.3
a. By government	2.6	2.7	2.2	2.6	3.1	3.5
b. By private institutions	8.6	10.0	12.1	12.1	11.8	11.8
3. Fixed investment securities	2.6	2.5	3.2	3.8	4.3	5.4
a. Government	1.4	0.7	0.5	1.2	1.7	2.6
b. Private	1.2	1.7	2.7	2.7	2.6	2.7
4. Insurance	0.7	0.9	1.3	1.4	1.4	1.6
5. Trade credit	4.5	5.5	7.7	8.8	7.3	6.7
6. Corporate stock	3.9	6.4	5.0	3.6	4.6	4.2
7. Other	1.9	1.8	0.7	2.8	3.0	3.3
8. Total financial assets	34.9	40.3	44.6	47.5	48.1	50.1
			III. National assets			
1. National assets	100.0	100.0	100.0	100.0	100.0	100.0

SOURCE: Table 7-40.

rises in land prices, from more than two-fifths of national assets in 1955 to one-fourth in 1977, or from two-thirds to one-half of tangible assets—all very high ratios for a developed country. The decline, the second main change in the structure of the national balance sheet, was due entirely to a fall in the share of agricultural land from more than one-fourth of national assets and two-fifths of tangible assets in 1955 to only 5 and 11 percent, respectively, in 1977, a movement consonant with economic development. The share of nonagricultural land actually increased from one-sixth to more than one-fifth of national assets, or from one-fourth to two-fifths of tangible assets after having reached a peak of more than one-fourth of national, and one-half of tangible, assets in 1965. Among reproducible assets, the share of inventories fell sharply from 7 percent of national assets in 1955 to 3 percent in the 1970s and even more sharply from more than 30 to 12 percent of reproducible assets, the third main structural change. The share of dwellings increased from an average of about 3½ percent of national, and 15 percent of reproducible, assets between 1955 and 1970 to 5 and 20 percent, respectively, in 1977. Whether this will turn out to be a fourth major change in the structure of the national balance sheet remains to be seen. The share of consumer durables stayed throughout the period close to 1½ percent of national assets and 6 percent of all reproducible assets, reflecting the much less pronounced increase in their prices. Nonresidential structures and equipment, finally, increased their share from 11 to 15 percent of national assets, but stayed close to one-half of reproducible assets.

Changes were less pronounced among financial assets. The most important one, possibly qualifying as the fifth major change in the structure of the national balance sheet, is the decline in the share of corporate stock between 1960 and 1977 from 6½ to not much more than 4 percent of national assets and from 16 to 8 percent of financial assets. The share of long-term bonds doubled in relation to national assets but only increased from 6 to nearly 11 percent of all financial assets, the increase being shared about equally between government and private issues. The shares of the other main financial assets showed no trend, only some short-term fluctuations. Thus currency and deposits and loans each accounted for approximately one-fourth and trade credit for about one-eighth of all financial assets throughout the period.

The movements of the ratios of the components of the national balance sheet to national product in table 7–42 show the same movements as the shares in table 7–41, but they refer to a different basis, which is supposed to reflect the size of the economy. The outstanding feature in this relationship is the increase in the ratio of national assets to national product from less than 7 in 1955 to nearly 10 in 1977. All of the increase occurred in the second half of the 1950s, continuing the even sharper advance of the first half of that decade, and the first half of the 1970s, both periods of relatively slow growth of national product, whereas the movement came to a halt in the 1960s. The increase was much more pronounced for financial assets, for which the ratio more than doubled from 2.3 to 4.8, than for tangible assets. Advancing only fractionally from 4.3 to 4.8, tangible assets declined in the case of land from 2.8 to 2.4 but advanced substantially from 1.5 to 2.4 for reproducible assets, the capital-output ratio as conventionally defined, and more than doubled for nonresidential structures and equipment and for dwellings. Among financial assets, only the ratios of debt securities and insurance, both secondary, advanced considerably more rapidly than the aggregate, and in their case the rise continued throughout the period.

The analytical value of national balance sheets is greatly increased if they are available for the main economic sectors, as well as for the economy as a whole. For this study, the preparation of sectoral balance sheets was possible for only the 1970s; the sectoral balance sheet for 1977 is shown in table 7–43.[79]

The main difference among the four main sectors, of course, is the virtual absence of tangible assets in the balance sheets of financial institutions, whereas they constituted in 1977 between 60 and 70 percent of all assets for the personal and government sector and for nonfinan-

---

79. The figures in table 7–43 differ slightly from those in table 7–40 because they are taken from a different source. Tables similar to 7–43 could be prepared from *ARNA*, pp. 427 ff. for every year from 1969 to 1977.

TABLE 7-42. National Balance Sheet, 1955–1977

	1955 (1)	1960 (2)	1965 (3)	1970 (4)	1975 (5)	1977 (6)
			I. Tangible assets			
1. Land	262.7	315.9	363.5	245.5	253.9	230.6
a. Agricultural	161.3	136.9	107.0	59.3	56.9	49.9
b. Other	101.4	179.0	256.5	186.2	197.0	180.7
2. Fixed assets	95.9	102.8	151.4	139.7	194.7	197.4
a. Dwellings	21.8	19.1	31.4	26.8	43.9	46.0
b. Consumer durables	8.7	9.2	13.7	12.6	13.9	13.1
c. Other	65.4	74.5	106.2	100.2	136.9	138.3
3. Inventories	43.6	36.4	39.4	29.5	30.3	27.1
4. Domestic tangible assets	402.2	455.1	554.4	414.8	478.9	455.1
5. Net foreign assets	2.2	2.1	1.4	2.2	1.4	3.5
6. National wealth	404.4	457.2	553.0	417.0	480.3	458.6
			II. Financial assets			
1. Currency and deposits	63.4	81.1	99.3	98.5	117.8	124.3
2. Loans	69.3	97.0	113.6	116.7	137.2	140.5
a. By government	15.9	20.7	17.5	20.9	28.4	32.5
b. By private institutions	53.4	76.3	96.1	95.8	108.8	108.0
3. Fixed interest securities	15.9	18.8	25.5	30.4	39.4	49.0
a. Government	8.3	5.7	4.2	9.1	15.5	24.1
b. Private	7.6	13.1	21.3	21.3	23.9	24.9
4. Insurance	4.0	7.2	10.4	11.3	12.9	14.2
5. Trade credit	28.0	42.2	61.2	69.8	67.2	62.9
6. Corporate stock	24.3	49.9	39.9	28.2	42.8	38.8
7. Other	11.6	13.0	5.3	22.1	28.0	30.4
8. Total financial assets	216.5	309.2	355.2	376.9	445.4	460.1
			III. National assets			
1. National assets	620.9	766.4	797.1	793.9	925.7	918.7

SOURCE: Tables 7-1 and 7-49.

cial corporations. The share of the three main types of tangible assets, however, is very different among the three nonfinancial sectors. Land represents nearly one-fourth and fully one-third of tangible assets for the government and corporate sectors but nearly three-fourths for the personal sector; and the difference is equally pronounced in relation to total assets, about one-fifth for the government and corporate sectors but nearly one-half for the personal sector. As a consequence, the share of reproducible assets in the corporate and government sector is considerably higher than in the personal sector, where it consists mainly of dwellings. Liabilities represent a considerably higher percentage of assets in the government, particularly the corporate sector, than in the personal sector, where their share is not much above one-eighth.

The differences in the balance sheet structure of the various sectors are reflected in the differences in the distribution of the main balance sheet items among the four sectors, once the shares of the four sectors in total assets are kept in mind. It then appears that the personal sector's share is highest in land and net worth, fairly high in fixed assets and in financial assets, and very low in liabilities. The government's share is highest in fixed assets, corresponds approximately to its share in total assets for liabilities and net worth, and is considerably below it in the case of financial assets. Nonfinancial corporations own one-half of all reproducible assets, the country's capital stock, but only one-fourth of all financial assets and account for nearly two-fifths of liability. As a result, the household sector accounts directly for three-fifths of total national net worth, the general government for slightly more than one-tenth, and the corporate sector, whose equity is owned chiefly by the household and secondarily by the government sector, for one-fourth.

TABLE 7-43. Structure of Four-Sector National Balance Sheet, 1977 (Percent)

	All sectors	General government	Nonfinancial corporations[a]	Households[b]	Financial institutions
Distribution within sectors					
Tangible assets	49.5	68.7	59.8	63.6	2.9
Land	25.9	16.5	21.7	46.2	1.6
Net fixed assets	20.6	52.1	29.3	16.6	1.2
Inventories	3.0	—	8.8	0.7	—
Financial assets	50.5	31.3	40.2	36.4	97.1
Total assets	100.0	100.0	100.0	100.0	100.0
Liabilities	47.1	37.1	57.2	13.9	92.6
Net worth	59.9	62.9	42.8	84.1	7.4
Distribution among sectors					
Tangible assets	100.0	13.2	38.1	47.4	1.3
Land	100.0	6.1	26.5	66.0	1.4
Net fixed assets	100.0	24.1	44.8	29.7	1.3
Inventories	100.0	—	91.1	8.9	—
Financial assets	100.0	5.9	25.1	26.6	42.3
Total assets	100.0	9.5	31.6	36.9	22.0
Liabilities	100.0	7.5	38.3	10.9	43.2
Net worth	100.0	11.3	25.5	60.0	3.1

[a]Includes government enterprises.   [b]Includes unincorporated business and nonprofit organizations.

SOURCE OF BASIC DATA: *ARNA*, pp. 430 ff.

The distributions within, and particularly those among, sectors have not changed much since 1970, nearly the first date for which comparable figures are available, nor is this to be expected in the case of such large and slow-moving aggregates. There has been, however, a slight increase between 1970 and 1977 in the share of the public sector, now including public incorporated enterprises, in total assets from 16 to 19 percent, in fixed assets from 34½ to 36½ percent, in financial assets from 14 to 17½ percent, and particularly in liabilities from 17½ to 24 percent, partly as the result of heavy deficit financing.[80] It remains to be seen whether this is part of a trend.

The four most interesting aggregative ratios that can be derived from the national balance sheet are shown in table 7–44 for five quinquennial benchmark dates between 1955 and 1975 as well as for 1977: the financial interrelations ratio, the financial intermediation ratio, the capital-output ratio, and the ratio of national assets to national product.

The financial interrelations ratio, which measures in terms of market value the size of the financial superstructure in relation to that of the real infrastructure, has shown a steady upward trend from not much more than one-half in 1955 to unity in 1977, except for the early 1970s. The rapid rise in 1976 and 1977 is not likely to continue for long. The upward movement of the ratio is to be expected in a period of rapid financial and economic growth such as Japan experienced in the past quarter century,[81] but the level of the ratio even in the later half of the period is rather low for a country with the size and diversity of Japan's financial superstructure and can be explained, at least in part, by the extraordinarily high level of land prices and aggregate land values in Japan.

The position of financial institutions in the financial superstructure is reflected in the financial interrelations ratio. The ratio rises from one-third in 1955 to fully two-fifths in the 1970s, with most of the increase occurring in the 1960s, and points to a substantial increase in

80. Cf. data in *ARNA*, p. 446 ff.
81. Cf. Goldsmith, 1969, particularly chap. 7.

TABLE 7-44. National Balance Sheet Ratios, 1955–1977

| | Financial inter-relations ratio[a] (1) | Financial inter-mediation ratio[b] (2) | Capital output ratio[c] | | National assets |
			Broad[c] (3)	Narrow[d] (4)	National product (5)
1955	0.54	0.33	4.02	1.40	6.21
1960	0.68	0.32	4.55	1.39	7.66
1965	0.80	0.37	4.42	1.52	7.95
1970	0.91	0.41	4.15	1.69	7.94
1975	0.93	0.42	4.79	2.25	9.25
1977	1.01	0.43	4.55	2.24	9.19

[a]Financial assets : tangible assets.   [b]Assets of financial institutions : all financial assets.   [c]Tangible assets : gross national product (average of GNP of benchmark and following year).   [d]Reproducible assets : gross national product (average of GNP of benchmark and following year).

SOURCES OF BASIC DATA: Tables 7-1 and 7-39 and *BJFFA*, various issues, for col. 3.

the importance of financial institutions within the financial superstructure. With a value of slightly more than two-fifths in the 1970s, the ratio indicates that financial institutions act (excluding intrafinancial items), in about three-fourths of all financial assets, as either creditor or debtor—that is, holder or issuer.

The narrower version of the capital-output ratio (reproducible capital stock divided by national product), which is the one commonly used in economic analysis, was low in international comparison in postwar Japan until the 1970s, standing at only 1.7 in 1970. The reasons are far from clear, although the low ratio of the value of the stock of dwellings to national product (less than 0.5 even in the 1970s and below 0.3 in the 1950s and 1960s), which reflects the country's modest housing standards, has been a contributing factor. Whether the sharp rise between 1970 and 1975 to 2¼ is more than cyclical is as yet uncertain. In contrast, the broad capital-output ratio, which includes the value of land in the denominator, has been on a high level and has been increasing irregularly from 4 in 1955 to 4½ in 1977. The reason, of course, is again the absolutely and relatively high value of land in the national balance sheet.

The ratio of national assets to national product, which results from a combination of the financial interrelations ratio and the broad version of the capital-output ratio, has risen substantially from 5¾ in 1955 to a little more than 9 in 1977, all of the increase occurring in the second half of the 1950s and the first half of the 1970s, a movement that reflects the upward trend in the two components.

In conclusion, an attempt will be made to explain the level of approximate unity in the financial interrelations ratio in 1975, in order to show what factors are responsible for this specific value. This will be done by means of an elementary approximative formula, using a few simplifying, but, it is hoped, not distorting, assumptions.[82] According to this formula, the financial interrelations ratio is the product of (1) the new issue ratios of the nonfinancial (δ) and financial sectors (ϕ) and the rest of the world (ξ), allowing for revaluation changes of corporate stock (ν); (2) the inverse of the growth rate of national product in current prices (γ); and (3) the inverse of the capital-output ratio in its broad form (β), adjusted by a truncation ratio ($0 < \tau < 1$), which reflects the facts that the ratio is calculated on the basis of a limited period rather than on the basis of a period of infinite length and that it is negatively related to the length of the period and the rate of growth of national product in current prices; plus the ratio (ϵ) of the financial assets at the beginning of the period divided by the tangible assets at the end of the

82. Ibid., where a somewhat more detailed and, hence, more informative formula is used.

period, a ratio that recognizes the existence of financial assets at the beginning of the period. The τ and ϵ ratios affect the value of the core of the formula in opposite directions, τ reducing and ϵ increasing it, and have a tendency to approximately offset each other. Thus:

$$FIR = (\delta + \phi + \xi)(1 + \nu)(\delta^{-1} + 1)\beta^{-1}\tau + \epsilon$$

The formula shows that the value of the financial interrelations ratio is positively related to the new issue ratios (δ and ϕ) as well as to the importance of revaluations (ν), to the truncation ratio (τ), and to the period's initial financial assets (reflected in ϵ) but negatively related to the rate of growth of national product (γ) and the capital-output ratio at the end of the period (β). Inserting the appropriate values for the twenty-year period of 1956–75, one obtains:

$$(0.24 + 0.31 + 0.02) \times 1.06 \times 7.51 \times 0.21 \times 0.95 + 0.03 = 0.94$$

The value of the financial interrelations ratio for 1975 obtained by means of the formula is thus quite close to the observed value of 0.93. The formula identifies the factors responsible for the observed value of the financial interrelations ratio of slightly below unity for 1975 and shows that this value is not a random number. It shows that in international comparison, the present Japanese financial interrelations ratio is the result of, first, extremely high new nonfinancial and financial issue ratios, which in turn are related to the high capital formation and external financing ratios of the business sector and the high financial intermediation ratio; second, a very low multiplier, reflecting a growth rate of national product in current prices of 15 percent, which is the result of an extraordinarily high rate of growth of real national product of 10 percent and an inflation at an average rate of 5 percent; third, capital-output and revaluation ratios of common level, which in the case of the capital-output ratio reflects a combination of a low ratio of reproducible assets and a high ratio of land to national product; and, fourth, a very high truncation ratio and a very low ratio of the initial relative stock of financial assets, both reflecting the extremely rapid rate of growth of the financial superstructure.

List of Publications Cited

3ɔ: 3ʃ⒉

Adams, T. F. M. *Japanese Securities Markets*. Tokyo: S. Okuyama, 1953.
_____. *A Financial History of Modern Japan*. Tokyo: S. Okuyama, 1964.
_____, and Hoshii, I. *A Financial History of the New Japan*. Tokyo: Kodansha International, 1972.
Allen, G. C. *Japan's Economic Recovery*. London: Oxford University Press, 1958.
Asakura, K. "The Characteristics of Finance in the Meiji Period." *Developing Economies* 5 (1967).
_____, and Nishiyama, C., eds. *Nihon keizai no kaheiteki bunseki* [A monetary analysis and history of the Japanese economy]. Tokyo: Center for Modern Economics, Rikkyo University, Sobunsha, 1974.
Bank of Japan. *A Study of Flow-of-Funds in Japan*. Tokyo: Economic Research Department, Bank of Japan, 1959.
_____. *Economic Statistics of Japan*. Tokyo: Statistics Department, Bank of Japan, 1961.
_____. *Flow-of-Funds Accounts in Japan, 1954–1963, 1964–1971, 1970–1977*. Tokyo: Economic Research Department, Bank of Japan, 1964, 1972, and 1978, respectively.
_____. *Hundred-Year Statistics of the Japanese Economy*. Tokyo: Statistics Department, Bank of Japan, 1966.
_____. *Supplement to Hundred-Year Statistics of the Japanese Economy—English Translation of Explanatory Notes and Footnotes*. Tokyo: Statistics Department, Bank of Japan, n.d.
_____. *Analysis of Financial Statistics by Size of Corporation*. Tokyo: Statistics Department, Bank of Japan, annually.
_____. *Economic Statistics Annual*. Tokyo: Statistics Department, Bank of Japan.
_____. *Financial Statements of Main Industrial Corporations in Japan*. Tokyo: Statistics Department, Bank of Japan, annually.
_____. *Economic Statistics Monthly*. Tokyo: Statistics Department, Bank of Japan.
Bellah, R. N. *Tokugawa Religion*. New York: Free Press, 1957.
Benedict, R. N. *The Chrysanthemum and the Sword*. Boston: Houghton Mifflin, 1946.
Bisson, T. A. *Japan's War Economy*. New York: International Secretariat, Institute of Pacific Relations, distributed by Macmillan, 1945.
Blumenthal, T. *Saving in Post-war Japan*. Cambridge: Harvard University Press, 1970.
Boulding, K., and Gleason, A. H. "War as an Investment: The Strange Case of Japan." In K. Boulding and T. Mukherjee, eds., *Economic Imperialism*. Ann Arbor: University of Michigan Press, 1972.
Bratter, H. M. *Japanese Banking*. Washington, D.C.: U.S. Department of Commerce, Finance and Investment Division, Trade Promotion Series, 116, 1931.
Brochier, H. *Le Miracle Japonais, 1950–1970*. Paris: Calman-Levy, 1970.

Cameron, R., ed. *Banking in the Early Stages of Industrialization.* New York: Oxford University Press, 1967.

Caves, R. E., and Uekusa, M. "Industrial Organization." In H. T. Patrick and H. Rosovsky, eds., *Asia's New Giant: How the Japanese Economy Works.* Washington, D.C.: Brookings Institution, 1976.

———. *Industrial Organization in Japan.* Washington, D.C.: Brookings Institution, 1976.

Cohen, J. B. *Japan's Economy in War and Reconstruction.* Minneapolis: University of Minnesota Press, 1949.

———. *Japan's Postwar Economy.* Bloomington: Indiana University Press, 1958.

Cowan, C. D., ed. *The Economic Development of China and Japan.* London: Allen & Unwin, 1964.

Crawcour, E. S. "The Development of a Credit System in Seventeenth-Century Japan." *Journal of Economic History* 21, no. 3 (September 1961).

———. "Changes in Japanese Commerce in the Tokugawa Period." *Journal of Asiatic Studies* 22 (1963).

———, and Yamamura, K. "The Tokugawa Monetary System: 1787–1868." *Economic Development and Cultural Change* 18, no. 4 (July 1970).

Denison, E. F., and Chung, W. K. "Economic Growth and Its Sources." In H. T. Patrick and H. Rosovsky, eds., *Asia's New Giant: How the Japanese Economy Works.* Washington, D.C.: Brookings Institution, 1976.

———. *Why Has Japanese Economic Growth Been So Rapid?* Washington, D.C.: Brookings Institution, 1976.

Ehrlich, E. E. "The Role of Banking in Japan's Economic Development." Ph.D. dissertation, New School for Social Research, 1960.

Emi, K. *Government Fiscal Activity and Economic Growth in Japan, 1868–1960.* Tokyo: Kinokuniya Bookstore, 1963.

———. "An Approach to the Measurement of National Saving in Japan (1878–1940)." *Hitotsubashi Journal of Economics* 6 (1965).

———. *Capital Formation.* Vol. 4, *Estimates of Long-term Economic Statistics of Japan since 1868,* edited by K. Ohkawa et al., Tokyo: Toyo Keizai Shimposha, 1971.

Federation of Bankers' Associations of Japan [Zenkoku Ginko Kyokai Rengokai]. *Banking System in Japan.* Tokyo: Federation of Bankers' Associations of Japan, 1972.

Fujino, S. "Permanent Income and the Transactions Demand for Money by Households." *Hitotsubashi Journal of Economics* 5 (1964).

———. "Business Cycles in Japan, 1868–1962." *Hitotsubashi Journal of Economics* 7 (1966).

———. *A Neo-Keynesian Theory of Income, Prices and Economic Growth.* Tokyo: Kinokuniya Bookstore, 1975.

Goldsmith, R. W. *Financial Structure and Development.* New Haven, Conn.: Yale University Press, 1969.

———. "Prolegomènes à l'analyse comparative des structures financières." *Revue d'économie politique* 80 (1970).

———. "The Development of Financial Institutions during the Postwar Period." *Banca Nazionale del Lavoro Quarterly Review,* no. 97 (June 1971).

———. "A Synthetic Estimate of the National Wealth of Japan, 1885–1973." *Review of Income and Wealth,* ser. 21 (1975).

———. "A Correction: Japan Is Different." *Review of Income and Wealth,* ser. 22 (1976).

———. *Institutional Investors and Corporate Stock: A Background Study.* National Bureau of Economic Research, 1973.

Goto, S. *Nippon no kinyu tokei* [Japanese financial statistics]. Tokyo: Toyo Keizai Shimposha, 1970.

Hadley, E. M. *Antitrust in Japan.* Princeton: Princeton University Press, 1970.

Hall, J. W. *Das Japanische Kaiserreich*. Frankfurt: Fischer Bücherei, 1968.

――――, and Jansen, M. B., eds. *Studies in the Institutional History of Early Modern Japan*. Princeton, N.J.: Princeton University Press, 1968.

Hara, Y. "From Westernization to Japanization: The Replacement of Foreign Teachers by Japanese Who Studied Abroad." *Developing Economies* 15 (1977).

History of Banking in Japan. Vol. 4, *A History of Banking in All Leading Nations*. New York: Journal of Commerce & Commercial Bulletin, 1896.

Hoekendorf, W. "The Secular Trend of Income Velocity in Japan 1879–1940." Ph.D. dissertation, University of Washington, 1961.

Honjo, E. *The Social and Economic History of Japan*. Kyoto: Institute for Research in Economic History of Japan, 1935.

――――. *Economic Theory and History of Japan in the Tokugawa Period*. New York: Russell & Russell, 1965.

Hoselitz, B., ed. *The Role of Small Industry in the Process of Economic Growth*. The Hague: Mouton, 1968.

Institute for Developing Economies. *One Hundred Years of Agricultural Statistics in Japan*. Tokyo: Institute for Developing Economies, 1969.

International Monetary Fund. *International Financial Statistics,* monthly.

Ishii, R. *Population Pressure and Economic Life in Japan*. London: P. S. King & Son, 1937.

Ishiwata, S. *Military Capital in Japan before World War II*. Tokyo, 1967.

Japan, Bureau of Statistics. *Family Income and Expenditure Survey, 1969*. Tokyo: Bureau of Statistics, Office of the Prime Minister, 1970.

――――. *Family Saving Survey, 1974*. Tokyo: Bureau of Statistics, Office of the Prime Minister, 1975.

Japan, Economic Planning Agency. *Annual Report on National Accounts*. Tokyo: Economic Planning Agency.

――――. *Annual Report on National Income Statistics*. Tokyo: Economic Planning Agency.

――――. *1970 National Wealth Survey*. Tokyo: Economic Planning Agency, 1975.

Jefferies and Co., Inc. *Investment Seminar*. Tokyo, 1970.

Jorgenson, D. W., and Nishimizu, M. "U.S. and Japanese Economic Growth: An International Comparison." *Economic Journal* 88 (1978).

Kato, Y. "Development of Long-term Agricultural Credit." In K. Ohkawa et al., eds., *Agricultural and Economic Growth: Japan's Experience*. Princeton, N.J.: Princeton University Press, 1970.

Kelley, A. C., and Williamson, J. G. *Lessons from Japanese Development: An Analytical Economic History*. Chicago: University of Chicago Press, 1974.

Klein, L., and Ohkawa, K., eds. *Economic Growth: The Japanese Experience since the Meiji Era*. Homewood, Ill.: Irwin, 1968.

Komiya, R. "The Supply of Personal Savings." In R. Komiya, ed., *Post-war Economic Growth in Japan*. Berkeley: University of California Press, 1966.

――――, ed. *Post-war Economic Growth in Japan*. Berkeley: University of California Press, 1966.

Kosobud, R., and Minami, R., eds. *Econometric Studies of Japan*. Urbana: University of Illinois Press, 1977.

Kotake, T. "'Unyo-Azukari' Loan and the Yamaichi-Securities Scare." *Keio Business Review* 5 (1966).

Lockwood, W. W. *The Economic Development of Japan: The Japanese Experience since the Meiji Era*. Princeton, N.J.: Princeton University Press. 1954.

――――, ed. *The State and Economic Enterprise in Japan*. Princeton, N.J.: Princeton University Press, 1965.

Maddison, A. *Economic Growth in Japan and the USSR*. New York: Norton, 1969.

Matsukata, M. *Report on the Adoption of the Gold Standard in Japan*. Tokyo: Government Press, 1899.

Mazelière, M. de la. *Essai sur l'histoire du Japon*. Paris, 1899.

Mikitani, R. "Corporate Investments and Sources of Funds—An Experience of Japanese Large Corporations." In J. Yao, ed., *Monetary Factors in Japanese Economic Growth*. Kobe: Research Institute for Economics and Business Administration, Kobe University, 1970.

Minami, R. *The Turning Point in Economic Development: Japan's Experience*. Tokyo: Kinokuniya Bookstore, 1973.

Miyamoto, M.; Sakudo, Y.; and Yazuba, Y. "Economic Development in Preindustrial Japan, 1859–1894." *Journal of Economic History* 25 (1965).

Mizoguchi, T. "High Personal Saving Rate and Changes in the Consumption Pattern in Post-war Japan." *Developing Economies* 8 (1970).

——. *Personal Savings and Consumption in Post-war Japan*. Tokyo: Kinokuniya Bookstore, 1970.

Mizushima, K. "Insurance Industry in the Formative Stage of Modern Industries during the Meiji Period of Japan." In Kobe Baigaku, *The Annals of the School of Business Administration*. Kobe: Kobe University, 1967.

Morley, J. W., ed. *Dilemmas of Growth in Pre-war Japan*. Princeton, N.J.: Princeton University Press, 1971.

Moulton, H. G. *Japan: An Economic and Financial Appraisal*. Washington, D.C.: Brookings Institution, 1931.

Nakamura, J. I. *Agricultural Production and the Economic Development of Japan, 1873–1922*. Princeton, N.J.: Princeton University Press, 1966.

Nakane, C. *Japanese Society*. Berkeley: University of California Press, 1972.

Nishimizu, M., and Hulten, C. R. "The Sources of Japanese Economic Growth: 1955–71." *Review of Economics and Statistics* 60 (1972).

Noda, T. "Savings of Farm Households." In K. Ohkawa, et al., eds., *Agricultural and Economic Growth: Japan's Experience*. Princeton, N.J.: Princeton University Press, 1970.

——. *Commodity Prices and Wages*. Economic Growth Conference, session A, paper 1 (1972).

Norman, E. H. *Japan's Emergence as a Modern State*. New York: International Secretariat, Institute of Pacific Relations, 1940.

Ogawa, G. *Expenditures of the Russo-Japanese War*. New York: Oxford University Press, 1923.

Ohkawa, K. *The Growth Rate of the Japanese Economy since 1878*. Tokyo: Kinokuniya Bookstore, 1957.

——, and Rosovsky, H. *Japanese Economic Growth: Trend Acceleration in the Twentieth Century*. Stanford, Calif.: Stanford University Press, 1973.

——, and Hayami, T., eds. *Papers and Proceedings on Japan's Historical Development Experience and the Contemporary Developing Countries: Issues for Comparative Analysis*. Tokyo: Nihon Keizai Shimbunsha, 1978.

——, et al., eds. *Estimates of Long-term Economics Statistics of Japan since 1868*. Tokyo: Toyo Keizai Shimposha, 1965–.

——, et al., eds. *Agricultural and Economic Growth: Japan's Experience*. Princeton, N.J.: Princeton University Press, 1970.

Okita, S. "Saving and Economic Growth in Post-war Japan." *Asian Studies* 2 (1964).

Okuma, S. *Fifty Years of New Japan*. London: Smith, Elder, 1910.

Ono, G. *Expenditures of the Sino-Japanese War*. New York: Oxford University Press, 1922.

Otsuki, T., and Takamatsu, N. "An Aspect of Size Distribution in Pre-war Japan." In K. Ohkawa and T. Hayami, eds., *Papers and Proceedings on Japan's Historical Develop-*

ment Experience and the Contemporary Developing Countries: Issues for Comparative Analysis. Tokyo: Nihon Keizai Shimbunsha, 1978.

Ott, D. "The Financial Development of Japan, 1878–1958." Ph.D. dissertation, University of Maryland, 1960.

_____. "The Financial Development of Japan, 1878–1958." *Journal of Political Economy* 69 (1961).

Patrick, H. T. "The Bank of Japan: A Case Study in the Effectiveness of Central Bank Techniques of Monetary Control." Ph.D. dissertation, University of Michigan, 1960.

_____. *Monetary Policy and Central Banking in Contemporary Japan*. University of Bombay, Series in Monetary and International Economics, no. 5, 1962.

_____. "External Equilibrium and Internal Convertibility: Financial Policy in Meiji Japan." *Journal of Economic History* 25 (1965).

_____. "Japan 1868–1914." In R. Cameron, ed., *Banking in the Early Stages of Industrialization*. New York: Oxford University Press, 1967.

_____. "The Financing of the Public Sector in the Post-war Japan." In L. Klein and K. Ohkawa, eds., *Economic Growth: The Japanese Experience since the Meiji Era*. Homewood, Ill.: Irwin, 1968.

_____. *Financial Intermediation in Japan*. Yale University Economic Growth Center, Discussion Paper no. 70, 1969.

_____. "The Economic Muddle of the 1920s." In J. W. Morley, ed., *Dilemmas of Growth in Pre-war Japan*. Princeton, N.J.: Princeton University Press, 1971.

_____, and Rosovsky, H., eds. *Asia's New Giant: How the Japanese Economy Works*. Washington, D.C.: Brookings Institution, 1976.

Ranis, G. "The Financing of Japanese Economic Development." *Economic History Review* 11, no. 3 (April 1959).

Rathgen, K. *Japan's Volkswirtschaft und Staatshaushalt*. Leipzig: Duncker and Humblot, 1891.

Reischauer, E. *Japan—Past and Present*. New York: Knopf, 1964.

Rosovsky, H. *Capital Formation in Japan, 1868–1940*. New York: Free Press of Glencoe, 1961.

_____. "Capital Formation in Pre-war Japan: Current Findings and Future Problems." In C. D. Cowan, ed., *The Economic Development of China and Japan*. London: Allen & Unwin, 1964.

_____. "Japan's Transition to Modern Economic Growth, 1868–1885." In H. Rosovsky, ed., *Industrialization in Two Systems*. New York: Wiley, 1966.

_____, ed. *Industrialization in Two Systems*. New York: Wiley, 1966.

Sakurai, K. *Financial Aspects of Economic Development of Japan, 1868–1958*. Tokyo: Science Council, Division of Economics, Commerce and Business Administration, 1964.

Shibagaki, K. "The Early History of the Zaibatsu." *Developing Economies* 4 (1966).

Shinjo, H. *History of the Yen*. Kobe: Research Institute for Economics and Business Administration, Kobe University, 1962.

Shinohara, M. *Growth and Cycles in the Japanese Economy*. Tokyo: Kinokuniya Book Store, 1962.

_____. *Structural Changes in Japan's Economic Development*. Tokyo: Kinokuniya Book Store, 1970.

_____. "A Survey of the Japanese Literature on Small Industry." In B. Hoselitz, ed., *The Role of Small Industry in the Process of Economic Growth*. The Hague: Mouton, 1968.

Shiomi, S. *Japan's Finance and Taxation, 1940–1956*. New York: Columbia University Press, 1957.

Singer, K. "The Currency of Japan: Dimensions and Proportions." *Economic Journal* 46 (1936).

————. *Mirror, Sword and Jewel.* New York: Braziller, 1973.

Smith, T. C. *Political Change and Industrial Development in Japan: Government Enterprise, 1868–1880.* Stanford, Calif.: Stanford University Press, 1955.

————. *The Agrarian Origins of Modern Japan.* Stanford, Calif.: Stanford University Press, 1959.

Soyeda, J. "Banking and Money in Japan." *History of Banking in All Leading Nations, Journal of Commerce.* New York, 1896.

Spaulding, R. M., Jr. *Imperial Japan's Higher Civil Service Examinations.* Princeton, N.J.: Princeton University Press, 1967.

Suzuki, Y. *Money and Banking in Contemporary Japan: The Theoretical Setting and Its Application.* Translated by John G. Greenwood. New Haven and London: Yale University Press, 1980.

Taira, K. *Economic Development and the Labor Market in Japan.* New York: Columbia University Press, 1970.

Takahashi, K. *The Rise and Development of Japan's Modern Economy.* Tokyo: Siji Press, 1969.

Takao, T. "The Financial Policy of the Meiji Government." *Developing Economies* 3 (1965).

Takizawa, M. *The Penetration of the Money Economy in Japan.* New York: Columbia University Press, 1927.

Teranishi, J., and Patrick, H. "The Establishment and Early Development of Banking in Japan: Phases and Policies to World War I." In L. Klein and K. Ohkawa, eds., *Economic Growth: The Japanese Experience since the Meiji Era.* Homewood, Ill.: Irwin, 1968.

Thorp, W. L. *Business Annals.* New York: National Bureau of Economic Research, 1926.

Tiedemann, A. E. "Big Business and Politics in Pre-war Japan." In J. W. Morley, ed., *Dilemmas of Growth in Pre-war Japan.* Princeton, N.J.: Princeton University Press, 1971.

Tsuru, S. *Essays on Japanese Economy.* Tokyo: Kinokuniya Book Store, 1958.

Uchide, N., and Ikeda, K., eds. *Social and Economic Aspects of Japan.* Tokyo: Economic Institute of Seijo University, 1967.

U.S. Strategic Bombing Survey. *The Effects of Strategic Bombing on Japan's War Economy.* Washington, D.C.: Government Printing Office, 1946.

Wallich, H. C., and Wallich, M. "Banking and Finance." In H. T. Patrick and H. Rosovsky, eds., *Asia's New Giant: How the Japanese Economy Works.* Washington, D.C.: Brookings Institution, 1976.

Ward, R. E., and Rüstow, D., eds. *Political Modernization in Japan and Turkey.* Princeton, N.J.: Princeton University Press, 1964.

Yamada, S., and Hayami, Y. *Agriculture.* Economic Growth Conference, Tokyo, session A, paper A, 1972.

Yamaichi Securities Co., *History of Yamaichi Securities Co., Ltd.* Tokyo, 1958.

Yamamura, K. *Economic Policy in Post-war Japan.* Berkeley: University of California Press, 1967.

————. "Japan 1868–1930: A Revised View." In R. Cameron, ed., *Banking and Economic Development.* New York: Oxford University Press, 1972.

Yamasaki, K., and Ogawa, G. *The Effects of the World War upon the Commerce and Industry of Japan.* New Haven, Conn.: Yale University Press, 1929.

Yao, J., ed. *Monetary Factors in Japanese Economic Growth.* Kobe: Research Institute for Economics and Business Administration, Kobe University, 1970.

Yoshino, T. "The Creating of the Bank of Japan: Its Western Origin and Adaptation." *Developing Economies* 15 (1977).

Index

Agriculture: Tokugawa era, 4; share of, in national product, 10, 99, 148; labor force's share in, 11, 18, 39, 59; rural debt in transition period, 31; land prices, 44, 75, 99, 153; takeoff period financing, 59–60; *1914–31* period, 74, 99–100; *1932–45*, 128; new institutions for financing of, 160

Asset prices: takeoff period, 44

Balance of payments: WWI years, 72–73; *1920s*, 76, 82; *1932–45* period, 108, 113

Bank notes: Bank of Japan, 46, 82

Bank of Japan: organized, 25; first years characterized, 46–47; assets described, 59; discount rate, 75, 82, 114, 118; *1914–31* period, 82–83; financing military buildup, 112; financing the war, 117–18; changes in asset structure, 140–41, 160–61; government debt absorbed, 141–42; monetary policy *1954–75*, 151–53. *See also* Banks and banking

Bank of Tokyo, 118

Banks and banking: Tokugawa era, 6; pension commutation operation, 22–24; Meiji government banks, 24–27; "lendings," 48–49; concentration in, 49–50, 69, 119–20; takeoff period characterized, 55–56; *1927* runs on, 84; assets in financial institutions, 140, 167, overloan, 162. *See also* Bank of Japan; City banks; Commercial banks; Keiretsu; Long-term credit banks; National banks; Private savings banks; Quasi banks; Reconversion Finance Bank; Yokohama Specie Bank; Zaibatsu

Big Four: holdings, 126, 196

Big Ten, 6

Black market, 112–13

Bonds: commutation, 22–24, 59; financing public sector, 58–59; insurance company holdings, 87; corporate, 102; Telephone Company, 154

Bonuses: effect on saving, 202

British postal saving system, 51. *See also* Postal saving system

Business sector: Meiji transition period, 30–31; financing of *1914–31*, 94–97: *1932–45*, 124–27; new issue ratio, 129; government's cooperation with, 151; small business financing, 160; uses and sources of funds, 190–94; unincorporated business, 198–99. *See also* Government; Households; Personal sector; Public sector

Buzumi deposits, 154, 191, 199. *See also* Deposits

Call money: interest rates, 154

Capital expenditures: takeoff period characterized, 57; residential structures, 63; government and private, 77, 114–15; *1932–36* period, 125; by government *1946–53*, 141; nonfinancial corporations, 142–43; *1954–75* period, 157; stock issues to finance, 182–83; personal sector, 201

Capital formation: *1869–1975*, 11–12; transition period, 19; takeoff era characteristics, 41–43, 57; agriculture's share in, 59–60; and new issues, 66–67; WWI and *1920s* periods compared, 77–78; *1932–45* period, 114–15; *1951–53* ratio, 132; *1954–75*, 147, 148, 150–51, 156–57; financial instrument ratios, 178–79

Capital imports: related to national product, 19; takeoff period, 44; WWI and *1920s*, 78

Capital market: lagging development of, 70

Capital output ratio: takeoff period, 43; *1955–77*, 218

Capital stock. *See* Reproducible capital stock

Censuses: Tokugawa period, 3–4

China Incident of *1937*, 127

Chinese war indemnity, 36, 47

Chung, W. K., 13

City banks: asset structure, 162; loans by, 197. *See also* Banks and banking

Combines. *See* Keiretsu; Zaibatsu

Commerical banks: described and characterized, 47–50; *1914–31* period, 83–85; branch offices, 83–85, 119, 168; "earthquake" bills, 84; merger movement, 84–85; Big Five, 85; government securities' holdings, 98; *1932–45* period, 118–20; Big Four, 120; changes in asset structure, 140–41. *See also* Banks and banking

Commodity exchanges: Tokugawa era, 7
Commutation bonds, 22–24; as capital, 25–26
Concentration movement: banks, 49–50, 69,
   84–85, 119–20, 167–68; life insurance, 121,
   168. *See also* Life insurance; Zaibatsu
Consumer credit, 204
Consumer price index: WWI years, 72
Corporate administrators: asset holdings, 208
Corporate stock: distribution of holdings, 183; in
   national balance sheet, 215
Corporations: growth of (takeoff period), 60–62;
   profits and dividends *1914–31*, 95; issue ratio,
   179. *See also* Business sector; Government;
   Industry; Insurance companies; Loans;
   Manufacturing
Credit cooperatives: Tokugawa era, 6; Meiji peri-
   od, 27; assets, 85–87; agricultural financing,
   100; *1932–45*, 120; increase in share of finan-
   cial institutions, 167; issue ratio, 170. *See also*
   Deposit Bureau; Postal saving system; Thrift
   institutions
Currency: Tokugawa era, 6; expansion *1868–85*,
   20–21
Cyclical movements: development of, 38–39;
   WWI years, 72; *1920*s, 73; *1954–73*, 148, 159

Dai Ichi, 49, 196
Daimyo: pensions commuted, 22–24
Daiwa, 185
Debentures: long-term credit banks, 51; as asset of
   financial system, 163
Debt-asset ratio: and farmers, 128
Debt securities: characterized *1954–75*, 185–88
Deflation: Matsukata, 27–29; *1920*s, 74
Denison, E. F., 13
Deposit Bureau, 23; long-term credit bank issues,
   51; described, 52–53; assets, 86–87; holdings
   of local and central government securities,
   98–99, 120. See also Credit cooperatives; Post-
   al saving system; Thrift institutions
Deposit money banks: asset structure changes,
   160–66. *See also* Banks and banking
Deposits: takeoff period, 48; thrift institutions, 52;
   insurance companies, 54; *1932–45* period characterized, 119; as asset of financial institutions,
   163; personal sector, 202. *See also* Banks and
   banking
Dividends: nonfinancial corporations *1914–31*, 95
Dodge-Shoup fiscal reforms, 131, 133, 141
Domestic debt: takeoff period, 58–59

Economic Planning Agency: national wealth sur-
   veys, 13
Edo. *See* Tokyo
Elites: symbiosis of, 36, 147; disappearance of
   military and imperial court, 146
Entrepreneurs: asset holdings, 208
Environment: neglect of, 150
Exports: WWI years, 71; capital, 76, 78
External financing: ratio for financial instruments,
   178–80; sources of funds, 191

Feudalism: Tokugawa period, 3–5; rice levies, 21
Financial institutions: Meiji period summarized,
   27; takeoff period, 54–56; distribution of assets
   among institutions, 88–90, 121–23; *1914–31*
   period, 88–94; distribution of types of assets,
   90–91, 123; institutional holdings of securities,
   91–92, 123–24; issue ratios, 92–94, 102–03,
   124, 139, 168–75; financing government,
   98–99; inflation's effect, 138–41; structural
   changes in, 160; structure of assets and liabilities, 160–66; portfolio structure, 162; expansion and position of main types, 166–68;
   network of offices of, 168; relation of assets to
   national product, 175–76; borrowings from, 192
Financial instruments: issue ratios, 176–80; penetration into household portfolios, 208–09; distribution of ownership of, 210–13
Financial intermediation ratio: transition period,
   33; described, 64; takeoff period, 66; *1914–31*
   period, 102–03; *1932–45* period, 129;
   1955–77, 218
Financial interrelations ratio: transition period,
   32–33; described, 64; takeoff period, 68;
   1914–31 period, 103–06; *1955–77*, 217–19
Financial surpluses and deficits: sectoral analysis
   1954–75, 157–60
Fire insurance, 53. *See also* Insurance companies
Food grains: cultivation of, 10
Foreign Exchange Bank Law, 118
Foreign financing: transition period, 31; takeoff
   period, 39, 57, 70; *1914–31*, 97
Foreign trade: takeoff period, 39; *1914–31*, 82;
   postwar period, 149–50
Foreign trade bank. *See* Yokohama Specie Bank
Fuji bank. *See* Yasuda bank
Fujino, S., 13

Genro, 36
Ginkobatsu, 36
Gold: Tokugawa era, 6; Meiji period, 20
Gold standard: adoption of, 39; abandonment of,
   107, 114
Government: finance in transition period, 30; role
   described, 69; financing of *1914–31*, 97–99;
   1932–45, 127–28; *1946–53* period characterized, 141–42; business's cooperation with,
   151; external financing ratio, 180; debt securities, 186; new issue ratio, 189
—local government: issues *1914–31*, 98; capital
   expenditures cut, 114; debt securities, 186
Government bonds. *See* Bonds
Government securities: national banks' main assets, 26; takeoff period, 59; commercial banks'
   holdings, 117–18; financial institution's holdings, 123–24, 162, 164; portfolio structure, 190
Grain production: Tokugawa period, 4
Gray market: interest rates, 155
Great Depression: beginning in Japan, 2; effect,
   77
Great Inflation. *See* Inflation
Gross national product: growth rate, 8–9; determi-

nants of growth, 14–15; WWI years, 72; *1931–36*, 108; in *1953*, 132; *1954–77*, 147
Gumbatsu, 36

Hanbatsu, 36
Hans, 17; *han* notes, 25
Hokkaido Colonial (Takushoku) Bank, 51
Households: financing of, 31; takeoff period financing, 63–64; saving, 79–80, 116; *1932–45*, 128–29; issue ratio, 179; saving behavior, 204–10; entrepreneurial and employee compared, 206–07; upper income and wealthy, 207
Housing: flimsy nature of, 43, 51, 64; Great Inflation's effect on, 143; neglect of, 150; finance of, 203–04
Housing Loan Corporation, 203
Hybrid stock-flow ratio, 175–76
Hyperinflation. *See* Inflation—Great Inflation's effect
Hypothic (Kangyo) Bank, 51

Income: influence of, 206
Indebtedness: Tokugawa era, 6–7; agriculture, 60, 99–100, 128
Industrial Bank of Japan, 51, 121
Industry: share in national income *1868–85*, 18; government participation in, 24; takeoff period, 39; commercial bank loans, 49; WWI years, 71, 72; Zaibatsu in, 126
Inflation, 69; WWI years, 72; *1932–45* period, 108–09, 112–13; commercial banks as engine of, 118; acceleration after *1973*, 156
—Great Inflation's effect: described, 133–38; on financial institutions, 138–41; on government, 141–42; on households, 143; on nonfinancial sectors, 143–45; *1945–51* described, 151
Insurance companies: described, 53–54; *1914–31* period, 87–88; *1932–45*, 121; Zaibatsu in, 126; assets in financial institutions, 140; issue ratio, 170. *See also* Life insurance
Interest rates: *1868–85*, 21; takeoff period, 44–45; post-WWI, 75–76; *1932–45* period, 114; *1954–75* period, 153–56; call money, 154; Telephone Company bonds, 154; Gray market in, 155
Inventories: WWI period, 77
Investment: transition period, 29; cyclical movements, 38–39
Iwasaki: as Zaibatsu, 62, 194. *See also* Zaibatsu

Kambatsu, 36
Kanto earthquake: effects of, 74, 76, 77, 82, 83, 84, 97; "earthquake" bills, 84
Keiretsu: Zaibatsu contrasted, 196–98; intergroup shareholdings, 197–98. *See also* Zaibatsu
Korean War, 135
Kyoto: Tokugawa population, 4

Labor force: agriculture's share of, 4, 11, 18, 39, 74; growth rate, 10–11, 14; nonagricultural, 74; in *1953*, 131; expansion of, in *1954–75*, 147

Land: reclamation, 4; expansion of cultivation of, 11, 14; tax on, 21–22; farm and urban prices, 114, 153, 214–15; sales of, 198
League of Nations: Japan's withdrawal from, 109
Life insurance, 53; growth *1914–31*, 87–88; concentration movement, 121, 168; distribution of assets, 121–22. *See also* Concentration movement; Insurance companies
Lineage group. *See* Keiretsu
Loans: to whom made, 26, 87; commercial banks, 48–49, 119; long-term credit banks, 51; thrift institutions, 87; agricultural, 100; Reconversion Finance Bank, 141; as asset of financial institutions, 163; issue ratios, 176–78
Long-term credit banks: described, 51, 88; in *1932–45*, 121; assets in financial institutions, 140

Machinery and equipment, in *1954–75*, 157
Manchurian "incident," 107
Manufacturing: share in national product, 10, 148–49; indices *1874–85*, 18; takeoff period, 39; WWI years, 71, 72; loss of control, 124–25; sources of credit, 192–94
Marine insurance, 53
Matsukata deflation: described, 27–29
"Measure of ignorance": factors of, 15
Meiji Life Insurance Company, 53
Meiji Restoration: characterized, 16–17; central bank established, 24–27
Mexican silver dollar, 120
Military expenditures: Sino-Japanese war, 35–36, 57; Russo-Japanese war, 36, 57–58; WWI period, 71, 77; *1932–45* period, 107–14 passim; in capital formation, 114
Mitsubishi bank, 49–50, 194, 196, 198
Mitsui (house of), 7; government enterprises taken by, 24; banking house, 25, 26, 49–50; as Zaibatsu, 62, 126, 194, 196, 198. *See also* Zaibatsu
Money: Tokugawa era, 5; reforms *1868–85*, 19–21; volume in takeoff period, 45, window guidance, 153
—supply: Matsukata deflation, 28–29; modernization, 46; *1932–45* period, 109, 112; price levels related to *1946–53*, 135–38; components of, 137–38; Bank of Japan's policy re, 151–53
Money clique. *See* Zaibatsu
Money issue ratio: *1932–45*, 124; *1954–77*, 174
Moneylenders: Tokugawa era, 6–7; rural debt, 31
Mortgage banks. *See* Long-term credit banks
Mujin. *See* Credit cooperatives

National balance sheet: transition period, 32–33; takeoff period, 67–68; *1914–31* period, 103–06; *1932–45*, 129–30; financial developments analyzed *1955–77*, 213–19
National Bank Act, 25
National banks: established, 24–27; conversion to commercial, 47. *See also* Banks and banking
National income: origins of, 18

National issue ratios: transition period, 31–32
National product: Tokugawa period, 4; growth rate, 8–9; sectoral origin changes, 9–10; determinants of growth, 14–15; in *1868–85*, 18–19
National Survey of Family Incomes and Expenditures *1969*, 207
National wealth: surveys of, 13
New issue ratio: of financial institutions, 56, 92–94, 168–75; described, 64; takeoff period, 65; *1914–31* period, 103–04; *1932–45*, 124; nonfinancial sector, 129; *1954–77* period, 168–75; financial instruments, 176–80; debt securities, 185; government, 189
Nikko, 185
Nippon Kangyo Bank: long-term credit banks merged with, 88
Nomura, 185
Nonagricultural business. *See* Business sector
Nonfarm households. *See* Households
Nonfinancial business. *See* Business sector; Corporations
Notes: European type central bank, 25

Ohkawa, Kazushi, xiii, 19
Osaka: Tokugawa population, 4; Big Ten, 6; concentration of offices in, 168
Overloan: described, 162
Oyabun-kubun relationship, 3

Paper currency: Meiji era, 20; Matsukata deflation, 28; Bank of Japan, 47. *See also* Banks and banking; Currency
Parliamentary democracy: described, 35
Pawnbrokers: Tokugawa era, 6; Meiji period, 27; rural debt, 31
Pearl Harbor, 107
Peking incident, 107
Pensions: feudal pensions commuted, 22–24
Perry, Commodore Matthew C., 16
Personal sector: saving, 199–200; sources and uses of funds, 200–02; bonuses, 202; saving behavior, 204–10; *See also* Government; Households; Public sector
Politics: structural changes, 146
Population: Tokugawa period, 3–4; growth, 8; rural depopulation, 11; *1886–1913*, 37; in *1953*, 131
Portfolio structure: financial institutions, 162
Postal saving system, 52; assets, 85–87; rates paid on deposits, 114; *1932–45*, 120; assets in financial institutions, 140; issue ratio, 170
Post Office life insurance, 87; *1932–45*, 121
Prices: Tokugawa era, 7; takeoff period, 40–41, 44; agricultural land, 74; *1920*s, 74–75; stock, 75; price levels and money supply related, 135–38; *1954–75*, 153
Primary industries: share in national product, 9–10, 18
Private savings banks: described, 52. *See also* Banks and banking
Profits: nonfinancial corporations *1914–31*, 95
Public sector: financing *1886–1913*, 56–59; described *1965–77*, 188–90. *See also* Business sector; Government; Households; Personal sector

Quasi banks: described, 27; rural debt, 31; conversion to ordinary banks, 47. *See also* Banks and banking

Railroads: growth, 39
Raw materials: imports, 111
Real estate prices, 113–14
Reconversion Finance Bank: financing of, 141
Reproducible capital stock: growth, 12–14; takeoff period, 43; *1913–30*, 77–78; war damage to, 130, 147
Residential construction expenditures: takeoff period, 43, 63; *1932–45*, 114, 128–29
Residual: factors of, 15
Rice: as linchpin of economy, 5; land tax payable in, 5, 21; commutation of rice rents, 22–24
Roads: neglect of, 150
Rural depopulation, 11
Russo-Japanese War: as watershed date?, 2; expenses of, 36; financing of, 40, 57, 58

Samurai: civilization and demilitarization of, 17; pensions commuted, 22–24
Sangyobatsu, 36
Satsuma rebellion, 16, 20
Saving: transition period, 29–30; takeoff period, 44; postal saving system, 52; private savings banks, 52, 85, 120; agriculture, 59–60; corporate, 61, 78–89; WWI and *1920*s periods, 78–82; *1932–45*, 115–16; *1954–75*, 157; personal sector, 199–200, 204–10
Savings banks. *See* Banks and banking
Securities: in Tokugawa era, 6; foreign holdings of, 40; stock prices, 44; commercial banks' holdings, 83; insurance company holdings, 87, 121; financial institutions' holdings of, 91–92; growth of companies in, 184–85; debt, 185–88
Seitobatsu, 36
Sekigehara battle, 1
Shibusawa: as Zaibatsu, 62. *See also* Zaibatsu
Shimbun, Asahi, 20
Shoup. *See* Dodge-Shoup fiscal reforms
Silver: Tokugawa era, 6; Meiji period, 20
Sino-Japanese War of *1895–96*, 36; financing of, 57
Slogans: substance of, 37
Small business. *See* Business sector
Standard of living: in *1886–1913*, 37; *1920*s, 74
Stock market: growth of, 75; in *1930*s, 113; new institutions connected with, 160; issue ratio, 170; market described, 176; developments in *1954–75*, 180–85
Stock ratios, 176
"Sturm und Drang" era, 35
Suicides: and Matsukata deflation, 28, 29
Sumitomo bank, 49; as Zaibatsu, 62, 194, 196, 198. *See also* Zaibatsu

Takeoff period: financial achievements of, 68–70
Taxation: land, 5, 21–22

Technology: government advancement of, 24; importation of, 147, 151
Teikoku bank, 120
Telephone Company bonds: interest rates, 154
Thrift institutions: described, 51–52; *1914–31* period, 85–87; *1932–45,* 120, 121. *See also* Credit cooperatives; Deposit Bureau; Postal saving system
Tokugawa period: end of, as watershed, 1; characterized, 3–5; isolation of, 5; Western Europe compared, 7; demise summarized, 16
Tokyo: Tokugawa population, 4; concentration of offices in, 168
Tokyo Fire Insurance Company, 53
Tokyo Marine Insurance Company, 53
Tokyo stock exchange, 75, 183, 185. *See also* Stock market
Total Mobilization Law, 109
Trade credit, 64, 65, 101–02; issue ratios, 176–77; use of funds, 190
Transition period: financial achievements, 33–34
Transportation insurance, 53
Trust accounts: growth rates *1931–44*, 120; issue ratio, 170
Trust Fund Bureau, 52; debt securities, 187
Tsuru, S., 20

Unincorporated business: puzzle of finances of, 198–99. *See also* Business sector

Urbanization: Tokugawa period, 4; effect on banking, 85; on land prices, 153

Welfare: neglect of, 150
Western-type organizations: government establishment of, 24; long-term credit banks, 51; insurance companies, 53–54; Japan's imitation of, 69
Window guidance: money policy, 153
World War II: effect on saving, 115; economic effects, 147

"Xenodoulophobia," 17

Yamaichi, 185
Yasuda bank, 49; as Zaibatsu, 62, 194, 196. *See also* Banks and banking; Zaibatsu
Yen: introduction of, 19–20; disagio of, 27, 29, 39
Yokohama Specie Bank, 23; organized, 26; described and characterized, 50–51; *1914–31* period, 83; liquidation of, 118; war role of, 118
Yoshimune, 3

Zaibatsu: as an elite, 36; and conversion of partnerships, 61; growth and features of, 62–63; at end of takeoff period, 69; and life insurance companies, 88; decelerating growth of, 125–26; dissolution of, 180, 183, 194–96; and Keiretsu contrasted, 196; intergroup shareholdings, 197–98. *See also* Concentration movement; Elites; Life insurance